TUTANKHAMUN AND CARTER

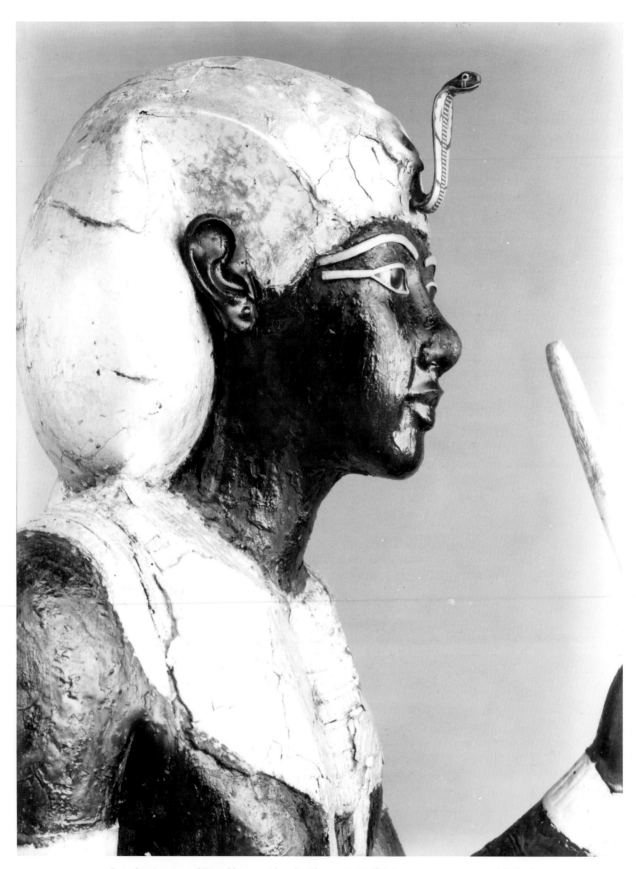

'Guardian' statue of Tutankhamun (detail). Photo: © Griffith Institute, University of Oxford.

TUTANKHAMUN AND CARTER

ASSESSING THE IMPACT OF A MAJOR ARCHAEOLOGICAL FIND

Edited by

ROGÉRIO SOUSA, GABRIELE PIEKE AND TINE BAGH

OXBOW | books
Oxford & Philadelphia

Published in the United Kingdom in 2024 by
OXBOW BOOKS
81 St Clements, Oxford OX4 1AW

and in the United States by
OXBOW BOOKS
1950 Lawrence Road, Havertown, PA 19083

Paperback Edition: ISBN 979-8-88857-067-8
Digital Edition: ISBN 979-8-88857-068-5 (epub)

A CIP record for this book is available from the British Library

Library of Congress Control Number: 2024936532

Printed in the United Kingdom by Short Run Press

Typeset in India by Lapiz Digital Services, Chennai.

For a complete list of Oxbow titles, please contact:

UNITED KINGDOM
Oxbow Books
Telephone (0)1226 734350
Email: oxbow@oxbowbooks.com
www.oxbowbooks.com

UNITED STATES OF AMERICA
Oxbow Books
Telephone (610) 853-9131, Fax (610) 853-9146
Email: queries@casemateacademic.com
www.casemateacademic.com/oxbow

Oxbow Books is part of the Casemate Group

Front cover: The funerary mask of Tutankhamun *in situ* (colourised digitally). Photo: © Griffith Institute, University of Oxford.
Back cover: The Golden Throne of Tutankhamun: a depiction on the backrest displays the royal pair in an intimate pose. Photo: Sandro Vannini.

This work is financed by national funds through FCT – Foundation for Science and Technology, I.P, in the scope of the projects UIDB/04311/2020 and UIDP/04311/2020.

Contents

List of contributors

VALENTIN BOYER
École du Louvre

KATJA BROSCHAT
Leibniz-Zentrum für Archäologie (LEIZA)

JENNY CASHMAN
Polytechnic School, Pasadena

JASMINE DAY
The Ancient Egypt Society of Western Australia Inc.

SALIMA IKRAM
American University in Cairo

GHADA MOHAMED
Faculty of Archaeology, Cairo University

DANIELA PICCHI
Museo Civico Archeologico di Bologna

VALENTINA SANTINI
University of Birmingham; CAMNES

MANON Y. SCHUTZ
University of Münster

ROGÉRIO SOUSA
Centre for History, School of Arts and Humanities – University of Lisbon

ANDRÉ J. VELDMEIJER
American University in Cairo

Foreword

On 16–17 February 2023, one hundred years after the official opening of the burial chamber of Tutankhamun, the conference *Tutankhamun and Carter: Assessing the Impact of a Major Archaeological Find* was held in Lisbon, organized by the Centre for History of the University of Lisbon and the Calouste Gulbenkian Foundation, with the invaluable cooperation of CIPEG, the ICOM International Committee for Egyptology.

The conference gathered together scholars presenting various aspects of the impact of this archaeological discovery on both scientific and popular audiences. After Carter and his team opened the tomb in November 1922, it soon became clear that the spell cast by the objects from the tomb hindered, rather than aided, the scientific study of this unique find. Despite the huge impact they have had on the study of the ancient world, the media and popular culture, these antiquities remain to this day very inadequately studied.

This book was prepared to showcase the variety of perspectives currently to be observed in the study of objects from the tomb of Tutankhamun. This applies in particularly to the 'ordinary' items found in the tomb, which have not received as much attention as the 'treasure'. A wide range of 'daily life' objects, such as baskets or leather artefacts, have been largely overlooked over the years, and only recently their study has received the attention they deserve. However, even famous masterpieces, such as the golden throne of the king, have remained poorly studied from the technical standpoint, in particular owing to their popularity and 'charisma'. The planning for the Grand Egyptian Museum and the move of the Tutankhamun objects from the Egyptian Museum at Tahir Square to Giza has given various experts more access to these objects and made it possible to look at them in new lights, particularly in terms of materiality and craft techniques. Incidents such as the attack on the Egyptian Museum in Cairo during the revolution in 2011, and the detachment of the divine beard from the golden mask of the king, also opened windows

of opportunity for first-hand examination and restoration of precious objects which otherwise would have remained out of reach.

Although disturbed in antiquity, the tomb of Tutankhamun is the only Egyptian royal tomb at Thebes to have been found essentially intact. This circumstance gives us the unique opportunity to consider the role of the objects that belonged to/were deposited in royal burials, which in the remaining tombs of the Valley of the Kings is only possible through small fragments and scattered objects. The antiquities found in the tomb of Tutankhamun thus provide unrivalled sources for the study of the complex set of rituals and magical beliefs regarding the afterlife of the king, a subject that remains largely overlooked despite the extraordinary wealth of material provided by the tomb. The transitional character of the reign of Tutankhamun, between the reign of Akhenaten and the rise of the 19th Dynasty, makes it a real treasure-trove in terms of how the Amarnian legacy was reintegrated into a more traditional Egyptian structure. In all these aspects, the immense contribution of Howard Carter is evident. He created archaeological methods and invited the best scholars of Anglophone Egyptology to work on the objects. It was through him that the find was salvaged, allowing its scientific study by generations to come.

Another side to the material culture of the tomb of Tutankhamun approached in this publication is its ability to interact with 20th-century and contemporary audiences. This covers a wide swathe, ranging from the media, to cinema, literature and comics, making the young king, who was hardly acknowledged by the Egyptian sources themselves, into the most famous pharaoh of Egypt. These aspects are today so closely intertwined in the objects of Tutankhamun that they are now inseparable.

As editors of the book, we are deeply grateful for all the contributors to this volume. They truly gave shape to our goal and intent, and illustrated the exceptional and inexhaustible field of research provided by the objects found in the tomb of Tutankhamun. A special word of acknowledgement is addressed to Aidan Dodson who kindly reviewed the text, as well as to Tom Hardwick. We are much indebted to their efforts.

A note of appreciation is addressed to José Horta and to Nuno Simões Rodrigues from the Centre for History of the University of Lisbon, who encouraged us to set up the conference. An especial word of acknowledgement is addressed to Stefano Scaramuzzino, from the Istituto Italiano di Cultura di Lisbona, and to João Carvalho Dias, from the Calouste Gulbenkian Foundation for the support they provided the conference. The sponsorship of the colour plates published in this book is due to the generous support of the Calouste Gulbenkian Foundation.

We could not finish without acknowledging the paramount role played by the Griffith Institute of the University of Oxford in supporting this publication so generously. Special thanks are owed to its Director, Richard Parkinson, and to the Archive Curator, Francisco Bosh-Puche, for his patience and support. A final word of recognition goes to the wonderful team from Oxbow Books, in particular to Julie Gardiner, for their immense support and back up.

The Editors
Lisbon–Mannheim–Copenhagen, 27 January 2024

Preface: Tutankhamun's never-ending story can continue

Daniela Picchi

Over the past four years, countless events have celebrated King Tutankhamun and the discovery of his tomb. It is impossible to list them all, but as a starting point, in 2018, we can recognize the travelling exhibition *Tutankhamun. Treasures of the Golden Pharaoh/Le trésor du Pharaon*, which the documentary film *Tutankhamun: The Last Exhibition* further publicized by using two famous singers, Iggy Pop and Manuel Agnelli, as narrating voices. Many, perhaps too many, have spoken and written about the young king. In any case, the Lisbon colloquium showed just how much there is still to be said about him and his tomb's discovery, both archaeologically and historically. This covers the grave goods as a whole, as well as the individual categories of materials, and the cultural phenomenon that we call Tut-mania. Three very distant historical periods, Tutankhamun's, Carter's and our own, are inexorably intertwined in any modern research into the exploration of the undeniable fascination for an event that remains exceptional.

It is worth mentioning what Richard B. Parkinson pointed out in his preface to the exhibition catalogue *Tutankhamun: Excavating the Archive* (Oxford, Weston Library, 13 April 2022–5 February 2023), namely that 'the historical reality of both the king's burial and its excavation by Howard Carter and his team is not as straightforward as people often assume'. A re-examination of the archival documents preserved at the Griffith Institute, as well as of the archaeological finds, is an essential starting point, and can still reveal much, including deliberate and unconscious omissions, especially in the light that these documents shed on their colonial(ist) context. Before we indulge in revisionist crusades against the past, however, as some scholars are wont to do, it is good to remember that the past, even if we do not like it, cannot be changed. It can be only interpreted through new understandings, remembering that, without wishing to question the intellectual honesty of scholars, our re-reading is itself a partial product of our own historical context.

Awareness of the past, nation by nation, cultural context by cultural context, recognizes that not all countries have the same past and the same responsibilities. This is something worth remembering, and should serve as a basis for taking a new and better look at the present and future of our discipline. The considerations of the European presence in Egypt during the early 1900s, which Parkinson introduced when dealing with Edward Morgan Forster's experience in the country,[1] are also addressed by Ahmed Al-Hout in his 'E.M. Forster in Egypt'.[2] This highlights that, already in the 1920s, some British voices were being raised against the 'nationalist' manner of collecting antiquities. In any case, moving from a personal level or that of specific areas of interest to a national level, from the past to the present, the possibility of radical political change, subject to economic, social as well as military power-logic, is a challenging goal to achieve, if we still speak of decolonization. Broadening our awareness as Egyptologists beyond the purely academic approach should be imperative, as should be the study of modern history, political science and economics, which inform the present study of the ancient Near East. If one of the main objectives of the Oxford exhibition was to move the focus from Carter to the unnamed members of the Egyptian team, thus restoring the narrative of what had been neglected by the culture of the time, another important objective was to remind the public that Tutankhamun is not just gold.

There is still much to be said about the objects found inside the tomb, the total number of which remains not wholly known. We know for sure that Lord Carnarvon and Carter kept some objects for themselves, which, after the archaeologist's death, were then sold on the antiquities market, or returned to Egypt. The impossibility of accurate quantification of the king's shabti figures and their miniature agricultural implements, for example, can be partly attributed to this, as well as cataloguing shortcomings, owing to the large quantity of material and the complex situation to be managed. Even though Carter's discovery of Tutankhamun's tomb represented a pivotal moment in the history of Egyptian archaeology, his methodology has been little debated, nor properly contextualized. The main archaeology manuals do not mention Carter's excavations, whose archaeological practices influenced him, nor the tools and techniques he used in the field. The replication of the entire burial chamber, which Factum Arte carried out in 2014, and its funerary equipment would not have been possible without Carter's detailed notes, Harry Burton's photographs, the documentation produced by the architects Walter Hauser and Lindsley Foote Hall, and the field experience of the analytical chemist Alfred Lucas. The latter set up a rudimentary laboratory in the nearby tomb of King Sety II to clean, repair and stabilize for transfer to Cairo Tutankhamun's artefacts. He documented all his interventions, a milestone for subsequent excavations, the broader public appreciation of conservation work and the development of the field of conservation. This remains one of the principal challenges facing those working in field archaeology.

Another question to investigate is whether the modern understanding and terminology of the objects found inside the tomb, which Carter introduced in the conceptual framework of his time, is appropriate for material deriving from ancient Egypt. Many scholars attending the Lisbon conference emphasized the need to go beyond the interpretations introduced by Carter and a mere typological study of the king's furniture and objects, to understand their daily, ritual and symbolic meaning with regard to beds, chairs, thrones and the many different types of miniatures. In-depth studies on these artefacts cannot ignore broader comparisons with the remaining typological classes in identifying the reasons for the choice of materials, techniques and the context of their place and modes of production. Some of these may have been common, employing the same craftsmen or workshop, or perhaps a wider group of collaborating workshops.

The transformations undergone by inscriptions on metal or gilded objects reveal technical characteristics of the interventions, which may be traceable back to specific craftsmen or workshops. In this case, one cannot exclude a close relationship between technical processes and an *a priori* choice of what to preserve and what to erase from an original inscription. One therefore cannot disregard the content aspects of the text to be changed, in many cases the king's name itself. All this said in the knowledge that some objects belonged to different and previous owners, as evidenced by inscriptions with the names of Tutankhamun's family members or stylistic elements. Starting with two blue faience bracelets of Neferneferuaten 'who is beneficial for her husband', with the exact size and design of an Akhenaten bracelet, and a tunic probably from Tutankhamun's tomb, colloquium participants debated at length on the identification and status of this enigmatic female king and her relationship to Tutankhamun.

Many materials from the royal funerary equipment testify to both the Amarna experience and its transition back to the traditional framework of Egyptian funerary religion, of which Tutankhamun's reign represents a crucial moment. Amarna's new beliefs led to a renewal of the Egyptian visual culture of the afterlife, evident in the king's funerary equipment, as well as in the architecture of the private tombs and in the production of anthropoid coffins and sarcophagi of the time.

Visual art also means artistic portraits of Tutankhamun, which influenced more or less the many and different reconstructions of his physical appearance. The preservation of the king's body, which Carter and his team divested of its bandages, made available his actual physical features. From this, one may reflect on matters of portraiture in ancient Egyptian art and, more precisely, in the field of the so-called Amarna and post-Amarnian art, how one might characterize the portraits of Tutankhamun, as well as portraiture in ancient Egyptian art in general.

The man behind the mask has often been relegated to second place to the mask itself and the other gold jewellery, to the point of removing the shroud and bandages from the body. In Carter's time, this practice was not uncommon and, still today, addressing the ethical issue of the approach to human remains, their preservation and display, starting with ICOM recommendations, is a challenging archaeological and museum matter.

The finding of the tomb and its 'wonderful golden things' created the myth of the young 'Pharaoh Tut' and the phenomenon called Tut-mania, which an unprecedented international media campaign amplified. This even reached Portugal, which in the early 1920s had no direct connection with archaeological activity in Egypt, and whose press mainly focused on domestic politics. Tut-mania permeated the whole of society at the time, without distinction of social classes or sectors of interest, giving rise to a long-standing international obsession, which has sometimes slipped, and still slips, into economic speculation. The uniqueness and importance of such an archaeological discovery influenced the antiquities market of the time, increasing the value of Egyptian artefacts, towards which the interest of many collectors was now turned. Improved transport and new expectations of archaeology created by the so-called 'Age of Mass Communication' increased the number of people travelling to Luxor to experience the excavations first hand. The endless manifestations of Tut-mania ranges from hundreds of ex libris with Egyptian motifs to plaques depicting the mask and other archaeological sources from the king's tomb; from the Bohemian glass beads and cabochons produced in Gablonz by Max and Norbert Niger to the influence of the discovery of Tutankhamun's tomb on contemporary Hollywood films, Marvel comics, novels – including famously some of those of Agatha Christie – fashion, music and art.

The economic aspect of the Tutankhamun phenomenon has always been relevant in all its different manifestations, including those with diplomatic, scientific, cultural and social implications. The words 'treasures' and 'gold' have been associated with this pharaoh in particular through exhibitions, such as those of the 1972–1981 world tour, in the wake of the richly documented volume *The Treasures of Tutankhamun*, published by Penelope Fox in 1951. These events magnified and consolidated what we might call an almost 'personal' relationship between different audiences and the only pharaoh whose tomb has been found nearly intact in the Valley of the Kings.

Celebrating 16 January 1923 with this colloquium, the organizers picked up the thread of history from the partial demolition of the south wall of the burial chamber, completed about a year later on 1 December 1923, to contribute to 'A No Longer Gilded Chronicle' of the discovery of Tutankhamun's tomb and its historical era. Ranging across academic interpretation and understanding of the past, and focusing on how the material culture of the tomb influenced scientific approaches and popular views on Tutankhamun, much has been said, but much will be said. Tutankhamun's never-ending story continues.

Notes

1   Richard B. Parkinson, '"Old things belonging to the nation": Forster, Antiquities and the Queer Museum', *Polish Journal of English Studies* 7.2 (2021), 54–71.

2   Ahmed Al-Hout, 'E.M. Forster in Egypt', *International Journal of Arabic–English Studies* 4 (2003), 31–48.

1

Archives and artefacts: studying objects from Tutankhamun's tomb

André J. Veldmeijer and Salima Ikram[1]

Abstract

Tutankhamun's tomb produced a wealth of artefacts, which Carter and his team documented. This article provides an overview of their recording methodology in terms of how it affects the research of subsequent scholars who work with the materials from the tomb. Our contribution is based on the experience of several research projects that were undertaken during the last two decades.

Keywords: Tutankhamun, Carter, leather, basketry, sandals, shoes, stick, staff, chariot, workshop, archaeological documentation

Introduction

Tutankhamun is most famous for the discovery of his virtually untouched tomb that Howard Carter found in 1922. The tomb captured the popular imagination due to the richness of its contents and the diverse objects found within. These finds could shed light on the religious beliefs of ancient Egyptian royalty and epitomize the assemblage of objects that the ancient Egyptians considered crucial for inclusion in a royal tomb.

It took Carter and his team 10 years to empty the tomb and document their findings. While three volumes about the tomb and its excavation were published,[2] unfortunately, Carter never completed the detailed scientific study of the finds as he had intended.[3] Consequently, the published information produced by the excavation team is limited. Fortunately, Carter and his team kept careful records, including photographs, which are now housed at the Griffith Institute in Oxford. This documentation has formed the basis for a wide variety of studies of the finds, including a series of monographs published by the Griffith Institute and others. These studies focus on different groups/genres of objects from Tutankhamun's tomb.[4]

The present brief communication explores the issues of using an archive together with actual artefacts, and the challenges that exist for researchers who are working on material that was excavated almost 100 years ago. This contribution is based on our experience with working intensively with the material from the tomb, the documentation of the excavation by Carter and his team, as well as scientific literature related to the objects. The projects that contribute to this paper include the Tutankhamun's Sticks and Staves Project (TSS),[5] Tutankhamun's footwear[6] as part of the Ancient Egyptian Footwear Project (AEFP),[7] Tutankhamun Basketry Research (TBR),[8] the study of the leatherwork from the tomb as part of the Ancient Egyptian Leatherwork Project (AELP),[9] a separate project that focused on the famous cuirass,[10] another on the victuals mummies,[11] and one that is currently underway concerning food. In addition, for comparative reasons, work carried out on weaponry, such as the clubs, boomerangs and throw-sticks, bows and chariots (as part of the chariot gold foil project)[12] and, finally, boxes,[13] also contribute to this article.

Excavation standards and Carter's methodology

Howard Carter was not what is nowadays defined as a trained archaeologist. However, for his time he was meticulous, thoughtful and insightful, and he knew the value of

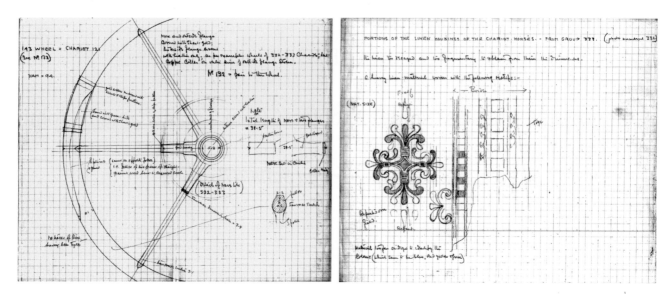

Fig. 1.1. Example of find cards by Carter and his team (chariot wheel and linen housing respectively). © Griffith Institute, University of Oxford.

consulting experts when the need arose. While there were other contemporary excavators employing high standards, for example, as exemplified by George A. Reisner's excavation of Queen Hetepheres tomb at Giza,[14] this was an exception rather than the rule.

Carter's initial training was as an artist and draughtsman,[15] though, by the time he worked for Lord Carnarvon and excavated Tutankhamun's tomb, his experience of 30 years in the field had far exceeded that of an artist or indeed his contemporary archaeological/Egyptological colleagues. He was not only a superb artist/draughtsman, but also had considerable experience working with material culture in his roles as excavator, antiquities consultant and inspector for the Antiquities Service.

Carter's thoughtfulness and precision as an excavator is shown by the way he organized the work in the tomb.[16] When he realized that Tutankhamun's tomb was (virtually) intact, he developed a system to document the tomb and its contents in such a way that the specific findspots could be traced. This system consisted of giving a unique number to the objects *in situ*.[17] The numbers were first placed with the objects in the tomb and photographed. In the laboratory (the tomb of Seti II) objects were sub-numbered, if necessary. Find cards were produced with descriptions and notes, complemented with sketches or even scale drawings (Fig. 1.1). Carter compiled a team of scientists and colleagues with different specialities and qualities to work on the assemblage.[18] Besides writing the find cards, these team members took meticulous notes in their diaries and notebooks and documented or studied some of the material in more detail, such as Walter Segal's on some of the chairs from the tomb.[19] These documents provide

additional valuable information about the excavation and objects, further enhanced by plans and drawings. Additional snippets of information are gained from letters sent home to family and friends. The main documentation, however, is the find cards.[20] Although many find cards were produced, not all objects had individual cards as sometimes groups of objects were combined under a single entry. In addition, the finds were photographed in situ and most of them separately as well. Photography was carried out by a professional photographer from the Metropolitan Museum of Art in New York, Harry Burton, who had been 'lent' by the Museum to Carter for this purpose.[21] Possibly, some objects were also photographed after their initial conservation. From the beginning Alfred Lucas, a chemist who worked for the Antiquities Service as a conservator, was involved as the main conservator. He probably also attended to the objects once they had reached the Egyptian Museum (Tahrir) in Cairo (EM). Lucas employed cutting edge technologies of the time, insofar as possible in the field in Luxor, to stabilize and conserve the objects, some of which were severely decayed.[22]

Displaying unusual initiative and foresight for the time, Carter sometimes made use of specialists who were not part of his team. Thus, authorities in philology, physical anthropology and archaeobotany were consulted. Some of them visited the site to examine materials, while in other cases queries or even samples were sent abroad for analyses that would not only identify an object, but help in its conservation. A list was compiled in order to keep track of all of these interactions.[23] For example, several samples of leatherwork were sent to England (probably Northampton) for identification, which was carried out by R.H. Pickard,

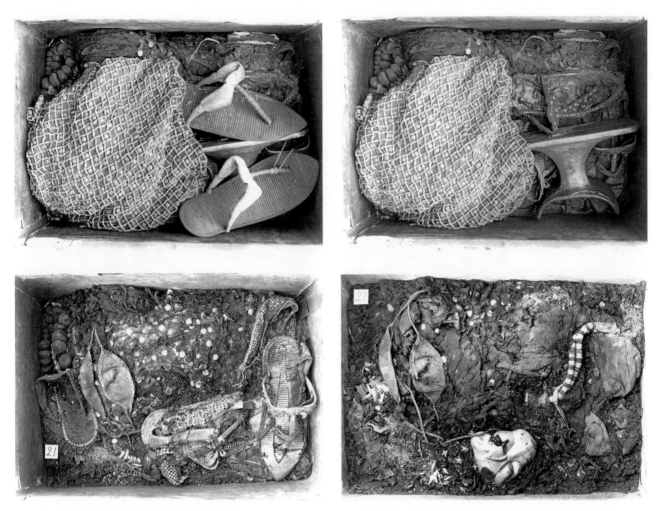

Fig. 1.2. Successive stages of emptying box 021. Photos: Harry Burton. © Griffith Institute, University of Oxford.

Director of The British Leather Manufacturers' Research Association in Northampton. Samples of the botanical materials were sent to Kew Gardens in London.

Carter and his team were meticulous, and the description of their work in the laboratory can serve as an example even for many modern-day excavators.[24] In the tomb, the ancient Egyptians had not only stacked up the goods haphazardly, but also, even within individual containers, jumbles of objects had been pushed into spaces that were either too small or too large, posing a variety of complicated challenges for the excavator. Carter and his team's patience, careful way of working and documentation remain exemplary. The step-by-step emptying of the famous so-called 'painted box' (021)[25] is a good example of how difficult the work often was. The box itself presented specific problems, being made of wood covered with a layer of gesso that was painted. The humidity affected the wood, causing the gesso to chip. The paint was also flaking off and fading in places. When the box was first opened, the complexity of excavating the contents was immediately

understood (Fig. 1.2): it was filled to the rim with a wide variety of objects that were made of vastly different materials. It contained leather open shoes (embellished with gold, glass and beads), beadwork, sandals made of vegetal material (grass, palm and papyrus), as well as textiles. Different materials meant various levels of preservation, necessitating diverse approaches to retrieval, consolidation and conservation.

Present-day researchers can still draw upon the diverse and rich sources of information left by Carter and his team that document the removal and analysis of the finds from Tutankhamun's tomb. The high quality of the documentation makes it indispensable. Additionally, the find cards are crucial to the understanding of how the tomb was excavated but also what the material looked like when it was discovered. One should note that, once a sealed tomb is opened, degradation of the material begins, no matter how careful archaeologists and conservators might be.[26] Thus, the notes of Carter and his team, especially of conservators, such as Alfred Lucas, are key resources for modern researchers.

The Crowd of Egyptian Visitors Coming from Cairo to Pay a Visit to the Scene of the Discoveries

Special SPHERE *pictures*

Although at first the Egyptians were curiously unperturbed by the great discoveries at Thebes, the vernacular press, by its many articles, has at last shown them the importance of Lord Carnarvon and Mr. Howard Carter's excavations. Great numbers of native visitors journey to Thebes daily to the valley of the Tombs of the Kings, and especially to the tomb of Tutankhamen

b

Fig. 1.3. Egyptian visitors to the tomb of Tutankhamun. From: The Sphere. *Courtesy: Peggy Joy Egyptology Library.*

Documentation in action

Professional as a system may be, and regardless how meticulously the work was carried out, the documentation of the materials from Tutankhamun's tomb was neither flawless nor exhaustive. Anyone who has actually worked on an archaeological mission knows that, despite one's best intentions, human error, exacerbated by heat, cold, dust, wind, flies and exhaustion, can affect recording. No doubt, some of these elements impacted the recording of Carter and his team. These were worsened by additional political and financial tribulations. Moreover, the constant stream of VIPs, such as the Belgian queen, who of course required special attention, in addition to groups of Egyptian students (Fig. 1.3), the curious hordes of tourists hanging about the tomb entrance and clamouring newshounds, added to the excavators' burdens. It was the intention to provide the first observations of the objects since Carter had assumed that further work by specialists (as well as himself) would be carried out when the tomb assemblage had been moved to the EM, where laboratories and a cleaner and calmer environment would provide a salubrious working space. Unfortunately, much of this was only to take place far in the future, long after Carter's demise.

Thus, some objects are documented in a much more comprehensive way than others (and this might also depend on who was filling out the find cards), and there are errors and omissions. Nonetheless, the documentation proved

helpful in several cases where, over the years and due to a variety of reasons, objects could not be linked with their original Carter number anymore. An example is derived from the so-called lotiform sticks, the condition of which has generally deteriorated during the many years since their recovery and prior to the study by the present authors. The main reason seems to be the use of large quantities of animal-based soft tissue: leather for the knobs and the appliqué, and probably animal-based glue to adhere the decoration.[27] Carter and his team were good observers, but not a single card pertaining to any of these sticks mentions the construction of the knobs: strips of leather wound around a wooden core in a stair-step fashion (Fig. 1.4). The present authors are convinced that this was not mentioned because, at the time, the knobs were not visible. They were still pretty much intact and entirely covered with the appliqué decoration, which is usually described in some detail by the excavators. Often, the appliqué on top of the knobs had (nearly) entirely vanished by the time of our recent study. Subsequent to their entry to the EM and removal to the Grand Egyptian Museum (GEM) a number of sticks became separated from their excavation numbers. However, thanks to the descriptions and the sketches that were sometimes included on the cards, it was possible to reunite the object with its number. This was aided by the fact that some sticks bore inscriptions that had been noted and published, and thus it was easier to identify them.[28]

The lotiform sticks were distinct enough in their details to separate them from each other, in contrast to the basketry. Moreover, the documentation of the basketry by the excavators was generally not overly detailed. Over the years, 96 baskets from the tomb lost their original numbers assigned by Carter and his team.[29] In most cases, it proved impossible to link these baskets to their find card and original number because the descriptions on the card were not specific enough to differentiate one basket from another. Additionally, even with a more detailed description, many baskets are too similar in appearance and size to be easily distinguished. Thus, neither the *in situ* photographs nor Carter's basic description can help identify very similar baskets. The poor condition and attempted conservation treatment(s) carried out over the years further hampered our ability to identify them. Moreover, since the contents of the baskets have been removed, these could not help in identification. References on cards to the wrong type of basket sometimes added to the confusion. For example, in discussing basket No. 422, reference was made to a basket of a different shape altogether.[30] But for more distinctly shaped baskets the documentation was helpful. At the start of the Tutankhamun Basketry Research, the EM records stated that two of the three aryballoi baskets (Carter Nos. 364, 451) were lost.[31] Fortunately, the description of the specific decoration representing vineyards and grapes allowed for the identification of several fragments of the missing two examples. Also, the shape is so specific that even in fragmented state (they were complete when found by Carter, as also evident from the *in situ* photographs), they were easily recognized. However, it proved impossible to determine which fragments specifically belonged to each of the two baskets; at least, though, they are no longer listed as missing and it is hoped that the conservation department finds means to reconstruct the fragments.

An example of less careful documentation is the card on sandals that were found on the floor of the Annexe. A confusing reference was made to 32 pairs of sandals (Carter No. 620(119)).[32] Despite the phrasing of 'pairs' it is not at all clear whether these were actually found as 'pairs'. Actually, it is highly unlikely that these 'pairs' represent original pairs: as it turned out during the study by the Ancient Egyptian Footwear Project (AEFP), some 'pairs' consisted of two sandals for the same foot. Thus, it is probable that Carter and his team had put sandals together as sets of two, regardless of whether they were actual pairs or not. Of course, it is possible that at any point in time after their removal from the tomb, these 'pairs' might have been accidentally reorganized. In other words, we cannot even be certain whether the 'pairs' that were put together by the excavators are still the same pairs found in the Museum nowadays (that have been studied and published by the AEFP). Another uncertainty is that one of these '32 pairs' is a sewn sandal with

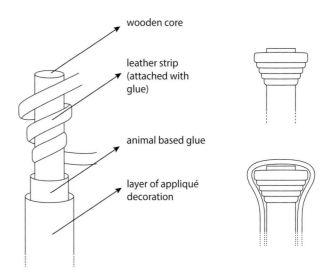

Fig. 1.4. The construction of the knob in the majority of lotiform sticks from the tomb was not documented by Carter and his team. Diagram by André J. Veldmeijer/Erno Endenburg.

the remains of a textile insole, of which the pair was not identified. Possibly, the insole of this second sandal was entirely separated from the sandal, or largely disintegrated and the remains removed during conservation interventions, and thus the sandal was not recognized. On the find card, reference is made to sandal No. 373, which is, indeed, a comparable sewn sandal. However, the card also refers to No. 453, B, which is not a sewn sandal at all, but rather a sandal strap that is made of rawhide and decorated with bark and gold foil.[33]

Sometimes the information on the cards is surprisingly rudimentary. This is the case with the cards of several of the chariots, but since Carter and his team described some in more detail, reference was made to those for the more general constructional features. A more puzzling case is the card for the leather and rawhide cuirass (No. 587a). The description of this unique object, the only surviving example from the Bronze Age in the region, consists of only two sentences and a sketch. On the card, reference was made to the only picture that was taken of this piece of armour lying crumpled in box No. 587 (Fig. 1.5). There are no Burton photographs of the object after its recovery from the box, before or after conservation, nor are there additional descriptions or notes. A third card, however, explains Lucas's treatment, which was unsuccessful and probably accelerated its decay,[34] resulting in the fragmentation of some portions. Nowadays, far less remains of the cuirass than when it was found, and one cannot but wonder whether the failed attempts to conserve/reconstruct the object were the reason that no more detailed documentation exists, or whether they might have found their way to a different part of Lucas's archive.

Fig. 1.5. The cuirass in the wooden box it was found in (587). Photos: Harry Burton. © Griffith Institute, University of Oxford.

Researching objects from Tutankhamun's tomb now

The excavation's archive, with all its documentation, should be the starting point of all research related to the tomb of Tutankhamun. Carter bequeathed this documentation to his niece Phyllis Walker, who gifted it to the Griffith Institute in Oxford. Nowadays, one can consult this documentation from anywhere in the world, as long as internet access is available, thanks to the initiative of the late Jaromir Malek. As former director of the Griffith Institute in Oxford, Malek made the notes, drawings, diaries and photographs relating to the excavation of Tutankhamun's tomb available to scholars, as well as anyone interested, via the World Wide Web: 'Tutankhamun: Anatomy of an Excavation' (Fig. 1.6).[35] The site is searchable by object name as given by the excavators, or browsable – as are the images.

It is only after a thorough investigation of the excavators' notes, drawings and photographs that one should proceed to the artefacts themselves. These should then be studied using all the means available to the scholar: macroscopic examination, written and visual documentation, archaeometrical analyses and a comparison with other similar objects.

Discussion

Egyptology and the world should consider itself fortunate that Howard Carter, with his attention to detail and knowledge of Egyptian history and material culture, was the one in charge of the excavation of Tutankhamun's tomb. While it is true that nowadays some different decisions might have been made, and we have far more tools to bring to bear when investigating material culture, one must remember that archaeological science was very different at the beginning of the 20th century. The contrast between Carter's work and that of others, such as Theodore Davis's of KV54, KV55 or the tomb of Yuya and Tjuiu, could not have been greater. While Carter's work and behaviour was not faultless,[36] in terms of the archaeology, the challenges that he faced were considerable and both the physical and psychological circumstances in which he and his team had to work were

Online resources

Archive Research Visits

Privileged Access Archive Tours

Image Rights & Fees

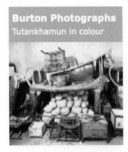

Burton Photographs
Tutankhamun in colour

Purchase prints of Harry Burton's photographs

Bookmark and Share

Tutankhamun: Anatomy of an Excavation

'Tutankhamun: Anatomy of an Excavation' is the definitive archaeological record of Howard Carter and Lord Carnarvon's discovery of the tomb of Tutankhamun.

On November 5th 1922, Howard Carter wrote in his pocket diary: 'Discovered tomb under tomb of Ramsses VI investigated same & found seals intact.' The subsequent excavation of the tomb of Tutankhamun captured the public imagination. The complete records of the ten year excavation were deposited in the Griffith Institute Archive shortly after Carter's death by his niece Miss Phyllis Walker.

This material is published here with full and free access, providing a comprehensive online resource for all audiences, from scholars to school children. One of the pioneering websites in Egyptology and archaeology, it has been running for more than 15 years and owes its foundation to Dr Jaromir Malek, the former Keeper of the Archive. As technology evolves, new presentation methods are being developed to assist all users in navigating this incredibly valuable resource.

Original concept & direction: Jaromir Malek, assisted by Sue Hutchison, Elizabeth Fleming, Diana Magee & Kent Rawlinson
Current concept & direction: Vincent Razanajao, assisted by Elizabeth Fleming, Francisco Bosch-Puche, Cat Warsi & Jenni Navratil

Fig. 1.6. The website dedicated to the archive of the excavations of the tomb of Tutankhamun. © Griffith Institute, University of Oxford.

extreme. And they were, like all of us, people, and people make mistakes.

It is only because of Carter's professional attitude towards the science of archaeology that we can still work with the tomb's contents and have a good idea of each artefact's context. The sampling and analyses of finds in order to better understand the nature of the materials used to fabricate objects, involving experts from all over the world, were exemplary and serve as a model for how contemporary archaeological investigations should be conducted. It is hoped that in the future more of the objects from Tutankhamun's tomb will be analysed and published.

However, regardless of the care taken by any excavator and the technologies brought to bear on recording objects, with or without computers and new technologies (perhaps even AI!), there are always going to be limitations and issues with the documentation. Despite these drawbacks, Carter and his team's find cards, papers and notes are key to our understanding of the objects. This is particularly true as, regardless of the care taken with material, there is a serious chance that it will deteriorate, making the initial documentation all the more valuable. The decline in an object's condition makes a hands-on study, in as holistic a way as possible, an essential part of any scientific research on objects. Thus far, researchers who wished to study the material excavated by Carter and his team have been able to access material in the EM and it is hoped that this will continue in the GEM, where the intention is to display all the objects from the tomb. This is also important as currently the numbers associated with the artefacts are changing because the objects are dispersed amongst museums throughout Egypt. It is expected that once the GEM opens, all of the artefacts that were found in Tutankhamun's tomb will be reunited there. Hopefully, the GEM's database will be able to provide links between its GEM numbers and Carter's excavation numbers, to the *Journal d'Entrée* (JE) numbers and other numbers of the EM as well as any (temporary) numbers associated with them when they were in other collections, such as the Sharm el-Sheikh Museum. Equally important is the availability of this information to scholars. Retaining links between the different numbers assigned to these objects is key as many have been published, even if cursorily, using the JE numbers.

Doubtless, the GEM's state-of-the-art conservation laboratories will be utilized to analyse more of the artefacts from the tomb in order not only to improve conservation methods, but also to enhance our knowledge of the objects' manufacturing, including the identification of materials. Thus far, only a few analyses have been permitted on Tutankhamun's belongings, thereby limiting the information derived from them. Scientific analyses of the artefacts coming from the king's tomb have the potential to provide modern scholars with a better understanding of the materials that were available to the ancient craftsmen and the technologies and methods that they employed to create the exquisitely detailed objects found in the young king's tomb. This will fill in lacunae in our knowledge of the use of raw materials and techniques used to make the artefacts (including the origin of the material as technologies), as well as contribute to a better understanding of the *chaîne operatoire* of the ancient Egyptian craftsmen who created such amazing objects for their royal client.

Notes

1 We would like to thank Maud Slingenberg for proofreading. Erno Endenburg is thanked for preparing the figures for publication. We are grateful to the Griffith Institute, and especially Francisco Bosch-Puche, for assistance and providing the relevant images for this publication.
2 Carter 1927; Carter 1933; Carter and Mace 1923.
3 Reeves 1990: 67.
4 For an overview, see Eaton-Krauss 2020.
5 Veldmeijer and Ikram 2020; Veldmeijer and Ikram 2021.
6 Veldmeijer 2011.
7 Veldmeijer 2019.
8 Veldmeijer and Ikram 2022.
9 Veldmeijer and Ikram in press.
10 Veldmeijer et al. 2022a.
11 Ikram 1995.
12 Bertsch et al. 2017.
13 For example, Veldmeijer et al. 2022b.
14 Reisner 1927; Reisner and Stevenson Smith 1955; Der Manuelian 2022.
15 James 1992.
16 Carter and Mace 1923, 164.
17 Carter and Mace 1923, 163–164; Murray and Nuttall 1963.
18 See for a list Reeves 2022: 90–97.
19 http://www.griffith.ox.ac.uk/gri/4segtut.html. (last accessed 20 March 2024).
20 See also Carter and Mace 1923, 164; http://www.griffith.ox.ac.uk/gri/carter/ (last accessed 20 March 2024).
21 http://www.griffith.ox.ac.uk/gri/carter/gallery/ (last accessed 20 March 2024).
22 http://www.griffith.ox.ac.uk/discoveringTut/conservation/ (last accessed 20 March 2024).
23 http://www.griffith.ox.ac.uk/discoveringTut/conservation/4lucas_samples.html (last accessed 20 March 2024).
24 Carter and Mace 1923, 151–177.
25 Though Carter and Mace used this as an example in their volume, the three volumes on the tomb devote considerable space on the methodology used in excavation, together with reflections on excavation techniques in general.
26 For an example, see Veldmeijer 2011: 37–40.
27 Veldmeijer and Ikram in press. See also Veldmeijer and Ikram 2021, 15–17.
28 Beinlich and Saleh 1989.
29 Veldmeijer and Ikram 2022, 14, 29.
30 Veldmeijer and Ikram 2022, 17.
31 Veldmeijer and Ikram 2022, 14, 29.
32 See Veldmeijer 2011, 19.
33 Veldmeijer 2011, 105–107.
34 Veldmeijer et al. 2022, 28.
35 http://www.griffith.ox.ac.uk/discoveringtut/ (last accessed 20 March 2024).
36 Brier 2022.

Bibliography

Beinlich, Horst, and Mohamed Saleh. 1989. *Corpus der hieroglyphischen Inschriften aus dem Grab des Tutanchamun. Mit Konkordanz der Nummernysysteme des 'Journal d'entrée' des Ägyptischen Museums Kairo, der 'Handlist to Howard Carter's catalogue of objects in Tut'ankhamūn's tomb' und der Ausstellungs-Nummer des Ägyptischen Museums Kairo.* Oxford: Griffith Institute.

Bertsch, Julia, Katja Broschat, Christian Eckmann, Salima Ikram, Nicole Reifarth, Florian Ströbele and André J. Veldmeijer. 2017. *Tutankhamun's Unseen Treasures: The Golden Appliqués.* Exhibition booklet, Egyptian Museum, Cairo.

Brier, Bob. 1922. *Tutankhamun and the Tomb that Changed the World.* New York: Oxford University Press.

Carter, Howard. 1927. *The Tomb of Tut.ankh.Amen. The Burial Chamber.* London: Cassel & Company.

Carter, Howard. 1933. *The Tomb of Tut.ankh.Amen. The Annexe and Treasury.* London: Cassel & Company.

Carter, Howard, and Arthur C. Mace. 1923. *The Tomb of Tut.ankh. Amen. Search, Discovery and Clearance of the Antechamber.* London: Cassel & Company.

Der Manuelian, Peter. 2022. *Walking Among Pharaohs: George Reisner and the Dawn of Modern Egyptology.* New York: Oxford University Press.

Eaton-Krauss, Marianne. 2020. 'Publications in Monographic Form of the "Treasure" of Tutankhamun, 1952–2020'. *Göttinger Miszellen* 262: 217–225.

Ikram, Salima. 1995. *Choice Cuts: Meat Production in Ancient Egypt.* Louvain: Peeters.

James, Thomas G.H. 1992. *Howard Carter. The Path to Tutankhamun.* London: Kegan Paul International.

Murray, Helen, and Mary Nuttall. 1963. *A Handlist to Howard Carter's Catalogue of Objects in Tut'ankhamun's Tomb.* Oxford: Griffith Institute.

Reeves, Nicholas. 1990. *The Complete Tutankhamun. The King. The Tomb. The Royal Treasure.* London: Thames & Hudson.

Reisner, George A. 1927. 'Hetep-Heres, Mother of Cheops'. *Bulletin of the Museum of Fine Arts, Boston* 25 (supplement May 1927): 2–36.

Reisner, George A., and William Stevenson Smith. 1955. *A History of the Giza Necropolis, The Tomb of Hetep-Heres the Mother of Cheops*, Vol. II. Cambridge, MA: Harvard University Press.

Veldmeijer, André J., with contributions by Alan J. Clapham, Erno Endenburg, Aude Gräzer, Fredrik Hagen, James A. Harrell, Mikko H. Kriek, Paul T. Nicholson, Jack M. Ogden and Gillian Vogelsang-Eastwood. 2011. *Tutankhamun's Footwear. Studies of Ancient Egyptian Footwear.* Leiden: Sidestone Press.

Veldmeijer, André J. 2019. *The Ancient Egyptian Footwear Project. Final Archaeological Analysis.* Leiden: Sidestone Press.

Veldmeijer, André J., and Salima Ikram. 2020. 'Tutankhamun's Sticks and Staves Project'. *The Scribe* (Spring): 8–13.

Veldmeijer, André J., and Salima Ikram. 2021. 'Walk the Line: Sticks and Staves from the Tomb of Tutankhamun'. In *Mehen. Essays over het Oude Egypte*, edited by Jan Koek, 8–23 [in Dutch]. Amsterdam: Mehen.

Veldmeijer, André J., and Salima Ikram., with a contribution by Lucy Kubiak-Martens. 2022. *The Basketry from the Tomb of Tutankhamun. Catalogue and Analysis.* Leiden: Sidestone Press.

Veldmeijer, André J., and Salima Ikram. In press. *Let a Cow-Skin be Brought. Armour, Chariots and Other Leather Remains from Tutankhamun's Tomb.* Leiden: Sidestone Press.

Veldmeijer, André J., Thomas Hulit, Lucy Skinner and Salima Ikram. 2022a. 'Tutankhamun's Cuirass Reconsidered'. 2020–2021. *Jaarberichten Ex Oriente Lux* 48: 125–156.

Veldmeijer, André J., Salima Ikram, Geoffrey Killen and Maud Slingenberg. 2022. 'Hoe een koning zijn spullen bewaart voor de eeuwigheid. Voorraadkisten in het graf van Toetanchamon'. *Ta-Merry* 14: 6–17.

The laboratory in the tomb next door: Alfred Lucas and the science of conserving Tutankhamun's treasures

Jenny Cashman

Abstract

The team working with Howard Carter on the excavation of the tomb of Tutankhamun (KV 62) was a dedicated group of Egyptologists, archaeologists and scientific experts. From the beginning, the participation of Alfred Lucas was crucial for the long-term survival of the objects that were excavated from the tomb. For his work, a rudimentary laboratory space was set up in the nearby tomb of Seti II (KV 15). There the artefacts were cleaned, repaired and stabilized for the long trip to Cairo. His notes from all nine seasons of work in the tomb provide insight into his processes. The contributions of Lucas are important not only to the Tutankhamun discovery but to the broader public appreciation of conservation work, and to the development of the field of conservation. In this paper, selected objects from the tomb are considered, including several boxes of jumbled and decomposed materials that Lucas painstakingly worked through. His notebooks and notations on Carter's notecards, along with Burton's photos, available online through Oxford's Griffith Institute Archive, provide an opportunity to continue to 'excavate' the tomb of Tutankhamun.

Keywords: Alfred Lucas, conservation, Tutankhamun

The enduring legacy of the discovery of the tomb of Tutankhamun in 1922 continues to evolve. Alfred Lucas, the analytical chemist who worked as a member of the team for nine seasons, and who cared for the objects in the Egyptian Museum in Cairo for decades afterwards, made unique contributions to the task at hand and to the emerging field of conservation science.

He was an unexpected trailblazer. Lucas was, first and foremost, a chemist and a scientist, and would become intimately familiar with the materials and chemical composition of ancient Egyptian artefacts. He may best be known as the author of the book, *Ancient Egyptian Materials* – in later editions renamed *Ancient Egyptian Materials and Industries*[1] – a book that is still a foundational work in Egyptology. His work on objects from the tomb of Tutankhamun would transform his knowledge, but what he brought to the

task was an approach full of determination and a scientific curiosity. 'Outspokenness, industry, generosity and a great kindness were the salient points in Lucas's character.'[2]

Born in Manchester, England, in 1867, he came to Egypt in 1898, working as a chemist for the Egyptian government, first in the Salt Department, later for the Geologic Survey. He was the first Director of the Government laboratory in Cairo, and then with the Department of Antiquities. His government work often intersected with archaeological investigations, and he developed an increasing interest in ancient Egyptian processes of working with materials.

Carter was very aware of the need to involve a chemist in the clearance of the objects from the tomb. The process of making the objects 'fit for transport and then for exhibition' would require a kind of 'first aid' without which Carter estimated that 'not one-tenth of the many hundreds of objects would have ever reached Cairo'.[3] Lucas's knowledge of materials was extensive, and he is credited with providing scientific guidance as well as hands-on work in conserving and preserving many objects that would not otherwise have survived. He worked closely with Arthur Mace, who Carter had brought onto the dig also at the beginning, thanks to A. Lythgoe. Mace was a well-established archaeologist connected with the Metropolitan Museum, one of several experienced people that Lythgoe loaned to Carter. Mace had a reputation for detailed work and reconstruction, and was a highly respected member of the Metropolitan Museum. His publication of excavations of the North Pyramid and cemetery at Lisht had earned him professional respect, and the work on the jewellery boxes of the Princess Sithathori-unet from Lahun was a masterful reconstruction from trays of fragments.[4] From the beginning, Carter brought Mace into the work as more of a partner, and a co-author for the first volume published on the tomb.[5]

Carter knew as soon as he glimpsed inside the tomb that the task ahead would take an enormous amount of work and he needed experienced people. The 'first and pressing need' in Carter's mind was photography, and so his first request was to ask Lythgoe at the Metropolitan Museum if he would loan Harry Burton for the project. Lythgoe's reply not only confirmed Burton's services, but also offered other assistance from the Metropolitan, notably the services of Arthur Mace, and also draughtsmen Hall and Hauser, whose plans and drawings were to prove invaluable in documenting the intricacies of the tomb's objects.

The idea of adding a chemist to an excavation, however, was something new. And it is most likely that even though the publication[6] of the excavation presents the necessity of a chemical expert as though it were a planned part of the team, Lucas's involvement was something that evolved and happened more due to circumstance and Lucas's willingness and interest. The fact that Lucas joined Carter's team had a long-term impact on the emerging field of conservation, in which he would prove to be an important pioneer and a dedicated, life-long contributor to its development.

There was a general acceptance in archaeology of the importance of some knowledge of chemical processes and how that impacted the preservation of objects. Flinders Petrie's *Methods and Aims*, published in 1904, devoted a chapter to preservation, and proposed that:

> Some familiarity with chemistry and physics and properties of materials, is one of the first requisites for an excavator. All this applies in a lesser degree to the difficulties of transport, which is also part of the preservation of the antiquities.[7]

Not only would Carter have read Petrie's work, but he had worked with him in the field, as had Mace.[8]

After the official opening of the tomb on 29 November 1922, Carter's plans began to take shape. His trip to Cairo in early December was an extended shopping list:

> Dec. 7: Arrived Cairo. Ordered from Rostaing steel gate for inner doorway of tomb. Purchased wadding & calico for transport and packing of antiquities. Ordered nests of cardboard boxes, Stationery etc. and bandages.[9]

While in Cairo, he also noted a meeting in his pocket diary:

> Dec. 9: Saw Lucas in regard of chemical preparations for preserving objects, and textiles.[10]

That meeting turned into something more than a discussion of how to deal with chemical issues in the upcoming excavations. It resulted in 'a piece of luck'[11] due to Lucas's interest and availability. Carter's entry in his journal for that same day briefly notes:

> Dec. 9: Saw Lucas (Director of Chemical Dept. of Egyptian Government) and he offered services for Winter.[12]

Lucas was also a forensic specialist and testified as a forensic witness in some high-profile trials in Egypt. His detailed scientific approaches to problem solving led to his being referred to in the press as 'The Sherlock Holmes of Egypt'.[13] In 1921, the year before the discovery of Tut-ankhamun's tomb, Lucas published a textbook on forensic chemistry, in which he laid out his approach to assessing and problem-solving forensics in what he called the 'Six golden rules of forensic chemistry': 1. Go slowly; 2. Be thorough; 3. Take notes; 4. Consult others; 5. Use imagination; 6. Avoid complicated theories.[14]

The first three principles were also central to good archaeological excavation techniques and documentation. The importance of consulting others with specific expertise was part of archaeological practice, which is by nature a collaborative enterprise. The last two 'rules' are an interesting addition for a scientist's work. The use of 'imagination' is not something normally associated with scientific analysis. What he meant was not 'uncontrolled' imagination, but rather, 'a disciplined imagination [...] which enables inferences and deductions (to be verified or discarded at a later stage) to be made from slender and incomplete premises'.[15]

These core concepts were principles that he applied in other aspects of his life, as they can be seen in the ways he approached his work on objects from archaeological contexts. In the forensic context:

> Forensic or legal chemistry may be defined as chemistry applied to the solution of certain problems which arise in connection to the administration of justice [...] [it] deals not only with purely chemical questions, such as the nature, composition and quality of materials as determined by analysis [...][16]

What is important here to understand about Lucas is that his experience included the application of chemical knowledge and analyses to a particular set of problems. In the archaeological setting, he would now apply his knowledge and skill to devise and implement new methods. Lucas as a scientist also added to the team, as his credentials as a scientist supported Carter's own concept and promotion of the tomb clearance as a 'scientific investigation', a phrase he used often in his own notes and in public presentations.

In this particular archaeological investigation, Lucas's experience in forensic analysis was immediately called upon as soon as he arrived in Luxor. Carter's initial investigations of the tomb suggested that tomb robbers had disturbed the contents, and the jumbled nature of the box contents, often containing parts from objects located elsewhere in the tomb, suggested that someone had repacked boxes with things left of the floors by the robbers. Carter concluded it was administration officials, since the tomb had been resealed with official seals, presumably after the discovery and 'tidying up' that had been done. One of the first things Carter asked Lucas to do was to analyse the tomb in terms of evidence of the robbery.

From Carter's journal:

> Dec. 20: Lucas arrived and began experiments on 21st. Also made inspection from criminological point of view. Permission from Government to use Tomb no. 15 as laboratory.

The work was under way. Lucas was to work most closely with Arthur Mace, as the two of them dealt with the objects in the laboratory in KV 15. Other experts also came and went during the field seasons, Alan Gardiner and James Breasted to work on inscriptions, Percy Newberry for the botanical objects and later Dr Alexander Scott and Harold James Plederleith from the British Museum. But the core team of the first season was Carter and Callender in the tomb, Burton taking photos in the tomb and of the objects after processing in the laboratory, and Mace and Lucas in the laboratory that was set up in KV 15 (Fig. 2.1).

> Dec. 21: Lucas started upon chemical tests for preserving textiles, etc. Lucas made careful inspection of tomb from criminological point of view. Permission from Government to use Tomb no. 15 as laboratory.[17]

Arthur Mace, talking about Lucas, said: 'working in collaboration with Mr. Lucas, Director of the Government Chemical Laboratories, who most generously sacrificed three months' leave to come and help us, and whose chemical knowledge was invaluable [...]'.[18]

The laboratory in the tomb of Seti II, KV 15

It was clear from the beginning of the work in Tutankhamun's tomb, which was small and crammed with objects, that there needed to be an additional space for working on cleaning, conserving and repairing the objects so they could be packed and shipped to Cairo. The tomb of Seti II (KV 15) was near enough to make it workable, as it provided not only workspace but also much needed storage space for objects removed from the tomb.

The tomb had an entrance corridor that provided space enough to set up a workroom that was 3 metres wide by

Fig. 2.1. The team in 1923: (left to right) Arthur Callender, Arthur Mace, Harry Burton, Howard Carter, Alan Gardiner and Alfred Lucas, outside tomb KV 6. © Griffith Institute, University of Oxford.

18 metres long, with a ceiling that was 3 metres high. This allowed space to set up trestle tables for objects being brought over from Tutankhamun's tomb, and enough interior space to separate out and work on multiple objects from boxes, and even on larger objects.[19]

A table on the left-hand side of the entrance area was used for the treatment of individual larger objects, such as the guardian statues (see Fig. 2.14 showing Lucas and Mace working on Statue 22) and some of the pieces of furniture.[20]

The courtyard outside the tomb entrance provided space for even larger objects, and the area was improved over time. Before the second season, the courtyard area in front of KV 15 was levelled to allow for work on the chariots (Fig. 2.17), and the gate in front of the tomb was improved for better security.[21] When Dr Alexander Scott visited the tomb as a consulting chemist, at Carter's invitation, he noted that the laboratory itself was rudimentary.[22]

While there are no records of what Lucas stocked it with, one can gain a good idea of what he worked with from the treatment notes he made on the individual object cards. His treatment notes included whatever solution he was using to preserve, repair or consolidate the object, and how he was applying it. In the discussion of selected objects that follows, his treatment notes are quoted for each object to provide an understanding of those details. Materials often mentioned in the 'treatment' notes often included paraffin wax, acetone, ammonia, benzene, celluloid, Canada balsam and duroprene.

The detailed system for recording, documentation and photography included Lucas adding treatment notes onto the individual cards. The notes on the cards reveal a recording and notation system that include the following procedure:

(1) Measurements, scale drawings and archaeological notes.
(2) Notes on the inscriptions by Dr Alan Gardiner.
(3) Notes by Mr Lucas on the preservative treatment employed.
(4) A photograph, showing the position of the object in the tomb.

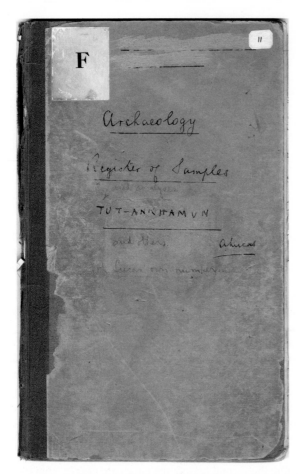

Fig. 2.2. Lucas's Register of Samples 1922–1932, recording samples taken and results of analyses. © Griffith Institute, University of Oxford.

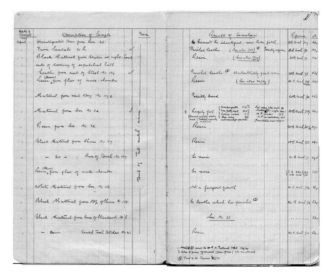

Fig. 2.3. Lucas's Register of Samples, entries on pages 6 and 7, from the first season work in the Antechamber. © Griffith Institute, University of Oxford.

(5) A scale photograph, or series of photographs, of the object itself.

(6) In the case of boxes, a series of views, showing different stages in the clearing.[23]

As Lucas began his work, he set up a book to keep track of samples taken and the results of his analyses. This 'Register of Samples' was, for him, the standard way to begin work with essential details: the date of the sample, the material to be analysed and the result of the work. He used this register throughout his work in the tomb of Tutankhamun, from 1922 to 1932 (Figs 2.2 and 2.3). It was a procedure he had used for his work in the government laboratories, and a system he recommended and detailed in his book on forensic chemistry. It remains a unique resource of data for an archaeological excavation, as it details not only the analyses he conducted on samples, but also where he sent samples for analysis in England. His work in KV 15 always was undertaken with a broader network of experts.[24]

After the first two seasons of work in Tutankhamun's tomb he published *Antiquities: Their Restoration and*

Preservation,[25] in which he shared what he had learned so far, and that book would impact conservators in museums and in the field.

> Much, however, can now be done in the field that formerly was thought to be impossible […] there are few objects, no matter of what kind, or how poor their condition, that cannot be preserved, and no object should be condemned as hopeless until it has been carefully studied and preliminary experiments made, since much that may appear at first sight to be beyond salvation can generally be consolidated and improved to at least some extent.[26]

More than a decade after the final season, Lucas published an article, 'Notes on Some Objects from the Tomb of Tutankhamun',[27] in which he provided a detailed list of corrections to the three popular books that Carter had published, a brief bibliography of publications he knew of objects from the tomb and other comments on a range of topics, from types of insects he had found in residue in vessels, to additional information on botanical specimens.

By that time the original team was gone – Arthur Mace had died in 1928, Howard Carter in 1939 and Harry Burton in 1940 – and Lucas, now 75 years old, wrote that he 'thought it would be useful to put on record a few facts that might help; facts that otherwise might be difficult to find, or that even might be lost'.[28]

A few years after that, he gathered up his notes from the nine seasons of work he had done in the tomb, and sent them off to the Griffith Institute. They are organized by season, but he did not date the individual entries, and even he was unsure about the dates that they covered. But by cross-referencing with the sequence of numbering of the objects discussed,

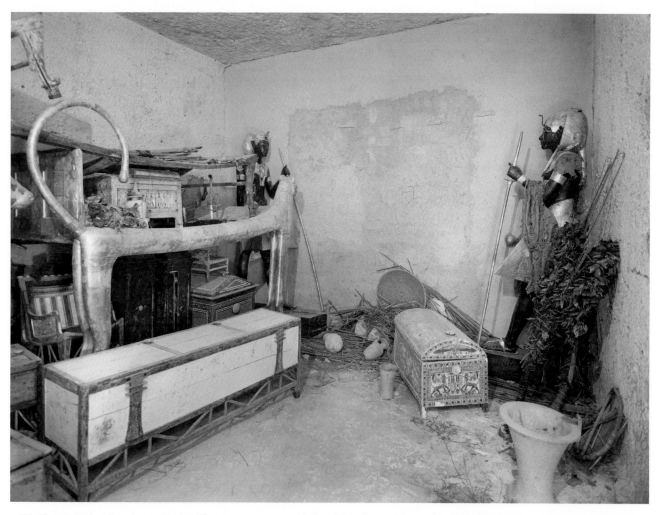

Fig. 2.4. Antechamber, facing Burial Chamber entrance, with Box 21 in front of Statue 22. © Griffith Institute, University of Oxford.

and in many cases with Arthur Mace's journal notes that mention when they began and ended working on specific boxes or objects, it is possible to determine when the notes were made.[29]

To explore the tomb's conservation work's processes and Lucas's contributions, we selected a small group of objects representative of the challenges they posed and what Lucas's notes reveal about the treatment techniques used. These objects are also chosen to represent the materials found on the four rooms within the tomb. Each example illustrates something about preservation issues in complex contexts and specific fragile materials. We have included information from notes that Lucas wrote that were in addition to the treatment summaries he noted on the excavation's cards (referred to here as Carter Cards), and some notes from Mace's journals. By introducing the objects in the order in which they were encountered in the tomb it is also possible to see something of the questions that Lucas asked, and the evolution of treatment methods.

Antechamber

The work in the Antechamber officially began on 27 December 1922 and would continue until mid-February 1923.[30] Lucas had arrived the week before, and immediately set up the lab in KV 15. The work began to the right of the entrance passageway, on the north end of the room where the two life-sized statues (object nos. 22 and 29) were stationed on either side of the doorway to the Burial Chamber (Fig. 2.4). The large doorway was plastered over, but the discoloration of the wall indicated the continuation of the tomb in that direction.

Although that doorway was not officially taken down until 16 February 1923, Carter, along with Lord Carnarvon and his daughter Lady Evelyn Herbert, had already surreptitiously entered the chamber before the clearing began, hiding the hole by which they gained access with a strategically placed basket and some rushes from the floor. Lucas wrote, decades later, that he knew of it after the fact, excusing Carter's conduct by claiming that he would have

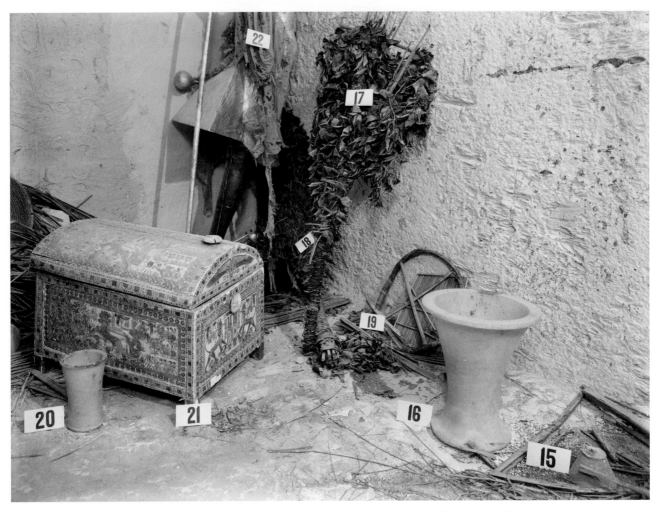

Fig. 2.5. Antechamber, Box 21 in situ, *showing numbered cards of objects. © Griffith Institute, University of Oxford.*

been 'pestered constantly by people wanting to go in' had the hole been visible.[31]

At the beginning, the plan was to implement a system of numbering objects as they were encountered, placing placards, taking photographs, documenting and proceeding step by step. A few objects had been numbered and noted from the entrance passageway, but the work really began in the Antechamber. In this discussion of the Antechamber, it is useful to compare the 'treatment' notes that Lucas added to each individual object record, usually on the last Carter Card documenting that object, with the lengthier personal notes he kept for his own reference.

Painted casket (object no. 21)

Lucas summarizes in just a few lines the treatment given to this famous casket painted with scenes of Tutankhamun in his chariot:

> Treatment (of box): Cleaned with soft brush and benzine: filled up small cracks and blisters with paraffin-wax

dissolved in benzene by means of a pipette: sprayed with a solution of celluloid in amyl acetate and finally coated box inside and out with melted paraffin wax. (Carter Card 021-4)

The box itself, which seemed relatively stable and in good condition when it was taken out of the tomb, packed onto a stretcher and carried over to the laboratory in KV 15, soon showed alarming signs of losing its beautiful paintings completely. The treatment summary on the documentation card, though accurate in relating the steps taken and substances used, does not capture the urgency, and Lucas's personal notes add considerable information to understanding the evolution of the problems with the box:

> [...] with the change of temperature and degree of humidity experienced when the box was taken out of the tomb the joints in the woodwork began to widen slightly and the painted gesso surface over the joints began to peel off. Every time the box was moved for photography, for the examination and removal of the contents or other purpose

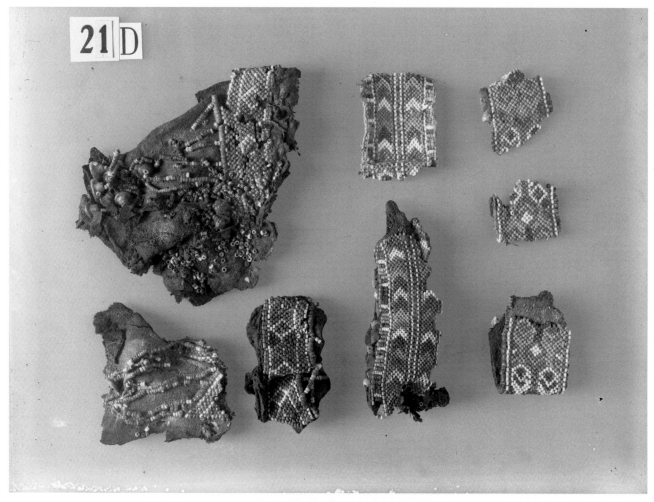

Fig. 2.6. Fragments of woven tapestry robe, consolidated with treatments of Canada balsam in xylol, then paraffin wax in benzene (Object no. 21d). © Griffith Institute, University of Oxford.

its condition became slightly worse, and after mature delib-eration and a preliminary experiment on one corner it was decided to treat the whole box with melted paraffin wax and this accordingly was done. The larger cracks were filled up with plasticine before applying the wax.[32]

Box 21 was the first box filled with items that was cleared, and thus it was the first chance for the team to see what challenges they would face (Fig. 2.5). The jumble of con-tents, which they deduced had been repacked after the tomb robberies, contributed to the difficulties:

> If we had searched the whole tomb through we should have been hard put to it to find a single object that created a greater number of problems […][33]

It took them three weeks to process the items and get to the bottom of that first box.[34] We will briefly discuss some of the artefacts found within this box and the problems they raised in terms of conservation.

Ceremonial robe (object no. 21d)

This beaded garment raised serious problems (Fig. 2.6). In Carter's Cards, Lucas summarizes his intervention in the following way:

> Treatment: Treated exposed portion of garment first with a solution of Canada balsam dissolved in xylene applied by means of a pipette, and afterwards with melted paraffin wax. Sprayed a few small portions of cloth from which ornamen-tation had dropped with a solution of celluloid dissolved in a mixture of amylacetate and acetone. (Carter Card 021d-14)[35]

Again, Lucas's notes provide a level of detail that allows the sequence of the procedures he adopted to be reconstructed (Fig. 2.6):

> Beaded Robe in Painted Box. No 21d. Plain Weave.

> Found crumpled in a heap at the top of the box. Beads and gold sequins (convex) were loose, the threads with which sewn having perished. Fabric of robe also perished.

Fig. 2.7. Decorated sandal (Object no. 21f), showing details of gold and beaded decorations. © Griffith Institute, University of Oxford.

Removed as much dust as possible by gentle blowing with small bellows and afterwards spraying with benzine.

Blue beads both long + round = glass Broke + examined

Treated repeatedly with solution of Canada balsam in xylol, allowing at least a day to elapse between treatments. The solution was applied by means of a small pipette.

Attempted to remove the robe but only a small portion came out intact, the rest falling to pieces. Consolidated this and some small pieces of borders of fine beadwork by saturating with a solution of paraffin in wax in benzine. Apart from the portion treated with wax it was only possible to keep intact a few small portions of the fabric from which the decoration had fallen and these were strengthened by spraying with a dilute solution of celluloid in amyl acetate and acetone.

After consolidating the piece of material mentioned above with wax in benzine, poured over it hot molten paraffin wax to consolidate further.

From Lucas's notes:

The robe was incredibly fragile, disintegrating at the touch, and in the end, only a few fragments could be saved.

Decorated sandal(s) (object nos. 021f[36] and 021g)

Extricating the object from the surrounding objects was a challenge. The sides of the sandals, made of tanned leather, had survived fairly well, though the threads on which the beads and sequins were strung had disintegrated, but the rawhide soles of the sandals had disintegrated and melted onto other objects. All the objects were jumbled together, and there was evidence that they had been crammed with force into the box, presumably by the officials who were tidying up after the robberies.

The decoration on this pair of sandals was not only elaborate, but it was the first object on which Lucas noted the variations of colours of the gold sequins, some more yellow, some more red (Fig. 2.7). Sandal 21f was the first entry into his Register of Samples in January 1923:[37]

With duck's heads in front. In very bad condition, the leather of the sole having perished and having become black and pitch-like and having stuck to other articles below. The leather of the sides had also perished and become brittle but has not stuck. Sole = new hide Sides = tanned leather.

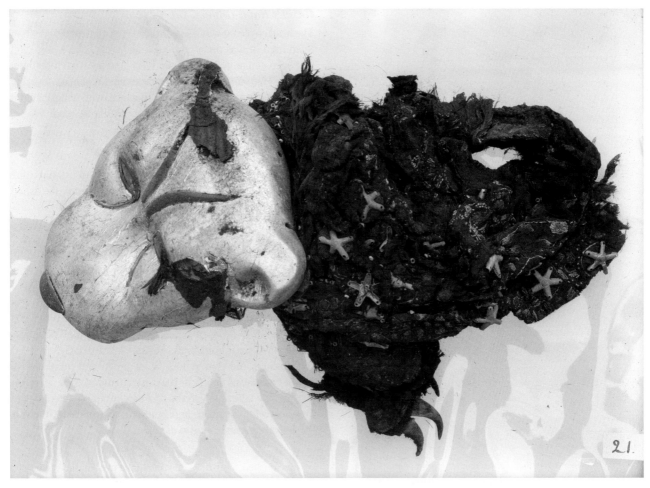

Fig. 2.8. Leopard head and cloak fragments, decorated with gold-star sequins and having silver claws (Object no. 21t). © Griffith Institute, University of Oxford.

A band of beadwork across the front was treated with a solution of Canada balsam in xylol applied with a pipette. The sides and bottoms were treated with a strong solution of celluloid in amyl acetate applied at first with a pipette and afterwards sprayed. On bottom this or any treatment was useless.

The sides were afterwards treated with a solution of Canada balsam in xylol applied with a pipette. This latter was fairly effective for the pieces of the sides remaining.[38]

The question of yellow gold and red gold continued to be something that Lucas turned to again and again:

The gold on which the scarlet occurs is always very yellow and bright and never tarnished. This may indicate a purer gold. That different qualities of gold were used is indicated by the grey appearance of some which is almost certainly due to silver chloride.

Coatings on Gold (Rathgen)

Silver Chloride formed by action of NaCl upon the Ag present. Removed by NH_3 or alternate use of $HCl + NH_3$ Red coating. Fe_2O_3. Due to extraneous deposits fixed by the AgCl. Removed by warming in HCl

(Rose) The surface colour of small particles of native gold is often apparently reddened by being coated with translucent films of oxides of iron.

Nature of Scarlet Colour

The colour is very easily rubbed off.

The colour is insoluble in: Water, Alcohol, Acetone, Benzine, Ammonia The colour is soluble in Hydrochloric acid (to a yellowish solution). Repeated <u>Agreed.</u>

The reddish brown colour is also insoluble in organic solvents but is soluble in HCl, forming a yellow solution. Repeated – colour only partly sol. in HCl.

The detailed notes he made and analyses he conducted during the fieldwork seasons allowed other researchers to have important data for continuing to explore this issue. The investigations and experimental work of Wood's experiments to replicate the purplish colour on gold, published in 1934, were directly related to Lucas's work.[39] Many decades later, Lucas's records continue to provide other researchers with both data and contexts to continue the discussion.[40]

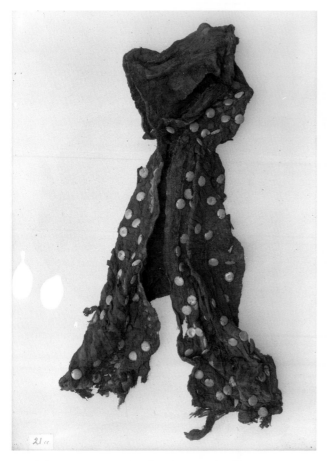

Fig. 2.9. Tapestry woven head covering, with gold sequins (Object no. 21cc). © Griffith Institute, University of Oxford.

Gilded leopard head and decorated cloth cloak (object no. 21t)

The photo Burton took of the second layer of the box's contents showed the jumble of materials, prominent among them a textile robe in the form of a leopard skin, decorated with applique five-pointed gold stars, silver claws and a leopard's head made of plaster covered with gold foil (Fig. 2.8).

Lucas Notes, no. 1, p9, from earliest season:

> Leopard's Head (plaster gilt) No 21t (Attached to Garment)

> Cloth ornamented with gold stars attached. – Sprayed with strong solution of celluloid in amyl acetate. Afterwards with celluloid in acetone. Gold much tarnished Head disfigured by patches of black patch-like material which had come from some other object. These were decomposed raw hide (from sole of sandal) + were softened and removed by water and a soft brush. Sprayed with solution of celluloid in amyl acetate to fix loose gilt. Gold of head yellow.

In Box 44 a similar leopard head (larger, more ornate and with a glass cartouche) was found attached to the remnants of a real leopard skin (object no. 44g), also decorated with gold sequins. Some additional scraps of leopard skin (object no. 46ff) were found in a bundle of other items.[41]

Child's hood (object. no. 021cc)

The head covering was a separate piece of cloth sewn on, about 8 cm high. It was open both back and front. The whole cloth had been elaborately decorated with tapestry woven coloured threads. This garment seemed to be some sort of head covering, child-sized, representing a protective bird, with wings hanging down behind (Fig. 2.9). In the Carter Cards we read:

> Treatment: Sprayed with solution of celluloid in amyl acetate.

For this item, Lucas's notes do not add any additional information, except to note that the gold sequins were tarnished, and that there were similarities to object no. 21x.[42]

'Guardian' statues (objects nos. 22 and 29)

Statues 22 and 29 are 'life-sized' statues which flanked the doorway to the burial chamber. Carter referred to them as 'sentinel' statues.

The description of the objects mentions: 'Wood, covered with gesso and black resin. The contrasting gold colour provided by an overlay of gold on gesso on cloth. The uraeus was bronze with gold inlay' (Carter Card 022-5).

Although the two statues were noted and numbered at the beginning of work in the Antechamber, they were not taken to the laboratory in the first batches of objects. Instead, they were left in place and boarded up to protect them as the burial chamber wall was taken down.

> By the middle of February our work in the Antechamber was finished. With the exception of the two sentinel statues, left for a special reason, all its contents had been removed to the laboratory, every inch of its floor had been swept and sifted for the last bead or fallen piece of inlay, and it now stood bare and empty.[43]

Mace's journal entries in early 1924, well into the second season, note dates of working on them, alone and with Lucas, and details some of the difficulties of carrying out the treatment process that had been determined:

> 7 Jan. 1924: Waxing head of Statue 22 slowly with a pipette. Care has to be taken to keep wax off the black parts, as the resin would melt & run.

> 10 Jan: Whole day on statue with Lucas.

> 19 Jan: Spent most of the morning photographing and wrapping statue 22. In afternoon finished and got it into its box.

> 23 Jan: Started work on second statue. Condition worst than the first in that black resin had melted & run down all over gold.

> 6 Feb: Finished waxing of statue 29, & waxed several sticks.

Burton photos show the statues in the laboratory, with Lucas and Mace working on them (Fig. 2.10). Although sturdier than the smaller objects, their packing was a complicated process of wrapping the limbs and the mace and staff that each held. A series of staged photographs captured the process of Carter and Callender wrapping Statue 29[44] and Statue 22[45] (Fig. 2.11).

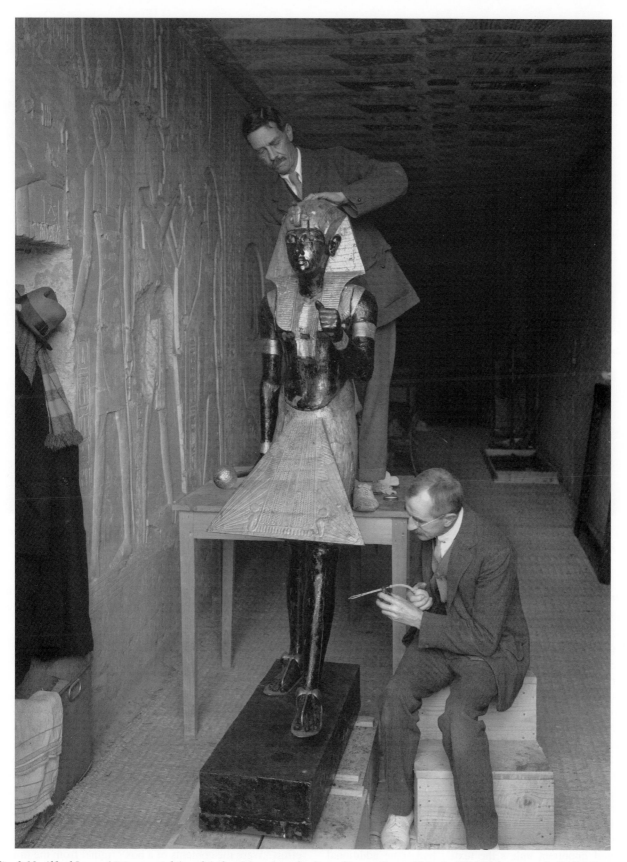

Fig. 2.10. Alfred Lucas (sitting on right) and Arthur Mace (standing), working on Statue 22 in the KV 15 laboratory. © Griffith Institute, University of Oxford.

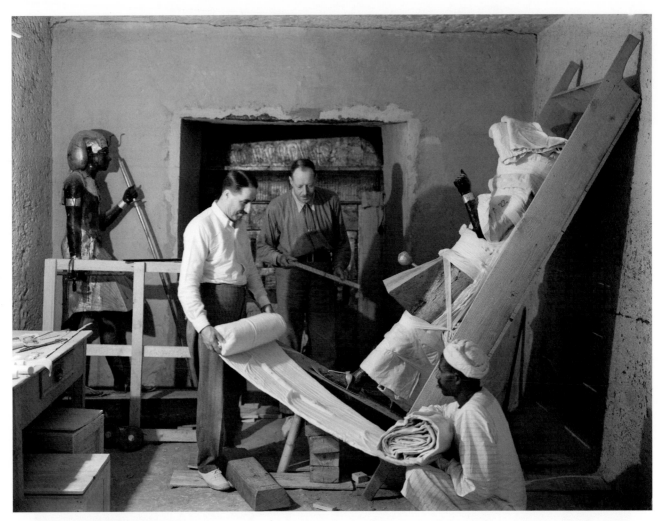

Fig. 2.11. Howard Carter and Arthur Callender in the emptied Antechamber, in front of entrance to Burial Chamber, wrapping Statue 22 for transport. © Griffith Institute, University of Oxford.

Linen covering (object. no. 22a)

The 'guardian' statues were wrapped in linen cloths. Although there are no individual photos of this linen wrapping, it can be partially seen in several of Burton's photos of Statue 22[46] and in the background photos taken of the corner of the Antechamber that included the numbered items around Box 21.[47] In one of the photos,[48] it appears that the covering may fall onto the kilt of the statue, or possibly wrap around the lower back of the statue and be looped over the right arm as well as the left.

The note card for Statue 29 states: 'This statue, like 22, had originally a fine linen covering' (Carter Card 029-3). This linen was not assigned its own object number, and there is no further information on it.

Textile wrappings around objects in the tomb were often only minimally recorded by the excavators, not being considered important unless the textile had some additional perceived value, such as inscription markings (such as object no. 261a, wrapped around the Anubis in the Treasury, which is discussed later in this paper). Lucas refers to it very briefly in the Carter Cards.

> Description: Remains of linen covering, hanging from L[eft] arm of Statue 22. In ragged condition, but cloth fairly strong. Packed to go to Cairo for experimental purposes.

There are no treatment notes added to the card by Lucas, and his personal notes do not discuss it.

Box 54

As the work in clearing the Antechamber continued, the team encountered more boxes that contained jumbled contents. Object documentation on the individual cards continued to include questions and attempts at answering contextual questions. Was the box or object in its original position, or had it been moved by either the robbers or the clean-up effort? Were the contents of a box original from the time of the burial, or altered by one of the other of the events? In

Fig. 2.12. Box 54, with blue nmst-*ewers on bottom, fragments of corslet and other objects in top layer. © Griffith Institute, University of Oxford.*

most cases, there was not enough information to do anything more than theorize, and notes on that appear on individual card notations.

Although the documentation system was an effective way to keep track of numerous objects, and the sub-numbering allowed for noting context of objects within a box or in a group of materials related by location, sometimes the groupings were arbitrary and there was not a built-in mechanism for comments on groups of objects or larger contexts.

Lucas's notes provide insight into questions he was considering and tests that he undertook but which did not necessarily relate to an individual object.

In the case of Box 54, a hieratic inscription on the lid,[49] lists its contents, which were present at the bottom of the box (Fig. 2.12).[50]

The jumble of materials on top of the original contents were from objects which were linked to so many different parts of the tomb that the excavators noted on the opening card that the box was 'a good illustration of the casual nature of the repacking'.[51] And, indeed, the contents of the box included chariot parts that probably

were originally associated with the stacks of chariots in the north end of the Antechamber, and the elaborate corselet (object no. 54k).

Combined corselet, collar and pectoral (object no. 54k)

The corselet was found broken into many pieces and scattered across the top of the faience vessels at the bottom of the box (Fig. 2.13). Parts of this object were found elsewhere in the tomb, such as:

1. Gold shrine (108)
2. 8 pieces in 12A & 4 in 12C
3. 13 + 10 in floor sweepings of the Antechamber, including ear, leg inlay from pectoral
4. One collar square from Dish 154, mixed with dates
5. One feather from Box 101
6. Three pieces of collar from Box 115
7. One feather with material from Chariot 122

The preliminary reconstruction of this object, which turned out to be a corselet of intricate gold and carnelian inlay

Fig. 2.13. Interior of Box 54, after cloth garment and other objects removed, revealing the corslet fragments scattered on top of the blue faience vessels. © Griffith Institute, University of Oxford.

with an attached collar of carnelian and faience beads, and open goldwork pectorals front and back, took Mace days of concentrated work and required calculated guesswork on how all the pieces fit together (Fig. 2.14).[52]

Lucas noted:

> Treatment: Stuck in a few of the larger loose pieces with celluloid cement: cleaned many of separate parts with benzine & soft brush & some with water & soft brush.

Lucas noted many years later that a new reconstruction had been done by Guy Brunton in the Cairo Museum, and that this was a more correct arrangement of the elements.[53]

Bronze snake with gold inlay (object no. 54b)

The bronze snake was found in the top layer of Box 54 (Fig. 2.15), along with other objects that were tossed in on top of the robe, including a scarab, a model knife, a pair of decorated throw sticks and other sections of woven fabric that covered the libation vessels. The snake

had three brackets on the underside that indicated it had been part of a larger object, possibly furniture, as noted on the card.

Later, once the chariots at the south end of the Antechamber had been removed and reconstructed, it was discovered that this snake was part of the interior decoration of the body of Chariot 122.[54] When restored to its original placement, it proved to be a hieroglyph beginning the word *Dt*, 'eternity'.[55]

Chariot (object no. 122)

This chariot was one of four that had been disassembled and stacked with parts of three other chariots (Fig. 2.16). The cleaning and restoration of this chariot was done in the courtyard of the laboratory tomb (Fig. 2.17),[56] where there was enough space for both Lucas and Mace to work on it.

The jumble of wheels and other chariot parts on the south side of the Antechamber presented numerous challenges.

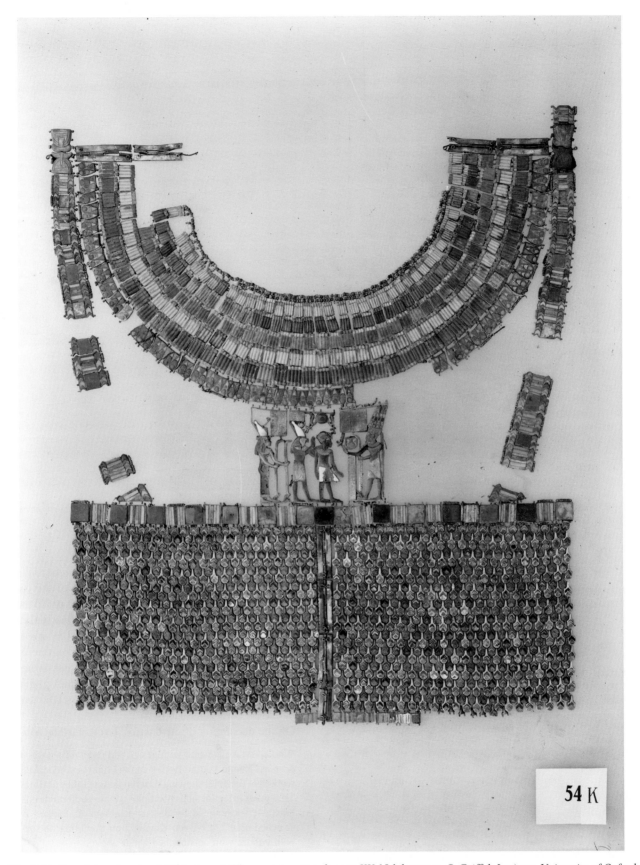

Fig. 2.14. Corselet and pectoral (Object no. 54K), reconstruction done in KV 15 laboratory. © Griffith Institute, University of Oxford.

Fig. 2.15. Interior of Box 54, showing bronze snake ornament (from Chariot 122), cloak and other objects, with nmst-*ewers underneath.* © *Griffith Institute, University of Oxford.*

Fig. 2.16. Southern end of the Antechamber, with four disassembled chariots on left, including Chariots 120 and 122. © Griffith Institute, University of Oxford.

Carter even noted that they had started the numbering system – and their work – on the opposite end of the room, 'thus putting off the evil day when we should have to tackle the complicated tangle of the chariots'.[57] For not only had the chariots been disassembled in antiquity to be able to fit into the tomb (the axles had been sawn off on one end), and then moved by the robbers, but all the leather harnesses and other trappings had disintegrated into a 'black glutinous mass [...] having rundown over everything [...] the leather has almost entirely perished'.[58]

On the decoration of the chariot, Lucas further notes:

Whole surface covered with gesso, and overlaid with gold & inlay. Round bottom twelve captive figures wonderfully worked in the gold, showing different nationalities or tribes. Triangular pieces at sides had first – at top – a floral design. Next ◇ surmounted by disk and plumes & flanked by crowned uraei. At bottom King as lion trampling on foes, with vulture with outstretched wings above.

Treatment: Cleaned with water & ammonia: loose inlay stuck in with glue and celluloid cement. Waxed.[59]

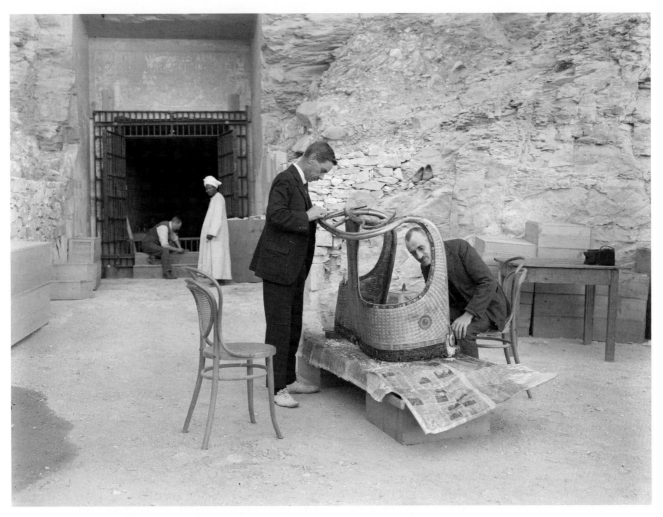

Fig. 2.17. In the courtyard in front of the laboratory in KV 15: Arthur Mace (standing) and Alfred Lucas (on right), cleaning and repairing Chariot 120. © Griffith Institute, University of Oxford.

The drawing of the floor plan, with various layers and objects indicated in red, provides a useful overview of the layers involved.[60] The documentation for Chariot 122 is the most complete for all the chariots in the tomb[61] and the first card notes this includes 'body, pole and two trays of fragments'.[62] Not all of the gold ornamentation and other embossed gold fragments belonged to this particular chariot but the pieces were so tangled together that they were assigned object no. 122 sub-numberings:

> Impossible to assign parts of the harness to any chariot in particular, so treated here under this number, as most of it was found in the neighborhood of body 122.[63]

It is important to note this arbitrary numbering assignment of fragments to the object no. 122 series, since some of the gold appliqués display the cartouches of both the kings' throne names – Tutankhaten and Tutankhamun – side by side, and interpretation of this might be further enhanced

if it could be determined whether only one of the chariots displayed these, or whether it was part of the decoration program of more than one chariot.[64]

Burial Chamber

In this section, three distinct materials found in objects from the Burial Chamber will be discussed. Their conservation raised challenges for Lucas. These materials were: natron (in faience cups in object no. 193), ostrich feathers (part of a fan a fan, object no. 242), and black unguents from the innermost coffin, object no. 255 (outside and inside).

Carter's drawing of the Burial Chamber provides a useful overview of the location of all of the objects in the areas around and between the shrines.[65] While Burton did take photos of the objects *in situ*, the limited space he had to work in the narrow walkway around the shrines did

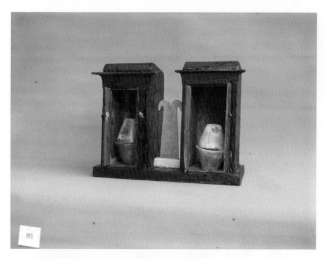

Fig. 2.18. Burial Chamber: Kiosks and peseshkef *on pedestal, with faience cups containing natron and resin (Object no. 193). © Griffith Institute, University of Oxford.*

not allow for recording the same types of photographic groupings that was done in the Antechamber.

Pair of Kiosks with Peseshkef (object no. 193) (Fig. 2.18)

A pair of kiosks coated with black resin, mounted on a platform, were found in the northwest corner of the chamber, between the wall and the outermost shrine. The kiosks flanked a *peseshkef* of slate that stood on a calcite base. The slate showed an ancient repair. This set of objects was at one end of the row of wooden oars (object nos. 182–192), and at the other end of the row was a similar, black-varnished wooden object, with a wooden *hes*-vase between two pylons (object no. 181).

Each of the kiosks contained a pair of small faience bowls, one turned over on the other to form a lid, and sealed with a black substance that Lucas identified as a resin similar to that which coated the kiosks. In the right-hand kiosk, a pair of pale blue cups held natron, while in the left-hand kiosk the dark blue faience cups contained resin. Lucas refer to these objects in these terms:

> Remarks [Treatment]:
>
> Cleaned with acetone sprayed after dusting with a brush. Feather cleaned with soap and warm water. Cups soaked in hot water.[66]

While the notecard identifies the slate object between the two kiosks as feathers,[67] the slate object may be identified as a *pesheskef*, a forked object associated with the Opening of the Mouth ceremony. The two cups on each side are in fact similar to those in the set of objects for the Opening of the Mouth ceremony. The presence of natron and resin in relation to this ceremony may be a new development in

Tutankhamun's reign.[68] The doors of the kiosks were closed with cord and sealed, though one seal was missing.

Long-handled fan with depiction of ostrich hunt (object no. 242)

This long-handled ostrich-plume fan was found lying on the ground between the third and fourth shrines. As an object it was spectacular, made of embossed gold, with the scenes upon it showing the king hunting ostriches on one side, and on the other side returning triumphant, with his attendants carrying the ostriches. For Lucas, this object provided a new opportunity and a new challenge. The ostrich feathers had been badly eaten by insects, but there were still some plumes left to try to preserve. Box 32 in the Antechamber had contained a few broken ostrich feathers (object no. 32w); perhaps visible in Burton photo p0094),[69] which Lucas had tried spraying with a solution of cellulose acetate in acetone.

With more material to work with from the fan, Lucas took some of the sections of the ostrich plumes, and tried spraying and treating them with eight different solutions to see what would work best:

> With this fan a mass of debris of insect-eaten ostrich feathers were found (see photo).[70] It has been cleaned with warm water and ammonia – the sheet gold where loose glued with scotch glue. Gold – cleaned with warm water and ammonia.

His notes show that most of these treatments either made the feathers too brittle or made them completely lose their 'fluffiness'. The best option ended up being duroprene in xylol, about ¼ original strength.

The Gold Coffin (object no. 255) and the consecration unguents

The process of opening, recording and then dismantling the four wooden shrines, and then removing the coffins from the sarcophagus, was full of engineering problems to navigate within the limited space of the Burial Chamber. This was where Callender's expertise was essential. In Mace's absence – his health prevented his return to Egypt after the second season – Lucas often worked in the laboratory alone, or with Carter helping with the recording and cleaning.

Carter's journals note Lucas's working on the first coffin, in particular:[71] '21 October: Lucas working on coffin lid – did a good job of it.' The chemist had become skilled at restoration work over the months of working on objects. But once the lid of the second coffin was raised, a new and daunting challenge presented itself.

The third coffin was covered with a thick layer of black pitch-like material, from the hands down the feet, apparently consecration unguents that had been poured during the funerary rites (Fig. 2.19). There was so much of it, buckets of it, that it filled the space between the two coffins up to the rim:

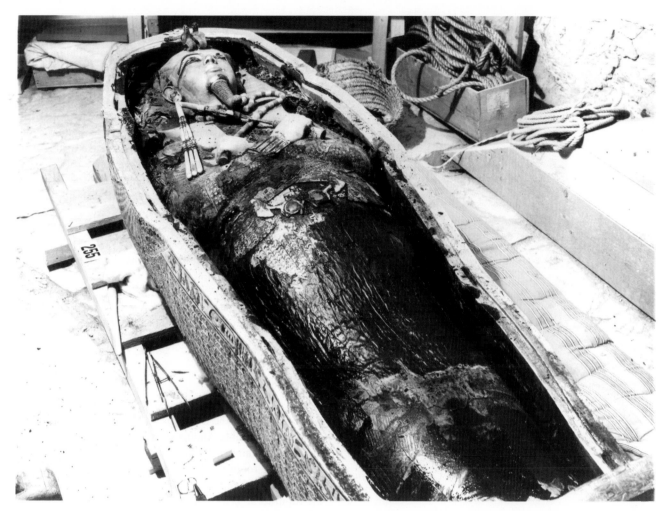

Fig. 2.19. Third coffin (Object no. 255) stuck inside second coffin (Object no. 254), showing hardened black unguents from the hands to the feet. © Griffith Institute, University of Oxford.

24 October 1925

It will be seen that our next problem, which is by no means an easy one, is to remove the third coffin firmly cemented by the libation to the interior of the second coffin without causing damage to either. To this subject and that of the future cleaning of the coffin, Lucas is now giving his attention.[72]

Lucas took samples of the black material, which had hardened on the coffin and had greatly damaged the mummy itself, and tried various solvents. More detailed and sophisticated analyses, processes that were beyond the rudimentary laboratory in KV 15, would take time, to send samples and await results. The results ultimately showed that the material contained resin and fatty matter, and other materials.[73] Various solvents were tried, but without success. And in the meantime, there was a looming deadline of the public investigation of the mummy, set for 11 November.

Lucas had an idea of the temperatures that could be generated by putting things out in full sun. He had collected data on temperatures, writing to Dr Hurst at the Ministry of Public Work in Cairo, for not only the usual values that a regular thermometer would provide, but also for black bulb temperature readings, which would provide temperatures outside in full sunlight. These high temperatures led him to experiment with sun as a possible heat source to melt the hardened unguents. But it was not enough to loosen the hardened material.

Carter's journal details the attempts:[74]

Nov 1

Removed the Royal Mummy to No. 15. It took ten men to bring out of the Tomb and carry it up. Placed in the sun for a few hours, while Lucas, Burton & self hammered off the black coating upon the lid of the third coffin. Heat of the sun not sufficient today to make any real impression upon the pitch-like material which has stuck fast the mummy & coffins.

Nov. 2

Found that the heat of the sun was of no avail in freeing the mummy from its coffin. In consequence, the examination of the Royal Mummy must necessarily take place as

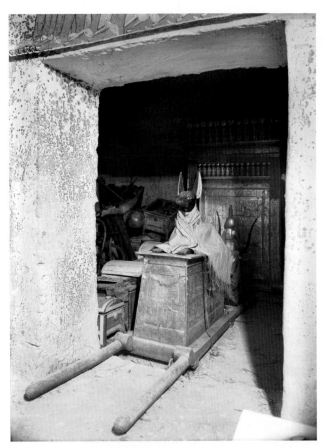

Fig. 2.20. Anubis shrine (Object no. 261) in doorway of Treasury, with carrying poles extending into the Burial Chamber. © Griffith Institute, University of Oxford.

it lies. Cleaned the greater part of the thick coating upon the third coffin.

In the end, the mummy remained anchored in the bottom of the gold coffin for the public event, and the temporary solution was to move the entire assemblage into the laboratory area inside KV 15, where the formal 'examination' was then conducted.[75]

After the ceremony, the work continued, and involved a series of trial-and-error attempts to heat the coffin enough to melt the unguents, but not cause damage. Lucas described the final process:

Treatment.

This pitch-like material hardened by age had to be removed by means of hammering, solvents and heat, while the shells of the coffins were loosened from one another and extricated by means of great heat; the interior being temporarily protected during the process by zinc plates – the temperature employed though necessarily below the melting point of zinc was several hundred degrees Fahrenheit. After the inner coffin was extricated, it had to be again treated with heat and solvents before the material could be completely removed.

Various solvents were tried on samples of the black substance, and various methods employed.[76] Once they moved beyond the Burial Chamber, they may have thought they were done with the problem of hardened consecration unguents. But they were to find this type of substance again inside the calcite canopic chest (object no. 266b) in the Treasury. One of the documentation cards noted that unguents had been poured over the four miniature gold coffins containing the viscera, 'as in the case of the royal mummy […] cementing the coffins in their receptacles'.[77] The black substance can be seen in one of Burton's photos (p1159), coating the insides of the compartments and spilling over on some of them, which Carter interpreted as evidence that the canopic chest had been moved after the rites had been completed and the chest sealed.[78]

Evidence that the unguents had hardened is only found in Carter's extended notes that he had made for the hoped-for future publication. In that draft he noted: 'a powerful solvent such as pyradine was applied for many days and as much heat as was prudent, but unfortunately they could not be extracted'.[79]

Treasury Room

What Carter called the 'Treasury' was not a sealed room, but was connected to the Burial Chamber by an open doorway in which a portable Anubis shrine was placed, facing into the Burial Chamber. Whether it was originally intended to be a sealed room is unknown, but the size of the Anubis shrine and the length of its carrying poles did not allow for the room to be bricked up like the other rooms. The tomb robbers had entered this room and many of the boxes had been opened, some left completely empty, while others were filled in the same haphazard way as in the Antechamber, with items replaced in the subsequent clean-up efforts of the officials.

We will focus on Lucas's analyses of two containers found in this room and on selected contents from them: the portable Anubis shrine, which was also a 'box' in the sense that it had a removable lid and compartments within it containing various objects; and object no. 271, an ornamental box that no longer had its original contents but had been filled with scribal palettes and other objects related to scribal activity.

Anubis figure and portable shrine (object no. 261)

The famous shrine was found in the doorway of the Treasury, facing into the Burial Chamber. The front carrying poles extended forward into the Burial Chamber (Fig. 2.20).[80] On the floor in front of the shrine, at the threshold between the two rooms, was a reed torch and magical brick (object no. 263), with a protection text inscribed on it.

The Anubis figure was draped in an outer linen covering (object no. 261a), under which the following objects were hidden from view: a 'muslin-like' inner covering (261b), flower garlands (261c) and a scarf (261d) around the neck; and between the forelegs was a painting palette inscribed with the name and titles of Meritaten (object no. 262).[81]

Lucas's notes on the Carter Cards did not provide any details about his conservation treatment to the Anubis figure itself, focusing instead on the shrine on which it rested:

> Remarks [treatment of pylonic shrine]: Though in fair condition the wood was much shrunk, the goldwork bulged in many places. Weak places filled in with wax and the whole surfaces completely waxed over. The gilding much tarnished.[82]

The object was in fact a box with interior compartments. The Anubis jackal figure is pegged to a board on the top that forms a lid for the box, and slides off to open it. The interior of the shrine was divided into one large compartment and a group of four smaller compartments at one end (Fig. 2.21).

The large compartment contained jewellery and an amulet (object no. 261i–p). Some of the pectorals were wrapped in a large piece of linen that seems to have been sealed but had been broken open.

The four smaller compartments (E, F, G and H) at the top contained groups of objects. Compartment H contained a pair of small cups (object no. 261h), again with one inverted over the other as in object no. 193 and containing a 'powdery substance' that is natron mixed with resin. The cups here were beakers, slightly smaller (top diameter 7.5 cm; bottom 3.5 cm; height 6.8 cm) and were made of calcite rather than faience.

Lucas's analysis of the substance reports:

> Contents.
>
> The bottom vase contained a very light brown-coloured material in the form of (a) very small tear-shaped particles, (b) thin rods of uniform diameter and (c) powder.
>
> The material consists of an intimate mixture of resin (probably gum-resin), common salt, sulphate of soda and a very small proportion of carbonate of soda (natron). It may be either a mixture of resin and salt (the latter contaminated with sulphate of soda and carbonate of soda) or it may be resin mixed with what was intended to be natron but which consisted essentially of salt and sulphate of soda with only a trace of natron. Although the resin when separated burns vigorously the mixture only lights with difficulty and soon goes out: the smell of the burning mixture is not fragrant. The evidence therefore seems against the mixture being for use as incense though the resin it contains may be incense. This will be further analysed in Cairo.

The other three of the four compartments held small amulets or cult objects individually wrapped in linen (object no. 261e–g). These four compartments appear similar in size and shape to the four hollowed-out compartments in which

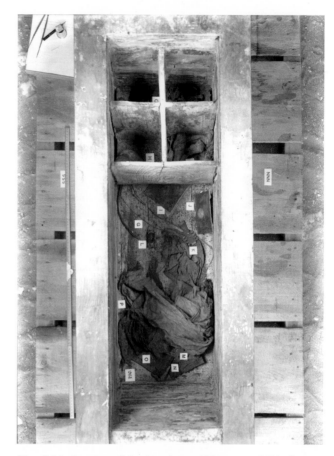

Fig. 2.21. Interior of Anubis shrine (Object no. 261) showing compartments and linen-wrapped objects. © Griffith Institute, University of Oxford.

the miniature coffinettes with Tutankhamun's mummified internal organs were placed, and then put into the calcite canopic chest (object no. 266b).[83]

The shrine itself may have been carried in the funeral procession, not only as a symbol of Anubis, but as a container for the embalmed viscera that were destined to ultimately be placed in the calcite canopic chest (object no. 266b). There is visual evidence from depictions of funeral processions in other tombs and Book of the Dead vignettes that show a similar Anubis shrine.[84] The inclusion of a very similar Anubis shrine on a sledge was depicted in the lengthy funeral procession on the Papyrus of Ani (19th Dynasty) following the funeral bier. The decorative design has alternating *djed* and *tjet* symbols, similar to the Anubis shrine in Tutankhamun's tomb.[85]

In the tomb of Roy (TT 225, 18th Dynasty, time of Horemheb), the funeral procession scene depicts an Anubis shrine, simply painted yellow with red bands, being carried by four men.[86] In the funeral procession of Pairy (TT 139, 18th Dynasty) a portable (on carrying poles) canopic shrine, of the shape of the calcite one in Tutankhamun's tomb, is carried behind the bier.

Fig. 2.22. Box 271 interior, showing royal scribal palettes (Object nos. 271b and 271e (2) on the left (linen wrapping visible). © Griffith Institute, University of Oxford.

Did the Anubis shrine in Tutankhamun's tomb serve that purpose, to transport the viscera under the protection of Anubis? The configuration of the interior of the shrine, and some of its contents, may offer some further data on this possibility.[87]

Pigments in royal palettes (object nos. 262, 271b, 271e)

Three palettes inscribed with royal names were found in the Treasury (Figs 2.22–2.23). The first (object no. 262) was a 'painting' palette, a designation given to a type of scribal palette that has multiple wells of pigments and pigment colours, more than the traditional black and red pigments of the scribe. This one was an ivory with six oval wells of pigments: it was inscribed a single vertical line of hieroglyphs running down the slot cover, and titles of Princess Meritaten, and was found between the forelegs of the Anubis figure on the shrine (object no. 261).

This box, like so many others, contained objects that had been tossed into it. In this case, though, it is clear, because of the construction of the box, that its original contents were gone. The bottom of the box was divided into 16 compartments, the edges of which were lined with ivory. In contrast to Box 54 in the Antechamber, which probably had the original contents at the bottom, this box in the Treasury contained none of its original materials.

The scribal palettes placed in this box, presumably after the robberies, are important objects partly because of their inscriptions: the gilded wooden one (object no. 271a) was inscribed with the Tutankhaten throne name and titles, while the ivory one next to it (object no. 271b) was inscribed with Tutankhamun's names and titles. The coexistence of these two inscriptions for Tutankhaten/ Tutankhamun in the context of writing instruments is

particularly intriguing, and these issues have been discussed elsewhere.[88]

The pigments on object nos. 271e(2) and 271b were black (carbon) and red (red ochre), the commonly used colours (and substances) of scribal activity. On object no. 262, Lucas analysed the black (carbon), red (red ochre), white (probably sulphate of lime, not carbonate of lime) and yellow (probably orpiment, sulphate of arsenic). The samples of white and yellow that he was able to take, without damaging the object, were too small for confirmation.

As he sampled other pigments on objects in the Treasury Room, especially on the model boats, he came to the tentative conclusion that the bright yellow was indeed orpiment, and he wondered if the presence of arsenic in the pigment kept fungus from forming on it, as it seemed those areas of the boats that were pained that yellow were not as affected by fungal growth.[89]

Annexe

The Annexe room was the last space to be cleared in the tomb, and the smallness of the space, combined with the chaos and destruction of the tomb robbers, and the lack of any kind of restoration of order, provided new challenges related to the conservation of objects. This final season of work was also a very short season, with hundreds of objects being removed within a period of just a few weeks in 1927: the season began on 30 November, and ended on 15 December.[90]

The written documentation of objects was in many cases minimal, and Burton took far fewer photos. The Annexe was originally the storeroom, the location for the pottery jars of wine, baskets of fruits and calcite vessels of oils.

To illustrate the conservation challenges of objects from this space, a few items are selected for discussion of Lucas's analyses and conservation. The floor was at a lower level, almost a metre below 'a jumble of every kind of funerary chattels, tumbled any way one upon the other, almost defying description'.[91]

Linen robe (object no. 367j)

This garment was badly crumpled up and cast into a wooden box (object no. 367). The fabric has suffered much but by being underneath the other robe it is in slightly better preservation. Lucas treated it with duroprene dissolved in xylol. The colours of the tapestry-woven ornament are difficult to discern exactly, but red and blue were present, as well as possibly green and black (Fig. 2.24).

This garment was later analysed and published by Crawford in 1941. In her article she talks about discussing the garment with Lucas at the Cairo Museum, and credits Lucas's help in suggesting an additional section of woven material from one of the boxes in the Antechamber. She never would have known about it if he had not told her, and it was crucial in her analysis of the garment.

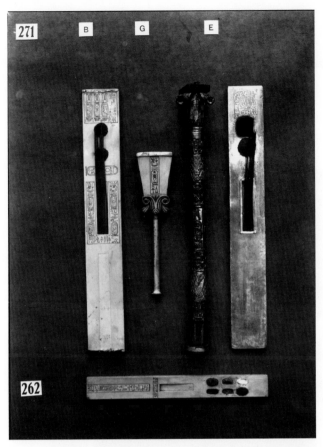

Fig. 2.23. Palettes inscribed with royal names: Tutankhaten (Object no. 271e (2)); Tutankhamun (Object no. 271b); and Meritaten (Object no. 262), with other scribal equipment from Treasury. © Griffith Institute, University of Oxford.

'Floor Rubbish' – objects nos. 620 (1) to 620 (123)

To illustrate how much destruction had taken place, presumably at the hands of the tomb robbers, we present here just the first 10 objects from the list of 620 numbers:

620 (1) 'Saucer' broken in several pieces with one fragment found in the Antechamber. Lid for object no. 435, an ornamental calcite vessel found in the Annexe (the inside of this vessels shows the finger marks of the thieves who had scooped out its contents (Burton photo, p1653)

620 (2) a calcite dish broken into 10 pieces

620 (3) calcite bowl or cover to a vase 'Broken in several pieces. Now mended'. Visible at least five pieces in the photo (p1281)

620 (4), (5) and (6) – ivory boomerangs, ends with gold caps partially torn off, found in dust on the floor

620 (7) and (8) – pair of gilt and faience throw sticks, tip broken off one

620 (9) blue faience throw stick broken in half

620 (10) blue faience throw stick, broken in four pieces.

Some finds within this category help make sense of earlier discoveries in the tomb. One of these is 620 (65), a grouping of 30 glass rods in various colours: turquoise-blue, violet-blue and yellow. Although initially entered as 'A number of sample rods of glass', a note added to the card later identified these glass rods to be the 'reeds' – representative pens – that had fallen out of some of the model scribal palettes (object nos. 367l, 367m and 367n) from Box 367, and from additional scribal palettes found amidst the debris on the floor of the Annexe.[92]

The wooden labels with hieratic inscriptions found 'scattered' in various places on the floor of the Antechamber are listed here in the 620s group: 620 (96) to 620 (109),[93] indicating that the 'Floor Rubbish' category was not only from the remains found on the floor of the Annexe, but what was left from earlier sweepings of the other chambers in the tomb.

Lucas and Tutankhamun's objects in Cairo

Lucas continued to work with and care for the objects that had been removed from the tomb and transported to the Cairo Museum. Some objects were exhibited right away, and he and Carter would meet at the Museum to discuss the exhibition process and how well the objects were doing in the new environment:

> Saw Lucas. We inspected the Tut.Ankh.Amen exhibits in the Museum, from the point of view of preservation. I think possibly there is a tendency of the throne darkening a little and we decided that late next spring we would treat it with wax which ought not only to brighten it up, but also help to make a permanent preservative.[94]

Carter also depended upon Lucas to help safeguard the Tutankhamun burial equipment in transit. When he was ready to bring the gold mask and gold coffin (object no. 255) to Cairo, he reserved a train car with an armed escort and Lucas joined him in it to bring the precious objects to Cairo.[95]

Lucas was also on hand to rescue the silver trumpet from the tomb when it was damaged in preparations for a BBC live broadcast in 1939. Lucas was there to be interviewed as a part of the programme. The day before the broadcast, the trumpeter who had been chosen to play the instrument rammed a modern mouthpiece (the ancient instrument did not have a mouthpiece) into the end of the trumpet, splitting it from end to end. Lucas spent the night soldering it back together, so the demonstration could go on.[96]

From 1923 onwards he was a chemist with the Department of Antiquities until his death in 1945,[97] and he made himself available to archaeologists, ending up consulting on and working with numerous projects. He not only worked on continuing to conserve and prepare the objects from the Tutankhamun tomb for exhibitions, he also played an

Fig. 2.24. Linen robe with tapestry woven decoration (Object no. 367j), from Box 367 in Annexe. © Griffith Institute, University of Oxford.

important role in assisting researchers who wanted to study the materials.

Two examples related to materials from the tomb of Tutankhamun illustrate this. Lucas was contacted by Wood, a chemist who was interested in trying to replicate the reddish or purplish colours of the gold, and sent him some samples that he had been given for experimentation. Wood had noticed similar gold films when working with optical properties of metallic granules, and thought the colour was produced at the time of manufacture. He experimented to see if he could reproduce it using methods that could have been employed at the time of Tutankhamun and was able to replicate it successfully.[98] Wood's experiments in turn informed the later work of Schorsch (2001) in wider consideration of the metal polychromy of objects from the tomb.[99]

Another example was further research done on one of the ceremonial robes found in the Annexe (object no. 367j), that was displayed between two sheets of glass in the Cairo Museum due to its fragility.

> [...] it would have been difficult to carry the study further if it had not been for the textile [Cairo 1045, Carter no. 54p] [...] As first recognized by Mr. Lucas, who pointed this out to me, this bears a strong resemblance to the patterned bands on the tunic [...] It was this that gave me the key to the weave of the bands [...] a weave which has not previously been described from ancient Egypt.[100]

Lucas's intimate knowledge of other objects from the tomb – including the small piece of woven textile from the top layer of Box 54 (the textile strip was 54p) – facilitated additional research.

Lucas's long career was founded from a belief that knowing about materials and processes made it possible to care for them appropriately, and to give them the opportunity to live again. He loved the objects themselves, was able to envision them whole and restored to their initial state at the time of their creation:

> The pleasure of the work needs to be known to be fully appreciated, but it is a real joy to see an object that has entered the workshop dirty, corroded and ugly gradually improving and finally becoming clean, healthy and beautiful.[101]

Notes

1. Lucas 1926, first edition. The second edition, published in 1933, was substantially expanded and included discussions about how the materials were worked with in ancient Egypt and therefore renamed to include 'Industries' in the title.
2. Brunton 1947, 6.
3. Carter and Mace 1923, 107–109.
4. Lee 1992, 13; Gardiner 1917, 203–206; Mace 1920, 151–156.
5. An initial draft of the first ten chapters of the book was in Mace's handwriting, and the first volume was initially published with both of their names on the cover. Mace was unable to continue work on the tomb after the first two seasons due to poor health which would ultimately lead to his early death in 1928; later publications left off Mace's name. Lee 1992, 95–97, 138–143.
6. Carter and Mace, 1923, Preface, xiii.
7. Petrie 1904, 85.
8. Petrie's dedication page at the beginning of *Methods and Aims* was a long list of Egyptologists who had been in the field with him, including Carter, Mace, Gardiner, Griffith and others.
9. Howard Carter journal, 1st Season, 7 December 1922.
10. Howard Carter pocket diary, 1st Season, 9 December 1922.
11. Howard and Mace 1923, 108 describes the unexpected and welcome addition of Lucas to the team.
12. Howard Carter journal, 1st Season, 9 December 1922.
13. Gilberg 1997, 33.
14. Lucas 1921, 9–10.
15. Lucas 1921, 10.
16. Lucas 1921, 2.
17. Howard Carter journal, 1st Season, 21 December 1922.
18. Mace 1923, 8.
19. Riggs 2021, 87–88; Carter and Mace 1923, 127–130.
20. A photo from the Times shows Lucas working on the throne, see Gilberg 1997, 36, Fig. 4; other photos and discussion of conditions in the laboratory in Lee 1992, 86–87.
21. Mace Journal, 2nd Season, 18 November 1923; for photo of the new gate see Gilberg 1997, 36, Fig. 2.
22. Scott 1927, 197.
23. Carter and Mace 1923, 164.
24. In 1945 he gave this book to the Griffith Institute, to be kept together with the Carter materials.
25. Lucas 1924.
26. Lucas 1924, 4n.
27. Lucas 1941, 135–147.
28. Lucas 1941, 135.
29. Lucas's notes on the cover sheet, dated 10/6/43, indicates six batches of notes, some on numbered loose-leaf pages, and some in notebooks.
30. Parkinson 2022, 130–131, provides a useful timeline of major events of work in the tomb.
31. Lucas 1941, 136.
32. Lucas Notes 1, 1–2.
33. The first volume of the popular books by Carter and Mace had an extensive discussion of this box and its contents (Carter and Mace 1923, 130–133).
34. Mace 1923, 10; Carter and Mace 1923, 133.
35. Usually, the treatment notes were recorded on the last card in the sequence for an object. Often these notes were in a thicker weight/darker, and that is probably Lucas's writing. (I have not done a detailed comparison of handwriting.) In this case, since what follows on the next three cards (Carter Cards 021-15 to 021-17) are detailed sketches and discussion of bead-work patterns, the treatment summary may well have been added to the card much later.
36. Sandal 21f is the first object listed in Lucas's Register of Samples, book, in the entry dated January 1923.
37. Lucas, Register of Samples.
38. Lucas Notes 1, 15.

39 Lucas sent to Wood some sequins from the Tutankhamun materials to do his experiments; there were presumably large quantities of such sequins that had fallen off textiles but had been kept (Wood 1934, 62).

40 The use and potential symbolic meanings of alternating colours or red and yellow gold and silver/silvery metals was examined by Schorsch, especially in Schorsch 2001; the sandals 21f and 21g, among others).

41 It is listed as another 'leopard-skin cloak' but there are only scraps of skin and no sequins or other decorative elements.

42 Lucas Notes 1, 11.

43 Carter and Mace 1923, 178.

44 Burton photos p0497, p0499.

45 Burton photos p0491, p0492.

46 Photos p0006, p0007.

47 Burton photos p0016 and p0017.

48 Burton p0320 (and p0321, which seems to be the same photo with slightly different lighting).

49 Černý 1965, 9, translates this inscription as 'What is in it – 17 blue *nmst*-ewers'.

50 Lucas Notes 1, 31; the coating contained salts.

51 Carter Card 054-2.

52 Mace's Journal, Season 2: he began work on it on 11 February and finally completed it on 23 February; though also working on other objects during this time, it seems to have been his main focus during this time.

53 Lucas 1941, 137.

54 Carter Card 122-12; Burton photo p0540; Parkinson 2022, 108–109 and Littauer, Crouwel 1985, 9 and 13–14.

55 Parkinson 2022, 108–109, provides a discussion of this along with Burton's photo showing it in place, and in which one can see the remains the 't' of the word, below the snake, formed in obsidian. Littauer and Crouwel 1985, 18, suggest that the bronze snakes on each side of the interior of the chariot body of Chariot 122 may have had a functional purpose, since Chariot 120 had gold bars in the same position in the interior of the chariot body.

56 The photo in Fig. 2.17 shows them cleaning Chariot 120, which was very similar to Chariot 122.

57 Carter and Mace 1923, 130.

58 Carter and Mace 1923, 132; preliminary nature of the treatment of the chariots before shipping to Cairo, 175.

59 Description of body, Carter Cards 122-05 through 122-13; treatment notes at bottom of Carter Card 122-13.

60 The drawing is Carter MSS i.G11 and can be viewed on the Griffith Institute website, but also see Parkinson's discussion and reproduction of it (Parkinson 2022, 12–13).

61 Leading Littauer and Crouwell 1985, 2, to make it the first chariot, 'A1' in their catalogue.

62 Carter Card 122-1.

63 Carter Card 122i; the number 122i is assigned to a pair of blinkers, the first of the objects on these trays. It is the only card that includes this information about the arbitrary assignment of numbers.

64 See Kawai 2022, 46–47, and Eaton-Krauss 2016, 26, for discussion of dual cartouches on these gold appliqués.

65 While Burton did take *in situ* photos of these objects, the limited space available meant the resultant photos do not provide a good overview of the spatial relationships. See the drawing, 'Burial Chamber: Objects *in situ*,' Carter MSS i.G.31, available on the Griffith Institute website.

66 Lucas did not seem to keep samples of materials once he has analysed them, unless he was sending the sample on to someone else for further analysis.

67 The Carter Card refers to them as feathers; Roth (1992) and Kaper (1994) both identify it as a *peseshkef* from the Opening of the Mouth ceremony.

68 Roth 1992, 135.

69 It appears only the shafts of the feathers remained.

70 In the photo of the fan *in situ* it is very difficult to see details, such as the remnants of the feathers; the photo must have been taken from the top of the shrine, looking downwards.

71 From HC Journal, 21 October 1925: 'Lucas working on coffin lid – did a good job of it'.

72 Howard Carter journal, 4th season, 24 October 1925.

73 Lucas, 2 January 1926, samples 1 and 2, *Register of Samples*; Plenderleith 1927, 215–216, reports on the results of analyses later done on the 'consecration fluid'.

74 Howard Carter journal, 4th Season, 1 and 2 November 1925.

75 Howard Carter journal, 4th Season, 2 and 11 November 1925; Parkinson 2022, 88–89, 94–95.

76 Lucas Notes 4: 3 and 7.

77 Carter Card 266b-10.

78 Carter Cards 266b-10 and 266b-11.

79 Carter n.d., 'Canopic Equipment notes'.

80 The carrying poles extend 74.2 cm in front and 75 cm behind the shrine, so there is not enough room for the shrine to have been placed completely in the Treasury.

81 The palette was hidden from view when the outer linen covering was in place, but visible after it was removed (see Burton photo p1674).

82 Carter Card 261-5.

83 No measurements are given for the interior, so my assessment of similar size is based on calculations of the objects and hollow spaces in both objects.

84 Falk's study of portable funerary furniture includes discussion of the Anubis shrine in this context (Falk 2015).

85 Russmann 2001, 197–198, no. 101; Goelet 1994, pls 5–6.

86 Porter and Moss 1960, 339; Schott photo archive, photo no. XIV, 55a.

87 Cashman forthcoming.

88 See Eaton-Krauss 2011 for this and other objects in the tomb with the Tutankhaten name. For a recent discussion and interpretation of the coexistence of the cartouches on a single object, see Kawai 2022. Also Cashman forthcoming.

89 Jones 1990, 7.

90 Timeline summarized in Parkinson 2022, 131.

91 Carter 1933, 98.

92 These palettes are discussed in detail in Cashman forthcoming.

93 Černý 1965, 15–17.

94 Howard Carter journal, 4th Season, 3 October 1925.

95 Lucas 1941, 135; Lucas notes the timing of this transport as spring 1926, while Carter's journal dates it to December 1924, which is probably more accurate.

96 Gilberg 1997, 39–40; Manniche 1976, 13; Kirby 1947, 40.

97 Brunton 1947, 1–2.

98 Wood 1934, 62–65.

99 Schorsch 2001, 55–71; includes discussion of the decorated sandals from Box 21.
100 Crowfoot and Davies 1941, 117.
101 Lucas 1924, 5.

Bibliography

Brunton, Guy 1947. 'Alfred Lucas, 1867–1943'. *Annales du Service des Antiquités de l'Égypte* 47: 1–6.

Carter, Howard. 1927. *The Tomb of Tut-ankh.Amen*, Vol. II. London: Cassell.

Carter, Howard. 1933. *The Tomb of Tut-ankh.Amen*, Vol. III. London: Cassell.

Carter, Howard, and A.C. Mace. 1923. *The Tomb of Tut-ankh. Amen*, Vol. I. London: Cassell & Company.

Cashman, Jenny. Forthcoming. 'Scribal Surprises in the Tomb of Tutankhamun: Anubis' Hidden Palette and Other Treasures'. Paper presented at the annual meeting of the American Research Center in Egypt, April 2022.

Černý, Jaroslav. 1965. *Hieratic Inscriptions from the Tomb of Tutankhamun*. Oxford: Aris and Phillips.

Crowfoot, Grace, and Norman de Garis Davies. 1941. 'The Tunic of Tut'ankhamūn'. *The Journal of Egyptian Archaeology* 27: 113–130.

Eaton-Krauss, Marianne. 2011. 'King Tutankhaten'. *Orientalia* 80 (3): 300–304.

Eaton-Krauss, Marianne. 2016. *The Unknown Tutankhamun*. London: Bloomsbury.

Falk, David Allen. 2015. 'Ritual Processional Furniture: A Material and Religious Phenomenon in Egypt'. PhD dissertation. University of Liverpool.

Gardiner, Alan. 1917. 'Review of Publications of the Metropolitan Museum of Art Egyptian Expedition, Vol. I. The Tomb of Senebtisi at Lisht, by A. M. Lythgoe, A. C. Mace, & H. E. Winlock'. *The Journal of Egyptian Archaeology* 4 (2/3): 203–206.

Gilberg, Mark. 1997. 'Alfred Lucas: Egypt's Sherlock Holmes'. *Journal of the American Institute for Conservation* 36 (1): 31–48.

Goelet, Ogden, 1994. *The Egyptian Book of the Dead, The Book of Going Forth by Day, being the Papyrus of Ani*. Translated by Raymond Faulkner. San Francisco: Chronicle Books.

The Griffith Institute. n.d. 'Anatomy of an Excavation'. http://www.griffith.ox.ac.uk/discoveringTut/ (last accessed 31 January 2024).

Jones, Dilwyn. 1990. *Model Boats from the Tomb of Tut'ankhamun*. Oxford: Griffith Institute.

Kaper, Olaf. 1994. 'The Door Sealings and Object Sealings'. In *Stone Vessels, Pottery, and Sealings from the Tomb of Tutankhamun*, edited by John Baines, 139–177. Oxford: Griffith Institute.

Kawai, Nozomu. 2022. 'The Time of Tutankhamun: What New Evidence Reveals'. *Scribe* 9: 44–53.

Kirby, Percival R. 1947. 'The Trumpets of Tut-Ankh-Amen and their Successors'. *The Journal of the Royal Anthropological Institute of Great Britain and Ireland* 77 (1): 33–45.

Lee, Christopher C. 1992. *... The Grand Piano Came by Camel: Arthur C. Mace, the Neglected Egyptologist*. Edinburgh: Mainstream Publishing.

Littauer, M.A., and J.H. Crouwel, 1985. *Chariots and Related Equipment from the Tomb of Tutankhamun*. Oxford: Griffith Institute.

Lucas, Alfred. 1921. *Forensic Chemistry*. London: Edward Arnold and Co.

Lucas, Alfred. 1924. *Antiques: Their Restoration and Preservation*. London: Edward Arnold and Co.

Lucas, Alfred. 1926. *Ancient Egyptian Materials*. London: Longmans, Green and Co.

Lucas, A. 1941. 'Notes on Some of the Objects from the Tomb of Tut-Ankhamun'. *Annales du Service des Antiquités de l'Égypte* 41: 135–147.

Mace, Arthur C. 1920. 'The Caskets of Princess Sat-Hathor-Iunut'. *The Metropolitan Museum of Art Bulletin* 15 (7): 151–156.

Mace, Arthur C. 1923. 'Work at the Tomb of Tutenkhamon'. *Metropolitan Museum of Art Bulletin* 18 (12), Part 2: The Egyptian Expedition 1922–1923: 5–11.

Manniche, Lise. 1976. *Musical Instruments from the Tomb of Tutankhamun*. Oxford: Griffith Institute.

Parkinson, Richard B. 2022. *Tutankhamun: Excavating the Archive*. Oxford: The Griffith Institute.

Plenderleith, H.J. 1927. 'Appendix V: Report on the Examination of Specimens from the Tomb of King Tut.Ankhamen'. In *The Tomb of Tut-ankh.Amen*, Vol. II, by Howard Carter, 214–216. London: Cassell.

Porter, B., and R.L.B. Moss. 1960. *Topographical Bibliography of Ancient Egyptian Hieroglyphic Texts, Reliefs, and Paintings*, Vol. 1, 2nd edition. Oxford: Griffith Institute.

Roth, Ann Macy. 1992. 'The Psš-Kf and the "Opening of the Mouth" Ceremony: A Ritual of Birth and Rebirth'. *The Journal of Egyptian Archaeology* 78: 113–147.

Russmann, Edna R. 2001. '*Book of the Dead*, Papyrus of Ani: The Funeral Procession'. In *Eternal Egypt: Masterworks of Ancient Art from the British Museum*, edited by Edna R. Russmann. No. 101, 197–198. Berkeley: University of California Press.

Schorsch, Deborah. 2001. 'Metal Polychromy in Egypt in the Time of Tutankhamun'. *Journal of Egyptian Archaeology* 87: 55–71.

Scott, Alexander. 1927. 'Notes on Objects'. In *The Tomb of Tut-ankh. Amen*, Vol. II, by Howard Carter, Appendix IV. London: Cassell.

Wood, R.W. 1934. 'The Purple Gold of Tut'ankhamūn'. *The Journal of Egyptian Archaeology* 20 (1/2): 62–65.

The furniture that shapes our world: a re-examination of Tutankhamun's beds, chairs and thrones

Manon Y. Schutz

Abstract

The tomb of Tutankhamun is one of the most famous archaeological discoveries of the last century. On the one hand, this is due to the fact that the burial of this previously little-known pharaoh was found nearly intact, which raises questions not only about the young king's death, but also his life and place within the Amarna period. On the other, this fascination is intrinsically linked to the afterlife, i.e., the reception, of this find, fuelled, for example, by thoughts of a murder plot and stories of a curse. Yet, even though the objects from the tomb are depicted in numerous books, shown in many documentaries, and have been displayed in museums and exhibitions around the world, more research needs to be done into the everyday and/or ritual use as well as the symbolic meaning of the various grave goods that accompanied Tutankhamun on his last journey. The aim of this paper is to reassess the furniture found in KV62, including the so-called beds, bier, couches, chairs and thrones, and to evaluate the general object categories in which these various pieces may be grouped. When cataloguing the contents of the tomb, Howard Carter and his team applied (knowingly or unknowingly) their own worldviews onto the ancient equipment by simply choosing different terms for what they perceived as different furniture items. This, of course, begs the question as to whether modern understandings and terminology of these items can correspond to their significance in ancient Egypt. Does similarity in form automatically entail similarity in function, and (as a consequence) difference in form suggest a difference in function? By re-examining the furniture discovered in the tomb, it may be possible to really see Tutankhamun's furniture through other eyes, not just as filtered through Carter's.

Keywords: furniture, burial equipment, (re-)classification

Introduction

Furniture – in the broadest sense of the word – is nowadays considered essential, accompanying us during each stage of our lives, from childhood to adulthood, from birth to death, and also during every activity, event and mood. It plays an important role in various domains, whether we are at home or at work, resting, sleeping, recovering, eating, celebrating or anything else! Usually, we are surrounded by several key pieces at once, designed and employed for specific purposes, such as beds, chairs, tables, desks, cupboards and shelves. The way in which we go about our days and nights influences our furniture, i.e., their shape, their location, their use; in other words, furniture reflects our way of life, our habits as well as, at least to some extent, our nature. Now, to reverse this, one might wonder whether the appearance, location and context of furniture could possibly convey the character of a person, a family, a community, a society or, indeed, a whole worldview. After all, even if the way of employing, displaying and interacting with objects is quite personal – there is no right or wrong approach – there are some tendencies that might indicate the practices of a particular household, e.g., the presence or absence of a certain type of furniture, the findspot, the integration with other equipment.

In the case of ancient Egypt, the employed furniture looks rather similar to its modern counterparts. Moreover, since it is also omnipresent in paintings and reliefs, archaeological contexts (mostly tombs, but also houses) and texts, it is often taken for granted, leading to the assumption of a certain universality regarding its meaning and use. Yet, the question arises of whether this is truly the case. Do similar shapes automatically suggest a likeness in function? Is there a typical classification of furniture, e.g., the differentiation between beds and chairs? The following paper tries to give an overview of furniture for reclining and seating in ancient Egypt, using the items found in Tutankhamun's tomb (KV 62) as the principal examples.

First, an attempt is made to broadly define beds, stools, chairs and thrones, presenting some of the issues arising from such an endeavour. Since Tutankhamun and his furniture do not stand at the beginning of the developmental line, but are the result of centuries of development, it is also necessary to look at items that derive from earlier periods and other geographic locations as well. Moreover, the chosen examples are meant to reflect a variety of owners from royal as well as non-royal contexts, including men and women, to get a more complete image of this particular object category. In other words, this selection is meant to highlight the features that can be considered as typical (if there is such a thing) for ancient Egypt. Afterwards, the beds and chairs from the burial of Tutankhamun are analysed, i.e., their types, their findspots, their possible relationships with each other as well as other objects. Questions posed include: what (if anything) can the arrangement within the tomb tell us about the meaning and usage of furniture more generally? Can the definitions and characterizations from the first section simply be applied to the various exemplars of this pharaoh? Do they help to put these pieces back into the religious-ritual landscape of Tutankhamun's world?

While the discussion about beds is based on the results of the author's doctoral thesis 'Sleep, Beds, and Death in Ancient Egypt. Studies on the Bed as a Female Entity',[1] the investigation of the chairs is still rather preliminary, requiring more research – research that cannot be accomplished within the framework of this article. Nonetheless, the following aims to provide a first impression of furniture, the many similarities between the varieties used for lying and/or sitting down, and the various possibilities an in-depth examination might offer not just for furniture studies, but the understanding of everyday and burial practices more generally.

Definition: attempts and issues

Before any discussion on beds, stools, chairs and thrones in ancient Egypt can happen, it is necessary to try to define these pieces of furniture – even if such a definition might seem superfluous from a modern perspective, considering that these objects are regarded by many people as quotidian, basic and familiar. The following considerations do not strive to be exhaustive, but merely aim to highlight some of the issues that arise when trying to describe such well-known items from a contemporary and, hence, biased point of view.

Beds

How can the object (or actually concept) 'bed' be defined? According to the *Oxford Learner's Dictionaries*, for example, a bed is 'a piece of furniture for sleeping on'.[2] The *Cambridge Dictionary*, to give another example, outlines it in a similar way, namely as 'a piece of furniture, or a place, to sleep on'; by adding 'or a place' and, thus, moving away from a strict object-centric notion, this lemma entry broadens the understanding of 'bed' in comparison to the *Oxford* one.[3] These might only be two definitions, but they already highlight the most typical characteristics of the item – or what is usually thought to be the most common features today. In fact, although the descriptions are rather short, they still give a general indication of the classification ('furniture' and 'place') as well as the purpose ('sleep') of the object.

In both lemmata, the *Oxford* as well as *Cambridge* one, the categorization of the bed as a piece of furniture takes centre stage. Again, while the term 'furniture' seems well known, even ordinary, grasping and describing such commonplace words is usually more difficult than it might appear at first. Whereas the *Oxford Learner's Dictionaries* define furniture as 'objects that can be moved, such as tables, chairs and beds, that are put into a house or an office to make it suitable for living or working in',[4] the *Cambridge* entry is rather short and nondescript, considering furniture as 'things in a house etc such as tables, chairs, beds etc'.[5] Furthermore, the *Online Etymology Dictionary*, which offers the explanation of 'chairs, tables, etc.; household stuff; movables required or ornamental in a dwelling-place', points out that the English expression, originally meaning an 'act of supplying or providing', appears isolated in the context of European languages, since a derivative from the Latin *mobile* 'movable' is common in most countries (e.g., the German 'Möbel' and the French 'mobilier').[6] In short, the umbrella term 'furniture' is elucidated by means of its individual parts in all these definitions, i.e., by specific examples of objects belonging to this particular group ('bed', 'chair', etc.). In a second step, the necessary, practical or purely decorative context of use of the item is frequently added, whether in the house (or, more general, dwelling place) as well as the office. Of course, this raises the question of whether these points could be valid for an ancient Egyptian setting as well.

The specimen of Queen Hetepheres I might serve as a good example for an ancient Egyptian bed (Fig. 3.1).[7] This piece of furniture was found in a poor state of preservation in the tomb (identified by some as a funerary deposit) of the royal woman, with little more than its sheet-gold covering lying collapsed on the floor next to the empty sarcophagus.[8] It is immediately striking that the piece of furniture looks quite similar to its modern counterparts – this article offers line drawings rather than photographs of the discussed objects, since they help focus on the most basic, primary components of the bed, i.e., its core elements, not the decorative additions, the used material, the colours in general. Hetepheres' gilded bed consists of a rectangular straight platform, contained by two long side bars with papyriform terminals at both ends and two cross poles that have been slotted into the former. While the reproduction of the item, made by Joseph Gerte in 1929 and housed in the Museum of Fine Arts in Boston (29.1858), has actual webbing, its leather strings attached to the frame by means of webbing slots, the original in the Egyptian Museum in Cairo is covered by wooden boards.[9]

Most scholars assume that this bed already served the queen during her lifetime, i.e., that it was a piece of furniture that was actively used in the everyday setting, and was only afterwards deposited into the tomb to function as equipment for her afterlife. However, as the wooden panels of the original would certainly not have added to the overall comfort of the sleeper, one might wonder whether this bed was constructed for a funerary role. It is also possible that the boards were installed only after Hetepheres' death, thus repurposing the object for the burial. The platform itself is carried by four gilded leonine legs, placed on beaded supports. Leonine furniture legs occur since the 3rd Dynasty; although they never entirely supplant their older bovine counterparts, documented since Predynastic times, they soon become the more popular type.[10] The front leg pair is significantly higher than the rear, causing the platform to slope towards the foot-end. The elevation of the head thus caused does not only improve the blood circulation,[11] but also refers symbolically to the waking up again in the morning, the rising of the head being likened to the rising of the sun.[12] In this way, the sleepers might have wanted to visually distinguish their position from that of the deceased, usually lying flat on their side or back. The legs were firmly attached to the frame by means of tenons as well as leather strings that were threaded through the two holes cut into the upper part of the thighs and eventually wrapped around the side poles. Afterwards, the leather would have been wetted, causing it to shrink and strengthen the connection.[13] Furthermore, the bed is equipped with a footboard, sitting atop the cross bar (yet not covering its entire width) and decorated with a feather and rosette pattern made of glazed composition (= Egyptian faience). This motif, suggesting embracing

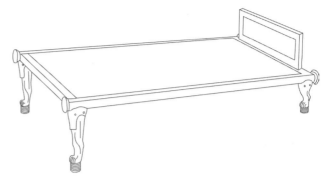

Fig. 3.1. The bed of Queen Hetepheres I (author's drawing).

wings, was certainly meant to emblematize the protection of the sleeper (or perhaps the deceased) resting on the platform. So far, the definition of 'bed' and 'furniture' offered by the *Oxford* and *Cambridge* dictionaries are applicable to Hetepheres' bed, at least to a certain degree: this object is indeed an element that can easily be moved around and offers enough space to accommodate a recumbent person.

The bed of Queen Hetepheres I is unique in that it is the only actual piece of furniture of this type that has survived from the Old Kingdom. The two-dimensional representations on contemporaneous tomb walls (especially as part of the so-called 'bed-making scenes') show that other members of the royal family and elite must have owned similar specimens, either with bovine or leonine legs. The most notable parallel for the exemplar of Hetepheres is the bed depicted in the tomb of Queen Meresankh III.[14] Yet, since these pieces of furniture do not only occur in these early times, it might be useful to present an example from the New Kingdom as well, to be able to compare both types. In the tomb of Tutankhamun, six beds were found that were certainly used by the king during his lifetime, as indicated by traces of wear and tear.[15] Five of these specimens belonged to the same type, a type that was also found in the tombs of Kha and Merit (TT 8) as well as Yuya and Tjuiu (KV 46).[16]

As in the case of Queen Hetepheres I, the platform of these beds consists of two long sides in between which the cross bars have been inserted (Fig. 3.2). Holes have been cut all around the interior surface of these four sides, so that the plant fibres could be threaded through and then woven to form the webbing. Characteristic for these New Kingdom – or, perhaps more precisely, 18th Dynasty – beds is the convex, i.e., downwards curving shape of their side poles, meaning that the lowest point of these bars lies in their centre. Once more, as in the Old Kingdom, the head-end constitutes the most elevated part. Of course, one might wonder whether the curvature of the wood might have occurred only after the discovery of these pieces. Could the environment in the museums have had a negative effect on the material and deformed it?[17] However, there are two observations that would speak against such an assumption: 1) early photographs of the objects, sometimes taken just

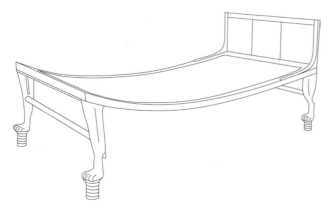

Fig. 3.2. Typical everyday bed type of Tutankhamun (author's drawing).

moments after the opening of the respective tombs, already show this curve; 2) the side bars of all the actual examples demonstrate the same form, i.e., the same amount of curvature, which rather indicates a planned act, i.e., a true bed type. Now, this platform stands over four leonine legs, equipped with beaded supports. It is noteworthy that the front and rear pairs are generally connected to each other by cross rods, adding to the overall stability of the furniture item. Moreover, instead of leather strips (used, e.g., in Hetepheres' exemplar), the legs were connected to the frame by means of the tenons on their 'heads' as well as wooden elbow angle brackets, one side of which was affixed to the inside of each thigh and the other to the cross poles at the head- or foot-end. The bed is further equipped with a footboard which occupies the entire width of the object's short side – it was notably shorter in the Old Kingdom specimen. Again, the method of fastening differs from the earlier exemplar: the footboard is fitted on both short sides with wooden angle brackets that were attached to the bedframe, strengthening the connection between both elements. Particularly noteworthy is the tripartite pattern of the footboard, a design that is typical for this period. Thus, this feature is subdivided into three panels that are either left plain or function as carriers of decoration. Visually, the separation between the sections is achieved by two papyrus stems that seemingly grow vertically from the top and bottom of the board towards its centre, their bulbous heads meeting in the middle. Frequent decorative motifs of the footboard include Bes, Taweret and lion-Bes, as well as floral designs such as papyrus, lotus and tall bouquets. One of Tutankhamun's beds even displays the *zmꜣ tꜣ.wi* motif, symbol of the unification of the two lands, in its central panel.[18] This emblem is intrinsically linked to kingship and occurs frequently in connection with royal chairs, as further discussed below.[19] For the sake of completeness, it should also be noted that Tutankhamun owned a travelling (or folding) bed,[20] a piece

of furniture that is basically unique in ancient Egypt: apart from this specimen, only a model of a folding bed has survived.[21] This bed type, likewise used during the king's lifetime, will not be examined in any detail here.

When considering Tutankhamun's and Hetepheres' exemplars, one might wonder how this investigation might add to the general definition of 'bed'. Although there are clear differences between the two described types, they share a basic structure, namely a rectangular platform with a raised head-end, carried by four legs. Moreover, both varieties (i.e., with straight and curved side bars) have footboards, this feature not being essential though. Another factor that unites the beds from both tombs is the movability, an important aspect in the definition of furniture: in theory, these wooden objects do not have to be kept in a single location within the house or palace. Yet, at the same time, one should bear in mind that both owners belong to the topmost strata of society, namely the royal family. In fact, the amount of everyday beds found in Tutankhamun's tomb might suggest that his pieces of furniture had fixed locations, for example, in a specific room, a specific palace or even during a specific period in the king's life – after all, the pharaoh could afford to have several beds and, hence, display his status via these furniture items. In contrast to these members of the elite, the majority of people would simply have slept on mats made of plant fibres. Two *talatat*-blocks, for instance, depict men sleeping around a campfire in the open, probably in the desert.[22] They lie on thin mats, their heads resting on headrests or their cupped hands. Their bodies are covered with apparently transparent blankets, showing the individuals underneath; in reality, they would have been made of thicker linen, probably, similar to the blankets found in the tomb of Kha and Merit.[23]

In short, these scenes represent the most important requirements when it comes to nightly sleep, namely the need for warmth and protection, e.g., from predators and insects. Of course, both depictions render a temporary reality, i.e., a reality that is only true for a limited amount of time, since it can be assumed that the men (perhaps guards or merchants) spent just one night in a specific camp before moving on. Nonetheless, it is generally assumed that the situation inside the houses would not have been much different, most people sleeping on mats that were placed on the ground or on a stone platform: such daises are found, for example, in the second room of Deir el-Medina houses. While such an architectural element or structure was obviously not movable, the mat (just like any piece of furniture) was easily transportable, storable (possibly in a rolled-up form) and could be employed in every location, inside as well as outside the house (e.g., on the roof), adapting to a person's needs, the season, the available space. Thus, the question arises of whether these mats, possibly equipped with headrests and blankets, can be considered furniture, more precisely beds. In other words: is it the compact wooden bedframe that defines a bed or the soft furnishings?

Thinking back to the definition of furniture in the *Oxford Learner's Dictionary*, characterising it as movable objects used in the house, the mat should certainly be attributed to this overarching category as well – after all, a bed is basically a framed mat carried by four legs. Furthermore, the aforementioned *talatat*-blocks have shown that the core concept 'bed' was far more than just the mat or, more generally, a platform on which one could lie down. For this reason, it is certainly not surprising that in Hetepheres' tomb (or deposit) the bed likewise did not occur on its own, but in conjunction with a headrest, a canopy and a box which might have stored the linen baldachin curtains and perhaps the bedding, i.e., typical bed accessories. Another interesting example that should be listed in this context is Merit's specimen, found in the tomb she shared with her husband Kha.[24] It stood inside the burial chamber, opposite its owner's coffin, and was equipped with linen covers and fringed blankets as well as a headrest wrapped in linen. These linen sheets likely served to cushion the platform, mattresses in our modern sense seemingly unknown in ancient Egypt or, at least, not having been used. Thus, the thick pillow-like cushions frequently rendered on beds in two-dimensional art might simply represent one or more such layers of linen; perhaps, their style and design were borrowed from the depictions of cushions on chairs, both furniture types often influencing each other.[25] It is clear that these furnishings play an important role, in the archaeological context as well as in paintings and reliefs. In fact, since most people did not even own a bedstead, the reclining surface as such (e.g., the ground, a mat, a wooden framework, a dais) was interchangeable: it is the accompanying accessories like headrest and blankets that truly constituted their bed.

After analysing the appearance of this piece of furniture, as defined in the *Oxford* and *Cambridge* dictionaries, it is also necessary to examine their statement about its perceived main function, namely as a sleeping platform. In general, the nightly rest is indeed foregrounded in our modern understanding of beds. Yet, there are still other contexts in which this object is employed nowadays, e.g., during sexual activities, birth, recovery from illnesses, death, but also to read a book, watch a movie and sometimes even to eat, depending on the owner's habits, means and available space. In other words, the use of beds can nowadays be quite individual, actually making it a multi-purpose item.

Of course, this raises the question of whether this multi-functionality would have existed in ancient Egypt as well. While it is difficult to grasp the individual use of beds and bed-like elements like mats and daises at that time, there are still some observations that can be made based on archaeological findings, two-dimensional tableaux as well as texts. These pieces of furniture were certainly used to sleep on, even in the funerary context in which this inactive state acquires a figurative meaning, being closely associated with death.[26] In the daily life setting, it seems that women spent the night together with their children, the men resting in another bed, perhaps even a different room, as possibly hinted at by figurines showing mothers and their offspring lying on a bed.[27] These objects are likely linked to the ideas of fertility and procreation, as often postulated in the literature, but they probably represent the lived reality of many ancient Egyptians first and foremost. Double beds are not attested, except for an unusual, damaged model;[28] in this case, however, it can be assumed that the object shows a concept rather than a reality.

Yet, as in modern times, beds were used not only for sleeping. In the tomb of Mereruka (Saqqara), for instance, dating to the 6th Dynasty, a scene shows the tomb owner sitting at the head-end of a leonine-legged bed, a pillow-like element supporting his back.[29] He holds a staff in his right hand, a flywhisk in his left. His wife Watetkhethor kneels at the foot-end, just in front of the footboard, and plays the harp for him. A similar tableau is also rendered in the tomb of Pepi at Meir (Tomb D1).[30] Such reliefs are usually understood in an erotic way, i.e., as alluding to sexual activities and, thus, symbolizing procreation and fertility. This interpretation is likely based on the general connection between beds and sexual intercourse, also encountered elsewhere. In the tomb of Khety at Beni Hassan (BH 7), for example, a cryptographic hieroglyph depicts a naked woman with yellowish skin lying on a bed with inverted leonine legs, while her head rests on a headrest.[31] An unclothed man, characterized by a reddish-brown skin tone, lies on top of her. Although the sign does not reveal many details, their activity is clear. This meaning certainly underlies the scene in Mereruka's relief as well, but the image should probably be read on a more basic level first, namely as portraying the bed as a place of leisure and social encounter.

Connected to these ideas are also the *Wochenlaube* (birth arbour) scenes that are mainly found on ostraca from New Kingdom (particularly Ramesside) Deir el-Medina.[32] They frequently show a bed that stands in the centre of a vegetal pavilion, decorated with ivy, lotus and/or papyrus stems. It is debated where this temporary structure would have been located, whether in the house, the garden, on the roof or even outside the settlement; actually, the depictions might merely be symbolic, the lotus and papyrus plants representing fertility, growth and life itself.[33] Moreover, the overall combination of bed and canopy is reminiscent of the burial equipment of Queen Hetepheres I, which likewise contained these two pieces of furniture. Thus, when it comes to the *Wochenlaube*-tableaux, the bed occurs once more in conjunction with specific accessories that serve a practical purpose, while also adding to the figurative meaning of these images – in the case of sleep, death and birth, the baldachins characterize the room within as a liminal space, a space of transition and transformation. Within the arbour, on the bed, sits the new mother with her infant, both recovering from the strains of the birthing process. Even though these beds are occasionally referred to as 'birthing beds' in the Egyptological literature, they were not used during active labour. In fact, ancient Egyptian women generally gave birth while squatting down, either on the ground or bricks.[34] However, it is possible that the mothers-to-be would have retreated to their beds in the case of exhaustion or complications, perhaps also between contractions, to regain some strength. At least, such an approach is documented in imperial China, where women likewise retreated to a purpose-built, temporary structure and gave birth while squatting.[35] From these few examples, it is already clear that beds did not only function as sleeping platforms in ancient Egypt, but were indeed multi-functional, used for sexual activities, social encounter, rest and recovery, while also acting as emblems of fertility and procreation as well as symbolically anticipating a successful birth.

When taking all the above observations into consideration, one might wonder how the ancient Egyptian bed can actually be defined. What, if anything, can the examples add to the *Oxford* and *Cambridge* descriptions? In a rather broad approach, one could see the bed as a rectangular platform, with or without legs, that can be contained by a frame. It is meant to accommodate a sleeping body, but also offers space for other activities like sitting, making music, recovering. At the same time, this framework is only rarely used on its own. It mostly occurs in conjunction with other objects, i.e., accessories, including linen sheets and blankets as well as headrests; in many cases, canopies likewise belong to the archaeological assemblages and tomb scenes that comprise beds. Of course, such a definition does not consider the symbolic understanding of beds which would have played a significant role in ancient Egypt – this symbolic function is discussed below in connection with Tutankhamun's funerary specimens.[36] Overall, an important factor to bear in mind is that similarity in form does not automatically entail similarity in function, just as similarity in function does not necessarily mean similarity in form. Moreover, the definition of 'bed' is not static, but varies from place to place, from period to period, from person to person; actually, it requires to be revaluated, redefined, adapted, changed with every new find.

The fact that the term has not been reassessed recently is reflected in the Egyptological literature, since it takes for granted definitions such as the ones listed in the *Oxford* and *Cambridge* dictionaries as well as, ultimately, the conventions established by early archaeologists, amongst them Howard Carter. Basically, in the Egyptological understanding, the word would indeed be employed to refer to the aforementioned specimens of Queen Hetepheres I, Tutankhamun and Mereruka: i.e., beds are perceived as everyday life objects. Yet, these pieces of furniture occur mainly in the funerary context, so that the ancient Egyptians would not

have slept on these platforms in the strictest sense of the word, having been placed on them only after their death. For this reason, as these objects did not really fit the modern description any more, the early Anglophone researchers addressed them with a different term, namely 'bier', still in use nowadays. Similarly, for example, German-speaking scholars also differentiate between 'Bett' for the quotidian objects and 'Bahre' for their funerary counterparts.

For the definition of 'bier', the same two dictionaries as before shall be consulted again: the *Oxford Learner's Dictionaries* consider the object to be 'a frame on which the dead body or the coffin is placed or carried at a funeral',[37] while the *Cambridge Dictionary* describes it in nearly identical words as 'a frame on which a dead body or a coffin is carried before a funeral'.[38] This idea of carrying, i.e., of other people carrying the deceased by means of this item, is already ingrained in the etymology of the word which is connected to the verb 'to bear'.[39] Besides the mere wish to differentiate between the everyday and funerary objects, the use of a bier during burial ceremonies would have corresponded to the lived reality of the Egyptologists that coined this terminology. At that time, the body of the deceased would have been placed (mostly without a coffin) on this platform during ecclesiastical ceremonies and transported with it to the tomb afterwards.[40] These biers were originally undecorated, uninscribed and the property of the deceased themselves. After having fulfilled their task, they were deposited into the tomb. However, the objects eventually moved into the possession of the church, their ornamentation increasing and becoming more elaborate; now, they were considered more valuable and repeatedly reused for the burials of community members. Of course, similar paraphernalia used to transport the departed are known in other cultures as well, but the understanding that underlies the Egyptological literature is mostly coined by early European and North American scholars. Hence, the term 'bier' has a very specific function and, as such, connotations – connotations that were often taken for granted and accepted within Egyptology.

Lastly, the designation 'couch' is employed to refer to the royal-ritual specimens, like the long-legged exemplars of Tutankhamun, discussed in more detail below. It is possible that this term was specifically introduced into the literature to differentiate these long-legged specimens from the short-legged funerary bed, the so-called 'bier', that was likewise found in the tomb of the young king.[41] This differentiation between funerary beds in the royal and non-royal contexts is a typical phenomenon of the Anglophone scholarship; in German, for example, this distinction is not made, both objects being called 'Bahre'. In studies of the ancient world, the term 'couch', originating from the same root as the French *se coucher* 'to lie down', generally denotes the Greco-Roman *kline*, i.e., the piece of furniture upon which the Greeks and Romans slept, sat and ate in this as well as the next life.[42] Another particularity of the expression, adding a new layer to the conversation, is that it developed into a synonym for 'sofa' in the modern parlance. Thus, the *Oxford Learner's Dictionaries* describe 'couch' as 'a long comfortable seat for two or more people to sit on',[43] the *Cambridge Dictionary* as 'a type of sofa for sitting or lying on'.[44] By adopting this word from the so-called classical studies like Classical Archaeology, it is not only the term as such that is introduced into the field, but also the specific expectations, concepts and ideas that come with it.

Hence, in short, the terms used within Egyptology for these pieces of furniture stem from a very particular context, a context that does not necessarily correspond to that of ancient Egypt. In fact, by applying modern terms to these ancient objects, the accompanying worldview is directly or indirectly, consciously or unconsciously transposed onto them as well. Words are not neutral, but always convey certain connotations. Of course, and this should be stressed, this does not mean that there are no points of contact between beds, biers and couches in the ancient and modern sense. It should merely be highlighted that the usage of different words for furniture used to lie upon in ancient Egypt, without being aware of their actual origin and meaning, automatically separates them into different object groups as well. This is not saying that furniture would not have been classified in one way or the other in antiquity already, only that such categorizations are not universal – various cultures attribute objects to different clusters. In other words, the choice of terminology alone can already divide elements that actually belong together. For this reason, the present article only uses the designation 'bed', no matter the setting in which the furniture piece occurs. Even though this term is not neutral either, coming with its very own set of connotations and preformed ideas, the use of a single term for this whole furniture category helps to approach the topic on a more unbiased note – or, at least, as unbiased as possible, considering that it is difficult (if not impossible) to completely disregard one's own worldview.

After this attempt at a definition of the term 'bed' – and a presentation of the issues that arise when doing so – one point should be particularly highlighted: the use of the bed as seating opportunity. This observation raises the question of how these pieces of furniture might relate to chairs which likewise serve as places for sitting. Could there be even more similarities between these two apparently different object categories? As in the case of beds, an attempt will be made to generally define seating furniture, i.e., stools, chairs and thrones, before investigating Tutankhamun's specimens and their meaning in more detail.

Stools, chairs and thrones

Beds are the earliest attested pieces of furniture which people could also (yet not exclusively) use to sit upon; as seen in the previous paragraphs, they were in fact multi-purpose

Fig. 3.3. *(Left) Stool of Neferetiabet; (centre) stool of Rahotep; (right) stool of Iry (author's drawings).*

objects in ancient Egypt. Only slightly later, objects emerge that were purpose-made to serve as seats, namely stools and chairs, which are discussed in this order in the following paragraphs. As in the case of furniture meant to lie upon, the *Oxford Learner's Dictionary* and the *Cambridge Dictionary* will serve as the main reference works. Thus, they define 'stool' as 'a seat with legs but with nothing to support your back or arms'[45] and, more shortly, 'a seat without a back'.[46] Etymologically, the noun 'stool' developed from the word root *sta, 'to stand, to make or be firm'.[47] This probably refers on the one hand to the object itself, meant to hold its occupant firmly in place, on the other to the firm, i.e., stable, consolidated position of the person sitting on such a piece of furniture: after all, the usage of this object reflected the elevated status of its owner, visually as well as symbolically. For this reason, the term 'stool' initially designated the throne, i.e., the seat of a worldly or religious dignitary, discussed in more detail below.[48] Here, several stools are examined, all the presented examples of seating furniture stemming from the typical offering table scenes which show the deceased on a stool or chair in front of a table. On the stela of Neferetiabet, for instance, the owner sits on a bovine-legged stool with papyri- or lotiform terminals, placed upon beaded supports in the shape of truncated pyramids (Fig. 3.3).[49] A similar, vaguely contemporary piece of furniture with bovine legs atop beaded supports and papyrus/lotiform terminals is also depicted in a relief of Rahotep (Fig. 3.3).[50] In this case, the object is not portrayed in true profile, since its platform is rendered in shortened top view. This wish to depict the stool in its entirety is also palpable, for example, on 2nd Dynasty stelae from Helwan, showing that it is an ancient convention;[51] eventually, this way of representation disappears from the repertoire. Moreover, in contrast to the case of Neferetiabet, Rahotep does not sit directly on the seat, but on a thin cushion, adding to his overall comfort. Contrary to the 'mattresses' of the beds, pillows are actually attested in ancient Egypt, even though it might still be folded linen that is referenced in the reliefs. Nefer, to give another example, sits on a bovine-legged chair that is reminiscent of the Neferetiabet's exemplar in form, yet is equipped with an additional pillow as in the case of Rahotep; the various elements can thus variously be combined with each other.[52] As a final stool type of the Old

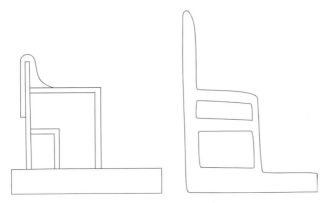

Fig. 3.4. (Left) Throne of Osiris, as shown in the papyrus of Hunefer; (right) chair of Nesuheqet (author's drawings).

Kingdom, the carved scene of Iry and Inet, portraying both of them seated on identical stools, may be cited (Fig. 3.3).[53]

While the aforementioned exemplars were bovine-legged, these seats are carried by four leonine legs atop the typical beaded supports, shaped like truncated pyramids. The side-pole, ending in a lotus terminal, is decorated with two (inlaid?) sections, displaying a crisscross pattern. Again, the platform is cushioned with an apparent pillow, although perhaps folded linen. Even though the shape of the legs as well as the decorative details might change, these pieces of furniture all have in common that they do not have back- or armrests. Animal heads and tails are likewise absent. The optional cushioning of the seat adds to the overall comfort, but certainly also highlights the owner's elevated status even further.

The use of a chair presents another option to highlight someone's higher rank and power. The *Oxford Learner's Dictionaries* consider a chair to be 'a piece of furniture for one person to sit on, with a back, a seat and four legs'.[54] In this case, the definition of the *Cambridge Dictionary* is less detailed: 'a movable seat for one person, with a back to it'.[55] In other words, a chair is basically a stool with a back. The fact that the word 'chair' can also refer to the seat and/or office of an authority, for example a professor, a bishop or even the leader of a meeting, indicates once more that these pieces of furniture represent an object, that literally and figuratively elevates their owner – just like the bed and stool.[56] Moreover, another observation that can be made based on the *Oxford* lemma is that the chair is described as 'a piece of furniture', i.e., with the same words as the bed, the main difference lying in the function ('sit' versus 'sleep'). According to Geoffrey Killen, the chair emerges from these stool forms during the 2nd Dynasty.[57] However, it should be clarified that this refers to four-legged specimens, since a block-like chair is already depicted on the Narme(he)r Macehead,[58] carrying the king himself.[59] This chair type develops into a characteristic attribute of kings and gods.[60] In the *Book of the Dead* papyrus of Hunefer, for example, Osiris attends the deceased's weighing of the heart, while

sitting on such a cuboid chair, the main body of the object being adorned with horizontal bands in green, blue and yellow (Fig. 3.4).[61] Particularly noteworthy are the strips on top and at the front as well as the ornamental square in its bottom rear corner, a decorative type that is known since the 4th Dynasty.[62] Klaus P. Kuhlmann already pointed out that the appearance of this piece of furniture is reminiscent of the *ḥw.t*-hieroglyph, leading to its designation as *ḥw.t* block-chair ('*ḥwt*-Blockthron') – an outer resemblance that is certainly not coincidental.[63] By sitting on this specific furniture item, the occupant might originally have been characterized as the owner of such a *ḥw.t* '(larger) house, estate, temple'.[64] Kuhlmann mainly attributes a religious, divine character to the *ḥw.t* in this case, explaining why the king or a god would preside over it; in fact, these block chairs are only rarely found outside the royal-divine sphere and, if so, exclusively in connection with the deceased.[65] Furthermore, taking the depiction of this furniture type on the Narme(he)r Macehead into account, it seems as if the development went from a royal to a divine attribute, its reinterpretation perhaps based on the old age of this type, possibly being associated with a mythical, primordial period. To give a possible parallel from a completely different context, one could cite the identification – or, again, reinterpretation – of the tomb of Djer (Abydos, Umm el-Qa'ab) from the 1st Dynasty as the burial place of Osiris.[66] Coming back to the seat of Osiris in Hunefer's papyrus, it should also be pointed out that a folded piece of cloth hangs over the backrest, that the piece of furniture itself stands on a blue dais with black, vertical zigzag lines, and that the scene is contained within a canopy. Hence, chairs (just like beds) often occur in connection with accessories that would have fulfilled a practical purpose, but also have added to the overall symbolic setting of the motif.

One of the earliest attested depictions of a four-legged chair is found on the stela of Prince Nesuheqet from Helwan (Tomb 964 H8), dating to the 2nd Dynasty (Fig. 3.4).[67] It shows a post-legged piece of furniture, characterized by a high back, and placed atop a rectangular base, further highlighting the distinguished position of the individual. Since this seat type is rather unusual within the Helwan corpus, most deceased sitting on bovine-legged stools, Zaki Y. Saad speculated that this particular specimen might already represent some sort of throne.[68] In other words, he assumed that it was this type of furniture that literally and symbolically lifted the prince out of the group. Moreover, due to the presence of the base and the rather stylized rendering of the furniture piece, there are visual ties to the block-chair, perhaps harnessing some of its meaning as well. In some cases, different seat types are also represented within the same scene, showing that the choice of design does not (or not entirely) depend on chronological or geographical preferences.

On the stela of Tjenti and Nefret, for example, the husband sits on a bovine-legged stool, cushioned with a pillow.[69] On the other side of the offering table, the wife sits on a chair. The form of this latter piece of furniture is not entirely clear, since it either consists of a thin platform carried by four post legs or a cuboid seat with a low back; a folded cloth is thrown over the back rest. Considering the royal-divine context of block-chairs, it would be unusual for Nefret to own such a cuboid seat, even if it is devoid of the particular *ḥw.t*-decoration. In general, one can assume that the chair of the woman is supposed to be less elaborate than the man's stool. This might not be surprising, as the status of Tjenti, the husband and tomb owner, would have been superior to that of his wife – a phenomenon that is observable throughout the history of ancient Egypt. Thus, it can be noted that the presence or absence as well as the height of the backrest *per se* does not reveal any information about the status and authority of its owner – the only constant in this scenario is the fact that the seating furniture does indicate the elevated position of its occupant, also in a social setting.

The most common chair type in offering table scenes, especially since the Old Kingdom, is certainly the four-legged leonine specimen. An early representation of this kind is found in the tomb of Mereruka. The relief in question shows Watetkhethor, the wife of the tomb owner, seated on a leonine-legged piece of furniture and sniffing a lotus flower.[70] The object is equipped with a low back, over which a piece of folded linen hangs, as well as supports in the form of truncated pyramids and stylized papyriform (or, possibly, lotiform) terminals. In this case, since no petals are indicated on the terminals, the relief otherwise being quite detailed, preference might be given to the interpretation as papyriform. In fact, the question arises of whether this feature could be based, at least originally, on early or less expensive chairs that were made of papyrus stems, the umbels perhaps being left on the shafts for decorative purposes – even if it should be noted that actual objects of this type are so far unknown from ancient Egypt, a *status quo* that could be due to the chance of preservation.[71] Hence, the symbolic nature of the papyrus would have become meaningful only in a secondary step.

Yet, at least at the time when the paintings and reliefs were executed, the various connotations of these faunal elements (e.g., connection to growth, fertility and life) must have already been foregrounded, since the often bovine- and leonine-shaped legs would not have occurred on a furniture piece made of plant material; here, the emblematic functions and interplay of the different components like the terminals and legs were clearly significant. Furthermore, other stools and chairs do have clear lotiform terminals.[72] This development (if it actually is a development, not a preference) could be based on a mere misunderstanding of the papyriform element and the reason for its existence or a deliberate reinterpretation of its shape and original meaning for artistic tendencies, and/or a shift in the symbolic

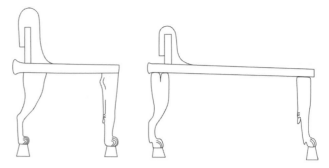

Fig. 3.5. (Left) Chair of Mentuweser; (right) 'bench' of Intef (author's drawings).

sphere. One might even wonder whether the appearance of the terminal was occasionally (or frequently?) left vague on purpose, so that the owner of the furniture item could benefit from the characteristics of both plants, papyrus and lotus, at the same time. To answer some of these questions, a more in-depth analysis of the terminals on stools and chairs throughout the various periods would be necessary, an analysis that unfortunately cannot be achieved within the framework of this paper. Of course, Watetkhethor's chair is not one-of-a-kind. The exact same chair style, to give more examples, is also represented on the stelae of Maati,[73] Mentuweser (Fig. 3.5)[74] and Sehetepibre.[75]

Interestingly, from the 11th Dynasty at the latest, a new way of representing these pieces of furniture seems to emerge. Thus, for example, on the stela of Intef (Fig. 3.5), the owner and his wife Iti sit on an alleged leonine-legged bench (or double chair).[76] The man sits at the front, his feet placed just before the forelegs of the object; he sniffs a lotus flower. His wife, following behind his back, has her legs dangling on the far side of the seat, while holding a floral bud in her right hand and embracing Intef with her left. Besides the unusual width of the platform, the leg type, the papyri- or lotiform terminal, and the low back with the folded linen hanging over it are clearly congruent with the aforementioned specimens of Maati, Mentuweser and Sehetepibre. Of course, the question arises of whether this really represents a single broad chair or whether this bench should actually be understood as two separate items. Since such a double seat would only be known from two-dimensional depictions, it is likely that the craftsmen wanted to portray the two separate pieces in this way to avoid the presence of too many overlapping legs, whether wooden or human in nature. Moreover, this artistic convention elevates Intef and Iti onto the same level, even though the hierarchy is clearly reflected by their seating arrangements – the man always sits in front, i.e., in the dominant position, while the wife is seated behind in a supportive as well as protective position.

Again, this example is not unique, such apparent benches being attested in other cases as well. For instance, on the stela of Siamun and his mother Amenhotep, both sit on

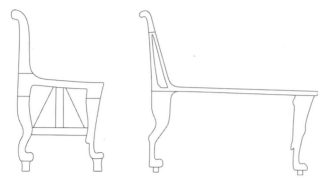

Fig. 3.6. (Left) Chair of Panakht; (right) 'bench' of Nakht (author's drawings).

such an apparent broad chair as well.[77] The colouring might differ (especially considering that Intef's specimen does not show any traces of paint), but the furniture form itself is identical to that of Intef and Iti's seat. The phenomenon of the presumed double chair is also encountered with other leonine-legged types. On the small round-topped stela of Panakht (Fig. 3.6), for example, the owner is shown on a seat with feline legs and a high back, while an offering table stands in front of him.[78] The legs are connected to each other by cross pieces as well as to the platform by means of an additional bar, adding to the overall stability of the construction. Now, a similar chair is also depicted in the upper register of the north wall in Nakht's tomb (Fig. 3.6), rendering the tomb owner and his wife resting on a bench-like furniture item.[79] The object is characterized by leonine legs and a high backrest, the upper part of which is painted yellow, i.e., gilded. Nakht sits in front, Taui behind her husband's back, her feet dangling down the side of the seat closest to the viewer. Through this arrangement, the wife is represented as literally and figuratively supporting and shielding her partner. In contrast to the chair of Panakht, this exemplar does not have any additional cross bars; it is likely that this representation is not based on reality, but again artistic conventions to avoid the furniture parts visually clashing with Taui's legs. Interestingly, a similar depiction, showing the couple before an offering table, is also painted in the lower register. However, the chair type differs in this case: here, the piece of furniture corresponds to that of Intef and Iti, i.e., a leonine-legged seat with a low backrest, over which a piece of cloth was thrown.

As previously mentioned, these apparent benches actually represent two individual chairs standing next to each other. This hypothesis is also confirmed by the banquet scene in the tomb of Ramose (TT 55) from the 18th Dynasty, which portrays several couples sitting together on bench-like pieces of furniture.[80] In general, these objects look similar to the one depicted in the upper register of Nakht's north wall. However, the seemingly long platform, equipped with a high back, is carried by three visible

leonine legs in this case, not the usual two, indicating that the element should indeed be interpreted as two chairs being placed side by side. The reason why the backrest of the first seat was omitted in the relief certainly has to do with aesthetic preferences once more, this element being less important than the clear and full rendering of the banqueteers.

Of course, the chair types described so far were also found as actual objects in the archaeological context. Thus, for example, the seat discovered in the burial chamber of Kha and Merit's tomb, characterized by four leonine paws and a high backrest, corresponds in design to that of Nakht as well as Ramose's banqueteers.[81] Interestingly, when discovered in front of Merit's rectangular coffin, a wooden statuette of the tomb owner was standing on its platform and looking towards the tomb entrance.[82] Claudia Näser compared this scenario to a painted scene in the tomb of Nakhtamun, which likewise renders a figurine on a chair.[83] In the case of this depiction, the piece of furniture is shown in conjunction with another chair carrying offerings and a man with an incense jar; the tableau clearly represents the continued supply with sustenance as well as a purification act, as mentioned in the accompanying inscription.[84] Although it cannot be ruled out completely that the statue of Kha was placed atop the chair for space-saving purposes, the burial chamber being rather small, the fact that the figure was not simply stored atop the piece of furniture – e.g., it was not lying down and surrounded by other objects – but apparently staged as if occupying the seat would speak against such a purely practical arrangement. The observation that the same scenario is also encountered in a two-dimensional form adds further weight to a more symbolic interpretation, even though practical and symbolic reasons are not mutually exclusive here. Hence, in the case of TT 8, the statuette on the chair seems to have likewise meant to indicate an eternalization of the offering rituals, putting the archaeological setting into direct parallel with the offering table scenes, discussed above.[85] This arrangement must have been of prime importance for Kha, since his tomb walls remained undecorated and he needed to guarantee his unending provision in another way.

When looking back at the offering table scenes presented here, it is noteworthy that the content of this motif does not change, only the form of the furniture pieces. Thus, it seems as if the choice of the seat, i.e., whether a stool, cuboid chair, four-legged chair with low or high back, was a personal choice (perhaps connected to status), the choice of the craftsmen and/or workshop or (at least partially) dependent on the period and geographical location. At least, it seems unlikely that the meaning and associated symbolism of the depiction would have changed significantly with the furniture shape. A more detailed analysis of the seating furniture would be needed, but cannot be provided in the framework of this paper. However, it is clear that the modern terminology focuses on the outer appearance of the objects, stressing their similarities and dissimilarities, while disregarding their context of usage – although it should be noted that the actual context is often lost, complicating the matter at hand. Yet again, as in connection with the beds, the question arises of whether the choice of different designations might separate objects that should be seen and treated together.

As an example for the importance of the context, the throne should be discussed here as well. According to the *Oxford Learner's Dictionary*, the throne is 'a special chair used by a king or queen to sit on at ceremonies',[86] while the *Cambridge Dictionary* defines it as 'the ceremonial chair of a king, queen etc, pope or bishop'.[87] In both cases, the throne is defined through its connection with the 'ordinary' chair from which it is merely distinguished by the owner and, ultimately, the context; the form, decoration and material do not play a role. The *Encyclopaedia Britannica* goes a step further by focusing not only on the seat itself, but also on its associated elements: 'chair of state often set on a dais and surmounted by a canopy' – the importance of such accessories was noticed in conjunction with ancient Egyptian beds and chairs as well.[88] The etymology of the term 'throne' is debated, but it is generally ascribed to the word root *dher, 'to hold firmly, to support'.[89] Thus, it has a similar core significance like 'stool', going back to *sta, 'to stand, to make or be firm'. If these definitions were now applied onto ancient Egyptian pieces of furniture, the word 'throne' would be suitable for the chair upon which the king and queen, perhaps also other dignitaries like the high priests, sit during ceremonies and rituals. The cuboid seat, often carrying deities, could likewise be added to this group. In the Egyptological literature, the term is generally employed for furniture items that are made with precious materials (e.g., gold, gemstones) and elaborately decorated. On the other hand, Marianne Eaton-Krauss uses the term for those seats that name the king and display 'motifs associated exclusively with kingship'.[90] However, this raises the question of whether every chair, every stool occupied by a royal or divine individual can be considered a throne or whether the term is only appropriate in certain circumstances, i.e., in specific political or religious settings. At least in the latter case, a classification as throne (rather than a 'simple' chair) is difficult, because the archaeological context is often lost and cannot be reconstructed. In two-dimensional depictions, the general framework of the scenes is usually clearer. Nonetheless, for example, one might wonder how the stool/chair in the offering table scenario should be assessed.

As the deceased undergo a transformation after the successful completion of the funerary rites, evolving into divine beings, it might be possible that their chairs are elevated onto a higher level as well. Should the chair of a justified departed likewise be regarded as some sort of throne? Does the chair found in TT 8 act as a throne for the statuette and, by extension, Kha himself? Since the offering table scenes occasionally include family members, friends

and/or servants who approach the seated owner while, e.g., pouring libations, handing sustenance, burning incense or having their hands raised in adoration, there are clear visual parallels with depictions in which a deity is worshipped. This is certainly no coincidence. An object which seems to directly compare the divine and funerary spheres is the stela of Kha: while Osiris and Anubis sit on cuboid thrones, standing on a blue *mȝꜥ*-dais, in the upper register, the deceased and his wife are seated on leonine-legged chairs, placed on blue mats, in the lower half.[91] Even though the pieces of furniture as well as their bases are quite different, the idea of elevating the main actors further from the floor (or even preventing them from touching it directly) is palpable in both cases, especially since the other performers stand on the ground.[92] Overall, one might thus query whether the chairs of the deceased were supposed to serve as thrones in the funerary-ritual context, the owner clearly being the focus of attention and, hence, comparable to a royal or divine person. After all, as seen, the departed can also be rendered on the block-chairs, a typical royal-divine attribute.

At the end of these observations on stools, chairs and thrones, it may be seen that the terms for seating furniture are not as clear-cut in Egyptology as those for reclining shapes. In general, the differentiation between beds, biers and couches is based on the perceived context of their usage, not the outer form. The same can be said about 'throne' which is not tied to any particular form either, the throne (just like the couch) being simply connected to a royal owner in the modern thinking. In contrast, the designations 'stool' and 'chair' are entirely dependent on the appearance of the objects, more precisely the presence or absence of a back-rest – a distinction that is, however, not always as strictly followed as it appears at first.[93] An issue which might arise from such an argumentation and the different categories thus created (e.g., everyday life versus funerary-ritual, royal versus non-royal) is that they are rooted in a modern worldview, i.e., a world separated according to modern categories, not ancient ones. At the same time, terminology describing the outer appearance of an object is probably the most neutral, especially since the original context is frequently lacking. Even though the burial of Tutankhamun is generally viewed as atypical for a king, based on criteria such as the size, layout and wall decoration, but also the fact that the young pharaoh likely died unexpectedly and was buried in haste, an analysis of the various pieces of furniture meant to carry the recumbent and seated king might help to further elucidate our understanding of this object category; after all, his tomb contained the best-preserved and most extensive royal equipment of the New Kingdom.

Furniture fit for a king: the case of Tutankhamun

After these more theoretical and general thoughts on furniture, the attempt at a definition as well as the discussion of

Fig. 3.7. Tutankhamun's bedsteads: (a) Ebony Bedstead, Carter-no. 047 (JE 62016 and 62714); (b) Wooden Bed, Carter-no. 080 (JE 62017); (c) Bedstead, Carter-no. 377 (JE 62015); (d) Bedstead, Carter-no. 466 (JE 62014). © Griffith Institute, University of Oxford.

the possible pitfalls when applying our own understanding onto ancient Egyptian objects and beliefs, the following paragraphs examine Tutankhamun's items in more detail and test the preliminary results gained from the previous sections against his assemblage – an assemblage that, at least in a fragmentary state, is also attested in other tombs in the Valley of the Kings, e.g., those of Ay (WV 23) and Horemheb (KV 57).[94] Looking at this equipment, questions are raised of how well (if at all) the various definitions fit the king's specimens, if characterizations need to be adapted and what their meaning might have been in the context of the tomb. Are the pieces of furniture merely practical, inanimate objects or do they have a deeper, symbolic meaning?

The many beds of Tutankhamun

In the young king's tomb, 10 pieces of furniture were found that were meant to accommodate a recumbent body. These items, which were all formerly kept at the Egyptian Museum

in Cairo and recently transferred to the Grand Egyptian Museum, were divided by Carter and his team into the three aforementioned groups, namely: beds (or bedsteads), biers and couches. Thus, these early researchers categorized Tutankhamun's objects as follows:

'Bed(stead)'

'Ebony Bedstead', Carter-no. 047; JE 62016 and 62714 [Fig. 3.7a].[95]
'Wooden {Couch} <Bed>',[96] Carter-no. 080; JE 62017 [Fig. 3.7b].[97]
'Bedstead (wood, stucco and gold-foil)', Carter-no. 377; JE 62015 [Fig. 3.7c].[98]
'Bedstead (covered with sheet gold)', Carter-no. 466; JE 62014 [Fig. 3.7d].[99]
'Bedstead', Carter-no. 497; unknown inv.-no.[100]
'Folding Bedstead', Carter-no. 586; JE 62018 [Fig. 3.8a].[101]

a

b

Fig. 3.8. Tutankhamun's bedsteads and bier: (a) Folding Bedstead, Carter-no. 586 (JE 62018); (b) Wooden Bier, Carter-no. 253a (JE 60669). © Griffith Institute, University of Oxford.

'Bier'

 'Wooden Bier', Carter-no. 253a; JE 60669 [Fig. 3.8b].[102]

'Couch'

 'Thoueris Couch', Carter-no. 137; JE 62012 [Fig. 3.9].[103]
 'Lion Couch', Carter-no. 035; JE 62011 [Fig. 3.10].[104]
 'Cow-headed Couch', Carter-no. 073; JE 62013 [Fig. 3.11].[105]

The leonine-legged 'beds' of Tutankhamun, i.e., the pieces of furniture that were likely already used during his lifetime, all belong to the same type, namely the one with the convex sides described and discussed in more detail above.[106] As already noted, the young pharaoh probably used these beds in different rooms, different palaces and/or different periods of his life; some of these items might even have originally belonged to someone else. The folding bed certainly constitutes a subcategory of these everyday life specimens, the king having used it during outings (Fig. 3.8a). Because such items are clear status-markers, elevating their occupant visually and symbolically (even when travelling), it would at least not be surprising for a pharaoh to own several such objects.

 While the actual purpose of a bed cannot always be ascertained from its mere form, especially since some

pieces were clearly repurposed after the death of their owners – for example, Merit's quotidian specimen was (re) painted white and an offering formula added in black ink to one of the long sides in a secondary step, preparing it for a funerary setting[107] – there are some elements that generally hint at an original use during the owner's lifetime. One of these features is the presence of a real webbing (mostly woven of plant fibres, occasionally leather) that acted like springs and, hence, augmented the comfort of the person sleeping or sitting on the platform. This was important, as 'mattresses' in the modern sense apparently did not exist at that time: the webbing was merely covered with linen sheets as suggested, for instance, by the textiles found on Merit's bed.[108] One might now wonder whether other material could likewise have been used to cushion the platform, for instance wool during colder times. So far, there is no evidence for New Kingdom use of woollen sheets (or even blankets), but wool is in any case generally rare in the archaeological record from pharaonic Egypt.[109] The absence of this material in tombs might be explained by a taboo, wool being seen as unclean, and not reflect everyday practices. Another characteristic of everyday exemplars is that they were never equipped with animal heads and tails, on the one hand because they might have been considered hindersome for the sleeper, on the other

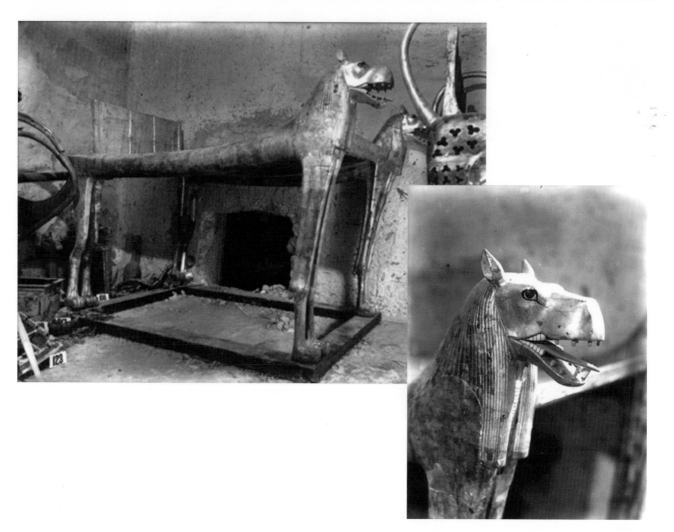

Fig. 3.9. Thoueris Couch, Carter-no. 137 (JE 62012). © Griffith Institute, University of Oxford.

because their symbolic meaning played an even greater role in the burial sphere.

The second type belonging to this furniture category is the so-called 'bier', a wooden object that stood inside Tutankhamun's stone sarcophagus and carried his three anthropoid coffins (Fig. 3.8b). Considering the enormous weight that this specimen had to support, the outer form is certainly fit for the purpose: the legs are rather short and sturdy compared to the king's everyday life beds, making it stronger and adding to its overall stability. Furthermore, since this exemplar fulfilled a purely funerary purpose, its webbing did not need to be real, so that it was merely carved into the platform – after all, comfort was not of the essence any more. The presence of leonine heads as well as tails, trailing behind the rear legs, is likewise remarkable, quotidian specimens generally being devoid of these features; in this case, the item is equipped with two heads and two tails, yet only four single legs, the doubling of the carrier-animal only being superficial.

These attributes, i.e., the carved webbing as well as animal attributes beyond the legs, are also found with the third furniture category of this kind from KV 62, named 'couches' by the early scholars (Figs 3.9–3.11). These objects are characterized by their long, thin leg pairs, the platform thus being carried by eight legs in total, as well as the addition of two animal heads and elevated tails. Here, contrary to the beings of the short-legged leonine bed, the doubling of the carrier animals is complete. The outer form of the legs already shows that the usage of these specimens would have differed from that of the short-legged leonine 'bier'. While the latter needed to carry a significant amount of weight, its long-legged counterparts were meant to hold the mummy of the deceased during the funerary rituals; their overall height would have eased the priests' tasks by preventing them from having to work in a constantly uncomfortable position, i.e., with an overly bent back. Moreover, it is unlikely that the anthropomorphic coffins were placed on these platforms at any time, as speculated

Fig. 3.10. Lion Couch, Carter-no. 035 (JE 62011). © Griffith Institute, University of Oxford.

for example by Horst Beinlich,[110] since it would have been too much weight for the priests to lift the chests onto the beds as well as for the pieces of furniture themselves to withstand the heaviness – the inner coffin alone weighs already 110.4 kg.[111] The tail position likewise indicates different functions. In the case of the short-legged specimen, the tail needed to hang down, as otherwise it would have been difficult to place the coffins onto the platform and close the sarcophagus lid without damaging this extremity. Because the long-legged exemplars only carried the much smaller and lighter body, the elevated tail would not have posed a problem. On the contrary: the encircling gesture of this element would have added to the protection of the deceased lying on the bed.

Tutankhamun owned three long-legged 'couches':

1. a composite specimen with a hippopotamus head, leonine paws, and a crocodile back and tail (Fig. 3.9);
2. a leonine exemplar with tear lines, a characteristic of cheetahs (Fig. 3.10).
3. a bovine piece, the cow heads carrying sun-discs between their horns (Fig. 3.11);

These were placed along the west wall of the Antechamber, all looking towards the north, i.e., the burial chamber in which the king rested (Fig. 3.12).[112] Owing to the hieroglyphic inscriptions found on the headboard of each bed, the identity of the goddesses that are represented through them and their roles are clear.[113] Indeed, these objects guarantee the eternal rejuvenation cycle of the sun and, by extension, the king, representing the three main steps of the solar journey.

First, Taweret-Ammit, often, yet imprecisely, described as a hippopotamus deity, swallows the aging sun and, as such, the king to initiate the rebirth process. She embodies the rite of separation or, in other words, the pre-liminal stage.[114] For this reason, this bed type is also placed furthest away from the sarcophagus room, the preliminary endpoint of the development – preliminary, because the solar journey is actually cyclical.

In a second step, the leonine *s.t-mḥ.tı̓.t* (perhaps 'the Place of the Caring One') protects the sun/deceased during their actual journey through the liminal sphere, assisting in their regeneration and transformation; in the literature, this goddess is often wrongly referred to as Isis-mehtet.[115] Since

Fig. 3.11. Cow-headed Couch, Carter-no. 073 (JE 62013). © Griffith Institute, University of Oxford.

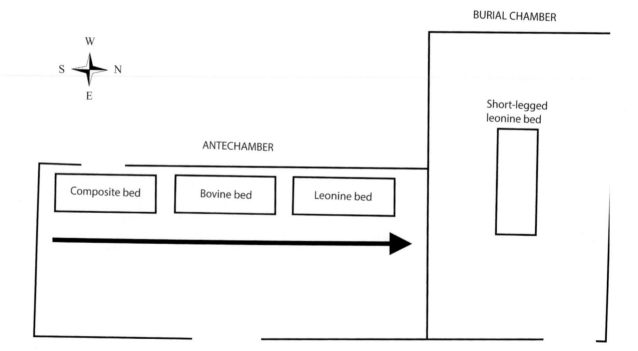

Fig. 3.12. Plan of Tutankhamun's Antechamber and Burial Chamber, indicating the location of the king's funerary beds (author's drawing).

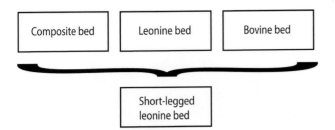

Fig. 3.13. Schematic representation of the relationship between Tutankhamun's funerary-ritual beds (author's drawing).

it is at this point that the departed acquires a divine nature, this piece of furniture corresponds to the rite of transition.

Eventually, the bovine bed, identified as Mehetweret, gives birth to the sun as well as the pharaoh and elevates them to the sky, carrying the solar disc between her horns, the mummy on her back. Thus, this specimen becomes a symbolic image for the temporary completion of the rebirth process, representing the rite of (re)incorporation and (re)integration, i.e., the post-liminal stage. In this context, it should be highlighted that the order of the leonine and bovine beds was reversed in Tutankhamun's tomb, possibly due to the general haste with which the tomb had to be equipped – the actual sequence is known from two-dimensional parallels, shown for example in the tomb of Seti I, further discussed below, and the *Book of the Fayum*.[116] Furthermore, the inscribed headboards of the two specimens were swapped by mistake as well, so that the text meant for the cow was found on the leonine bed and vice versa; this confusion likely happened when the pieces of furniture were reassembled after having entered the Antechamber at the time of the burial.

While the *Book of the Fayum* likewise depicts three entities, namely Taweret-Neith, a leonine bed and Mehetweret, and hence corresponds to the arrangement in the Tomb of Tutankhamun,[117] the relief in Seti I's Room J, a room adjacent to the burial chamber, shows two identical groups with four long-legged beds (usually referred to as 'couches') each.[118] Although the depictions are in a rather poor state of preservation, it is clear that these pieces of furniture reflect once more the expected order, i.e., a composite specimen followed by a leonine and a bovine one. However, it is a second leonine bed that concludes the sequence in this case, differing from the first merely through the black colour of its frame; the first exemplar was painted yellow. Of course, the question arises of how this additional feline specimen should be understood, considering that the preliminary part of the rebirth process was already marked by the cow. It is likely that this fourth bed is linked to Tutankhamun's short-legged 'bier' and its role. When shown in relief, there is no need to depict the latter in a different way than its long-legged counterparts, since it did not matter what its actual purpose was, i.e., how much weight it would have to carry *realiter*. In fact, a visual harmony, achieved by the overall symmetry of the scene and the identical appearance of the four pieces

of furniture, would have been more important. Seen from this point of view, it is hence probable that the 'couches' and the 'bier' actually belonged to the same object category for the ancient Egyptians, despite the differences in their outer form. If so, the short-legged bed might have acted as a *pars pro toto* for the entire group, i.e., some sort of abbreviation for the whole cycle (Fig. 3.13).

The transformative stage represented by the leonine type was likely seen as the most representative in this context, a true emblem of the rebirth process itself. Such an understanding would also explain why feline exemplars were the most commonly represented on tomb walls, coffins, stelae and other burial equipment, but also the most frequently found archaeologically in the non-royal environment. Apparently, private individuals only had access to the leonine type at that time, the long-legged bed group being a prerogative of the pharaoh in the New Kingdom. So far, only a single example for the latter ensemble has been found outside the Valley of the Kings, namely the relief from the tomb of an unknown queen in the Valley of the Queens (QV 40; possibly 19th Dynasty).[119] Furthermore, the short-legged bed of Tutankhamun may have served another purpose as well: by placing the pharaoh's coffins on the bed – an arrangement meant to last for eternity – the continuation of the rebirth process is guaranteed, i.e., eternalized.

This overview of Tutankhamun's beds shows that the modern terminology, chosen by the excavators, and the worldview it conveys are not necessarily compatible with the ancient Egyptian understanding of these pieces. In general, the apparent boundaries between the furniture categories of 'bed', 'bier' and 'couch' are rather blurry and flexible, if not to say artificial. When thinking about the role of Tutankhamun's funerary-ritual specimens and their close link to the solar cycle, i.e., the succession of light and darkness, it is noteworthy that everyday beds actually follow the same pattern: the rhythm of death and being reborn clearly mirrors that of sleep and waking up – a concept that is already encountered in the Pyramid Texts.[120] During the New Kingdom, this idea is even reversed, texts characterizing sleep as a form of death, during which the individuals immerse themselves into the primordial ocean at night in order to emerge rejuvenated and regenerated again in the morning.[121] For this reason, beds are essential in the daily routine as well as the afterlife of their owners, protecting them during their journey through the liminal space and guaranteeing a successful outcome. Moreover, if there would have been such a significant difference in meaning between a daily life and a funerary exemplar, a simple repurposing (as, e.g., attested in Merit's case) would have been unthinkable. Thus, the use of a single term like 'bed' allows us to consider the category of ancient Egyptian furniture for reclining as a group, without being influenced or prejudiced by the image conveyed through the terminology chosen by previous scholars.

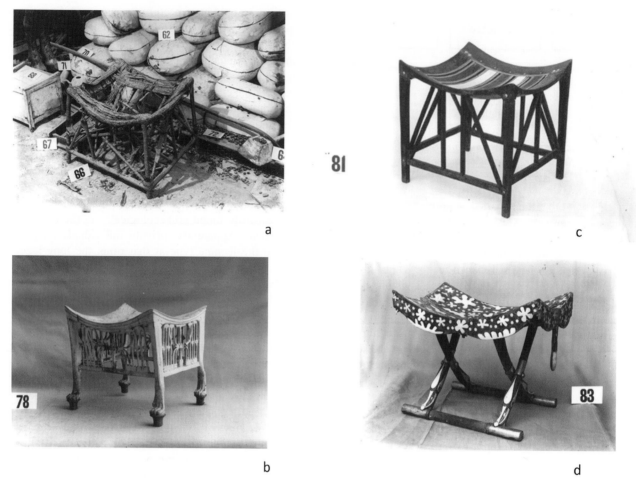

Fig. 3.14. Tutankhamun's stools: (a) Wood and Papyrus Stool, Carter-no. 066 (unknown inv.-no); (b) Wooden stool, Carter-no. 078 (JE 62039); (c) Wooden stool, with ivory and ebony decoration, Carter-no. 081 (JE 62041); (d) Stool of ebony and ivory imitating skin, Carter-no 083 (JE 62035). © Griffith Institute, University of Oxford.

The stools, chairs and thrones of Tutankhamun

While Howard Carter and his team categorized Tutankhamun's furniture meant for lying down according to their perceived context (bed versus bier and couch) and, to a lesser extent, form (long-legged couch versus short-legged bier), their classification of the young king's seats is mainly tied to their appearance, i.e., the presence or absence of a backrest, as well as, in rarer cases, to the owner and framework of use (ordinary stool/chair versus throne). The objects in question from KV 62, moved only recently to the Grand Egyptian Museum, were grouped in the following way:

'Stool'

'Wood and Papyrus Stool', Carter-no. 066; unknown inv.-no [Fig. 3.14a].[122]
'Wooden stool', Carter-no. 078; JE 62039 [Fig. 3.14b].[123]
'Wooden stool, with ivory and ebony decoration', Carter-no. 081; JE 62041 [Fig. 3.14c].[124]
'Stool of ebony and ivory imitating skin', Carter-no. 083; JE 62035 [Fig. 3.14d].[125]

'Stool of painted white wood', Carter-no. 084; JE 62040 [Fig. 3.15a].[126]
'Folding (?) Stool of ebony, ivory, gold & leather', Carter-no. 139; JE 62037 [Fig. 3.15b].[127]
'Folding (?) Stool of ebony, ivory, gold & leather', Carter-no. 140; JE 62036 [Fig. 3.15c].[128]
'Decorated Wooden Stool', Carter-no. 149 and 142b; JE 62042.[129]
'Faldstool', Carter-no. 351; JE 62030 [Fig. 3.16].[130]
'A three-legged stool (wood, painted white)', Carter-no. 412; JE 62043 [Fig. 3.17].[131]
'A four-legged stool (wood, painted white, and gold)', Carter-no. 467; JE 62038 [Fig. 3.15d].[132]
'Stool', Carter-no. 595; JE 62058.[133]

'Chair'

'Solid Ebony Chair (for a child)', Carter-no. 039; JE 62033 [Fig. 3.18a].[134]
'A Chair of Ebony and Papyrus', Carter-no. 082; JE 62031.[135]

Fig. 3.15. Tutankhamun's stools: (a) Stool of painted white wood, Carter-no. 084 (JE 62040); (b) Folding (?) Stool of ebony, ivory, gold & leather, Carter-no. 140 (JE 62036); (c) Folding (?) Stool of ebony, ivory, gold & leather, Carter-no. 140 (JE 62036); (d) Four-legged stool (wood, painted white, and gold), Carter-no. 467 (JE 62038). © Griffith Institute, University of Oxford.

'Carved Cedar (?) Wood Chair', Carter-no. 087; JE 62029 [Fig. 3.18b].[136]

'A Wooden Chair (painted white)', Carter-no. 349; JE 62032 [Fig. 3.18c].[137]

'Wooden stand (?)' [nowadays generally interpreted as a children's chair, possibly even a feeding chair], Carter-no. 033; JE 62057 [Fig. 3.16d].[138]

'Throne'

'Throne (or Ceremonial Chair)', Carter-no. 091; JE 62028 [Figs 3.19, 4.1].[139]

In the framework of this article, it is impossible to analyse every piece of seating furniture. For this reason, only two examples are discussed in more detail here, namely the so-called 'faldstool' and the 'throne', and some preliminary thoughts on them presented. The 'faldstool', found partially covered with linen strips in the Annexe, is characterized by a curved, somewhat crescent-shaped platform, which would have perfectly accommodated the rounded shape of a seated human body, possibly on a cushion (Fig. 3.16). Its frame made of ebony with inlaid ivory blotches is meant to imitate 'panther-skin', i.e., either leopard or cheetah, both being intrinsically linked in the funerary-religious context of ancient Egypt;[140] the separately worked head, tail and paws of the animal were originally attached to the seat as well, but are mostly lost nowadays.[141] The middle section of the seat is decorated with rectangular ivory panels, the patterns

Fig. 3.16. Faldstool, Carter-no. 351 (JE 62030).

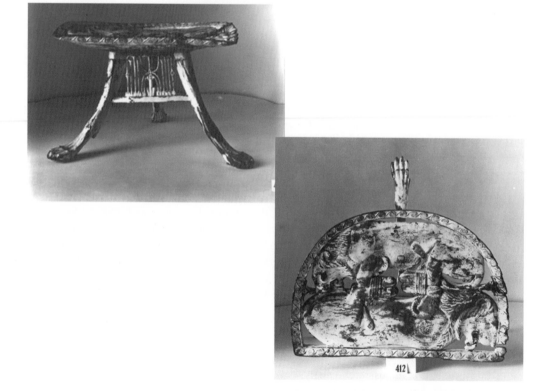

Fig. 3.17. Three-legged stool (wood, painted white), Carter-no. 412 (JE 62043). © Griffith Institute, University of Oxford.

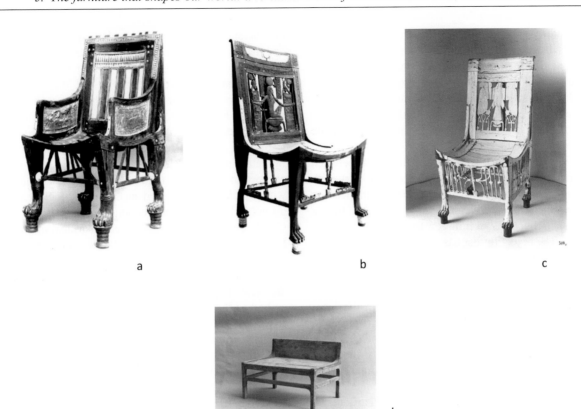

Fig. 3.18. Tutankhamun's chairs: (a) Solid Ebony Chair (for a child), Carter-no. 039 (JE 62033); (b) Carved Cedar (?) Wood Chair, Carter-no. 087 (JE 62029); (c) Wooden Chair (painted white), (d) Carter-no. 349 (JE 62032); Wooden stand (?), Carter-no. 033 (JE 62057). © Griffith Institute, University of Oxford.

Fig. 3.19. Throne (or Ceremonial Chair), Carter-no. 091 (JE 62028).

of which likewise imitate the hide of various animals. The platform itself is carried by four ebony legs that are arranged crosswise, similar to a modern camping stool – a comparison already made by the tomb's excavators – and end in duck heads. These animals seemingly bite into two cross bars, i.e., the actual feet of the object, adding stability to the overall construct and protecting the elaborate and fragile beaks from wear and tear.

The *zmꜣ tꜣ.wi* motif is prominently displayed between both chair leg pairs. Moreover, another back part with straight legs was added to the 'faldstool', frequently leading to the assessment that this element must have come from a different chair since the overall construction seems rather artificial.[142] The object further has an elaborately decorated back, displaying rows and panels with variously coloured inlays of glass and semi-precious stones. A frieze with sun-discs wearing uraei concludes the backrest on top, the snakes surrounding and seemingly moving away from the large sun-disc in its centre. The cartouches below this principal sun contain the name and titles of the Aten, indicating an Amarna period date, even though the usual rays with the little hands are missing. This dating is also confirmed by the fact that the royal cartouches alternately contain both names, i.e., Tutankhaten and Tutankhamun. Particularly noteworthy also is the horizontal panel beneath this uraeus frieze which contains the depiction of a large female vulture with outspread wings. In each claw, the bird of prey holds an ostrich feather fan and an *šn*-ring, further strengthening the animal's protective role. In fact, whenever the king sat on this chair, the bird would have symbolically surrounded his head with its wings, similar to Horus in the case of the well-known Khafre statue.[143]

The question now arises of why this piece of furniture was originally assessed as a 'faldstool'. According to the *Collins Dictionary*, a faldstool is 'a chair or seat, originally one capable of being folded, used by a bishop or other prelate when officiating in his own church away from his throne or in a church not his own', as well as the stool 'placed at the south side of the altar, at which the kings or queens of the U.K. kneel at their coronation'.[144] As such, the faldstool is related in form and function to the *sella curulis* of the Roman magistrates who used this type of seat (with a low backrest or none at all), placed on a *suggestus* (= a tribune or otherwise elevated place), during important meetings, e.g., court hearings or assemblies of the senate.[145] Due to its light weight and the ability to be folded, the *sella curulis* was meant to be carried around by the official's servants, further highlighting his high status and authority. Thus, in general, the term 'faldstool' does not necessarily refer to a stool *per se*, i.e., a seat without a back, but rather to a piece of furniture that expresses a certain authority – the choice of word is certainly connected to the original meaning of 'stool', namely as a throne. In this case, it is obvious that the designation, chosen because of structural similarities with

the ancient Egyptian object, displays specific connotations and acts in a particular environment, an environment that is not automatically compatible with the original purpose of Tutankhamun's seat.

Of course, this does not mean that there are no points of contact between the 'faldstool' and the pharaoh's chair, as both pieces of furniture certainly represent the elevated status and authority of their owner in a literal as well as figurative meaning. However, one might wonder what the purpose of this chair might have been. The various names with which it is addressed in the Egyptological literature do not help to elucidate its actual purpose. For example, Carter refers to the item as an 'ecclesiastical throne' in the final publication, an expression that basically appears like a synonym for 'faldstool' in this case, reflecting once more its outer appearance rather than its context.[146] At the same time, the excavator assumed that this particular piece of furniture embodied the king's role as the highest religious authority. It seems likely that this interpretation was (whether consciously or unconsciously) influenced by the similarities in form between the ancient object and the 'faldstool' of bishops, i.e., a piece of furniture with which the modern, especially British, scholars would have been quite familiar.

Eaton-Krauss, to give another example, rejects Carter's understanding. In fact, she believes that the 'inlaid ebony throne', as she calls this furniture piece, was 'associated particularly with festive domestic use, rather than for a public display of authority and prestige'.[147] This interpretation derives from the so-called *ḥmsi nfr* scenes that are known from the lintels of Ramesside houses and focus on a man resting on a piece of seating furniture, the type of which can differ; some examples actually render a folding chair.[148] Family members and friends are frequently shown offering floral bouquets, libation vessels and other goods. Moreover, since there are depictions of this kind that also include an additional offering table, their outer form is comparable with the above-described offering table scenes from the funerary context. Yet, even if there are clear parallels between the two scene types, the former are usually interpreted as belonging to this world, because the lintels likely stem from the interior of houses, i.e., from the domestic context. Thus, the phrase *ḥmsi nfr*, translated as 'well-seated' or 'sit well!', might be a written invitation to every visitor entering the house and wanting to join the festivities within, the festive character being visually evoked by the drinks and flowers of the pictorial decoration.[149]

At the same time, the expression *ḥmsi nfr* was occasionally also inscribed on the backrests of funerary seats associated with private chapels at Deir el-Medina, that is, places that were frequented during festivities in honour of the deceased.[150] In these ritual-ceremonial situations, the boundaries between this and the next life as well as between the human and divine spheres are blurred, even abolished.[151] For this reason, the pertaining to the purely festive domestic sphere that Eaton-Krauss assumes for this chair might not be as clear-cut as commonly thought. As in the case of the offering table scenes, there are different seat types that can occur as part of these *ḥmsi nfr* tableaux, the folding chair only being one option. Thus, the choice of chair was not central to the meaning of the depictions as such; it is actually the other way around, the context of the scenes providing the pieces of furniture with their symbolic aspects. Furthermore, although the 'faldstool' was likely built and decorated for the king's enjoyment in life, it might still have acquired a funerary dimension, e.g., serving Tutankhamun during festivities in the afterlife.

Another question that arises now is whether 'throne' would be the most fitting term, if the chair were really used in the domestic, private context; after all, a throne is linked to the monarch's demonstration of status and authority at ceremonies, such official (e.g., political and/or religious) ceremonies often happening in the presence of a chosen audience. Martin Metzger doubts that this object was ever used as a throne.[152] Of course, one could also revert to the argument that every elaborate chair in the possession of a ruler is automatically a throne. In this particular case, the inclusion of the *zmȝ tȝ.wi* and the cartouches into the decorative programme indeed characterize this chair as pertaining to the royal sphere, perhaps even as a throne.

Yet, as seen, the emblem for the unification of the two lands as well as the cartouches are also found on beds: should they then be considered thrones as well? One might also wonder whether the fact that Tutankhamun's seat imitates a folding chair could be significant in this case. Actually, folding furniture (of which Tutankhamun's travelling bed is an example) was meant to be easily transportable, to be carried around and to follow the king on his outings, highlighting his authority even outside the palace. Could this object hence be a portable throne, serving the king when travelling around the country? Already Kuhlmann has suggested that it was perhaps used in the field ('Feldthron'), although he did not exclude the possibility that it played a role inside the palace.[153] In fact, it has even been suggested that this chair would have been used by Tutankhamun during his hunting activities, the animal hide decoration being seen as evidence for this assumption.[154] However, besides the circumstance that the 'faldstool' was made rigid, it was certainly also heavier (and thus more impractical) than most folding chairs due to the extensive inlay work, making such a specific function rather improbable. In general, this sort of interpretation might also arise from the fact that folding furniture is apparently only owned by men.[155] The sole statement that can be made with any certainty in this case is that the chair was meant to underline its owner's power and wealth through the use of precious materials as well as the elaborateness of the craftsmanship. Furthermore, considering the aforementioned multi-functionality and purpose of beds, it is also possible that such a chair could have acted

in different ways, in different contexts, in different rooms, in different places (in- and outside the palace).

The second chair of Tutankhamun that is discussed in this article is the so-called 'throne', found standing below the composite bed in the Antechamber and likewise being equipped with linen strips; the leonine heads are directed towards the entrance (Figs 3.19, 4.1). Perhaps, it was constructed for the king in a similar life stage to the 'faldstool', this object also mentioning both Tutankhaten and Tutankhamun. This 'throne' is actually a gilded chair with leonine legs, placed on beaded supports. The four legs are connected to each other by cross bars, each one serving as a basis for a (now only partly preserved) *zmȝ tȝ.wi* sign. Two feline heads with inlaid eyes sit on the front corners of the seat, their manes falling down the platform and reaching the upper part of the thighs – they are clearly reminiscent of the heads on the headend of Tutankhamun's leonine 'couch'. Interestingly, the actual seat does not consist of the expected webbing, but of a gessoed and gilded surface, the chequerboard pattern of which merely imitates the woven plant fibres.[156] One might wonder whether the leonine heads in combination with the imitation webbing could indicate a purely ritual, perhaps even funerary purpose, as suggested by the general *status quo* of the beds.

Indeed, it is noteworthy that such additional animal parts seem to only occur in connection with the king's and, to a lesser extent, the queen's chairs, not in a non-royal context.[157] Furthermore, the piece of furniture is equipped with a back and two armrests, the latter usually being a prerogative of the pharaoh.[158] The armrests are reminiscent of wings surrounding the king on his chair, evoking images like those of Isis standing behind Osiris' throne and spreading her wings protectively around him. For this reason, it is certainly not surprising that the armrest is decorated with a winged snake on a *nb*-basket, wearing the double-crown and guarding the king's cartouche – and, implicitly, the pharaoh on the platform himself – with its wings. Two further uraei (one wearing the white, the other the red crown) are also placed on the rear corners and would likewise have flanked and guarded Tutankhamun. Eventually, four cobras, wearing sun-discs on their heads, sit threateningly at the back of the chair, seemingly placed in front of a papyrus thicket with emerging ducks. Particularly noteworthy is the decoration on the inside of the backrest, i.e., the part that would have been in direct contact with the pharaoh sitting on the seat.

The main scene portrays Tutankhamun sitting in a relaxed position on a chair with a high, partially gilded back, on which he rests his right arm; his feet stand on a footstool. A brown cushion was placed on the piece of furniture to increase the king's comfort. Moreover, the *zmȝ tȝ.wi* symbol is visible between the leonine legs of the object, in a way copying the actual design of the 'throne'. Ankhesenamun stands in front of her husband, bending slightly towards him and touching his left shoulder with her right hand. In her left hand, she holds a vessel. Traditionally, this scene is understood as the queen anointing her husband, an interpretation that has since been doubted by Eaton-Krauss: she believes that the queen is offering her husband a drink.[159] To the right of the couple is a stand decorated with garlands and carrying a broad collar.[160] The figurative scene itself is framed by a palace facade motif at the bottom and a uraeus frieze on top; the latter further encloses a large Aten-disc with its accompanying cartouches in its centre, its rays reaching down towards the couple. Furthermore, a tall floral bouquet concludes the panel on each side. In a way, the composition of the image is reminiscent of the aforementioned *ḥmsì nfr* scenes.

Again, one might wonder whether the designation 'throne' is appropriate in this case. In general, it can be assumed that the term was chosen by the early scholars to indicate that this particular chair seemed to be the most elaborate and valuable for them, i.e., a piece of furniture fit for a king, especially in a ceremonial context.[161] However, this line of argumentation presupposes that a throne always has to consist of precious materials like gold and that each ruler only possesses one chair that is used in this function. In the case of Tutankhamun, it is particularly likely that he owned several seats for several occasions, since Eaton-Krauss has pointed out that the 'golden throne' is of a rather flimsy construction and would not have been able to safely carry the king on a daily basis; she assumes that it only played a role during special events.[162] Another question that might arise is whether the seat shown in the scene on the backrest should be called a 'throne' as well. If so, it is noteworthy that the two chairs indeed share similarities, but that the object in the two-dimensional rendering seems somewhat plainer, less precious. Yet, both items are equipped with leonine legs, and a high back as well as the *zmꜣ tꜣ.wì*. Hence, the backrest is perhaps a necessary element of a throne, since it protects the back of the ruler, the back otherwise being one of the most vulnerable and exposed parts.

The other element that might characterize a chair as a throne (or, at least, as belonging to a pharaoh) is the association with the *zmꜣ tꜣ.wì*, emblem of the unification of the country, a task that clearly lies in the hands of the king and, by extension, the throne. If this motif were really accepted as an indicator of a royal-ritual piece of furniture, this would also mean that the 'faldstool', presented in more detail above, would be on the same level as the gilded leonine seat, just like the chairs with the Carter nos. 349 and 087 as well as the stools registered as Carter nos. 078, 412, 467, and 595 – the latter are never thought of as thrones.[163] A different approach may be needed here. As defined by the *Encyclopaedia Britannica*, a 'throne' is usually more than just the furniture for seating: it comprises the combination and interplay of all its accessories. Thus, a feature that has not yet been mentioned but might be significant in the overall context is the footstool, i.e., 'a low piece of furniture used

for resting your feet on when you are sitting'[164] or, in other words, 'a low support on which a person who is sitting can place their feet'.[165] In fact, both the 'throne' and the 'faldstool' have low, rectangular footstools that are closely linked to them.[166] The decoration of the two objects is rather similar: bound captives are rendered lying on top of the piece of furniture, so that the king would have trampled his enemies, whenever sitting on the respective chair. Could the footstool thus have been a prerequisite for a throne? In the end, Tutankhamun likely owned more than one throne. He could have possessed several thrones that were used in different palaces, rooms, contexts or at different points during the young king's life. Hence, the stools with the *zmꜣ tꜣ.wì* signs might have belonged to him when he was still a prince, i.e., at a time when elements like the backrest and perhaps the footstool with the constrained foreigners were not yet as important on a symbolic-ritual level; of course, some of the stools could also have belonged to another member of the royal family. Overall, it is difficult to categorize the objects discovered within KV 62, since the original context of use is mainly lost.

When it comes to Tutankhamun's stools and chairs, it is noteworthy that the original designations chosen by Carter and his team are not as strictly followed by modern scholars as in the case of the beds. This paper does not aim to solve the issues surrounding furniture and furniture terminology, but would like to suggest that the terms employed for seating furniture should first be based on their outer form, rather than their context of use – especially since the specific setting and occasion are often unknown and, hence, based on personal interpretation. Thus, more neutral expressions like 'stool' and 'chair', referring to the presence or absence of a backrest, are preferable to words like 'throne', often laden with specific connotations. Of course, one could add further descriptions and/or the perceived context in a secondary step, so that the 'throne' could for example be called 'a leonine chair that was likely used in an official/ceremonial context'. At the same time, as also mentioned in connection with the beds, one should bear in mind that such objects are often multi-purpose and able to move between spheres, fulfilling a practical function as well as acting on a symbolic level.

Beds and thrones: similarities and dissimilarities

Following this overview of the various furniture types used for reclining and seating, the close ties between beds and chairs/thrones according to the ancient Egyptian worldview should be highlighted. On a basic level, both objects consist of a platform carried by four legs, often in the shape of animal limbs (bovine or leonine). They are luxury goods that visually underline the status and wealth of their owners, since the majority of people would simply have slept and sat on mats placed on the ground – for this reason, the man kneeling on the floor (𓀀) is the typical determinative for the broadly applicable verb *ḥmsi*, 'to sit, to occupy', while the individual on the seat (𓀎) is reserved for an elite setting, e.g., for words like *špss*, 'to be noble, to be esteemed, to be rich'.[167] Hence, they literally and symbolically elevate their occupants above anyone else. Of course, the individual furniture items would have further differed in the material used (e.g., gold foil, semi-precious stones, glass) and the elaboration of the decoration, depending on the means of the owner, perhaps also the context of use. For example, Tutankhamun's funerary beds generally appear more prestigious than his everyday life specimens; the addition of animal heads and tails to ritual furniture is especially noteworthy. Thus, one might wonder whether similar observations might apply to chairs as well. Does the presence of the leonine heads on the king's 'golden throne' indicate and even strengthen its possible ritual function – a function that is discussed in more detail below?

Another feature shared by both pieces, at least in their most complete form, is a panel that is attached perpendicularly to the platform: the footboard in the case of beds, the back and armrests in connection with the chairs (Fig. 3.20). Both features display a tripartite pattern in the New Kingdom. The central section often contains the main, i.e., the most important decoration, while the two sides play a subordinate role and are often decorated with an identical motif. In the case of the footboards, the same scene or element can be shown in all three parts. The close connection between bed and chair is also highlighted by the fact that the same motifs frequently occur in the decorative programmes of both objects, e.g., Taweret, Bes and lion-Bes, as well as floral motifs like tall bouquets, lotus flowers and papyrus thickets. It should further be stressed that beds and chairs are rarely placed directly on the ground, but rather on mats, supports or daises.[168] Moreover, they are often contained within a canopy, the basic form of which conveys the image of the celestial platform.[169] The overall composition thus creates a microcosm within which the king acts.

Now, the question arises of whether these similarities between beds and chairs in form and decoration could be coincidental – a possibility which, however, seems highly unlikely. Beds are older than chairs and were certainly also used for seating right from the start. Actual seating furniture, i.e., a piece of furniture that was specifically made for a sitting person, only developed in a secondary step from their bigger counterparts. At the same time, it is noteworthy that bed platforms can be rather short in Pre- and Early Dynastic times, in fact just long enough to accommodate a body sleeping in a foetal position.[170] This reduced size might have eased the emergence of the single stool and chair, but also actively blurred the boundaries between the two types of furniture, boundaries with which depictions like the aforementioned scene in the tomb of Mereruka play as well. The fact that beds and stools/chairs were originally understood as belonging to the same object

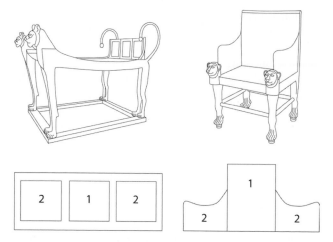

Fig. 3.20. *Visual comparison between Tutankhamun's funerary-ritual bed and his ceremonial chair (author's drawing).*

category, displaying many similarities in form, is also visible through the term *s.t*, variously translated as 'place, seat, throne, residence, position, rank'.[171] Interestingly, the expression *s.t-(n-)ḫt*, literally '*s.t* of wood' can also designate beds, as evidenced by determinatives accompanying the word in the Old Kingdom.[172] Thus, the core noun *s.t* refers to furniture of both types, indicating that both are part of the same group; if needed, the word could be specified by adding short descriptions like *(n-)ḫt* 'of wood', *ḥmsi* 'for sitting' or *sḏr* 'for lying down'.[173]

A surge of terms, used to label both beds and chairs, in particular thrones, is palpable in the Greco-Roman period. Particularly noteworthy in this context is an inscription from the temple of Edfu, unfortunately preserved in a rather fragmentary state. This text with the title 'Knowing the Day of the Birth of Horus' narrates how Seth experiences the very moment of Horus' birth at night: *wn.in stš rs* [...] *mn[m] n zmꜣ(.t)=f ḥr=f nwr ib=f* [...] 'Then, Seth woke up [...] his *zmꜣ(.t)* shook under him and his heart trembled [...]'.[174] Considering the overall situation, it is possible to translate the term *zmꜣ(.t)* in two ways here. On the one hand, the *zmꜣ(.t)* can be understood as a bed, since Seth's sleeping activity (or rather its interruption) is highlighted and the birth occurs at night. Yet, the interpretation as a throne would make sense as well; after all, the mere existence of Horus does not only threaten his uncle's nightly sleep, but also (most importantly!) his reign, emblematized through the throne.[175] Even the image of the *zmꜣ tꜣ.wi*, conjured through the use of *zmꜣ(.t)*, is of no help: as seen, this emblem can decorate both furniture pieces. One might wonder whether the meaning of the term remained ambiguous on purpose, bundling the role and symbolism of both bed and (ceremonial) chair.

Is it possible that the two objects are more closely related to each other than our modern understanding might suggest? Although this phenomenon cannot be discussed in any detail here, it is noteworthy that beds and the seating furniture of rulers (i.e., 'thrones' in the widest sense of the word) are frequently associated with each other around the world. On the so-called garden relief of Ashurbanipal, for example, the king is shown resting on a *kline*-like piece of furniture, drinking from a bowl held in his right hand.[176] His wife sits next to him on an elaborate chair, perhaps even a throne, likewise sipping from a drinking bowl. While the queen sits on the 'throne', there is no doubt that it is the reclining Ashurbanipal who represents the highest form of authority in this context, the *kline* elevating him significantly above everyone else. His power is further stressed by the severed head of Teumman, the king of Elam, hanging in one of the trees. Overall, it is clear that this relief does not depict a peaceful banquet scene. It portrays Ashurbanipal's power play, the bed serving as the scene for the display of his power, authority and wealth.

The more recent Sun Throne, also called Takht-e Tavoos or Peacock Throne (not to be confused with the Peacock Throne of the Great Mughal in Delhi), stood inside a room known as the Council Chamber in the Golestan Palace, Teheran – it has been exhibited in the Central Bank of Iran alongside the Iranian crown jewels since 1980.[177] Its name derives from a rotating diamond sun with emanating rays, attached to the back of the furniture piece. The throne itself, made by Mohammed Husein Khan, Sadr of Isfahan, for Fath Ali Shah in 1798, consists of a large platform, carried by seven legs and covered in precious stones (e.g., rubies and emeralds).[178] The Shah would have kneeled on this seat, cushioned by pillows.[179] Considering the appearance and dimensions of the seat, the object does not represent a typical throne in the sense of a chair, but clearly displays features of a bed as well. In fact, George N. Curzon, who analysed the throne in detail, describes it as a 'platform, or, as Tavernier calls it, a Field-bed Throne; as were the majority of those employed by the sovereigns of the East'.[180] The expression 'Field-bed Throne', to which Curzon refers, stems from the publication *The Six Voyages* by Jean-Baptiste Tavernier (1605–1689). This early French traveller described the throne of the Indian Mughal as follows:

> The Throne is a little Bed, with four Columns, about the bigness of one of our Field-Beds, with a Canopy, Backpiece, Boulster and Counterpoint, all embroider'd with Diamonds. Besides all this, when the King comes to sit upon the Throne, they throw over the Bed a Coverlet of Cloath of Gold, or some other richly-embroider'd Silk; and he ascends by three little steps, two-foot-board.[181]

Thus, it is not only the outer form of the Sun Throne as such that is reminiscent of a bed, but also the equipment, including pillows and covers.

A last specimen that should be discussed here is the bed-throne of the Ethiopian emperors, representing a large platform that is likewise equipped with textiles and cushions.[182] The importance of this piece of furniture is also highlighted by the title of the crown prince, i.e., *alga warash* 'the heir to

the bed', attested until the abolition of the Ethiopian monarchy in 1974.[183] In fact, the shape and meaning of this object reflects the general practice in Ethiopia to use beds as seats, even though stools and chairs are found in households as well.[184] Thus, many patriarchs would possess a bed that no one else was allowed to use; if someone sat down on this piece of furniture without explicit allowance, it was considered a crime – in the case of the bed-throne even high treason.[185] After the death of its owner, this status symbol was either destroyed and placed on their tomb or passed on to the eldest son, i.e., the heir.[186] The *kline* of Ashurbanipal, the Sun Throne of the Shah, and the bed-throne of the Ethiopian emperors may only represent a few examples, but they show that the confines between beds and thrones are not always as clear-cut as generally assumed, especially not in the royal sphere. Of course, this does not mean that the ancient Egyptians would not have made any distinction between the two types of furniture, only that their beds should be seen through a different lens than their modern counterparts, i.e., not just as a platform to sleep on, but as a means of expressing wealth, power and the highest authority.

Hence, from the point of view of the form and function, there are many similarities between beds and chairs. Now, this raises the question of whether their symbolism might be comparable as well in ancient Egypt. So far, the type of the leonine chair with heads has been variously interpreted. While Constant de Wit understood this seat as a microcosm, in which the king is reborn daily like the sun, and the lions as representatives of the Eastern and Western horizons,[187] Kuhlmann rejects this theory because the queen's ceremonial chair could be equipped with leonine heads as well, the queen never being likened to Re.[188] Instead, he suggests that the lion might be an apotropaic animal on the one hand, a manifestation of the ruler himself on the other.[189] He further argues that occasionally the leonine heads are replaced by female ones on the queen's chair for this very reason, the heads always representing the occupants themselves (in this case the queen) – the chair of Sitamun is examined as an example below. In general, he interprets this leonine type as a symbol for the secular, everyday kingship and, hence, contrasts it with the block-throne, embodying a more sacred, divine reign.[190] In the following, Tutankhamun's golden seat is analysed in conjunction with the pharaoh's ritual beds with which it shares many similarities, perhaps adding another aspect to the overall construct 'throne'.

In both instances, the shape of the two objects, i.e., the platform carried by four legs, is reminiscent of the sky-sign and, as such, Nut who bends over the earth and touches it with her four extremities; the four furniture legs as well as the goddess's arms and legs represent the four cardinal points.[191] For this reason, it is not surprising that the bed – and likely also the royal chair – is intrinsically linked to the solar cycle and, by extension, the daily rebirth of its owner in the funerary-ritual context.

This connection of furniture item and celestial vault was particularly noted in the case of Tutankhamun's three long-legged specimens which, as representatives of different mother-goddesses, would swallow the sun and, hence, the king every night to give birth to them again in the morning. As one of the characteristics of these ritual pieces of furniture, the addition of animal parts, i.e., heads and tails, was highlighted. Since the young pharaoh's 'golden throne' is equipped with leonine heads as well, one might wonder whether it could be associated with mother-goddesses as well. The fact that this chair seems devoid of elevated tails would not contradict such an interpretation, since the backrest perhaps assumes their position visually and figuratively.

The motif of the chair with two leonine heads is already attested in the Old Kingdom. One of the best-known examples of this kind is certainly the seated statue of Khafre with a falcon behind his neck, perched on the backrest of the chair and spreading its wings protectively around the back of the king's head.[192] This piece of furniture appears block-like at first, but the carvings suggest a four-legged chair. The main body of the object is comprised of a platform with a high, undecorated backrest, yet without armrests. Each foreleg represents the front of a standing lion, the heads being part of the leg itself – in the case of Tutankhamun, the heads were worked separately and then placed on the front corners. Thus, in contrast to the specimen from KV 62, the seat was carried by four leg pairs, i.e., eight individual limbs; here, the doubling of the carrier animal is complete. Furthermore, the space between the leonine paws is decorated with the *zmꜣ tꜣ.wi* symbol on both sides, another element that will become standard for most royal chairs in the official context.[193] If the combination of high back, leonine heads and *zmꜣ tꜣ.wi* characterized the throne, i.e., the most important ceremonial chair in the case of Tutankhamun, then the seat of Khafre should likewise be identified as such. Now, in connection with the role of the ritual beds, this furniture type with all its features might actively guarantee the renewal of the pharaoh and his power on a daily basis, just like that of the sun, and protect him throughout the different phases. At least, such a symbolic function would be quite fitting for a throne.

Of course, the rather fragile nature of Tutankhamun's chair should be borne in mind, as highlighted by Eaton-Krauss. It is possible that it was only used on special occasions, e.g., during particular (perhaps funerary?) rituals, but was still active on a symbolic level even when not in use. In fact, the pharaoh's effigy on the back might have acted as his replacement in these instances. One could even go a step further: should this 'throne' be seen as a more elaborate parallel of the chair found in TT 8? In contrast to Kha and Merit, who had to repurpose some of their everyday objects for the funerary context, Tutankhamun was able to afford purpose-made ritual items, amongst them probably the 'golden throne'. Since it was assumed that the arrangements in the tomb of Kha, i.e., the placing of his statuette

on the seat, was meant to symbolize a materialization of the offering table scene and an eternalization of the offerings, the decoration on the back of Tutankhamun's chair might fulfil the same function, especially if the scene should really be understood as Ankhesenamun offering the king a drink. Moreover, it might be significant that both chairs were turned into the direction of the tomb entrance, i.e., oriented towards the world of the living and the origin of the offerings.

The so-called throne of Princess Sitamun, found in the tomb of Yuya and Tjuiu, is an interesting example for a chair from the royal sphere as well.[194] While the chair is supported by four single leonine legs, it displays human instead of animal heads, attached to the front corners of the object. Each protome renders the gilded head and neck of a woman, wearing a floral, polos-like crown and collar. Her short hair, or wig, is comprised of many little curls and reaches down to her chin. She further wears a decorative band around her head. As the chair belonged to Sitamun, daughter of Amenhotep III and Tiye, these heads are thought to represent the owner herself. On the back of the chair, the princess, characterized by the sidelock of youth, is represented twice in the centre of the scene, seated back-to-back on a chair. A female servant approaches her, offering her a collar. The tableau on the backrest as well as the two heads certainly indicate Sitamun's ownership of the chair. At the same time, it can perhaps be assumed that the heads are meant to fulfil the same role as the lionesses, i.e., representing the mother-goddess and assisting in the ritual rebirth; certainly, male heads are never found in this position. These two explanations are not mutually exclusive: Sitamun perhaps wanted to deposit her own chair into the tomb of her grandparents to take part in and guarantee their daily regeneration, at least to some extent.

If this interpretation is correct, one might even go further and extend this understanding to royal seated statues that show women standing in front of the throne's legs, especially in the New Kingdom. In the case of the Memnon Colossi, for example, Queen Tiye is rendered next to Amenhotep III's right leg, Mutemwia next to the left: as the wife and mother of the pharaoh, these two women would certainly have constituted the most important female influence during his reign.[195] In other cases, the king's daughters can be depicted in this position as well. Overall, it might thus be conceivable that the presence of these royal mothers, wives and daughters in these statues would not just be a means of including them into the family portrait, so to speak. They perhaps played a more active role in the cyclical regeneration and strengthening of the royal power than generally assumed. After all, every king needs a queen, every male aspect a female counterpart – a queen that supports her husband, a mother that supports her son just like a chair (and bed) supports its occupant.

Of course, these are just some preliminary thoughts on furniture categorization and the symbolic function of beds and chairs. A more in-depth investigation of chairs and thrones is definitely needed, the above observations having shown that there is still potential in analysing apparently familiar objects.

Preliminary conclusion(s)

The aim of this paper was to give a brief overview of the various furniture types that existed in ancient Egypt for the purposes of lying and sitting down. In this framework, the burial equipment of Tutankhamun functioned as the main example since it is the most completely preserved group. Of course, one should bear in mind that this arrangement was certainly not typical for its time due to the untimely (and probably unexpected) death of the king and that such a narrow corpus also limits the possibilities of understanding. The results gleaned from KV 62 are not necessarily applicable to non-royal individuals, different periods and geographic locations. Nonetheless, the ensemble allows us to get an insight into the use and symbolic meaning of these pieces of furniture. One of the difficulties that presented itself was the attempt of a definition. Because beds, stools and chairs share clear similarities in form and usage with their modern counterparts, they often appear familiar, commonplace, well known. To a certain degree, the visual and functional parallels even make us blind to the disparities. As we seemingly comprehend these items and their use well, we apply our own terms and (indirectly as well as unconsciously) connotations onto these ancient objects, often obfuscating their actual original function and meaning. In a way, we will never be able to completely let go of our lived experiences as well as our own view and understanding of the world, but it is important to constantly make ourselves aware of our biases, to challenge them. We need to be conscious of which words we use in which context, as words are never neutral. After all, we see the world around us through words – words create and words bring into existence. For this reason, it has been suggested to choose designations based on the outer form of an object, i.e., 'bed', 'stool', 'chair'. In contrast, words like 'bier' and 'throne' only acquire meaning through their context, so that they are already loaded with connotations and preformed ideas; however, since the context is frequently lost in ancient Egypt, such an approach proves difficult.

Another point that has been highlighted here is the many similarities between beds and chairs in form, purpose, decoration and possibly symbolism. Even though this aspect still needs a more thorough analysis, the results so far being only preliminary, there are clear indications for the fact that the borders between these two four-legged object categories were understood in a different way in ancient Egypt – such delimitations and classifications are not universal. This discussion has shown how challenging it can be to take a step back and try to look at everyday, seemingly familiar items

with fresh eyes. At the same time, such questions open up paths for further research. Thus, for example, the approach of examining Tutankhamun's long-legged leonine bed and his 'golden throne' in conjunction might reveal previously unnoticed connections, leading to a better understanding of both furniture items and their respective contexts. There could be even more. Considering the ability of beds and chairs to carry and elevate, one might wonder whether furniture pieces like the sedan would have belonged into this object category as well and shared the same general symbolism. Could the ensemble found in the tomb (or deposit) of Hetepheres, consisting of a bed, two chairs and a litter, represent more than just burial equipment and constitute a ritual group?

In the end, looking at 'well-known' pieces of furniture like beds and chairs, testing their common modern definitions against ancient evidence and (if necessary) adapting them is a useful and important approach that might bring us closer to understanding the lives – and deaths – of the ancient Egyptians.

Notes

1   University of Oxford, 2023.
2   https://www.oxfordlearnersdictionaries.com/definition/english/bed_1?q=bed (last accessed 17 June 2023).
3   https://dictionary.cambridge.org/dictionary/english-german/bed (last accessed 17 June 2023).
4   https://www.oxfordlearnersdictionaries.com/definition/english/furniture?q=furniture (last accessed 19 June 2023).
5   https://dictionary.cambridge.org/dictionary/english-german/furniture (last accessed 19 June 2023).
6   https://www.etymonline.com/word/furniture (last accessed 24 June 2023).
7   Cairo, Egyptian Museum of Antiquities, JE 52261; now Grand Egyptian Museum, GEM 6364; from Giza, G 7000 X; 4th Dynasty. http://giza.fas.harvard.edu/objects/54942/full/ (last accessed 18 July 2023); Reisner 1929, 88–89; Baker 1966, 43–45, 47, Fig. 37; Killen 2017, 39–40, pl. 36, no. 7.
8   For the discussion of tomb versus deposit, see Münch 2000.
9   For the reproduction, see https://collections.mfa.org/objects/147125 (last accessed 3 July 2023).
10 Baker 1966, 51; Metzger 1985, 11; Eaton-Krauss 2008a, 35.
11 Asprey 2018, 149–150.
12 For the link between head and sun, see Hellinckx 2001.
13 Cf. e.g. Killen 2017, 36.
14 Giza, G 7530–7540; 4th Dynasty. Dunham and Simpson 1974, 5, Fig. 8; Baker 1966, 43, Fig. 32.
15 For these beds, see also 'Furniture fit for a king: The case of Tutankhamun'.
16 Kha and Merit: Turin, Museo Egizio, S. 8327 and S. 8629; from Thebes, Deir el-Medina, TT 8; 18th Dynasty. Baker 1966, 119, 123, Fig. 170; 124, Fig. 171. Yuya and Tjuiu: Cairo, Egyptian Museum of Antiquities, CG 51108, 51109, and 51110; from Thebes, Valley of the Kings, KV 46; 18th Dynasty. Baker 1966, 71–74, figs 82–85.
17 I would like to thank the anonymous reviewer for bringing up this caveat.

18 Cairo, Egyptian Museum of Antiquities, JE 62014, now Grand Egyptian Museum; from Thebes, Valley of the Kings, KV 62; 18th Dynasty.

19 'Furniture fit for a king: The case of Tutankhamun' discusses this motif in connection with stools and chairs.

20 Cairo, Egyptian Museum of Antiquities, JE 62018, now in the Grand Egyptian Museum; from Thebes, Valley of the Kings, KV 62; 18th Dynasty.

21 New York, Metropolitan Museum of Art, 20.2.13a–c; unknown provenance; 18th Dynasty. Baker 1966, 104–105, figs 136–137; Reeves 2022, 373–374, Fig. on p. 372. For the model folding bed, see https://www.metmuseum.org/art/collection/search/545758 (last accessed 17 July 2023); Hayes 1990, 203, Fig. 118; Baker 1966, 104–105; Scott 1965, 145, Fig. 41; Reeves 2022, 373.

22 Boston, Museum of Fine Arts, 67.921; from Hermopolis, 18th Dynasty: https://collections.mfa.org/objects/46211/talatat-sleeping-man?ctx=44d51c8e-13c2-4f2e-8c79-4ca7d-00d7c3e&idx=0 (last accessed 18 July 2023); Aldred 1973, 141, no. 65. Brooklyn, Brooklyn Museum, 64.148.3; unknown provenance; 18th Dynasty: https://www.brooklynmuseum.org/opencollection/objects/3729 (last accessed 18 July 2023); Aldred 1973, 145, no. 70. For a related *talatat* in a private collection, see https://www.christies.com/en/lot/lot-6382007 (last accessed 18 July 2023). A discussion of these blocks is also found in Schutz 2024 (forthcoming).

23 See Turin, Museo Egizio, S. 8632; from Thebes, Deir el-Medina, TT 8; 18th Dynasty: https://collezioni.museoegizio.it/en-GB/material/S_8632/?description=merit&inventoryNumber=&title=&cgt=&yearFrom=&yearTo=&materials=&provenance=&acquisition=&epoch=&dynasty=&pharaoh= (last accessed 18 July 2023); and Turin, Museo Egizio, S. 8633; from Thebes, Deir el-Medina, TT 8; 18th Dynasty: https://collezioni.museoegizio.it/en-GB/material/S_8633/?description=merit&inventoryNumber=&title=&cgt=&yearFrom=&yearTo=&materials=&provenance=&acquisition=&epoch=&dynasty=&pharaoh= (last accessed 18 July 2023).

24 Turin, Museo Egizio, S. 8629; from Thebes, Deir el-Medina, TT 8; 18th Dynasty: https://collezioni.museoegizio.it/en-GB/material/S_8629/?description=merit&inventoryNumber=&title=&cgt=&yearFrom=&yearTo=&materials=&provenance=&acquisition=&epoch=&dynasty=&pharaoh= (last accessed 18 July 2023); Baker 1966, 124, Fig. 171.

25 For the many similarities between beds and chairs, see 'Beds and Thrones: Similarities and dissimilarities'.

26 The role of the beds in the funerary context is further discussed in 'Furniture fit for a king: The case of Tutankhamun'.

27 See e.g. Meskell 2002, 75, Fig. 3.7.

28 London, Petrie Museum of Egyptian Archaeology, LDUCE-UC16601; unknown provenance; 18th Dynasty: https://collections.ucl.ac.uk/Details/collect/32052 (last accessed 18 July 2023); Petrie 1937, 9, no. 193; Meskell 2002, 75, Fig. 3.7. Petrie actually mentions a second 'double couch', found in Thebes, Sheikh Abd el-Qurna (1937, 9, no. 194).

29 Baker 1966, 55–56, Fig. 53, colour pl. III; Kanawati et al. 2010, pls 52, 99.

30 Vandier 1964, 186–187, Fig. 77.

31 Kanawati and Woods 2010, pls 9, 11.

32 For a thorough discussion and a catalogue of these scenes, see Backhouse 2020. For the meaning of the bed in these *Wochenlaube*-scenes, see also Schutz 2024 (forthcoming).

33 See e.g. Backhouse 2020, 74–74, 78–79; Meskell 2002, 70–71; Nifosi 2019, 205–216; Arnette 2015, 25–36; Kleinke 2007, 31–33.

34 Nifosi 2019, 56–60.

35 Furth 1987, 17; Lee 2005, 234–241.

36 See 'Furniture fit for a king: The case of Tutankhamun'.

37 https://www.oxfordlearnersdictionaries.com/definition/english/bier?q=bier (last accessed 6 July 2023).

38 https://dictionary.cambridge.org/dictionary/english/bier (last accessed 6 July 2023).

39 https://www.etymonline.com/search?q=bier (last accessed 7 July 2023).

40 For the development of the bier in this context, see Jürgensen 2014.

41 For Tutankhamun's ritual-funerary beds, see 'Furniture fit for a king: The case of Tutankhamun'.

42 https://www.etymonline.com/search?q=couch (last accessed 7 July 2023). See also von Stülpnagel 1997, 35–37.

43 https://www.oxfordlearnersdictionaries.com/definition/english/couch_1?q=couch (last accessed 7 July 2023).

44 https://dictionary.cambridge.org/dictionary/english-german/couch (last accessed 7 July 2023).

45 https://www.oxfordlearnersdictionaries.com/definition/english/stool?q=stool (last accessed 23 June 2023).

46 https://dictionary.cambridge.org/dictionary/english-german/stool (last accessed 23 June 2023).

47 https://www.etymonline.com/word/stool (last accessed 24 June 2023).

48 https://www.etymonline.com/word/stool (last accessed 24 June 2023).

49 Paris, Musée du Louvre, E 15591 and E 22745; from Giza, Mastaba G 1225; 4th Dynasty: https://collections.louvre.fr/en/ark:/53355/cl010005261 (last accessed 27 June 2023); Ziegler 1990, 187–188, no. 29; Ziegler 1999, 242–244, no. 51; Der Manuelian 2003, 12–13, pls 11–12; 58–62.

50 London, British Museum EA1242; from Beni Suef; 4th Dynasty; Fig. 3.3b: https://www.britishmuseum.org/collection/object/Y_EA1242 (last accessed 28 June 2023); Baker 1966, 53–54, Fig. 50.

51 Saad 1957, 12, figs 7–8; 14, figs 9–10; 16, figs 11–12; 18, Fig. 14. See also Schäfer 1974, 140, Fig. 122.

52 Rome, Museo di Scultura Antica Giovanni Barracco; unknown provenance; 4th Dynasty: https://artsandculture.google.com/asset/stele-of-the-dignitary-nefer/MgG2GK8p-bQHCCQ (last accessed 28 June 2023).

53 London, British Museum, EA1171; from Giza; 4th Dynasty; Fig. 3.3c: https://www.britishmuseum.org/collection/object/Y_EA1171 (last accessed 27 June 2023); Robins 1993, 158, Fig. 66; Russmann 2001, 72–73, no. 6.

54 https://www.oxfordlearnersdictionaries.com/definition/english/chair_1?q=chair (last accessed 17 June 2023).

55 https://dictionary.cambridge.org/dictionary/english-german/chair (last accessed 17 June 2023).

56 https://www.etymonline.com/word/chair#etymonline_v_8391 (last accessed 24 June 2023).

57 Killen 2017, 91.

58   Although the name is generally rendered as Narmer, there is evidence that it should actually be read as Narmeher: Quack 2003, 113–116; Quack 2022, 271–289; Rother 2015, 2.

59   Oxford, Ashmolean Museum, AN1896–1908 E.3631; from Hierakonpolis, Main Deposit; 0 Dynasty. Quibell 1900, 8–9, pl. XXVI.B; Metzger 1985, 5, pl. 1.1.

60   For this throne type and its role more generally, see Kuhlmann 1977, 51–61, 81–85.

61   London, British Museum, EA9901,3; unknown provenance; 19th Dynasty: https://www.britishmuseum.org/collection/object/Y_EA9901-3 (last accessed 8 July 2023).

62   Metzger 1985, 14–15.

63   For this chair type, see Kuhlmann 1977, 57–60, 82–83.

64   Kuhlmann 1977, 82–83.

65   Kuhlmann 1977, 59.

66   See e.g. Budka 2019, 15, with further references.

67   Saad 1957, 8–10, no. 3; Killen 2017, 91–92, Fig. 24.

68   Saad 1957, 9, figs 4 and 5.

69   Chicago, Art Institute, 1920.265; from Giza, probably G 3035; 4th Dynasty: https://www.artic.edu/artworks/121737/stela-of-tjenti-and-nefret (last accessed 24 June 2023); Teeter 1994, 18, no. 1; Eaton-Krauss 2008b.

70   https://www.flickr.com/photos/manna4u/30464941158/ (last accessed 28 June 2023).

71   I would like to thank the anonymous reviewer for this suggestion.

72   See e.g. the stela of Qenmen and Henut (Turin, Museo Egizio, 1513; unknown provenance, 11th Dynasty; https://collezioni.museoegizio.it/en-GB/material/Cat_1513/?description=henut&inventoryNumber=&title=&cgt=&yearFrom=&yearTo=&materials=&provenance=&acquisition=&epoch=&dynasty=&pharaoh= (last accessed 1 January 2024) and the stela of Harbes (Turin, Museo Egizio, S. 17161; provenance unknown; 25th or 26th Dynasty: https://collezioni.museoegizio.it/en-GB/material/S_17161/?description=harbes&inventoryNumber=&title=&cgt=&yearFrom=&yearTo=&materials=&provenance=&acquisition=&epoch=&dynasty=&pharaoh= (last accessed January 2024).

73   New York, MET, 14.2.7; from Thebes, probably El-Tarif; First Intermediate Period, 11th Dynasty: https://www.metmuseum.org/art/collection/search/544005?pkgids=331&pos=2&nextInternalLocale=en&pg=1&oid=544005&rpp=4&exhibitionId=%7B-36bfd863-bd71-4d58-b1b2-f3f865084dbb%7D&ft=* (last accessed 8 July 2023); Scott 1965, 140, Fig. 25; Hayes 1953, 153, Fig. 91; Scott 1965, 140, Fig. 23; Arnold and Arnold 2015, 43–44, no. 2.

74   New York, MET, 12.184; probably from Abydos; 12th Dynasty: https://www.metmuseum.org/art/collection/search/544320?pkgids=331&pos=62&nextInternalLocale=en&pg=2&oid=544320&rpp=60&exhibitionId=%7B36B-FD863-BD71-4D58-B1B2-F3F865084DBB%7D&ft=* (last accessed 28 June 2023); Hayes 1953, 298, Fig. 195; Grajetzki 2015, 125–127, no. 60.

75   New York, MET, 65.120.1; unknown provenance; Middle Kingdom, 13th Dynasty: https://www.metmuseum.org/art/collection/search/558084 (last accessed 8 July 2023); Yamamoto 2015, 266–267, no. 202.

76   New York, MET, 57.95; unknown provenance; Middle Kingdom, 11th Dynasty: https://www.metmuseum.org/art/collection/search/545393 (last accessed 8 July 2023); Arnold and Jánosi 2015, 58–60, no. 10.

77   New York, MET, 1970.49; unknown provenance; 18th Dynasty: https://www.metmuseum.org/art/collection/search/555406?searchField=All&sortBy=relevance&ao=on&ft=egypt+offering&offset=180&rpp=20&pos=189 (last accessed 28 June 2023).

78   Paris, Musée du Louvre, E 16367; from Thebes, Deir el-Medina; Ramesside period. https://collections.louvre.fr/en/ark:/53355/cl010025210 (last accessed 27 June 2023); Bruyère 1952, 103, Fig. 175, pl. XXIV, no. 233; Andreu 2002, 140, no. 84.

79   Thebes, Sheikh Abd el-Qurna, TT 52; 18th Dynasty. For the copy by Norman de Garis Davies, see https://www.metmuseum.org/art/collection/search/548578 (last accessed 27 June 2023).

80   Davies 1941, pls VIII–XII.

81   Turin, Museo Egizio, S. 8333; from Thebes, Deir el-Medina, TT 8; 18th Dynasty: https://collezioni.museoegizio.it/en-GB/material/S_8333/?description=chair&inventoryNumber=&title=&cgt=&yearFrom=&yearTo=&materials=&provenance=&acquisition=&epoch=&dynasty=&pharaoh= (last accessed 9 July 2023); Baker 1966, 117, Fig. 160.

82   Turin, Museo Egizio, S. 8335; from Thebes, Deir el-Medina, TT 8; 18th Dynasty: https://collezioni.museoegizio.it/en-GB/material/S_8335/?description=kha&inventoryNumber=&title=&cgt=&yearFrom=&yearTo=&materials=&provenance=&acquisition=&epoch=&dynasty=&pharaoh= (last accessed 9 July 2023); Näser 2008, 466, Fig. 8.

83   Also named Amunnakht in the literature; Thebes, Deir el-Medina, TT 335; 19th Dynasty.

84   Bruyère 1926, 135, Fig. 91; Näser 2001, 381; Näser 2008, 466–467. For further examples, see Näser 2001, 380–381.

85   Näser 2001, 381; Näser 2008, 467.

86   https://www.oxfordlearnersdictionaries.com/definition/english/throne?q=throne (last accessed 17 June 2023).

87   https://dictionary.cambridge.org/dictionary/english-german/throne (last accessed 17 June 2023).

88   https://www.britannica.com/topic/throne (last accessed 17 July 2023). See also Kuhlmann 1977, 3.

89   https://www.etymonline.com/search?q=throne (last accessed 24 June 2023).

90   Eaton-Krauss 2008a, 21, note 3.

91   Turin, Museo Egizio, 1618; from Thebes, Deir el-Medina, TT 8; 18th Dynasty: https://collezioni.museoegizio.it/en-GB/material/Cat_1618/?description=kha&inventoryNumber=&title=&cgt=&yearFrom=&yearTo=&materials=&provenance=&acquisition=&epoch=&dynasty=&pharaoh= (last accessed 9 July 2023); Vandier d'Abbadie and Jourdain 1939, 13–14, pl. XI; Tosi and Roccati 1972, 38–39, 263, no. 50007.

92   For daises and mats below the throne in general, see Kuhlmann 1977, 70–71, 90; Metzger 1985, 93–99.

93   For example, Z. Y. Saad uses the word 'chair' to refer to backless seating furniture as well (see e.g. Saad 1957, 12, 14, 16, 18, 20–21, 22, 24, 26, 28, 30, 34, 36, 38, 40, 41, 46, 49, 51).

94   For the ritual beds in the tomb of Ay, see e.g. Schaden 1984, 54, Fig. 34; Price 2016, 281. For Horemheb's exemplars, see

e.g. Davis 1912, 103–104, pls LXXXI–LXXXIII; Reeves and Wilkinson 1996, 132–133; Martin 2016, 98, 103, Fig. 4; Price 2016, 281; Mohammed Hussein Ahmed 2022, 218–219, figs 2–3.

95 http://www.griffith.ox.ac.uk/perl/gi-ca-qmakesumm. pl?sid=80.152.217.177-1688964715&qno=1&curr=047 (last accessed 10 July 2023); Baker 1966, 103–104, figs 134–135; Reeves 2022, 371–372, Fig. on p. 370; Killen 2017, 42, pl. 40, no. 12.

96 The term 'couch' was written first, but then crossed out and replaced by the designation 'bed', added above the line. This might indicate that the differentiation between the furniture categories was perhaps somewhat artificial and confusing for Carter's team as well – at least at the beginning.

97 http://www.griffith.ox.ac.uk/perl/gi-ca-qmakesumm. pl?sid=80.152.217.177-1688964715&qno=1&curr=080 (last accessed 10 July 2023); Baker 1966, 105, Fig. 139; Reeves 2022, 372; Killen 2017, 42, pl. 39, no. 11.

98 http://www.griffith.ox.ac.uk/perl/gi-ca-qmakesumm. pl?sid=80.152.217.177-1688964715&qno=1&curr=377 (last accessed 10 July 2023); Baker 1966, 105, Fig. 138; Reeves 2022, 372.

99 http://www.griffith.ox.ac.uk/perl/gi-ca-qmakesumm. pl?sid=80.152.217.177-1688964715&qno=1&curr=466 (last accessed 10 July 2023); Baker 1966, 101–103, figs 132–133; Reeves 2022, 372–373; Killen 2017, 42–43, pl. 41, no. 13.

100 http://www.griffith.ox.ac.uk/perl/gi-ca-qmakesumm. pl?sid=80.152.217.177-1688964715&qno=1&curr=497 (last accessed 10 July 2023); http://www.griffith.ox.ac. uk/perl/gi-ca-qmakesumm.pl?sid=80.152.217.177-1688964715&qno=1&curr=576 (last accessed 10 July 2023); Reeves 2022, 373.

101 http://www.griffith.ox.ac.uk/perl/gi-ca-qmakesumm. pl?sid=80.152.217.177-1688964715&qno=1&curr=586 (last accessed 10 July 2023); Baker 1966, 104–105, figs 136–137; Reeves 2022, 373–374, Fig. on p. 372; Killen 2017, 43–44, pls 42–43, no. 14.

102 http://www.griffith.ox.ac.uk/perl/gi-ca-qmakesumm.pl?si d=80.152.217.177-1688964715&qno=1&curr=253a (last accessed 10 July 2023).

103 http://www.griffith.ox.ac.uk/perl/gi-ca-qmakesumm. pl?sid=80.152.217.177-1688964715&qno=1&curr=137 (last accessed 10 July 2023).

104 http://www.griffith.ox.ac.uk/perl/gi-ca-qmakesumm. pl?sid=80.152.217.177-1688964715&qno=1&curr=035 (last accessed 10 July 2023).

105 http://www.griffith.ox.ac.uk/perl/gi-ca-qmakesumm. pl?sid=80.152.217.177-1688964715&qno=1&curr=073 (last accessed 10 July 2023).

106 See 'Definition: Attempts and issues'.

107 Turin, Museo Egizio, S. 8629; from Thebes, Deir el-Medina, TT 8; 18th Dynasty: https://collezioni.museoegizio.it/en-GB/ material/S_8629/?description=merit&inventoryNumber=&-title=&cgt=&yearFrom=&yearTo=&materials=&prove-nance=&acquisition=&epoch=&dynasty=&pharaoh= (last accessed 10 July 2023); Baker 1966, 119, 124, Fig. 171.

108 See Turin, Museo Egizio, S. 8634; from Thebes, Deir el-Medina, TT 8; 18th Dynasty: https://collezioni.museoegizio.it/en-GB/ material/S_8634/?description=merit&inventoryNumber=&-

title=&cgt=&yearFrom=&yearTo=&materials=&prov-enance=&acquisition=&epoch=&dynasty=&pharaoh= (last accessed 1 January 2024) and Turin, Museo Egizio, S. 8635; from Thebes, Deir el-Medina, TT 8; 18th Dynasty: https://collezioni.museoegizio.it/en-GB/ material/S_8635/?description=merit&inventoryNum-ber=&title=&cgt=&yearFrom=&yearTo=&materials=&prov-enance=&acquisition=&epoch=&dynasty=&pharaoh= (last accessed 1 January 2024).

109 Strauß-Seeber 1986, 1285–1286.

110 Beinlich 2006, 29, with note 54.

111 Reeves 2022, 219.

112 For the find situation in general, see Carter and Mace 1923, 112–120.

113 For these texts, see Beinlich and Saleh 1989, 15, no. 35; 31, no. 73; 61, no. 137. These beds and their perceived specific functions are also discussed in Beinlich 2006, 29.

114 For these rites, see van Gennep 1960, 146–165; Turner 1997, 94–95.

115 See e.g. Reeves 2022, 369. The goddess's name is not recorded in Leitz 2002.

116 Beinlich 1991, 96–103, figs 35, 37, 39.

117 Beinlich 1991, 96–103, figs 35, 37, 39.

118 Hornung 1991, 242, Fig. 178.

119 Beinlich 1991, 101, note 188; Leblanc and Siliotti 2002, 68, Fig. 2.

120 See e.g. Sethe 1910, 476, PT 670 (1975a–b): 'You went (away), may you return. You slept, may you wake up (again). You moored (= died), may you live (again)'.

121 De Buck 1939, 28; Hornung 1956, 63, 65–66; Assmann 2010, 244.

122 http://www.griffith.ox.ac.uk/perl/gi-ca-qmakesumm. pl?sid=217.91.228.146-1689014302&qno=1&curr=066 (last accessed 10 July 2023); Reeves 2022, 390; Eaton-Krauss 2008a, 21, 110–111.

123 http://www.griffith.ox.ac.uk/perl/gi-ca-qmakesumm. pl?sid=217.91.228.146-1689014302&qno=1&curr=078 (last accessed 10 July 2023); Reeves 2022, 390; Eaton-Krauss 2008a, 102–104.

124 http://www.griffith.ox.ac.uk/perl/gi-ca-qmakesumm. pl?sid=217.91.228.146-1689014302&qno=1&curr=081 (last accessed 10 July 2023); Baker 1966, 86–87, 88, Fig. 101; Reeves 2022, 390; Eaton-Krauss 2008a, 106–109; Killen 2017, 67, pl. 77, no. 25.

125 http://www.griffith.ox.ac.uk/perl/gi-ca-qmakesumm. pl?sid=217.91.228.146-1689014302&qno=1&curr=083 (last accessed 10 July 2023; Baker 1966, 87–89, Fig. 102; Reeves 2022, 390, Fig. on p. 391; Eaton-Krauss 2008a, 116–119; Killen 2017, 63–64, pl. 64, no. 13.

126 http://www.griffith.ox.ac.uk/perl/gi-ca-qmakesumm. pl?sid=217.91.228.146-1689014302&qno=1&curr=084 (last accessed 10 July 2023); Baker 1966, 86, 88, Fig. 100; Reeves 2022, 390; Eaton-Krauss 2008a, 109–110.

127 http://www.griffith.ox.ac.uk/perl/gi-ca-qmakesumm. pl?sid=217.91.228.146-1689014302&qno=1&curr=139 (last accessed 10 July 2023); Baker 1966, 88–89, Fig. 103; Reeves 2022, 390; Eaton-Krauss 2008a, 112–116.

128 http://www.griffith.ox.ac.uk/perl/gi-ca-qmakesumm. pl?sid=217.91.228.146-1689014302&qno=1&curr=140 (last

129 accessed 10 July 2023); Baker 1966, 88–89, Fig. 103; Reeves 2022, 390; Eaton-Krauss 2008a, 112–116.

129 http://www.griffith.ox.ac.uk/perl/gi-ca-qmakesumm. pl?sid=217.91.228.146-1689014302&qno=1&curr=149 (last accessed 10 July 2023); http://www.griffith.ox.ac.uk/perl/ gi-ca-qmakesumm.pl?sid=217.91.228.146-1689014302&qn o=1&curr=142b (last accessed 10 July 2023); Reeves 2022, 390; Eaton-Krauss 2008a, 119–120.

130 http://www.griffith.ox.ac.uk/perl/gi-ca-qmakesumm. pl?sid=217.91.228.146-1689014302&qno=1&curr=351 (last accessed 10 July 2023); Carter 1933, 111–113; Reeves 2022, 388, Fig. on p. 389; Eaton-Krauss 2008a, 75–91; Killen 2017, 100, 102, pls 100–101, no. 10.

131 http://www.griffith.ox.ac.uk/perl/gi-ca-qmakesumm. pl?sid=217.91.228.146-1689014302&qno=1&curr=412 (last accessed 10 July 2023); Baker 1966, 90–91, Fig. 105a–c; Reeves 2022, 390, Fig. on p. 391; Eaton-Krauss 2008a, 122–125; Killen 2017, 65–66, pl. 71, no. 19.

132 http://www.griffith.ox.ac.uk/perl/gi-ca-qmakesumm. pl?sid=217.91.228.146-1689014302&qno=1&curr=467 (last accessed 10 July 2023); Baker 1966, 87, colour pl. VII; Reeves 2022, 390, Fig. on p. 391; Eaton-Krauss 2008a, 104–106; Killen 2017, 67, pl. 78, no. 26.

133 http://www.griffith.ox.ac.uk/perl/gi-ca-qmakesumm. pl?sid=217.91.228.146-1689014302&qno=1&curr=595 (last accessed 10 July 2023); Reeves 2022, 390; Eaton-Krauss 2008a, 21, 112.

134 http://www.griffith.ox.ac.uk/perl/gi-ca-qmakesumm. pl?sid=217.91.228.146-1689014330&qno=1&curr=039 (last accessed 10 July 2023); Baker 1966, 84, 86, 87, Fig. 99; Reeves 2022, 384; Eaton-Krauss 2008a, 93–96; Killen 2017, 100, pl. 99, no. 9.

135 http://www.griffith.ox.ac.uk/perl/gi-ca-qmakesumm. pl?sid=217.91.228.146-1689014330&qno=1&curr=082 (last accessed 10 July 2023); Reeves 2022, 387; Eaton-Krauss 2008a, 96–98.

136 http://www.griffith.ox.ac.uk/perl/gi-ca-qmakesumm. pl?sid=217.91.228.146-1689014330&qno=1&curr=087 (last accessed 10 July 2023); Baker 1966, 83–85, figs 95–96; Reeves 2022, 386; Eaton-Krauss 2008a, 57–67; Killen 2017, 98, pl. 97, no. 7.

137 http://www.griffith.ox.ac.uk/perl/gi-ca-qmakesumm. pl?sid=217.91.228.146-1689014330&qno=1&curr=349 (last accessed 10 July 2023); Baker 1966, 83–84, 86, figs 97–98; Reeves 2022, 387; Eaton-Krauss 2008a, 68–74; Killen 2017, 98, pl. 96, no. 6.

138 http://www.griffith.ox.ac.uk/gri/carter/033.html (last accessed 17 July 2023); Reeves 2022, 388; Eaton-Krauss 2008a, 100–102.

139 http://www.griffith.ox.ac.uk/perl/gi-ca-qmakesumm. pl?sid=217.91.228.146-1689014344&qno=1&curr=091 (last accessed 10 July 2023); https://egypt-museum.com/gold en-throne-of-tutankhamun/ (last accessed 11 July 2023); Carter and Mace 1923, 117–119; Baker 1966, 77–80, figs 89–90, colour pls VI–VII; Metzger 1985, 78, 80, pl. 35–36, no. 253; Reeves 2022, 379, Fig. on p. 378; Eaton-Krauss 2008a, 25–56; Killen 2017, 101, fig. 32, 102, pl. 102, no. 11.

140 For the term 'panther' and its meaning in this context, see Westendorf 1982, 664–665; McDonald 2009, 359–366.

141 Eaton-Krauss 2008a, 87. For the discussion on the animal's identification, see Eaton-Krauss 2008a, 87–88.

142 Eaton-Krauss 2008a, 84–86.

143 This statue is discussed in more detail in 'Beds and Thrones: Similarities and dissimilarities'.

144 https://www.collinsdictionary.com/de/worterbuch/englisch/ faldstool (last accessed 11 July 2023).

145 https://www.rdklabor.de/wiki/Faldistorium (last accessed 12 July 2023).

146 Carter 1933, 111–112. See also Eaton-Krauss 2008a, 90.

147 Eaton-Krauss 2008a, 91.

148 Eaton-Krauss 2008a, 91. For an example, see Berlandini 1982, 171, Fig. 29. For these scenes in general, see Budka 2001, 15–20.

149 Eaton-Krauss 2008a, 90–91.

150 Budka 2001, 19. For more details, see Bomann 1991, 57–76.

151 Assmann 1969, 250–262, in particular 259; Assmann 1989, 14–15; Budka 2001, 19.

152 Metzger 1985, 83.

153 Eaton-Krauss 2008a, 90; Kuhlmann 1977, 65–66, note 6.

154 https://egypt-museum.com/ceremonial-throne-of-tutankhamun/ (last accessed 13 July 2023). See also Metzger 1985, 83.

155 Eaton-Krauss 2008a, 90, 115.

156 Reeves 2022, 380; Metzger 1985, 78; Eaton-Krauss 2008a, 28.

157 Kuhlmann 1977, 69, 86.

158 Kuhlmann 1977, 69, 86.

159 Carter and Mace 1923, 117; Kuhlmann 1977, 65; Eaton-Krauss 2008a, 50–51.

160 See also Eaton-Krauss 2008a, 47.

161 E.g., Carter 1933, 111; Metzger 1985, 84. See also Eaton-Krauss 2008a, 25.

162 Eaton-Krauss 2008a, 54, 56.

163 For the *zmꜣ tꜣ.wi* in connection with seating furniture, see Metzger 1985, 26–32 (Old Kingdom), 36–43 (Middle Kingdom), 99–114 (New Kingdom).

164 https://www.oxfordlearnersdictionaries.com/definition/eng lish/footstool?q=footstool (last accessed 13 July 2023).

165 https://dictionary.cambridge.org/dictionary/english/footstool (last accessed 13 July 2023).

166 See Metzger 1985, 91; Kuhlmann 1977, 69–70, 89. For the footstool associated with the 'throne' (Carter no. 090; Cairo, Egyptian Museum of Antiquities, JE 62046; now in the Grand Egyptian Museum), see http://www.griffith. ox.ac.uk/perl/gi-ca-qmakesumm.pl?sid=80.152.217.177-1689278827&qno=1&curr=090 (last accessed 13 July 2023); Carter and Mace 1923, 119; Baker 1966, 83, Fig. 93; Eaton-Krauss 2008a, 130–131; Reeves 2022, 380. More information on the footstool connected to the 'faldstool' (Carter no. 378; Cairo, Egyptian Museum of Antiquities, JE 62045; now in the Grand Egyptian Museum) is found here: http://www.griffith. ox.ac.uk/perl/gi-ca-qmakesumm.pl?sid=80.152.217.177-1689278827&qno=1&curr=378 (last accessed 13 July 2023); Baker 1966, 83, Fig. 94; Eaton-Krauss 2008a, 132–133; Reeves 2022, 388.

167 Kuhlmann 1977, 7.

168 For more details, see Kuhlmann 1977, 70, 75–80, 90, 93–95.

169 Kuhlmann rejects any connection between sky and canopy (1977, 71–75, 90–92).

170 See e.g. Scott 1965, 145, Fig. 39; Killen 2017, 33, no. 1.

171 https://thesaurus-linguae-aegyptiae.de/lemma/854540 (last accessed 18 July 2023); Kuhlmann 1977, 22–23. For *s.t* in general, see Kuhlmann 1977, 16–28.

172 See e.g. https://thesaurus-linguae-aegyptiae.de/lemma/125410 (last accessed 4 April 2024); Murray 1905, pl. I; Brovarski 1996, 141–144, note g.

173 https://thesaurus-linguae-aegyptiae.de/lemma/125380 (last accessed 4 April 2024); Kuhlmann 1977, 23; Brovarksi 1996, 144–146, note h.

174 Chassinat 1931, 219.8–10; Kurth 2004, 390; Smith 2009, 408. For the term as such, see also https://thesaurus-linguae-ae-gyptiae.de/lemma/134310 (last accessed 18 July 2023).

175 Smith 2009, 408. For the word *zmꜣ.t*, see also https://thesau-rus-linguae-aegyptiae.de/lemma/134310 (last accessed 4 April 2024); https://thesaurus-linguae-aegyptiae.de/lemma/134280 (last accessed 4 April 2024); Kuhlmann 1977, 11.

176 London, British Museum, 124920; from Iraq, Niniveh, North Palace; Neo-Assyrian, 645–635 BCE: https://www.britishmu-seum.org/collection/object/W_1856-0909-53 (last accessed 14 July 2023); von Stülpnagel 1997, 30–32, Fig. 4.

177 https://www.metmuseum.org/art/collection/search/652100 (last accessed 15 July 2023); https://www.iransafar.co/iran-na-tional-jewels-museum/ (last accessed 15 July 2023); Curzon 1892, 317–318, Fig. on p. 319.

178 Curzon 1892, 318–320, 321.

179 https://www.iranchamber.com/museum/royal_jewels/national_iranian_jewels08.php (last accessed 15 July 2023).

180 Curzon 1892, 328.

181 Tavernier 1678, 46.

182 Asserate 2017, 37, 42–43; Haberland 1965, 121–122. For pictures of Empress Zauditu sitting on her bed-throne, see https://commons.wikimedia.org/wiki/File:Zauditu_of_Ethio-pia-empress-onasofa.jpg (last accessed 15 July 2023); https://commons.wikimedia.org/wiki/File:Zewditu_and_favored_priest.png (last accessed 15 July 2023).

183 Haberland 1965, 122.

184 Haberland 1965, 121.

185 Haberland 1965, 121.

186 Haberland 1965, 121.

187 De Wit 1978, 158–161.

188 Kuhlmann 1977, 86. See also Eaton-Krauss 2008a, 36.

189 Kuhlmann 1977, 87; Metzger 1985, 12.

190 Kuhlmann 1977, 84; Eaton-Krauss 2008a, 36.

191 For a more detailed discussion on the connection of Nut and beds, see Schutz 2024 (forthcoming).

192 Cairo, Egyptian Museum of Antiquities, CG 14, JE 10062; from Giza, Valley Temple of Khafre; 4th Dynasty. Borchardt 1911, 14–16, pl. 4, no. 14; Kuhlmann 1977, 61, pl. II.3a. This statue was not unique, see e.g. Borchardt 1911, 9–10, no. 9; 13–14, no. 13.

193 Baker 1966, 50–51, Fig. 45.

194 Cairo, Egyptian Museum of Antiquities, CG 51113; from Thebes, Valley of the Kings, KV 46; 18th Dynasty. Quibell 1908, 53–54, pls XXXVIII–XLIII; Baker 1966, 63–67, figs 68–72; Metzger 1985, 80; Eaton-Krauss 2008a, 47.

195 Kozloff and Bryan 1992, 43.

Bibliography

Aldred, Cyril. 1973. *Akhenaten and Nefertiti*. New York: The Brooklyn Museum.

Andreu, Guillemette. 2002. *Les artistes de Pharaon. Deir el-Médineh et la Vallée des Rois*. Paris: Brepols.

Arnette, Marie-Lys. 2015. 'Purification du post-partum et rites des relevailles dans l'Égypte ancienne'. *Bulletin de l'Institut Français d'Archéologie Orientale* 114: 19–72.

Arnold, Dieter. 2015. 'A New Start from the South: Thebes during the Eleventh Dynasty'. In *Ancient Egypt Transformed: The Middle Kingdom*, edited by Adela Oppenheim, Dorothea Arnold, Dieter Arnold and Kei Yamamoto, 38–53. New York: The Metropolitan Museum of Art.

Arnold, Dieter, and Peter Jánosi. 2015. 'The Move to the North. Establishing a New Capital'. In *Ancient Egypt Transformed: The Middle Kingdom*, edited by Adela Oppenheim, Dorothea Arnold, Dieter Arnold and Kei Yamamoto, 54–67. New York: The Metropolitan Museum of Art.

Asprey, Dave. 2018. *Game Changers. What Leaders, Innovations and Mavericks Do to Win at Life*. London: Harper Wave.

Asserate, Asfa-Wossen. 2017. *King of Kings. The Triumph and Tragedy of Emperor Haile Selassie I of Ethiopia*. London: Haus Publishing Ltd.

Assmann, Jan. 1969. *Liturgische Lieder an den Sonnengott. Untersuchungen zur altägyptischen Hymnik*, Vol. 1. Berlin: Verlag Bruno Hessling.

Assmann, Jan. 1989. 'Der schöne Tag. Sinnlichkeit und Vergänglichkeit im altägyptischen Fest'. In *Das Fest*, edited by Walter Haug and Rainer Warning, 3–28 (Poetik und Hermeneutik 14). München: Fink, Wilhelm.

Assmann, Jan. 2010. *Tod und Jenseits im alten Ägypten*. München: C.H. Beck.

Backhouse, Joanne. 2020. *'Scènes de Gynécées'. Figured Ostraca from New Kingdom Egypt: Iconography and Intent*. Archaeopress Egyptology 26. Oxford: Archaeopress.

Baker, Hollis Seibe. 1966 *Furniture in the Ancient World. Origins & Evolution 3100–475 B.C.* London: The Connoisseur.

Beinlich, Horst. 1991. *Das Buch vom Fayum. Zum religiösen Eigenverständnis einer ägyptischen Landschaft*. Ägyptologische Abhandlungen 51. Wiesbaden: Harrassowitz.

Beinlich, Horst. 2006. 'Zwischen Tod und Grab: Tutanchamun und das Begräbnisritual'. *Studien zur Altägyptischen Kultur* 34: 17–31.

Beinlich, Horst, and Mohamed Saleh. 1989. *Corpus der hieroglyphischen Inschriften aus dem Grab des Tutenchamun. Mit Konkordanz der Nummernsysteme des 'Journal d'Entrée' des Ägyptischen Museums Kairo, der Handlist to Howard Carter's catalogue of objects in Tut'ankhamūn's Tomb und der Ausstellungs-Nummern des Ägyptischen Museums Kairo*. Oxford: Griffith Institute.

Berlandini, Jocelyne. 1982. 'Portes d'édifices privés et de bâtiments de service. Problèmes de typologie'. In *L'Égyptologie en 1979. Axes prioritaires de recherches*, Vol. 1, edited by Jean Leclant, 169–173 (Colloques Internationaux du Centre National de la Recherche Scientifique 595). Paris: Centre National de la Recherche Scientifique.

Bomann, Ann H. 1991. *The Private Chapel in Ancient Egypt. A Study of the Chapels in the Workmen's Village at el Amarna with Special Reference to Deir el Medina and Other Sites.* London: Kegan Paul International.

Borchardt, Ludwig. 1911. *Statuen und Statuetten von Königen und Privatleuten. Teil I: Nos 1–1294.* Catalogue Général des Antiquités Égyptiennes du Musée du Caire. Berlin: Reichsdruckerei.

Brovarski, Edward. 1996. 'An Inventory List from "Covington's Tomb" and Nomenclature for Furniture in the Old Kingdom'. In *Studies in Honor of William Kelly Simpson*, Vol. 1, edited by Peter der Manuelian, 117–155. Boston: Museum of Fine Arts.

Bruyère, Bernard. 1926. *Rapport sur les Fouilles de Deir el Médineh (1924–1925).* Fouilles de l'Institut Français d'Archéologie Orientale du Caire 3.3. Cairo: Imprimerie de l'Institut Français d'Archéologie Orientale.

Bruyère, Bernard. 1952. *Rapport sur les Fouilles de Deir el Médineh (1935–1940).* Fouilles de l'Institut Français d'Archéologie Orientale du Caire 20.2. Cairo: Imprimerie de l'Institut Français d'Archéologie Orientale.

Budka, Julia. 2019. 'Re-Awakening Osiris at Umm el-Qaab (Abydos)'. In *Perspectives on Lived Religion. Practices – Transmission – Landscape*, edited by Nico Staring, Huw Twiston Davies and Lara Weiss, 15–25. Leiden: Sidestone Press.

Carter, Howard, and Arthur C. Mace. 1923. *The Tomb of Tut-Ankh-Amen. Discovered by the Late Earl of Carnarvon and Howard Carter*, Vol. 1. London, New York, Toronto and Melbourne: Cassell and Company Ltd.

Carter, Howard. 1933. *The Tomb of Tut-Ankh-Amen. Discovered by the Late Earl of Carnarvon and Hoard Carter*, Vol. 3. London, Toronto, Melbourne and Sydney: Cassell and Company Ltd.

Chassinat, Émile. 1931. *Le Temple d'Edfou*, Vol. 6. Mémoires publiés par les membres de la Mission archéologique française au Caire 23. Cairo: Imprimerie de l'Institut Français d'Archéologie Orientale.

Curzon, George Nathaniel. 1892. *Persia and the Persian Question*, Vol. 1. Cambridge: Cambridge University Press.

Davies, Norman de Garis. 1941. *The Tomb of the Vizier Ramose.* Mond Excavations at Thebes 1. London: The Egypt Exploration Society.

De Buck, Adriaan. 1939. *De Godsdienstige Opvatting van den Slaap Inzonderheid in het Oude Egypte. rede uitgesproken bij het aanvaarden van het ambt van buitengewoon hoogleeraar in de Egyptologie en de geschiedenis van de antieke godsdiensten aan de Rijksuniversiteit te Leiden op 20 October 1939.* Mededeelingen en Verhandelingen van het Voorziatisch-Egyptisch Gezelshap Ex Oriente Lux 4. Leiden: Brill.

Der Manuelian, Peter. 2003. *Slab Stelae of the Giza Necropolis.* Publications of the Pennsylvania-Yale Expedition to Egypt 7. New Haven and Philadelphia: Oxbow Books.

De Wit, Constant. 1978. *Le rôle et le sens du lion dans l'Égypte ancienne. 2ième édition avec nouveaux addenda et corrigenda.* Luxor: Gaber Aly Hussein.

Dunham, Dows, and William Kelly Simpson. 1974. *The Mastaba of Queen Mersyankh III.* Giza Mastabas 1. Boston: Museum of Fine Arts.

Eaton-Krauss, Marianne. 2008a. *The Thrones, Chairs, Stools, and Footstools from the Tomb of Tutankhamun.* Griffith Institute Publications. Oxford: Griffith Institute.

Eaton-Krauss, Marianne. 2008b. 'An Offering Table Scene in the Art Insitute, Chicago'. *Göttinger Miszellen* 219: 19–24.

Furth, Charlotte. 1987. 'Concepts of Pregnancy, Childbirth, and Infancy in Ch'ing Dynasty China'. *The Journal of Asian Studies* 46 (1): 7–35.

Grajetzki, Wolfram. 2015. 'The Pharaoh's Subjects. Court and Provinces'. In *Ancient Egypt Transformed: The Middle Kingdom*, edited by Adela Oppenheim, Dorothea Arnold, Dieter Arnold and Kei Yamamoto, 120–159. New York: The Metropolitan Museum of Art.

Haberland, Eike. 1965. *Untersuchungen zum Äthiopischen Königtum.* Studien zur Kulturkunde 18. Wiesbaden: Franz Steiner Verlag.

Hayes, William Christopher. 1953. *The Scepter of Egypt. A Background for the Study of the Egyptian Antiquities in The Metropolitan Museum of Art. Part I: From the Earliest Times to the End of the Middle Kingdom.* New York: Abrams.

Hayes, William Christopher. 1990. *The Scepter of Egypt. A Background for the Study of the Egyptian Antiquities in the Metropolitan Museum of Art. Part II: The Hyksos Period and the New Kingdom.* New York: Abrams.

Hellinckx, Bart R. 2001. 'The Symbolic Assimilation of Head and Sun as Expressed by Headrests'. *Studien zur Altägyptischen Kultur* 29: 61–95.

Hornung, Erik. 1956. 'Nacht und Finsternis im Weltbild der Alten Ägypter'. Unpublished PhD thesis, Tübingen.

Hornung, Erik. 1991. *The Tomb of Pharaoh Seti I. Das Grab Sethos' I.* Zurich and Munich: Artemis Verlag.

Jürgensen, Martin Wangsgaard. 2014. 'The Ever-Present Death Behind the Church Door: On the Funeral Bier and Its Emblematic Qualities'. *Journal of Early Modern Christianity* 1: 91–114.

Kanawati, Naguib, and Alexandra Woods. 2010. *Beni Hassan. Art and Daily Life in an Egyptian Province.* Cairo: The American University of Cairo Press.

Kanawati, Naguib, Alexandra Woods, Sameh Shafik and Effy Alexakis. 2010. *Mereruka and his Family. Part III:1. The Tomb of Mereruka.* The Australian Centre for Egyptology Reports 29. Warminster and Oxford: The Australian Centre for Egyptology.

Kleinke, Nira. 2007. *Female Spaces: Untersuchungen zu Gender und Archäologie im pharaonischen Ägypten.* Göttinger Miszellen. Beihefte 1. Göttingen: Seminar für Ägyptologie und Koptologie.

Kozloff, Arielle P., and Betsy M. Bryan. 1992. *Egypt's Dazzling Sun. Amenhotep III and his World.* Cleveland: The Cleveland Museum of Art.

Kurth, Dieter. 2004. *Edfou VII. Die Inschriften des Tempels von Edfu I/3.* Wiesbaden: Harrassowitz.

Lee, Jen-Der. 2005. 'Childbirth in Early Imperial China'. *NAN NÜ* 7 (2): 216–286.

Leitz, Christian (ed.). 2002. *Lexikon der Götter und Götterbezeichnungen*, Vols I–VII. Orientalia Lovaniensia Analecta 110–115. Leuven: Peeters.

Martin, Geoffrey T. 2016. 'Re-Excavating the Tomb of Horemheb in the Valley of the Kings'. In *Valley of the Kings since Howard Carter. Proceedings of the Luxor Symposium November 4, 2009*, edited by Mamdouh Eldamaty, 95–106. Cahier des Annales du Service des Antiquités de l'Égypte 40. Cairo: Ministry of Antiquities.

McDonald, Angela. 2009. 'The Curiosity of the Cat in Hieroglyphs'. In *Sitting Beside Lepsius. Studies in Honour of Jaromir Malek at the Griffith Institute,* edited by Diana Magee, Janine Bourriau and Stephen Quirke, 361–379. Orientalia Lovaniensia Analecta 185. Leuven, Paris and Walpole, MA: Peeters.

Meskell, Lynn. 2002. *Private Life in New Kingdom Egypt.* Princeton and Oxford: Princeton University Press.

Metzger, Martin. 1985. *Königsthron und Gottesthron. Thronformen und Throndarstellungen in Ägypten und im Vorderen Orient im dritten und zweiten Jahrtausend vor Christus und deren Bedeutung für das Verständnis von Aussagen über den Thron im Alten Testament.* Alter Orient und Altes Testament. Veröffentlichungen zur Kultur und Geschichte des Alten Orients und des Alten Testaments 15. Neukirchen-Vluyn: Verlag Butzon & Bercker Kevelaer, Neukirchener Verlag Neukirchen Vluyn.

Mohammed Hussein Ahmed, Seham. 2022. 'Another Perspective on the Set of Gilded Couches of Tutankhamun'. *Égypte Nilotique et Méditerranéenne* 15: 217–232.

Münch, Hans-Hubertus. 2000. 'Categorizing Archaeological Finds: The Funerary Material of Queen Hetepheres I at Giza'. *Antiquity* 74: 898–908.

Murray, Margaret alice. 1905. *Saqqara Mastabas*, Vol. I. Egyptian Research Account 10. London: Gilbert and Rivington Ltd.

Näser, Claudia. 2001. 'Zur Interpretation funerärer Praktiken im Neuen Reich: Der Ostfriedhof von Deir el-Medine'. In *Begegnungen. Antike Kulturen im Niltal. Festgabe für Erika Endesfelder, Karl-Heinz Priese, Walter Friedrich Reineke, Steffen Wenig von Schülern und Mitarbeitern,* edited by Caris-Beatrice Arnst, Ingelore Hafemann and Angelika Lohwasser, 373–398. Leipzig: Verlag Helmar Wodtke und Katharina Stegbauer.

Näser, Claudia. 2008. 'Jenseits von Theben – Objektsammlung, Inszenierung und Fragmentierung in ägyptischen Bestattungen des Neuen Reiches'. In *Körperinszenierung – Objektsammlung – Monumentalisierung: Totenritual und Grabkult in frühen Gesellschaften. Archäologische Quellen in kulturwissenschaftlicher Perspektive,* edited by Christoph Kümmel, Beat Schweizer and Ulrich Veit, 445–472. Tübinger Archäologische Taschenbücher 6. Münster, München, Berlin et al.: Waxmann Verlag GmbH.

Nifosi, Ada. 2019. *Becoming a Woman and Mother in Greco-Roman Egypt. Women's Bodies, Society and Domestic Space.* Medicine and the Body in Antiquity. London and New York: Routledge.

Petrie, William Matthew Flinders. 1937. *The Funeral Furniture of Egypt.* British School of Archaeology in Egypt and Egyptian Research Account 43. London: Aris & Phillips Ltd.

Price, Campbell. 2016. 'Other Tomb Goods'. In *The Oxford Handbook of the Valley of the Kings,* edited by Richard H. Wilkinson and Kent R. Weeks, 274–289. Oxford and New York: Oxford University Press.

Quack, Joachim Friedrich. 2003. 'Zum Lautwert von Gardiner Sign-List U 23'. *Lingua Aegyptia* 11: 113–116.

Quack, Joachim Friedrich. 2022. 'Nochmals zum Lautwert von Gardiner Sign-List U 23'. *Lingua Aegyptia* 30: 271–289.

Quibell, James Edward. 1900. *Hierakonpolis*, Vol. 1. Egyptian Research Account 4. London: Bernard Quaritch.

Quibell, James Edward. 1908. *Tomb of Yuaa and Thuiu. Nos 51001–51191.* Catalogue Général des Antiquités Égyptiennes du Musée du Caire. Cairo: Imprimerie de l'Institut Français d'Archéologie Orientale.

Reeves, Nicholas. 2022. *The Complete Tutankhamun*, revised and expanded edition. London: Thames & Hudson Ltd.

Reeves, Nicholas, and Richard H. Wilkinson. 1996. *The Complete Valley of the Kings. Tombs and Treasures of Egypt's Greatest Pharaohs.* London, New York, Sydney and Toronto: Thames and Hudson.

Reisner, George Andrew. 1929. 'The Household Furniture of Queen Hetep-heres I. Restored by Mr. W.A. Stewart and now in the Cairo Museum'. *Bulletin of the Museum of Fine Arts* 27: 83–90.

Robins, Gay. 1993. *Women in Ancient Egypt.* London: British Museum Press.

Rother, Christian. 2015. *Die Erfindung der Schrift. Ägypten zur Zeit der 1. Dynastie.* Hamburg: disserta Verlag.

Russmann, Edna. R. 2001 *Eternal Egypt. Masterworks of Ancient Art from the British Museum.* Berkeley and Los Angeles: University of California Press.

Saad, Zaki Youssef. 1957. *Ceiling Stelae in Second Dynasty Tombs from the Excavations at Helwan.* Supplément aux Annales du Service des Antiquités de l'Égypte 21. Cairo: Imprimerie de l'Institut Français d'Archéologie Orientale.

Schaden, Otto. 1984. 'Clearance of the Tomb of King Ay (WV-23)'. *Journal of the American Research Center in Egypt* 21: 39–64.

Schäfer, Heinrich. 1974. *The Principles of Egyptian Art,* translated by J. Baines. Oxford: Clarendon Press.

Schutz, Manon Y. 2024 (forthcoming). 'Beyond the Grave: The Use and Meaning of Beds in New Kingdom Daily Life Settings'. In *Living in the House. Researching the Domestic Life in Ancient Egypt and Sudan,* edited by Fatma Keshk. Warsaw Studies in Archaeology. Turnhout: Brepols.

Scott, Nora. 1965. 'Our Egyptian Furniture'. *The Metropolitan Museum of Art Bulletin,* New Series 24 (4): 129–150.

Sethe, Kurt. 1910. *Die altägyptischen Pyramidentexte, nach den Papierabdrücken und Photographien des Berliner Museums neu hrsgg. und erläutert II Text, zweite Hälfte Spruch 469–714 (Pyr. 906–2217).* Leipzig: Hinrichs'sche Buchhandlung.

Siliotti, Alberto, and Christian Leblanc. 2002 *Nefertari e la Valle delle Regine.* Florence: Giunti Editore.

Smith, Mark. 2010. 'The reign of Seth: Egyptian Perspectives from the First Millennium BCE'. In *Egypt in Transition. Social and Religious Development of Egypt in the First Millennium BCE. Proceedings of an International Conference, Prague, September 1–4, 2009,* edited by Ladislav Bareš, Filip Coppens and Květa Smoláriková, 396–430. Prague: Oxbow Books.

Strauß-Seeber, Christiane. 1986. 'Wolle'. In *Lexikon der Ägyptologie,* Vol. VI, edited by Wolfgang Helck and Wolfhart Westendorf, 1285–1286. Wiesbaden: Otto Harrassowitz.

Tavernier, Jean-Baptiste. 1678. *The Six Voyages of John Baptiste Tavernier, a Noble Man of France now living, through Turky into Persia and the East-Indies, finished in the Year 1670. Giving an Account of the State of those Countries.* London: R.L. and M.P.

Teeter, Emily. 1994. 'Egyptian Art'. *Art Institute of Chicago Museum Studies* 20 (1): 14–31.

Tosi, Mario, and Alessandro Roccati. 1972. *Stele e Altre Epigrafi di Deir el Medina n. 50001– n. 50262.* Catalogo del Museo Egizio di Torino – Serie Seconda – Collezioni 1. Turin: Edizioni d'Arte Fratelli Pozzo.

Turner, Victor. 1997. *The Ritual Process. Structure and Anti-Structure.* New Brunswick and London: Aldine Transaction.

Vandier, Jacques. 1954. *Manuel d'archéologie égyptienne IV. Bas-Reliefs et peintures. Scènes de la vie quotidienne.* Paris: Éditions A. et J. Picard.

Vandier d'Abbadie, Jeanne, and Geneviève Jourdain. 1939. *Deux tombes de Deir el-Médineh I. La chapelle de Khâ. II La tombe du scribe royal Amenemopet.* Mémoires publiés par les membres de la Mission archéologique française au Caire 73. Cairo: Imprimerie de l'Institut Français d'Archéologie Orientale.

Van Gennep, Arnold. 1960. *The Rites of Passage.* Chicago: The University of Chicago Press.

Von Stülpnagel, Karl-Heinrich. 1997. 'Frühformen des Bettgestells'. In *Bettgeschichte(n): Zur Kulturgeschichte des Bettes und des Schlafens*, edited by Nina Hennig and Heinrich Mehl, 25–42. Heide in Holstein: Verlag Boyens.

Westendorf, Wolfhart. 1982. 'Panther'. In *Lexikon der Ägyptologie*, Vol. IV, edited by Wolfgang Helck and Wolfhart Westendorf, 664–665. Wiesbaden: Otto Harrassowitz.

Yamamoto, Kei. 2015. 'Abydos and Osiris. The Terrace of the Great God'. In *Ancient Egypt Transformed: The Middle Kingdom*, edited by Adela Oppenheim, Dorothea Arnold, Dieter Arnold and Kei Yamamoto, 250–269. New York: The Metropolitan Museum of Art.

Ziegler, Christiane. 1990. *Catalogue des stèles, peintures et reliefs égyptiens de l'Ancien Empire et de la Première Période Intermédiaire. Vers 2686–2040 avant J.-C.* Paris: Editions de la Réunion des musées nationaux.

Ziegler, Christiane. 1999. 'Slab Stela of Princess Nefret-Iabet'. In *Egyptian Art in the Age of the Pyramids*, edited by John P. O'Neill and Carol Fuerstein, 242–244. New York: The Metropolitan Museum of Art.

4

*Tut*orial: 'How to change your predecessors' names into Tutankhamun'

Katja Broschat

Abstract

It is well known that many objects found in Tutankhamun's tomb once belonged to different, earlier owners. Some of these are inscribed with the names of members of Tutankhamun's family; in other cases, scholars suggest that stylistic elements like facial features and bodily proportions reveal earlier owners.

Another enigmatic category comprises objects whose inscriptions, generally the cartouches carrying the owner's name, have been changed. Objects made of many different materials – wooden, stone, gold and gilded – show this process. On stone and wood, as a rule, an earlier name had to be completely or at least partially ground off and the new name written on the now lower surface level. On gold and gilded surfaces, for technical reasons, various methods were applied.

This presentation focuses on objects made of metal or gilded, like Tutankhamun's golden throne, some of his pectorals, his mummy bands and his small canopic coffins. It traces the different processes that were used to alter their inscriptions and discusses the question of why different procedures were applied, identifying the technical characteristics of these processes from the traces remaining on the objects.

It illustrates remnants of original or previous inscriptions, and discusses what could be expected both to survive and not to survive from an earlier inscription.

Keywords: Tutankhamun, ownership, gilded materials

What's in a name? It situates you in the world. It can tell others who you are related to, what your plans as king are, what you believe in or how you wish to present yourself. It is widely known that various objects discovered in Tutankhamun's tomb carry names other than his. Among them, some display his previous name, Tutankhaten, or the names of his ancestors and family members.[1] In other instances, scholars propose that certain stylistic elements such as facial features or bodily proportions may indicate previous ownership.[2] A more intriguing category includes objects whose inscriptions, most notably the cartouches carrying the name of the owner or addressee, have been altered.[3] Objects in a wide variety of materials – wood,

ivory, stone, gold and gilding – are evidence of this process.

Typically on stone, wood or ivory, the previous names – when they were worked into the surfaces – had either to be completely or partially ground off (e.g., Carter 405),[4] and the new names had to be inscribed on the resulting lower surface (e.g., Carter 588),[5] or the earlier signs had to be filled and the new ones worked in (e.g., Carter 79 [box] and 574 [lid]).[6] Or – if the removal caused a deep recess, for example – a new piece of stone or wood with a new inscription had to be inserted.[7] On gold and gilded surfaces, various other methods were applied for technical reasons. A selection of objects from the tomb will illustrate these.[8]

The Golden Throne

In its lavish grandeur, the so-called Golden Throne (Carter 91) is undoubtedly the most impressive and recognizable piece among the furniture from Tutankhamun's tomb.[9] It is, of course, a gilded throne rather than a golden one: an armchair exquisitely ornamented with intricately crafted gold foils and gold and silver sheets over wood and gesso,[10] as well as prefabricated appliqués and coloured inlays (Fig. 4.1, Plate 1).[11]

The names of the royal couple, Tutankhamun and Ankhesenamun, are inscribed in gilded relief on the front of its backrest, replacing their earlier names Ankhesepaaten and Tutankhaten.[12] The same applies to the name of Tutankhamun on the interior of the left armrest's interior; elsewhere, the other names appear to be the original Ankhesenpaaten and Tutankhaten or Tutankhamun's prenomen Nebkheperure (which remained unchanged throughout his reign). The Aten cartouches were chased into the gilding and the names on the armrests' exteriors are made with coloured inlays.

Since this article focuses on the name changes on the backrest, some general information about making a gilded relief on wood will be given first. As a general practice, a gesso or a blend of gesso and binder, sometimes with an added layer of textile, was applied to the wood as a base for attaching the foils or sheets. Subsequently, patterns, motifs or signs were worked in relief into the gesso. The gold foils could be affixed onto the gesso with glue or resin and adjusted to the relief by for example rubbing and pressing. Further details or contour lines were worked into the gold surfaces using fine driving or chasing punches, which were often transferred to the surface of the gesso resin mixture.

As a result, these fine details are often still precisely recognizable even if the gold foil is lost (Fig. 4.2a–b).[13] Depending on the thickness of the gold sheet – the thicker, the more likely it is – some sheets must have been preformed by working into a mould or chasing from the back. This is possibly when a production variant, as described by I.E.S. Edwards, comes into play, which he proposes for the making of the small golden shrine (Carter 108):[14] that the motif or overall shape would be chased into the gold, followed by the application of a piece of fine linen on the verso of the pre-formed sheet, then a layer of gesso and sometimes another piece of fine linen as a support,[15] and this construction would be attached to the shrine.

On the throne, almost the entire front of the backrest was gilded by means of a single large sheet, bent around the side rails of the backrest and attached to the back with small gold pins. This sheet measures at least 57 × 52 cm (width × length) in total, which illustrates the capabilities of the craftsmanship of the time, since producing a sheet of this size is no simple undertaking.[16]

While gilded wooden relief can be made in a number of ways, a specific technique consistently seems to be employed in making alterations to them. For the erasure

of a king's name, the inscribed areas within the cartouche underwent partial or complete cutting, with the renewal of the gesso ground and modelling of the new name in raised relief. The resulting surface was then covered with a new piece of gold foil, which was rubbed or pressed onto it. Finally, contour lines and details were chased into the new gilding.

These newly added gold sheets are easily recognizable through visual examination alone. With minimal overlap, they were mainly positioned within the cartouches, as clearly demonstrated on the king's and queen's names (Fig. 4.3a–b). In general, they sometimes differ in colour from the main sheet, sometimes not. However, it is also true that they can be analytically distinguished from the surrounding gold sheet by their chemically different gold composition. This indicates that these sheets were newly produced, rather than being reworked and reused as frequently assumed.[17]

In comparison to Harry Burton's early photographs (Burton 163), it is evident that these added gold sheets fitted better at the time of the recovery – the signs were more pronounced and the gold sheet less wrinkled than they are today. This suggests a loosening – maybe resulting from the use of a weaker glue for the alterations – and reattachment of the sheets at a specific point after the recovery. It could also suggest an intentional partial detachment of the added sheets, maybe undertaken to look for an earlier inscription underneath.

The question of whether earlier inscriptions or palimpsests can be uncovered beneath added gold sheets has been addressed to us many times during our work on the objects. This is intriguing, but highly unlikely. The portions of the gesso that are usually renewed and remodelled make it very, very unlikely that any clues or traces of earlier characters would have survived. It should be noted that reattached sheets, even when in their original shape, will never achieve the same neat and crisp appearance as before detachment. Instead, they will inevitably appear crumpled and uneven to some degree due to the detachment.

The alteration process just described was executed identically to the cartouche inscribed on the inside of the left armrest, which now contains the later name Tutankhamun.[18] This is again reflected in the chemical composition of the newly added gold sheet, which differs from the surrounding sheet that originally covered the entire interior of the armrest except for the edge.

The earlier name Tutankhaten remained on the outer side of the right armrest (see, e.g., Burton 157)[19] and this is generally explained by the idea that the craftsmen did not take the time and effort to change it because it was made with a different technique and it would be much more difficult to make changes here.[20] In fact, it would not require significant effort to alter the cartouche on the exterior of this armrest, assuming you possess an assortment

Fig. 4.1. The Golden Throne of Tutankhamun. Photo: Harry Burton. © Griffith Institute, University of Oxford.

a

b

Fig. 4.2. At the centre brace on the back of the throne, the details of the basket (GSL V30) are still visible where the main part of the gold sheet is lost (a); another example is a circular attachment that is probably related to the chariots and/or horse harness (b). It is made from wood and gesso with the gilding mostly lost. Photos: Katja Broschat, Leibniz-Zentrum für Archäologie. Courtesy of the Egyptian Museum Cairo.

a

b

Fig. 4.3. The king's cartouche has new gold foil inside the ring, the edges overlapping it (a); to change the queen's name to Ankhesenamun, only the lower portion of the foil was replaced (b). At the time of the throne's discovery, the foil adhered more firmly and evenly to the surface than it does today. Photos: (a) Eid Mertah, Egyptian Museum Cairo; (b) Christian Eckmann, Leibniz-Zentrum für Archäologie. Both courtesy of the Egyptian Museum Cairo.

of different inlays or can have them made relatively easily. The modification would simply require the removal of the gilding and the inlays within the loop of the cartouche, the refilling of the gesso base and the subsequent new gilding.

Moreover, the hollows for the new hieroglyphs must be cut out, and the new, coloured inlays put in place.[21] However, currently, there is no evidence to suggest that the name of a predecessor has been overwritten.[22]

Pectoral of Nut

A pectoral depicting the goddess Nut (Carter 261p[1]) was found in the Anubis shrine (Carter 261) in the Treasury of the tomb. It is inscribed with a text she addresses to the king. The inscription provides an excellent example of well-preserved palimpsests from an earlier name that is possible to be read with relative ease (Fig. 4.4, Plate 2).

The cartouche located to the right of the goddess's head now contains Tutankhamun's nomen. Carter himself reported the cartouches 'were initially sketched as Akh-en-aten's names',[23] but the still visible remnants of the former inscription have recently been more plausibly reconstructed as the nomen of Neferneferuaten.[24] Darkened residues in the depths of the former signs – probably a conglomerate of dirt and waxy materials that were used in restoration – make it even easier for the modern reader to observe the palimpsest text.

During Tutankhamun's reign, inscriptions and decoration were made on gold by chasing, a technique that displaces and compacts the metal, but does not remove any (unlike engraving). It is possible to chase a line or character in such a way that it can be seen or read in raised relief – albeit mirrored – even from the reverse side. It is evident from the mirrored decoration on the backside of the pectoral that the craftsmen took advantage of this and deliberately created the text to be legible on both sides (the text reads left to right on the inlaid side, and right to left on the verso, but as hieroglyphs can be written and read in both directions neither side has textual primacy over the other). To accomplish this, the characters were driven into the gold sheet with punches and chisels with a certain amount of force, with the thickness of the gold sheet and the working surface influencing how clearly the characters also appear on the reverse. In this respect the choice of the working base was crucial: it could be a softer wood with or without a leather coating, for example, but more complex work required a chaser's pitch as a base, as can be seen in a beautiful piece in the collection of the Egyptian Museum in Berlin, which still gives a positive impression of the king and his spouse.[25] When heated, the pitch is soft enough to make a good contact with the metal surface – at room temperature, it is hard enough to adhere to the metal and hold it in place, but still plastic enough to give space to the driven gold.

When it comes to erasing or changing a chasing in metal, you can basically use the same techniques, tools and materials; complex shapes of objects can complicate the work and may require special measures. The flat shape of the pectoral allowed for easy handling and access from both sides. It appears that a highly polished, flat stone was used as a (re-)working basis, with the raised signs on the back being chased and pushed back beginning from the verso. Subsequently, the metal was chased somewhat from the front as well, with the aim of pushing the gold from the sides of the lines back towards their centres. These

Fig. 4.4. The pectoral of Nut includes an altered cartouche which displays less elegant and detailed writing than that of the main inscription. Photo: Christian Eckmann, Leibniz-Zentrum für Archäologie. Courtesy of the Egyptian Museum Cairo.

work steps may have been repeated, but this rather limited action does not necessarily require frequent re-annealing of the gold, a technique that helps to reduce internal stresses in the metal and keep it as soft and malleable as possible during the process.

However, if one wants to make more radical changes to the shape of the gold, reannealing becomes necessary. It requires temperatures of about 600 degrees, depending on the alloy. It may not always be possible to expose a piece to such high temperatures, particularly if it has delicate stone and glass inlays. This is also why it is not as simple as completely removing a section of the metal (by cutting it out with a sharp chisel) and replacing it with a newly inscribed piece that fits exactly and must be fixed by soldering at even higher temperatures.

Another option would be to take off the inscribed surface (or parts of it) by grinding, as though the metal surface were stone or wood. Even if the visible marks of this process are removed through meticulous finishing treatment and polishing, it can still be identified by the notably decreased thickness of the gold sheet. In addition, the raised characters on the back side would remain largely unchanged and visible unless the grinding is paired with additional techniques. Also, some thinner gold sheets do not allow this process anyway. Upon inspection of the verso of the pectoral, however, it can be observed that only minimal remnants of the previous inscription are visible.

On the contrary, it is remarkable how well-preserved palimpsests remained on the front, considering that the removal of the earlier name should have been relatively easy in this case. It is possible that the (new) inscription was enhanced with colour pigments, as can still be seen on other inscribed gold objects from the tomb.[26] This visual highlighting would have emphasized the new inscription

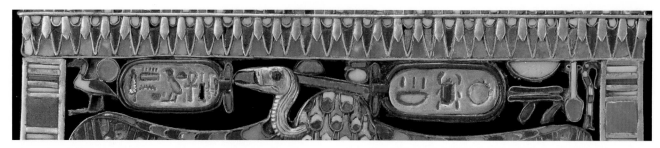

Fig. 4.5. Pectoral depicting the goddess Nut as a vulture (detail). The right order of the cartouches is reconstructed in this picture. Photo: Christian Eckmann, Leibniz-Zentrum für Archäologie. Courtesy of the Egyptian Museum Cairo. Reconstruction: Katja Hölzl, Leibniz-Zentrum für Archäologie.

in contrast to the plain (but now dirty) gold palimpsests of the earlier inscription.

Another pectoral of Nut

Another pectoral (Carter 261p[3]) found in the Anubis shrine was also reinscribed for Tutankhamun.[27] It shows a vulture with widespread wings. Inlaid cartouches to the left and right of its head, reading into the centre of the pectoral, contain the praenomen and nomen of Tutankhamun flanking the name of Nut. The cartouches are, however, incorrectly arranged with respect to their titles, and the names are also written 'backwards' within the cartouches (Fig. 4.5, Plate 3). If the contents of the cartouches were swapped around, they would be correct as to name, title and orientation of script. This arrangement already suggested that a change might have been made here, and made incorrectly.[28]

Inlaid metalwork decoration can be divided into two types: inlays set into pre-made recesses in the metal, and compartmental inlays created by using individually shaped small strips of gold that were soldered vertically onto a base sheet to form cells for the inlays. The second technique was used to manufacture the pectorals discussed here.[29]

And, indeed, the earlier cartouches were typically removed here by cutting them out with sharp chisels, including the gold sheets that supported the surface decorations and bore the respective cartouches (chased) on the verso. The resulting voids were simply covered by gluing pieces of rather awkwardly shaped gold sheets to the backs (Fig. 4.6).

Because the chased decoration on their backs mirrors (with few exceptions) again the design on the front of the pectorals, the new cartouches were first chased into these new gold sheets before they were glued in place. Subsequently, new inlayed cartouches were made and inserted at the fronts.[30] It should be noted that the reverse of the pectoral was lined with fabric when it was found,[31] maybe to enhance wearability, and this also concealed the somewhat crude modifications. Therefore, it may have been especially significant that the images and inscriptions were present on the reverse side, even if they were not visible or

Fig. 4.6. The replaced gold base sheet on the back of the pectoral, with parts of the earlier cartouche base still visible underneath. Other altered cartouches on this or the other three pectorals do not show this vestige. Photo: Christian Eckmann, Leibniz-Zentrum für Archäologie. Courtesy of the Egyptian Museum Cairo.

well executed. However, the textile could also have been exclusively applied for funerary purposes.

The side straps from the outer trappings of the mummy

The two side straps (Carter 256b[4])[32] as part of the outer ornamentation (Plate 4) on Tutankhamun's mummy are assembled with a vertical and four horizontal inlaid text bands (Carter 256b[3]), a pair of gold hands holding a crook and flail (Carter 256b[1]), a *ba*-bird amulet (Carter 256b[2]), and the gold mask (Carter 256a) which itself wore two necklaces (Carter 256a).[33] The side straps consist of five sections, each made in a different design, identically arranged on either side of the mummy.

The earliest mention of a name change here was again made by Carter, who noted

On the back of the cartouches, Uraei, and Rîshi and drop-pendant plaques of the first section of the ornamental

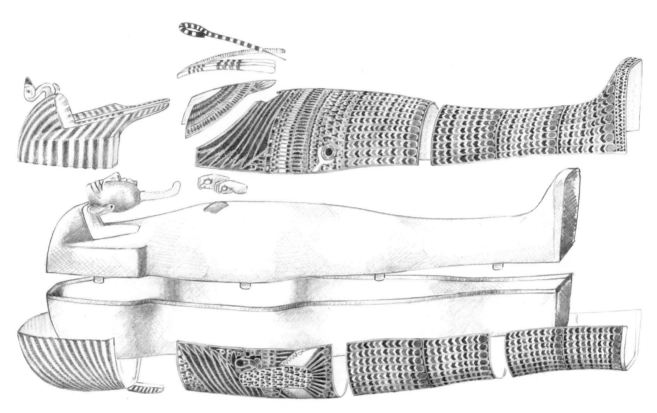

Fig. 4.7. Partially exploded drawing of the main parts of the canopic coffins. The ears and beard are also produced separately, but are shown attached to the face in the drawing for clarity. Drawing Michael Ober, Leibniz-Zentrum für Archäologie.

side straps are engraved hieroglyphic texts […], the reading of which is not consecutive. In some cases cartouches have been deliberately cut out, plain gold inserted in their place, but in one instance the original cartouche – which is that of Smenkh-ka-Ra – remains.[34]

A more recent comment reads 'the side straps […] were found to carry on the reverse texts containing the prenomen (occasionally cut out) of Neferneferuaten'.[35]

In fact, as Carter described it, only the upper sections of the side straps carry the inscription on their backs; the other parts exhibit a chased decoration, basically mirroring their front patterns on the verso. It is important to note that (roughly estimated) less than 8 per cent of the mummy bands (about 19 per cent of the side straps) can currently be considered to be reworked;[36] the status of the rest of the mummy bands cannot be established with certainty.

One cartouche is written on a segment of the side straps, a second one was discovered among the straps that secured a large resin scarab and was affixed to the burial mask before its recovery (see Plate 4).[37] These are most certainly other portions (of the flanking parts of the same side straps) that were joined with the scarab to form a necklace.[38]

Both authors erred in suggesting that further cartouches were cut out of the inscription on the verso; the text

fragments themselves probably give no reason to believe that names were previously written in these places.[39]

However, technically, we have the same situation here as on the last pectoral. The inlaid front decoration was modified by removing parts of the previous inlay sections, including their inscribed base sheets. The resulting voids were concealed by affixing pieces of gold sheet to the backs (Plate 5a and b), and the cartouches of Tutankhamun were subsequently inserted on the front.

This process applies to all cartouches in the inlaid decoration on the fronts. The 'ghosts' in the shape of cartouches that we see on the versos of the attached gold sheets are only imprints of their contours. It seems that no one cared to add the now missing parts of the inscription to these gold sheets beforehand, perhaps because, as Carter said, the text was no longer continuous anyway.[40] It is unclear whether the cut-out areas in the inlay decoration (on the fronts) previously contained cartouches or another motif.

The canopic coffins

The four canopic coffins (Carter 266g [1–4]), designed to preserve and protect the king's embalmed internal organs, were discovered in the alabaster (calcite alabaster) canopic chest (Carter 266b–f),[41] which was itself housed in a

Fig. 4.8. Selected cartouches from the canopic coffins (Carter 266g [1–4]). Some alterations went relatively well, with no negative effect on the shape of the gold sheet (a); others resulted in less smooth surfaces due to grinding (c) and/or more severe deformation to the whole area (d). The lower cartouche shows traces of pencil in the palimpsests. Few new inscriptions were made by engraving, which can be recognized by small edges and protruding gold that no one bothered to smooth out (b). Photos: Katja Broschat and Christian Eckmann, Leibniz-Zentrum für Archäologie. Courtesy of the Egyptian Museum Cairo.

gilded canopic shrine (Carter 266a). It is recognized that their interior inscriptions were altered, with the names of Neferneferuaten being erased and replaced with those of Tutankhamun.[42]

For a better understanding of the methods and processes utilized to eliminate earlier inscriptions on the coffins, it is imperative to initially comprehend their fundamental construction (Fig. 4.7).[43]

The coffins, not surprisingly, consist of a trough and a lid. Both parts are made of gold sheets that were hammered and chased into the desired shape, with separately made pieces for the faces (with ears) and hands soldered onto the lid. The base is also soldered to the lid and trough.

Attached to the lid and trough are multiple gold appliqués lavishly decorated in the compartmental inlay technique described above. The appliqués represent the *nemes* head-dress, the collar and the vulture and winged uraeus together with the lower *rishi* decoration; the 'footboards' of the coffins are not covered with appliqués.

The appliqués were attached to the coffin halves using small pins and potentially some additional wax or resin. This basic construction principle applies to all four coffins. It is evident that any hammering or chasing from the interior of the coffins is precluded as long as the decorative appliqués with their inlays of coloured glass and stone are still in place. Since the appliqués had to be taken off to ease the handling of the coffin halves for alteration, it is unsurprising that none of the small pins originally utilized fasten them to the lids and troughs are present any more and the holes that took them are empty today.

After the appliqués were taken off, the ancient gold-smiths attempted to remove the previous names on the now isolated gold trough and lid by chasing from both sides, as explained earlier. However, due to the object's convex or concave shape, which varies depending on how it is turned, this task proved to be much more challenging than reworking a substantially flat piece (such as the pectoral of Nut), and they ran the risk of buckling and distorting in the process (Fig. 4.8a–d). This is an unfortunate outcome, and is likely to have caused the current unsatisfactory fit of coffin parts[44] that were originally tailored to perfectly suit each other.

Consequently, the craftsman attempted further to obscure the inscriptions by grinding as well, with less risk of altering the general shape of the coffin parts. These are (so far) the only known examples of gold objects from the tomb that have undergone grinding in an attempt to change an inscription, and the whole endeavour has a bit of a trial-and-error feel to it. A special approach was also taken for some of the new inscriptions by engraving the new signs into the metal with sharp chisels instead of chasing them with blunt tools. Engraving is a rare technique during Tutankhamun's time that involves removing material, as opposed to chasing, which displaces the metal.

In the end, despite all efforts, the earlier inscriptions are still preserved inside the canopic coffins in the form of more or less legible palimpsests, as on the Nut pectoral discussed above. The palimpsest cartouches in the interiors of the coffins imply that the inlaid cartouches in the appliqués are also replacements, but the question of their potential modification has not been so widely discussed. Chemical analysis provides backing for this hypothesis by showing that these cartouches are composed of a gold sheet distinct from the rest; in addition, some of them exhibit a darker gold tint, although others do not. For this alteration, however, it is natural not to expect any palimpsests, since the removal of the inlaid inscriptions would be carried out differently (as discussed in the previous examples).

On the question of different gold hues

The question of gold colour variations remains a topic of interest in the field. It is easily subject to overinterpretation, for example, with reference to the search for altered names.[45] Therefore it is important to better understand why varying hues of gold may be present on an object, and whether they may or may not be indicative of alterations; their interpretation can be complex, and various factors and principles are often confused or misconstrued.

In general, the colour of gold primarily depends on its composition. Many variations in alloy (with and without visibly different colours) occur naturally, depending on the source they come from, but can also be produced artificially by mixing the metals in different ratios.

To put it simply, a higher content of copper and/or silver can shift the colour noticeably into the silvery-yellow or reddish range, but as long as there is more than 80 per cent gold, and equal quantities of silver and copper, the colour will not change very much to the naked eye.[46] The quantity of silver in the alloy primarily affects the hardness and malleability of gold, while a greater copper to gold ratio lowers the melting temperature of the alloy.

Egyptian craftsmen were aware of these different characteristics and effects and exploited them, and were able to make a hard solder blend seamlessly with the main gold of an object, while capitalizing on its lower melting temperature from its higher copper content.[47]Also, it may be preferable for certain construction elements, such as clasps, to match the metal colour of the main object while being more harder and more resistant to wear than the rest of the piece.

Ageing processes can unintentionally alter the colour of gold alloys, as evident for example from the first (Carter 207) and second shrine (Carter 237) from the tomb (Fig. 4.9).[48] The corrosion on the doors' interiors results from a thin film of silver-gold sulphide minerals that developed on some gold sheets.[49] This does not necessarily mean that new sheets were placed here.

It is theoretically also possible for substances such as an antique varnish or dyes from textiles that were once wrapped around objects to influence or trigger this process, but there has not yet been a proper study to confirm this and objective evidence on this matter is currently lacking.

However, during (and for some time after) the creation of the shrine, the various gold sheets probably appeared identical (or at least very similar) to the naked eye, and today's distinct colour variations were likely neither seen nor intended.

Of course, there is also metal polychromy. This technique uses the deliberate combination of different metals and their colours, such as gold, silver, copper or alloys of these, such as electrum, to add details and meaning to an object.[50]

Another colour phenomenon is the so-called pink gold (or purple gold), which appears, with a few exceptions, mostly among the belongings of Tutankhamun.[51] It is the result of an intended colour manipulation, typically employed in combination with granulation (Plate 6). Experimental work showed that it is possible to create this effect by adding iron to small amounts of molten gold,[52] but the process is not yet fully understood.

Egyptian goldworkers may also have used a sort of staining technique to achieve different colours.[53] However, this can only be speculated on, and cannot currently be explained.

An example of misinterpreting the gold colour to indicate a modification can be seen on the gilded throne. A reddish hue in the gold above the stand with the collar does not relate to the alteration of the cartouche above it,[54] since no physical or causal connection exists between the discoloration of the gold beneath Ankhesenamun's cartouche and the newly applied sheet within the cartouche.

The colour of the gold also seems to have played a significant role in identifying alterations made to gold objects. In discussions with a number of Egyptologists regarding the canopic coffins, it was suggested that certain parts of the previous names were removed and 'new gold' was added

Fig. 4.9. The optical corrosion phenomena match nicely the shape of some gold sheets that were used for the gilding of the shrine, but it can also occur in certain parts of a sheet only. Photo: Harry Burton. © Griffith Institute, University of Oxford.

in these areas by pouring it on. This would be evident by the different colours of the gold. Maybe this idea pertains to the few darker and somewhat greyish cartouches one can observe even in the historic pictures by Harry Burton (e.g., Burton 1757 and 1759), but scientific analysis shows very similar alloys here and thus does not suggest any addition with another gold. In one case traces of grey in the palimpsests of the earlier characters are also visible, but these seem to be simply modern pencil marks and not related to any alteration.

Reworked areas also often keep a rougher surface that easily traps dirt and is more susceptible to possible corrosive influences. In short, it is important not to overestimate the significance of gold hues in relation to alterations but rather to consider them as potential initial indicators that should be weighed against other factors.

Résumé

How probable is it to identify previous names with respect to the various techniques utilized for their removal? As discussed above, the details provide the clues. To summarize, it can be stated that the altered or modified gold items from the tomb consistently display very clear signs of their reworking procedures, whether in the form of palimpsests or other technical details. This applies not only to modifying inscriptions, but also to decorative and/or stylistic changes.[55] The various metalworking methods each leave distinguishable marks, but surprisingly none of them were used or combined to such an extent that the previous inscriptions are now unreadable.

However, in cases of altered decorations created using inlay techniques, it is impossible to determine what was shown or written previously. This naturally also applies to the replaced gold sheet parts, such as those on the backs of the pectorals or mummy band segments.

We have not encountered any instances of a previously cut out piece of sheet or gold being reworked and reused on the original object again among the tomb finds. High temperatures are also generally not used on any finished gold works with inlay decoration.

On gilded objects, any name changes should be primarily noticeable by identifying newly added gold sheets that overlap the surrounding originals. This is true unless larger portions of the decoration were altered and larger parts or the entire gilding renewed. While specific or inconsistent colour deviations may indicate these replacements, they are not necessarily a guarantee.

The likelihood of discovering pre-existing inscriptions underneath newly added and inscribed gold sheets is vanishingly small due to the renewed and remodelled gesso underneath, and therefore does not justify measures such as the removal of these added gold sheets or foils, which will always have an unsightly aesthetic effect. Ultimately, and as a basic principle of object study, it is always necessary to prioritize observation before assigning meaning, rather than the reverse.

Notes

1   Carter 1923, 1927, 1933; Reeves 2022.
2   See, e.g., Reeves 2022.
3   See, e.g., Eaton-Krauss 1993; Allen 2010; Gabolde 2016; Reeves 2022.
4   Loeben 1991. Since the objects from the tomb are about to be moved or already moved to the Grand Egyptian Museum and their future accession number is not yet known, the Carter excavation numbers are given as they are the most reliable reference for all subsequent catalogues. All objects from the tomb mentioned in this article can be found by their Carter numbers in the archives of the Griffith Institute, University of Oxford, including *in situ* and object photographs by Harry Burton as well as the descriptions on the Object Cards, in Carter's journals and Lucas's and Walter Segal's notes (http://www.griffith.ox.ac.uk/discoveringtut/ [last accessed 13 September 2023).
5   Object Cards 588-1+3.
6   Object Cards 79-3, 574-1; Reeves 2022.
7   As suggested, e.g., for the inlaid ebony throne (Carter 351; Eaton-Krauss 2008). Reeves implies this praxis for the canopic chest (Reeves 2022), but the continuous veining of the stone between the chest and most cartouches shows that stone inserts were not used here (see also note 41).
8   My observations stem from various collaborative studies with Eid Mertah and Christian Eckmann on a variety of gilded objects and goldsmith's works, especially on the mummy equipment. I thank them warmly for allowing me to highlight some of the details here. The analytical data will be presented and discussed in detail elsewhere and are only briefly mentioned here with regard to their informative impact on the alterations. I also wish to thank Tom Hardwick for his linguistic help and fruitful discussions.

9   See, e.g., Object Cards 91-1 to 91-10; Carter and Mace 1923; Carter 1933; Walter Segal's notes 1935; Baker 1966; Reeves 1990; Eaton-Krauss 2008; Gabolde 2016; Bartos 2021; Reeves 2022.
10   The term 'gesso' is a general designation that lacks precision. Its key components consist of calcium carbonate or calcium sulphate, blended with an organic binder (Hatchfield and Newman 1991). In Egypt, this material is primarily used with wooden or non-metallic bases (e.g., Rifai and El Hadidi 2010; Abdrabou et al. 2019).
11   A detailed study about the lavish and extravagant combination of decoration techniques on the throne is currently being prepared (Broschat et al. 2024).
12   Segal 1935; Eaton-Krauss 2008; Reeves 2022.
13   For the different gold layers on the stile of the throne in Fig. 2a and other areas on the throne as well as on other objects from the tomb, see Broschat et al. 2024.
14   Carter 1923; Eaton-Krauss and Graefe 1985.
15   Edwards 1972. He does not consider the possible use of resins or glues, which function as a fixing material.
16   Only one row of pins was identified on the back of the backrest (left side). Therefore, we cannot rule out the possibility that a single sheet of gold, twice the size, was wrapped around the entire backrest (with the exception of the headrail on the back).
17   See, e.g., Gabolde 2016. Of course, this may be reused gold, but just not from the initial main gold sheet.
18   Harris 1992; Gabolde 2016.
19   See also, e.g., James 2000.
20   Eaton-Krauss 2008; Gabolde 2016; Reeves 2022.
21   For those who may think that there was also a change in name from a predecessor to Tutankhaten, it may be important to know that the composition of the gold sheet within the cartouche is identical to that of the single large sheet which covers the outside of the armrest.
22   As proposed by Reeves (2022). The details of changes in the decoration from gilded raised relief to coloured inlaid decoration will be discussed in Broschat et al. 2024.
23   Object Card 261p1-3.
24   Gabolde 1989, 2009; Allen 2010. This counts for both cartouches and as a predecessor name has been changed here, the two prenomen have also been updated to refer to Tutankhamun.
25   Hackbeil 2012.
26   Broschat and Eckmann 2022.
27   Eckmann et al. 2023; see also Reeves 2022. The technique of alteration described for this pectoral also applies in principle to three other pectorals also found in the shrine – 251m, Carter 261i and 261n.
28   Reeves 1990.
29   Both techniques are commonly called *cloisonné*, although the former is actually closer to *champlevé*. Both terms are problematic because technically they refer to the use of enamel, which was not commonly known in pre-Ptolemaic Egypt (Teeter 1981, 319; Andrews 1990, 82–82; Müller 1999, 153; Ogden 2000, 166). There are other, more detailed differentiations of the inlay techniques, but they are irrelevant here.

30 It is theoretically possible that the cartouches were prefabricated in one piece with the carrying gold sheets and inserted from the back using a single gluing operation.

31 Object Card 261p3-2; see also Burton 1136.

32 It was not possible to study the mummy bands in person and the observations described in this study were made from photographs alone.

33 Broschat and Eckmann 2022.

34 Object card 256b-05.

35 Reeves 2022.

36 For a different description see Reeves 2022.

37 See also Object Cards 256-1, 256a-4–256a-6; e.g., Burton 744; Broschat and Eckmann 2022; Reeves 2022.

38 More specifically, of the three rows that make up the side strap segments, these are only parts of the flanking vertical rows. As can be determined from a comparison of pictures (Burton 744, 750a with 761), the order of these strap segments was altered during the process of recovery and reconstruction. At some point after the object left Luxor, the segment carrying the cartouche was interchanged with one from the side straps, possibly in an effort to restore the original wording (author's observation).

39 For the text, see Beinlich and Saleh 1989.

40 To add Tutankhamun's names, like in the examples mentioned earlier, would therefore be senseless in this case.

41 Carter 1933. Reeves (2022) identified alterations of the names on the chest too (by inserts of new stone pieces?), but the continuous veins from the calcite alabaster that cross most cartouches make this seem unlikely. The surfaces give no reason to assume a reworking too.

42 Gabolde 1988; Allen 2010.

43 This description provides only a brief overview; a detailed study of the canopic coffins including the scientific data will be published with Eid Mertah and Christian Eckmann elsewhere.

44 Object Cards 266g-1, 266g-3.

45 Besides the example mentioned below, it is noteworthy to note Reeves's observations regarding, as he suggests, the exchange of the face of the mummy mask from Tutankhamun (Reeves 2015 a and b). He claims to be supported by a scientific study conducted by Uda et al. 2007 and 2014, that seems to have identified different colours/alloys of the gold. However, a recent study has not confirmed his ideas (Eckmann et al. 2023).

46 Rehren et al. 2022.

47 See, e.g., Broschat et al. 2022; Rehren 2022; Guerra 2023.

48 Piankoff 1955 or Burton 603aLS and 632a.

49 Frantz and Schorsch 1990. For a chemical characterization of corroded gold surfaces also Tissot and Guerra 2023.

50 Schorsch 2001 or, e.g. Gänsicke et al. 2023. A striking example of this is a pectoral (Carter 269k) with intricate decorative work. The piece shows a night barque supported by lotus blossoms and buds, with the moon and a crescent below, and is interpreted as a nocturnal voyage of the barque on the 'heavenly waters'. The moon disk shimmers with a light, almost silvery gold tone, whereas the night boat is represented in 'yellow gold'.

51 Schorsch 2001.

52 Wood 1934; Plenderleith and Werner 1971; Frantz and Schorsch 1990.

53 See, e.g., a ring bezel with a group of figures (Carter 44j). The tiny standing baboons have bright and light-coloured faces and dark furs; the headdress of the worshipping figure also seems to have been intentionally darkened.

54 Eaton-Krauss 2008.

55 Boschat et al. 2024.

Bibliography

Abdrabou, Ahmed, Nesrin M.N. el-Hadidi, Safa Hamed and Medhat Abdalla. 2019. 'Multidisciplinary Approach for the Investigation and Analysis of a Gilded Wooden Bed of King Tutankhamun'. *Journal of Archaeological Science: Reports* 21: 553–564.

Allen, James P. 2010. 'The Original Owner of Tutankhamun's Canopic Coffins'. In *Millions of Jubilees: Studies in Honor of David P. Silverman*, Vol. 1, edited by Zahi Hawass and Jennifer Houser Wegner, 27–41. Cairo: Conseil Suprême des Antiquités.

Andrews, Carol A.R. 1990. *Ancient Egyptian Jewellery*. London: British Museum Publications.

Baker, Hollis S. 1966. *Furniture in the Ancient World: Origins & Evolution. 3100–475 B.C.* London: The Connoisseur.

Bartos, Ilinca. 2021. 'Tutankhamun's Golden Armchair: Its Original Owner and Shape Reconsidered'. *Égypte Nilotique et Méditerranéenne* 14: 273–284.

Beinlich, Horst, and Mohamed Saleh. 1989. *Corpus der hieroglyphischen Inschriften aus dem Grab des Tutanchamun: mit Konkordanz der Nummernsysteme des 'Journal d'Entrée' des Ägyptischen Museums Kairo, der Handlist to Howard Carter's Catalogue of Objects in Tut'ankhamun's Tomb und der Ausstellungs-Nummer des Ägyptischen Museums Kairo.* Oxford: Griffith Institute.

Broschat, Katja, Christian Eckmann and Eid Mertah. 2024. 'Conceived, Created, Changed? An Armchair Study of the Golden Throne of Tutankhamun'. *Journal of the American Research Center in Egypt*, 60.

Broschat, Katja, Florian Ströbele, Christian Koeberl, Christian Eckmann and Eid Mertah. 2022. *Iron from Tutankhamun's Tomb*. Cairo and New York: American University in Cairo Press.

Carter, Howard. 1927. *The Tomb of Tutankhamen, Discovered by the late Earl of Carnarvon and Howard Carter*, Vol. II. London: Cassell.

Carter, Howard. 1933. *The Tomb of Tutankhamen, Discovered by the late Earl of Carnarvon and Howard Carter*, Vol. III. London: Cassell.

Carter, Howard, and Arthur Mace. 1923. *The Tomb of Tutankhamen, Discovered by the late Earl of Carnarvon and Howard Carter*, Vol. I. London: Cassell.

Eaton-Krauss, Marianne. 1993. *The Sarcophagus in the Tomb of Tutankhamun*. Oxford: Griffith Institute, Ashmolean Museum.

Eaton-Krauss, Marianne. 2008. *The Thrones, Chairs, Stools, and Footstools from the Tomb of Tutankhamun*. Incorporating the records made by Walter Segal. Griffith Institute Publications. Oxford: Griffith Institute.

Eckmann, Christian, Katja Broschat and Tom Hardwick. 'Zur Frage einer möglichen Umarbeitung der Mumienmaske Tutanchamuns'. *Journal of the American Research Center in Egypt* 59: 39–67.

Edwards, Iorwerth Eiddon Stephen. 1973. *The Treasures of Tutânkhamun.* Foreword by Lord Trevelyan. New York and London: Viking Press; Michael Joseph.

Frantz, James H., and Deborah Schorsch. 1990. 'Egyptian Red Gold'. *Archaeomaterials* 4: 133–152.

Gabolde, Marc. 1998. *D'Akhenaton à Toutânkhamon.* Collection de l'Institut d'Archéologie et d'Histoire de l'Antiquité 3. Lyon: Université Lumière-Lyon 2, Institut d'Archéologie et d'Histoire de l'Antiquité.

Gabolde, Marc. 2009. 'Under a Deep Blue Starry Sky'. In *Causing His Name to Live: Studies in Egyptian Epigraphy and History in Memory of William J. Murnane,* edited by Peter Brand and Louise Cooper, 109–120. Leiden and Boston: Brill.

Gabolde, Marc. 2016. 'Le confort d'un roi'. *Orientalistische Literaturzeitung* 111 (1): 1–9.

Gänsicke, Susanne, Monica Ganio, Arlen Heginbotham, Douglas Maclennan, Jeff Maish, Johana Herrera and Karen Trentelman. 2023. 'Mensa Isiaca: New Findings on its Composition, Construction, and History'. *Rivista del Museo Egizio* 7: 24–56.

Gardiner, Alan H. 1927. *Egyptian Grammar, Being an Introduction to the Study of Hieroglyphs.* Oxford: Clarendon Press.

Guerra, Maria Filomena, Marcos Martinon-Torres and Stephen Quirke. 2023. *Ancient Egyptian Gold. Archaeology & Science in Jewellery (3500–1000 BC).* McDonald Institute Monographs Series. Cambridge: University of Cambridge.

Hackbeil, Cornelius. 2012. 'Kat.-Nr. 47'. In *Im Licht von Amarna. 100 Jahre Fund der Nofretete,* edited by Friederike Seyfried, 270. Petersberg: Michael Imhof.

Harris, John Raymond. 1992. 'Akhenaten and Nefernefruaten in the Tomb of Tut'ankhamūn'. In *After Tut'ankhamūn: Research and Excavation in the Royal Necropolis at Thebes,* edited by Carl Nicholas Reeves, 55–72. London: Kegan Paul.

Hatchfield, Pamela, and Richard Newman. 1991. 'Ancient Egyptian Gilding Methods'. In *Gilded Wood: Conservation and History,* edited by Deborah Bigelow, Elisabeth Cornu, Gregory J. Landrey and Cornelis van Horne, 27–47. Madison, CT: Sound View Press.

James, Thomas Garnet Henry. 2000. *Tutankhamun: The Eternal Splendour of the Boy Pharaoh.* London and New York: Vercelli: Tauris Parke; White Star.

Kuhlmann, Klaus. 1977. *Der Thron im alten Ägypten: Untersuchungen zu Semantik, Ikonographie und Symbolik eines Herrschaftszeichens.* Abhandlungen des Deutschen Archäologischen Instituts Kairo, Ägyptologische Reihe 10. Glückstadt: J.J. Augustin.

Loeben, Christian E. 1991. 'No Evidence of Coregency: zwei getilgte Inschriften aus dem Grab von Tutanchamun'. *Bulletin de la Société d'Égyptologie de Genève* 15: 81–90.

Müller, Hans-Wolfgang, and Eberhard Thiem. 1999. *The Royal Gold of Ancient Egypt.* London: I.B. Tauris.

Ogden, Jack. 2000. 'Metals'. In *Ancient Egyptian Materials and Technology,* edited by Paul T. Nicholson and Ian Shaw, 148–176. Cambridge: Cambridge University Press.

Piankoff, Alexandre. 1955. *The Shrines of Tut-Ankh-Amon.* Edited by Natacha Rambova. Egyptian Religious Texts and Representations 2; Bollingen Series 40. New York: Pantheon Books for the Bollingen Foundation.

Plenderleith, Harold James, and Alfred Emil Anthony Werner. 1971. *The Conservation of Antiquities and Works of Art, Treatment, Repair and Restoration,* 2nd edition. London and New York: Oxford University Press.

Reeves, Carl Nicholas. 1990. *The Complete Tutankhamun: The King, the Tomb, the Royal Treasure.* London: Thames and Hudson.

Reeves, Carl Nicholas. 2015a. 'Tutankhamun's Mask Reconsidered'. *Bulletin of the Egyptological Seminar* 19: 511–526.

Reeves, Carl Nicholas. 2015b. 'The Gold Mask of Ankhkheperure Neferneferuaten'. *Journal of Ancient Egyptian Interconnections* 7 (4): 77–79.

Reeves, Carl Nicholas. 2022. *The Complete Tutankhamun. 100 Years of Discovery,* revised and expanded. London: Thames & Hudson.

Rehren, Thilo, Katja Broschat, Myrto Georgakopoulou and Stavroula Golfomitsou. 2022. 'Die Goldanalysen'. In *Tutanchamuns Mumienmaske – Chronographie einer Ikone,* edited by Katja Broschat and Christian Eckmann, 147–167. Monographien des RGZM, Band 162. Mainz: Verlag des Römisch-Germanischen Zentralmuseums.

Rifai, Mai M., and Nesrin M.N. El Hadidi. 2010. 'Investigation and Analysis of Three Gilded Wood Samples from the Tomb of Tutankhamun'. In *Decorated Surfaces on Ancient Egyptian Objects, Technology, Deterioration and Conservation,* edited by Julie Dawson, Christina Rozeik and Margot M. Wright, 16–21. London: Archetype Publications.

Schorsch, Deborah. 2001. 'Precious-Metal Polychromy in Egypt in the Time of Tutankhamun'. *Journal of Egyptian Archaeology* 87: 55–71.

Segal, Walter. 1935. MSS 1.1–31: http://www.griffith.ox.ac.uk/gri/4segtut.html (last accessed 13 September 2023).

Teeter, Emily. 1981. 'Enameling in Ancient Egypt?' *American Journal of Archaeology* 85: 319.

Tissot, Isabel, and Maria Filomena Guerra. 2023. 'The Corrosion of Precious Metals: The Case of Egyptian Goldwork'. In *Ancient Egyptian Gold: Archaeology and Science in Jewellery (3500–1000 BC),* edited by Maria Filomena Guerra, Marcos Martinon-Torres and Stephen Quirke, 175–184. Cambridge: McDonald Institute for Archaeological Research.

Uda, Masayuki, A. Ishizaki and Masahiro Baba. 2014. 'Tutankhamun's Golden Mask and Throne'. In *Quest for the Dream of the Pharaohs: Studies in Honour of Sakuji Yoshimura,* edited by Jiro Kondo, 149–177. Cairo: Ministry of Antiquities.

Uda, Masayuki, Sakuji Yoshimura, A. Ishizaki, D. Yamashita and Y. Sakuraba. 2007. 'Tutankhamun's Golden Mask Investigated with XRDF'. *International Journal of PIXE* 17 (1 & 2): 65–76.

Wood, Robert William. 1934. 'The Purple Gold of Tut'ankhamūn'. *The Journal of Egyptian Archaeology* 20 (1): 62–65.

Searching for light: on the rise of yellow coffins

Rogério Sousa

Abstract

Until the reign of Amenhotep III, anthropoid black coffins were the prevalent type of body container in high elite burials. The festive dress type of coffins represented a deep break with this tradition which probably originated at Amarna. Attempts to integrate the festive dress type of coffins into the Osirian scheme of decoration of the black type can be detected as early as the reign of Tutankhamun, particularly in the production of anthropoid sarcophagi and coffins at Saqqara. In Thebes, this trend progressed even further, playing a decisive role in the subsequent evolution of coffin decoration. The goal of this paper is to characterize this trend and to better understand the corpus of the Ramesside proto-yellow coffins which eventually led to the creation of the yellow corpus. The genealogy of this phenomenon reveals the paramount role performed by the artisans from Deir el-Medina, who developed these concepts in the craftsmanship of their own coffins before they had slowly spread towards other Theban contexts.

Keywords: yellow coffins, black pitch, varnish, New Kingdom

Coffin decoration in ancient Egypt is a multi-layered phenomenon revealing not only important clues to the understanding of religious beliefs, but also workshop practices, socioeconomic relations and political ideologies.[1] Although this can be observed in any period of the pharaonic history, this process is particularly unclear during the New Kingdom, given the scarcity of archaeological records when compared to other periods. In this paper we will approach this subject aiming to clarify the symbolic meaning, as well as the social and political dynamics associated with the craftsmanship of coffins.

Black coffins

From the time of Hatshepsut/Thutmose III to that of Amenhotep III, private anthropoid coffins were crafted after the so-called 'black type'. The most distinctive feature of these coffins is the presentation of the deceased in mummiform shape, with their surfaces coated in black pitch or sometimes partially or entirely gilded (Fig. 5.1).[2]

High elite burials of the 18th Dynasty frequently involved a nest of up to three anthropoid containers and a rectangular coffin shaped as a *per-nu* shrine (Fig. 5.1).[3] Besides this wealth of body containers, typically the burial equipment of the black type also included a funerary mask and a gilded cartonnage openwork mummy-board, sometimes with depictions of the Sons of Horus.[4] The funerary mask was often designed as a cartonnage version of the headboard of the lid, showing the deceased wearing a striped tripartite wig and a small collar between the lappets.[5] A well-defined repertoire of texts and images is included in the decoration of these coffins. On the lid, the underside of the footboard presents the image of Isis, and the crown of the headboard is decorated with Nephthys.[6] On the box, the texts and images depicted on the sides refer to the Sons of Horus and Anubis. Together, these features reproduce the deities shown in the

Fig. 5.1. Burial assemblage of Yuya (Egyptian Museum, Cairo). Composition by the author.

vignette of Chapter 151 of the Book of the Dead, aiming at identifying the deceased with Osiris.[7] Other features are solar related, such as the winged goddess Nut depicted over the chest of the lid, or the image of Thoth on the box alluding to Chapter 161 of the Book of the Dead, referring to the triumph of the sun god Re over his enemy Apophis, and to the opening of the sky by Thoth enabling the sun god to ascend to the heavens.[8] This scheme of decoration remained very stable.

Black pitch and gold played a particularly important role in this type of coffins. Ideally, the innermost coffins were entirely gilded, while the outer containers were coated in black pitch and had only their inscriptions and images covered with gilded foil. In the finest examples, texts and images were moulded in plaster before being coated in gold foil. These objects often display exquisite levels of crafts-manship,[9] using a wealth of inlaid stones or glass.[10] The sculptural work is outstanding, especially in the treatment of the faces, often crafted separately in imported wood, and

feature many anatomical details such as kneecaps, shinbones and the contour of the legs and buttocks.[11] Beards,[12] as well as other gender-markers, are rare, as the deceased is always depicted as an idealized Osiris.[13] In exceptionally luxurious burials, the black scheme was even used when carving anthropoid sarcophagi in stone.[14]

Cheaper objects involved improvised solutions: the texts and images are directly carved in the wood[15] and the gilded foil is simply substituted by yellow paint if the purpose was to emulate a gilded coffin,[16] or by black paint to imitate black pitch.[17] As already mentioned, regardless of these differences in terms of quality, black coffins did not differ much in terms of iconography. This stability allowed workshops to carry out most of the work without close supervision, as long as a model was provided.

It is likely that the use of black pitch in the private burials might have followed royal funerary archetypes. In the tombs of Horemheb (KV 57), Ramesses I (KV 16), Seti I (KV 17) and Ramesses IX (KV 6) were uncovered a large number of wooden statues coated in black pitch depicting deities of the netherworld with obvious relation to the imagery of the Book of the Amduat.[18] Although these objects are much later, they probably followed a tradition that went back to the earlier 18th Dynasty, as similarly black coated objects were found in the tomb of Thutmose III (KV 34).[19] The use of black pitch on private coffins might have had the purpose of identifying the deceased with the underworld deities, associating him with the nightly journey of the sun and the mystery of cosmic renewal that occurred in the netherworld, a phenomena with which the deceased longed to be associated.

Black pitch was probably applied during the funerary ritual itself and this was certainly the reason why the decoration had to be covered with gilded foil, so that it could remain visible after the application of black pitch.[20] If so, the design of black coffins was heavily determined by the ritual context of the funerary ceremonials. In any case, pictorial representations of these objects make clear that black coating was a fundamental aspect of their definition, as this feature is universally represented in the representation of coffins until the reign of Amenhotep III (Fig. 5.2).[21]

Festive dress coffins

During the reign of Akhenaten, the Osirian beliefs were almost entirely obliterated from the official discourse and religious practices. This is particularly clear in the *Great Hymn of Aten*, where death itself is ignored, as well as the netherworld with all its mythological inhabitants.[22] Everything in the reform of Amarna revolves around light and the visibility of the natural phenomena. Hence, not surprisingly, the rich imagery related to the Book of the Amduat was obliterated in the visual culture unfolded in the royal tomb of Amarna. Both in the royal and private tombs of Amarna, iconography is entirely focused on the daily existence of the inhabitants of this city. However, this 'daily life', as shown in the tomb scenes in Amarna, does not revolve around mundane events, as we see in the Old Kingdom private tombs until the reign of Amenhotep III, but rather focuses on divine festivals and royal events.[23] Although there is no explicit discourse on this subject, it is likely that the afterlife in Amarna was seen as an ongoing existence in the sacred city of the god Aten, where light and life were continuously celebrated.

Given this new mindset, body containers of Amarna had to be entirely redesigned. Unfortunately, in this regard, the archaeological evidence is particularly scarce. The short time span of the city's necropolis, the heavy destruction that followed, and the lack of interest in these materials by modern excavators certainly explain this lacuna. Recently, fragments of body containers have been found in the South Tombs Cemetery of Amarna, providing a glimpse on the burial customs of the inhabitants of Amarna. These fragments belonged to rectangular coffins painted in black with figures

Fig. 5.2. Opening of the mouth ritual. Tomb of Nebamun and Ipuki (TT 181). Photo by the author.

outlined in yellow simply showing offering scenes without featuring any deity. This 'godless' decoration clearly shows that new designs were being formed in Amarna, ones that were consistent with the theological values of the period.[24]

The highest elite tombs from Akhetaten did not provide any evidence in this regard. However, their scenes may help to shed light on the shape and form of contemporary coffins. In the Royal Tomb itself, the king and queen are shown mourning the princess Meketaten (Fig. 5.3a). The deceased princess is lying on a funerary bier, with the arms alongside the body, showing the corpse as if suspended over a raised platform.[25] As we have noted elsewhere,[26] this scene, which is normally interpreted as the depiction of the corpse, may actually represent the type of coffin in use for the Amarnian highest elite, showing the lid designed after the living image of the deceased and an undecorated box. Similar examples are known from other iconographic sources. The fragments of the sarcophagus of Djehutymes show the deceased both upon the funerary bier and standing (Fig. 5.3b). In the latter scene, the deceased is mourned by the widow squatted at his feet, exactly in the same way that coffins are depicted in mourning scenes.[27]

With the lid shaped after the living image of the deceased, this new type of coffin was designed as a hollow statue, featuring the deceased attired to attend the sacred festivals in the Temple of Aten. Gender differentiation of the coffins, which would persist henceforth, was thus introduced in these

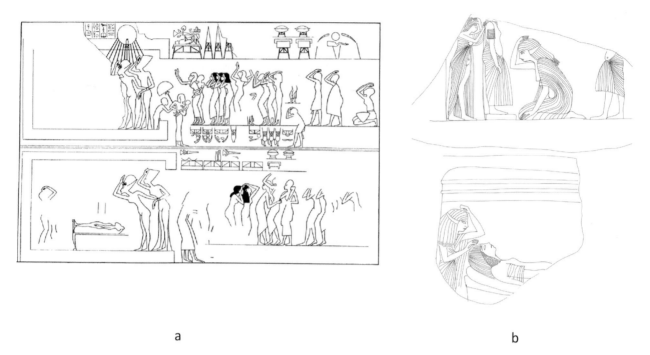

a   b

Fig. 5.3. Mourning scenes. Composition by the author. (a) Room Y, royal tomb of Amarna; (b) Fragments of the sarcophagus of Djehutymes (Kaiser Wilhelms-Universität, Strasbourg, no. 1393, Museo Camposanto, Pisa, no. 2).

coffins.[28] As to the box, it was probably simply painted in white. The only known example of a 'pure' coffin of the festive dress type is that of the prince Amenemhat (Fig. 5.4a), found in Deir el-Bahari and now in the Metropolitan Museum of Art, New York (inv. no. 19.3.207a–b). The lid shows a very simplified layout of the festive linen garments: no drapery of the festive pleated garment is shown, and it was merely painted in white, and the same procedure was applied to the box. This stylized treatment of the garment suggests that this is a later object, surely following an early model.

Another example of a later revival of the 'pure' festive dress coffin is found in the coffin of Tairsekheru (National Museums Scotland, Edinburgh, no. 1887.597). This coffin, probably found in the tomb of Sennedjem (TT 1),[29] has the sides of the box simply decorated with red and yellow stripes. Instead of the usual deities, the texts only mention the names of the deceased child, and her mother, Iyneferty (Fig. 5.4b). Only the striped headboard of the box, as well as the deities depicted on the underside of the footboard of the lid and box provide hints of the usual repertoire of the black type, suggesting that this is a later revival of the Amarnian model.

So far, Amarnian coffins of this type remain unattested in the archaeological records, but some other pieces of evidence suggest that such models did exist at least by the end of the Amarna period.[30] The *rishi* coffin found in KV 55 (Egyptian Museum, Cairo, JE 13247) shows a ceremonial

braided 'Nubian' wig instead of the divine tripartite head-dress, and the same can be said of the lids of the canopic vases found in the same tomb.[31] This, of course, is not the first attestation of braided wigs in coffin decoration. During the reign of Amenhotep III, braided wigs had already appeared both in coffins[32] and in shabtis.[33] A particularly interesting example is provided by the anonymous coffin of a prince wearing a sidelock, which already reveals a focus in the representation of the deceased as a living being.[34] This coffin was found in Deir el-Medina but its dating is uncertain. The style, the face in particular, seems consistent with the reign of Amenhotep III. The *rishi* coffin from KV 55 differs from these examples by the use of a ceremonial wig, suggesting that a new type of coffin featuring the deceased in festive garments, and not as an Osirian deity, had already been formed.

Also intriguing, is the use of unguent cones in the funerary equipment of the mummies found in Amarna. In the South Tombs Cemetery of Amarna, human remains adorned with unguent cones were discovered.[35] Unguent cones are a traditional motif in festivals, but its use in the mummification itself remains unique to Amarna, suggesting that during this period the mummy was attired as to integrate a sacred ceremony.

Shabtis, which have always been designed after the shape of the coffins in use, also reveal a sudden change during the Amarna period. The shabti of Hatsherit, datable to the reign of Akhenaten,[36] conspicuously displays the deceased

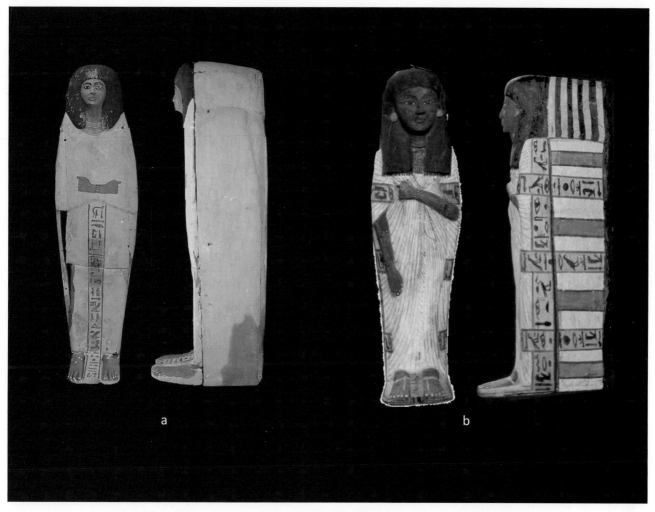

Fig. 5.4. Festive dress coffins. Composition by the author. (a) Coffin of Amenemhat (Metropolitan Museum of Art, New York, inv. no. 19.3.207a, b); (b) Coffin of Tairsekheru, from TT 1 (Royal Museum of Scotland, Edinburgh, inv. no. 1885.597).

in festive garments (Fig. 5.5). An interesting feature of this object is the polychrome decoration: the garments are painted in white, the long hair is blue and the skin of the female deceased is painted red. This feature is particularly intriguing as it does not follow the traditional colour code, which reserved yellow for women, and it is often found in Amarnian art.[37] This colour code recalls, as we will see below, the red paint used in Ramesside coffins of the festive dress type and so the latter may find its roots in the Amarna festive dress type. It is thus likely that the putative festive dress coffins of Amarna already featured polychrome decoration. The question of knowing if the yellowish varnish was also used in these coffins remains unclear.

As we mentioned, the creation of these coffins introduced a deep break with the former tradition. Such a break followed the set up of new workshops in the capital city. Despite the clear rupture with the Osirian tradition, it is interesting to detect in this reformative impetus the recovery of ideas from the Old Kingdom funerary culture that had long been discarded, such as the preparation of the mummy to look like a statue of the Ka. The festive dress coffin actually provided the deceased with a statue of his/her Ka, with the implied statement that he/she was no longer seen as an Osirian deity, as previously occurred in the black type. It is thus clear that the new model of coffins conveniently contributed to reassert the political agenda of Akhenaten, as it removed to the deceased the very possibility of deification through his/her identification with Osiris.

Body containers from the reign of Tutankhamun

After the Amarna period, the traditional Osirian archetype was back in favour and black coffins were reintroduced. This is particularly clear in the embalming cache of KV 63, where the coffins bear the beautiful style typically associated with

Fig. 5.5. Shabtis designed after the layout of the festive dress type. Photo: Composition by the author. (a) Shabti of Hatsherit (British Museum, EA 8644); (b) Funerary statuette of Sennedjem (National Museum of Egyptian Civilization, Cairo, JE 27221); (c) Shabti of Wepwautmes (National Museum of Antiquities, Leiden, AH 117); (d) Coffin and shabti inscribed for Amenmose (British Museum, EA 53892).

the reign of Tutankhamun. All of them show – in different degrees of complexion – the layout of the black type.[38]

In the royal tomb of Tutankhamun itself, miniature black coffins were used to bury the two stillborn children of the king and to keep the lock of hair of Queen Tiye (Fig. 5.6a–b).[39] These black coffinettes are used in nested assemblages together with *rishi* coffinettes as the innermost objects. It is interesting to point out that such association between the black type – normally used in private burials – with the royal *rishi* type remains unattested elsewhere.

Another example of a miniature coffin is provided by the small shabti figurine in wood nested in a rectangular coffin coated in black pitch, as was the usual practice in the early part of the 18th Dynasty. Shaped as a *per-nu* shrine, the object offers an exact replica of the outermost container of this kind (Fig. 5.17).

In the coffins of Tutankhamun themselves the use of black pitch – which is prevalent in the black type – is abundantly attested. It can be seen in the outer coffin where black pitch was applied over the footboard. This practice is also observed in the inner coffin, which seems to have been almost entirely coated in black pitch, as Harry Burton's photos suggest. Plate 10 shows the iconic photo presenting Howard Carter and his assistant cleaning the innermost

gilded coffin. When the photo was taken, Howard Carter had already cleaned the upper part of the torso down to the abdomen but the lower part is still much darkened. It is thus surprising that this outstanding golden object was in fact almost entirely coated with what is today perceived as a black and thick bitumen-like substance which completely hid its gilded radiance. Burton's photos also reveal that the interior of the second coffin was heavily coated in black pitch (Plate 9). This evidence shows that in the reign of Tutankhamun the patterns associated with the black type were fully back in favour, particularly in the royal burial.

However, despite this conservative observance of tradition, even in the tomb of Tutankhamun we find evidence that points to a change in the anthropoid coffin's layout. One of them is found in the outer coffin, where the king is not featured with the royal *nemes* headdress (Fig. 5.7). Instead, two lappets of braided hair provided with terminals are featured falling from his *khat*-headdress, forming an exceptional composition for a royal burial. Interestingly, the braided design found in this divine wig would become a fundamental feature of high elite yellow coffins produced from the end of the Ramesside period to beginning of the 21st Dynasty,[40] suggesting that this later trend was first introduced during the reign of Tutankhamun.

Fig. 5.6. Coffinettes from the Tomb of Tutankhamun (Grand Egyptian Museum, Cairo). (a) Coffinette holding the lock of hair of Queen Tye; (b) Coffinette holding the remains of a phoetus. Photos: © Griffith Institute, University of Oxford.

Another clue is found in the decoration of the royal burial chamber itself, particularly in the funerary procession scene (East wall), where the mummy of the king is depicted lying within a garland-bedecked shrine dragged by 12 high officials (Fig. 5.8).[41] This scene, otherwise unattested in royal tombs, was used in the repertoire of private tomb decoration from the reign of Hatshepsut onwards, always associated with black coffins (Fig. 5.9). In Tutankhamun's scene, however, the coffin is omitted – here we would expect to find a *rishi* coffin – and the mummy is displayed instead. The mummy, painted in white, is displayed on a lion bier adorned with a floral collar, a scarab pectoral and a funerary mask, all elements that were effectively used in the king's burial. Thus, the royal mummy is depicted as if the anthropoid coffins had become completely invisible. Interestingly, it is exactly in this same way that coffins begun to be represented from that moment onwards. Especially in private contexts, Ramesside depictions of coffins depict the layout of the mummy and no longer show the coffin itself, as if it had become truly 'invisible' (Fig. 5.10).

This change in the pictorial representation of coffins is consistent with the emergence of a new model of body container which was apparently based on the Amarnian revolutionary coffin type. In a small corpus of anthropoid sarcophagi carved from the reign of Tutankhamun to the early Ramesside period a mixture of features from the previous types of body containers is observed: the lid is designed showing the deceased in festive attire, but the box is fully designed after the black type.[42] This layout had lasting consequences as from then on, the lid and the box became formally independent and decorated as two completely independent pieces. The unity between the lid and the box of the body container was definitely broken.[43]

These developments are first seen in Saqqara, where most of the courtiers of Tutankhamun, who previously lived in Amarna, were eventually buried. In this small corpus, the decoration of the box follows the usual layout of the black type, showing the Sons of Horus, Thoth and Anubis, while the scheme of decoration of the lid combines the festive dress coffins with elements borrowed from the black type. The sarcophagus of Djehutyhotep (Louvre Museum, Paris, D3) shows the simplest composition of this corpus. The box is designed after the layout of the black type, while the lid presents the deceased, with bare feet, wearing a pleated ceremonial garment and long braided wig (Fig. 5.11a).

A similar design is detected in a small corpus of coffin lids crafted in wood, normally assigned to the Saqqara necropolis (Fig. 5.12b).[44] The layout of the boxes is unknown, as they are not preserved.[45] The lids show the deceased in full festive garments, with an unusually high

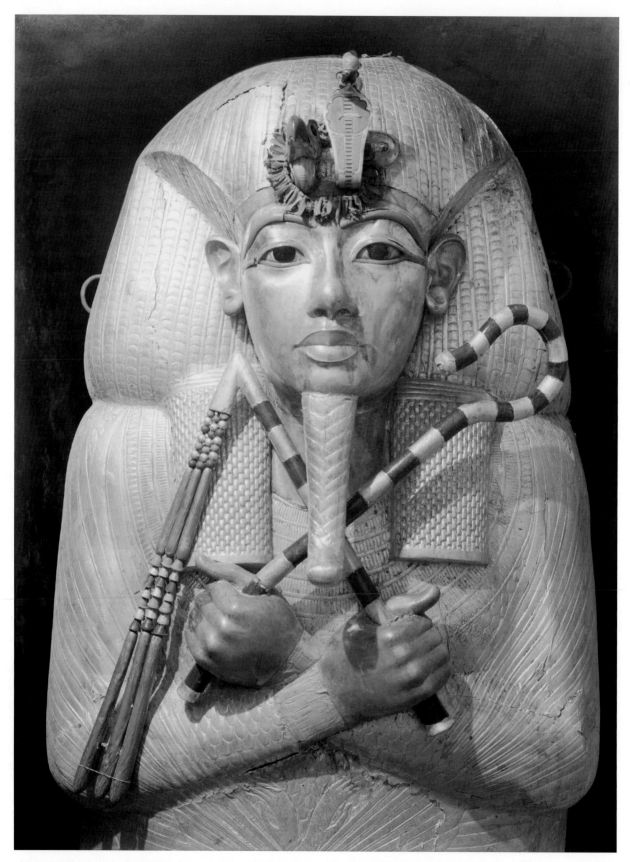

Fig. 5.7. The outer coffin of Tutankhamun (Grand Egyptian Museum, Cairo). Photo: © Griffith Institute, University of Oxford.

Fig. 5.8. The East wall of the burial chamber of Tutankhamun (KV 62). Photo: © Griffith Institute, University of Oxford.

Fig. 5.9. Funerary procession. Tomb of Pairi (TT 130). Photo by the author.

and rounded wig, probably imitating the layout of the stone objects. In some objects the polychrome decoration was not preserved, either due to the poor conditions of preservation or because they were cleaned up by modern dealers.[46] Vestiges of pigments were found on some of these objects, especially on the headboard and collar.[47] In the best-preserved examples, the wig, face and collar were plastered, painted and varnished.[48]

The male figures show the hands flat on the thighs, probably representing the gesture of adoration, *dw3*, while women show the left hand bent up to the chest, holding a ritual implement or flowers, while the other hand rests flat

Fig. 5.10. Funerary procession. Tomb of Roy (TT 255). Photo by the author.

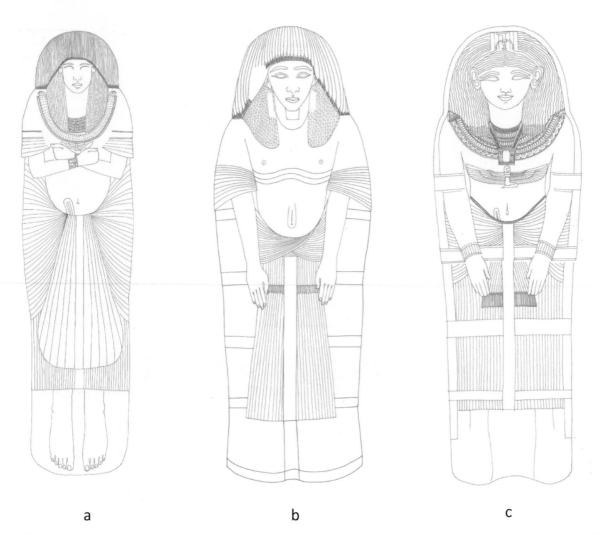

a   b   c

Fig. 5.11. Sarcophagi from Saqqara showing the lid carved after the festive dress type. Drawings by the author. (a) Sarcophagus of Djehuty (Louvre Museum, Paris, D 3); (b) Sarcophagus of Nia (Louvre Museum, Paris, D 2); (c) Sarcophagus of Senqed (Egyptian Museum, Cairo).

Fig. 5.12. Assemblage of objects of Northern origin using features from the festive dress type. Composition by the author. (a) Sarcophagus of Khay (National Museum of Egyptian Civilization, Cairo, JE 36454); (b) Lid of anonymous woman (Michael Carlos Museum, Atlanta, inv. no. L2003.14.38); (c) Anonymous male mask (Musées royaux d'Art et d'Histoire, Brussels, inv. no. E.6884).

on the thighs.[49] Female depictions show the curves of the female pubic triangle carefully carved.

The association with Saqqara may suppose that these coffins might have been used combined with anthropoid sarcophagi showing a similar design (Fig. 5.12a). However, most of them certainly formed independent sets. In any case, these are the first archaeological attestations of the use of the festive dress type in wooden coffins. These sets were certainly used together with a new type of cartonnage mask, one that featured the deceased with a heavy braided wig and with a larger *usekh*-collar (Fig. 5.12c).[50]

By the late 18th Dynasty, anthropoid sarcophagi already showed a heavy contamination of the black type in the festive depiction of the deceased on the lid (Fig. 5.11b): the bare feet were no longer depicted, being replaced by the usual footboard of the black type, and the bands of texts were displayed over the legs.[51] In some objects, the typical iconographic repertoire of the black type is eventually reintroduced over the lid, with the effigies of Nephthys, Nut and Isis depicted over the crown of the head, chest and feet, respectively (Fig. 5.11c).[52]

The reintegration of the black type progressed even further when the divine wig eventually replaced the festive one.[53] Once arrived at this point, one could think that the festive dress type and the conceptual framework associated with it was about to be completely forgotten. However, as we will see, this was not by all means what happened.

Proto-yellow coffins

The integration of both models progressed even further in the Ramesside period, eventually giving rise to a new type of body container, which we label as 'proto-yellow coffins'. Strictly speaking, these coffins form what can be considered a typological oddity. Due to the yellow coloration of the background, they are normally indifferently grouped with the 21st Dynasty yellow coffins.[54] Based on the same criterion, even objects dating from 18th Dynasty and showing clear features of the black type have been identified as belonging to the yellow type.[55]

In our view, this is too simplistic a way of looking at these objects as a cultural phenomenon. The fact that the box keeps being designed after the black scheme, with the background painted in yellow to imitate gilded foil, suggests that early Ramesside coffin decorators saw these objects as proper 'gilded' black coffins. A coffin set found in 2023 in Al-Gharifa (Tuna el-Gebel) shows a Ramesside burial within a rectangular box entirely coated with black pitch, both on the exterior and the interior walls, which is telling of how these objects were perceived. Nevertheless, unlike the coffins from the 18th Dynasty, the Ramesside boxes are flattened, which implies that they were no longer intended to be nested within a rectangular container.

These innovative inputs do not follow a consistent trend, implying an unstable design concept, where different degrees of interrelation of the festive dress layout with the traditional black type can be found. For this reason, we consider these objects as an intermediate category, actually closer to the black type than to the yellow corpus itself.[56]

Combining the black type with the festive dress layout was not a unilinear process and it involved several approaches and attempts, suggesting that different workshops approached this challenge in various ways. The evidence is here predominantly associated with the Theban necropolis. Our understanding of this process is severely limited by the small number of objects that have survived to the present. In the Theban Ramesside corpus alone, we have identified four main groups of coffins, which we label as A, B, C and D. Each one of these groups puts forward different ways of addressing the challenge of combining the festive dress type with the Osirian scheme of the black type and we will now briefly examine the features of each one of them.

Group A: coffins with lids showing the full-length depiction of the deceased in festive garments

This group gathers objects seemingly from Deir el-Medina (Plate 12). The coffin of Iset was found in the tomb of Sennedjem (TT 1). The coffin of Weretwahset (Brooklyn Museum, 37.47E-a), re-inscribed for Bensuipet, is said to have been found at Deir el-Medina and this is probably also the case for the coffin of Henutwati (Louvre Museum, E 18848).

These body containers reveal a heavy influence of the layout observed in the anthropoid coffins and sarcophagi of the late 18th Dynasty from Saqqara. As with the latter objects, they show the lid following the layout of the festive dress type and the sides designed after the black type. The result is a juxtaposition of both models in one single coffin.

However, unlike the body containers from Saqqara, these objects conserved the polychrome decoration. On the lid the deceased was clad in vivid white garments, with the skin painted in red regardless of his/her respective gender. More elaborate forms of these coffins show the deceased woman grasping a bunch of ivy leaves falling down the dress (Fig. 5.13).[57]

As usual, the box is painted in yellow, as an imitation of the gilded versions of the black type. This decorative scheme thus combined the chthonic imagery of the black type with the ideas revolving around the celebration of light embodied in the Amarnian festive dress type. The burial equipment of the mummies associated with these coffins included masks displaying festive wigs and floral collars.[58]

Group B: coffin sets with a full-length board showing the deceased in festive dress garments

Most of the coffins from this group were found in the tomb of Sennedjem (TT 1). Another coffin from this group, that of Paherpet, was found in the Royal Cache but, as with most of the coffins found there, it was reused from a previous burial.[59] In this group, the full depiction of the deceased in festive garments is displaced from the lid to an inner funerary plank that covered the mummy (Plate 13). This plank was seen as independent from the funerary mask, as the latter object is also found in these sets. The plank is provided with a footboard allowing its use in standing position, perhaps during the funerary rituals themselves.

The lid of the coffin shows the deceased again in fully Osirian guise, with only the braided wig as a faint reminder of the festive dress type. Most of its decorative features are designed after the black type scheme. For example, even the figures of Nephthys and Isis, typically found in the black type, are represented on the crown of the head and on the underside of the footboard (Fig. 5.14).[60]

This type of burial assemblage showing the deceased in festive garments on the funerary board and in mummiform shape on the lid seems to have been seen an established model, as it is reproduced even in shabtis (Fig. 5.5d).[61]

An interesting aspect of these sets is that the design of the lid is already evolving towards an arrangement in sections, which later will be a fundamental aspect of the yellow type. Actually, the most distinctive feature of this group is the design of the lower section and the footboard, where a variety of vignettes borrowed from the repertoire of the Book of the Dead is figured within the network of text bands. On Sennedjem's lid, the earliest of this group, two vignettes from the Book of the Dead were included over the footboard, featuring the deceased before the tree goddess (Fig. 5.14). On the proper left side, Sennedjem is figured with black hair, while on the right side he is depicted with grey hair, thus suggesting that he is represented both as a young and as an old man. These scenes provide the first attested examples of the use of the deceased's image

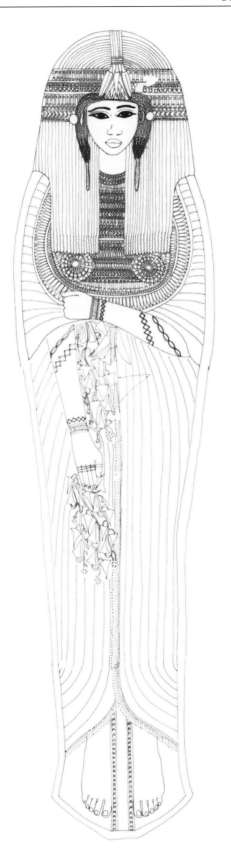

Fig. 5.13. Lid of Isis (National Museum of Egyptian Civilization, Cairo, JE 27309). Drawing by the author.

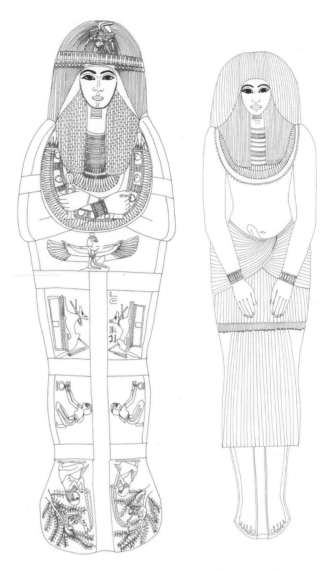

Fig. 5.14. Lid and full-length board of Sennedjem (National Museum of Egyptian Civilization, Cairo, JE 27308). Drawing by the author.

depicted as a living person (and not in mummiform guise) in the iconographic repertoire of the coffin.

These truly revolutionary scenes are shown on the coffin exactly in the same way as they are painted on the walls of the burial chamber and in the vignettes of the Book of the Dead (Plate 11). Integrating the depiction of the deceased as a living person in the iconographic repertoire of coffin decoration had important consequences, and with it an association with the repertoire of Book of the Dead was triggered, allowing in a very literal way the transfer of the scenes previously featured on tombs to the coffin's walls.[62]

The use of tomb scenes in coffin decoration, first witnessed in Sennedjem's coffin, was quickly expanded to the coffins of his family. In the coffin of Iyneferty,[63] the wife of Sennedjem, the lower section of the lid already presents a wealth of scenes borrowed from the repertoire of the

Book of the Dead, combined with more mundane banquet scenes, precisely as they are figured on Sennedjem's tomb walls, an exceptional circumstance that will remain unique to this group.

Besides the rich repertoire of scenes, this group excels in the pictorial resources it uses. The vivid compositions attest to the quality of the painters involved in this work, which are possibly the very same artists who worked on the decoration of the tomb of Sennedjem itself. The inner surfaces of these coffins are coated in black pitch, but on the exterior transparent varnish is used instead. This seems to be a Ramesside technical innovation. These are the first coffins where the use of varnish is well attested. It consists of pistacia resin, a substance also used as incense in temple ritual and which conferred the gleaming yellow colour, a godlike radiance, to the deceased.[64] The varnish would literally 'make divine' the deceased, hence its importance in coffin decoration.[65]

The provenance of most of these coffins from one single burial ground, TT 1, suggests that they have been produced to be used within the community of the villagers of Deir el-Medina.[66] Unlike the former examples, whose scheme remained relatively stable, the coffins from Group B result from an entirely experimental process, where the focus of this innovative input is concentrated on the lower section and the footboard of the lid. The vignettes displayed in these sections completed those of the burial chamber, and established an interplay between the coffin and the tomb that would be decisive to foster what René van Walsem labelled as 'architectonisation' of coffins,[67] i.e., the design of coffins provided with different symbolic spaces, a feature that will be further developed in the yellow type and in the stola corpus.[68] In other words, these vignettes attest that the coffin is no longer seen as just a body container, regarded as a sacred space in itself, but rather in symbolic/magical association with the tomb. This is particularly clear in the association between the lid of the coffin, the lid of the funerary canopy and the ceiling of the burial chamber (Plate 11). Each one of these elements was identified with the heavenly realm, in which the deceased is depicted in priestly garments (as he/she figures in the funerary plank).[69]

In this process, it is important to acknowledge the paramount role of the craftsmen themselves. Far from just following well-established trends, these craftsmen were creating an entirely new one. The fact that these craftsmen were involved in the creation of their own burial equipment and tomb must have played an important role to enhance the use of the Book of the Dead imagery in the decoration of coffins.

The burial equipment found in the tomb of Sennedjem documents how this process quickly evolved in a period of just two generations, suggesting that innovations seem to be mastered by the craftsmen themselves, who assessed the results of their own work and quickly foresaw innovative developments that were designed after their own expectations.[70]

Although it is likely that these highly skilled craftsmen may have worked for other people than their own family, the evidence of their activity outside Sennedjem's tomb is scarce, which suggests that their production may have been restricted to the circle of Deir el-Medina.

Group C: coffin sets with an open-work funerary board

Also dating from the early Ramesside period, another group of coffins has a most distinctive feature: the use of an open-work board that covers the lower part of the mummy (Plate 14). This object derives from the burial equipment of the black type, where it was used to include the depiction of the Sons of Horus in open-work.[71] In the Ramesside sets, however, this repertoire includes the deceased, who are shown in ritual scenes before the deities of the underworld, attired in festive garments.[72]

The arrangement of the scenes in the open-work boards usually follows a well-established pattern. Heading the object is the winged goddess Nut with her arms outstretched all along the width of the board. Two lateral partitions are figured below, showing a symmetrical arrangement. In the first register, the god Thoth offers the $wd3t$-eye to an enthroned god. There follow three registers below showing the deceased before the deities of the underworld. The object normally includes a small footboard featuring the mourning goddesses in reversed position. Another interesting feature of these open-work boards is the use of a linen canvas on the reverse side of the object, which once provided a vivid white background to the gilded/yellowish framework.

As with the sets from Group B, these assemblages are keen to include the deceased in the iconographic programme. However, while the former show the deceased in the vignettes that are displayed over the lid, the latter tend to show him/her in the open-work board, thus in the innermost object of the set.

The equipment of these sets is complemented with a funerary mask. The layout of this object is also interesting as it is actually an extension of a normal mask, depicting the head, collar and upper torso, including the forearms and hands.[73] Below the hands, which are crossed over the chest, is normally depicted a naophoric pectoral. In short, this 'mask' is nothing less than a shorter version of the full-length boards showing the deceased in festive dress garments as they were used in the sets in Group B. Due to this drastic reduction in size, the arms of the deceased are always crossed over the chest and not displayed along the body, as in the latter.

Unlike the sets in Group B, which normally use one single coffin, these assemblages often involve two coffins, as we see in the set of Tamutneferet (Louvre Museum, Paris, N 2631, N2571, N 2623, N 2620). Like the objects from Group B, these coffins show the deceased wearing the braided festive wig, a large floral collar and a winged goddess over the abdomen. However, in Group C the skin of the deceased is no longer painted in red: either it is gilded or it is painted yellow.[74] It is likely that some of these have been coated with varnish.[75]

Another major distinction from the objects in Group B is in the design of the lower section, where there is no consistent pattern: it can be shown either completely devoid of vignettes, or with these usually referring to the Sons of Horus or Osiris. These deities are always shown in centripetal direction, a rule that will be discontinued in the yellow type. The interior of the coffins is coated in black pitch.

The most distinctive feature of the sets from Group C is their affinity with the craftsmanship of the black type.[76] The combined use of a mask and an open-work funerary board directly follows the tradition of the black coffins from the 18th Dynasty. However, both the mask and the open-work board are updated after the inputs put forward by the festive dress type. The mask is extended to show the deceased clad in festive garments down to the abdomen, and the open-work board includes scenes where the deceased is featured in gala dress.

This suggests that the Theban workshops that previously mastered the production of black coffins were integrating the new design into their own schemes. As usual, these workshops worked for the Theban high elite, which is clearly documented by the use of gold found in some of these objects. In contrast to the coffins from the Group A and B, the pictorial work is not particularly good. However, its rudimentary use is somehow compensated by the sculptural work carried out in the open-work boards. Certainly not by chance, this aspect has always been mastered in the workshop tradition of the black coffins. Despite the above-mentioned innovations, the layout of these sets is much more conservative than those from Group B.

Group D: coffin sets with a mummy-board

By the mid-20th Dynasty, other transformations occur, again focused on the mummy-board (Plate 15).[77] At this stage, a full-length board reappears. In the earliest objects of this kind, a small footboard is preserved,[78] while in those of later dating, the footboard is completely excluded. Two types of design are attested in these objects.

The simplest layout presents the deceased with a long wig and a collar, with the rest of the body simply painted in white, and, at times, a long red belt, as an oversimplification of the festive dress planks discussed in the later forms of Group B.[79] This stylized depiction of the deceased in festive garments excluded the depiction of the feet, simply suggested by a short footboard, also painted in white. However, the most interesting aspect of these objects is the adoption of two motifs previously featured in the masks and boards of the sets from Group C: the winged goddess, usually seen

in the upper part of the open-work board, is here associated with the naophoric pectoral featured on the funerary masks, creating a composition with two registers.[80] This composition is the basic scheme of the central section of the yellow type, and shows that a new layout is taking shape. This trend was relatively short-lived and by the beginning of the 21st Dynasty it fell into disuse.

In the more elaborate boards, we find an even more extensive influence of the design of the masks and boards from the sets of Group C.[81] Thus, the upper section follows the design of the mask, showing the deceased wearing the braided wig and a large floral collar. The lower section of the mummy-board displays two longitudinal partitions where the deceased is figured in adoration scenes before the deities of the underworld, precisely as he/she was depicted in the open-work boards. The earliest mummy-covers of Group D conspicuously preserve a small footboard, as the open-work boards used in the Group C. As in the objects previously mentioned, the central section is formed by gathering the winged goddess that used to figure on the top of the open-work board with the sacred pectoral that figured at the lower part of the mask.

The creation of the mummy-board with the juxtaposition of the mask and open-work boards had already been suggested by Gábor Schreiber, who arrived at that conclusion through examination of the many fragments of cartonnage boards from the 20th Dynasty in TT 400.[82] With the rise of this kind of mummy-board, the funerary mask is for the first time excluded from the burial assemblages, which suggests that the magical role of these boards overlapped that of the masks.

This scheme of decoration detected in the mummy-board eventually dictated the layout of the lid itself, giving it the basic layout later maintained in the yellow type.[83]

A coffin set found in 2023 at Al-Gharifa (Tuna el-Gebel) provides an interesting glimpse of the importance that the mummy equipment from Group C played in this process. This is a Ramesside burial with a box entirely coated with black pitch, both on the exterior and interior walls. The mummy is equipped with an extended mask showing a ceremonial wig, a pleated garment and a large pectoral hanging from the chest. The open-work board shows the typical decoration showing the deceased before Osiris on the first register. Noteworthy is the abundant use of varnish which is rare in the Theban corpus that we are familiar with. However, the most interesting object of the set is the lid which is coated in black pitch and outlined in yellow, already showing features of the yellow type, namely the central section designed after the basic scheme. Moreover, the face is painted in green, and the eyes are inlaid. This provincial object, crafted for a chantress of Thoth from Hermopolis, shows that the new trends put forward in Thebes were being used elsewhere, as the main pieces of the burial were the objects that covered the mummy: the mask and the board. The box was left undecorated (which is perhaps a local trend?) but the decoration of the lid is clearly designed after the features of the mummy equipment, clearly resulting from the combination of the design of both objects.

In the Theban coffins, the layout of the boxes keeps repeating the black type, but this scheme would soon be challenged and the monotonous set motifs typically used in the black type replaced by an enormous wealth of new subjects, both on the exterior and the interior walls.[84] The interior of the boxes is for the first time decorated with the goddess of the West, showing a clear input from royal archetypes.[85] Altogether, these changes are the first true forms of the yellow type.

Coffins, workshops and craftsmen

When we look at the deep changes that occurred in coffin craftsmanship during the New Kingdom, it becomes clear that these different models involved entirely different ways of managing funerary workshops.

Black coffins required highly skilled carpenters, who truly carved the coffin as a 'hollow statue'. The planks were carved organically according to the shape of the planks themselves, combining the available materials with the desired shapes. Pieces of imported wood could, on occasion, be added separately to form the face or the hands, but as a rule these features were carved directly on the structural planks of the object. In the decoration of the coffins, these workshops used plaster, with which they moulded the texts and images in relief, and gold leaf, to cover the decoration, or the entire coffin, if it was gilded. Occasionally glass and stones were used to inlay the eyes, cosmetic lines, the straps of the wig or other details. A stable scheme of decoration, entirely codified by ritual needs, defined with accuracy the key features included in the coffin, and so the carpenters involved in the manufacture of the black coffins had a very clear idea of what would be expected from their work. These objects were commissioned privately and certainly affordable only for the highest elite. Given the high levels of standardization detected in these objects, it is unlikely that the commissioner had anything to say about the features of the coffin itself. However, the depiction of heart amulets, which at this time was a royal decoration,[86] may point to a certain degree of individualization of the decorative programme.

The materials used in the black coffins were selected having in mind the performance of the ritual of coating the coffin with black pitch. These materials, such as the gilded foil, could be covered with this dark resin without being hidden by it. Coffins that did not use gilded foil had to be 'ready' when leaving the workshop, and that prevented the re-enactment of the ritual of giving gleaming light to the coffin which was probably a very important step of the funerary ritual. It was precisely in these cheaper objects that painting

was sporadically used, and the first examples of coffins painted with yellow ground were produced to imitate gilded decoration. Due to this association, painting remained a 'poor' resource used in workshops that worked for the lower elite. These workshops certainly followed the traditions associated with the production of the white or the *rishi* coffins, produced in the early 18th Dynasty.

Black coffins were introduced during the reigns of Hatshepsut/Thutmose III in close association with the rich imagery related to the Book of the Amduat and to the Book of the Dead, which began to play such a paramount role in the funerary visual culture of the period.[87] Although rooted in previous developments, black coffins were put forward as a consistent model, fully equipped with the texts, images and materials that would be needed for the deceased's everlasting manifestation as an Osirian deity of the netherworld. In this model innovations were introduced *from above*, i.e., workshops received instructions from the kingly circles to produce coffins with the desired specifications. Thus, besides the obvious religious meaning, this model was deeply imbued with an ideological and political significance, contributing to define the status of the owner in regard to the pharaonic power structure of this time.

Another example of how innovations were introduced *from above* is provided by the festive dress coffins, during the reign of Akhenaten. Once again, the coffin layout is entirely reshaped in light of theological concepts serving ideological purposes under the reform put forward by this king. Although at this stage we cannot actually know how these coffins were crafted, as none have survived,[88] it seems clear that in terms of the organization of work they would not differ so much from the previous ones: also here the coffin would have to be crafted by carpenters as a 'hollow statue'. The main difference is that these workshops used paint to finish off their objects, instead of black pitch. As black coffins, the festive dress containers were crafted for the highest elite, and, as the former, were highly political objects, signalling the owner as someone close to the king, and conveying a vision of the hereafter where the deceased's deification was abolished. This might be the very reason why they disappeared from the archaeological record so drastically.

After the Amarnian reform, an interesting phenomenon occurred in terms of art history. This seems to have first taken shape in Saqqara.[89] Here, the revolutionary ideas put forward during Akhenaten's reign were not forgotten, as a conscious effort was carried out to adapt and bring them into the traditional Osirian framework. These efforts are first visible in the creation of anthropoid sarcophagi where the box was designed after the black type and the lid was shaped after the festive dress type. The intensity of the plundering activity focused on the New Kingdom tombs from Saqqara led to the almost complete eradication of contemporary wooden coffins from the archaeological record. However, there is enough evidence showing that a similar phenomenon took place in the craftsmanship of wooden coffins. These body containers were at least partially painted, and remnants of varnish have been found on them.[90]

From the point of view of material funerary pragmatics, during the Ramesside period the most important developments in coffin decoration are observed in the Theban necropolis. The integration of the festive dress coffins in Thebes probably took place after the arrival of new settlers in Deir el-Medina, in the beginning of the 19th Dynasty, giving rise to what we label the 'proto-yellow' coffins, i.e., objects showing the box designed after the black type and the lid displaying in varying degrees the deceased in festive garments. It is in this corpus that we find further and far more subtle attempts to achieve a meaningful synthesis between the black type and the festive dress coffins.

The examination of the proto-yellow corpus allowed us to isolate the activity of different groups of artisans. Groups A and B are obviously related to each other, and they seem directly related to the settlement of Deir el-Medina. Coffins from Group B seem to derive from the layout of Group A, which itself evolved from the developments carried out in Saqqara during the end of the 18th Dynasty. The introduction of coffins from Group A in the Theban necropolis thus seems to have resulted from the adoption of models put forward in the North, probably as the result of the arrival of new settlers in Deir el-Medina during the reign of Seti I. This may well have been the case of Sennedjem's family, whose burial equipment reveals a clear influence of the northern model.

The coffins from TT 1, especially those belonging to Group B, show a masterful combination of sculptural and pictorial work. A few techniques used in the black corpus are still used, such as the moulding of the texts in plaster, and the use of black pitch to coat the interior of the boxes. However, the breadth and scope of the pictorial work is unprecedented, both in the techniques and in the innovative arrangement of the design.

From a technical point of view, the most distinctive feature of the objects from Group B is the outstanding polychrome decoration covered by shiny yellowish varnish. The use of this coating material is deeply embedded in the magical search for solarization of the funerary equipment and was supposed to replicate the gilded decoration. Moreover, this varnish consists of *pistacia* resin, a substance also used as incense in temple ritual.[91]

Technically speaking, the use of varnish in coffin decoration had major consequences, as it had the advantage of adding gleaming light to the object, without hiding the pictorial work, as black pitch did. This transparent coating material allowed the coffin to be used literally as a canvas and, from this moment onwards, there is a clear input of techniques introduced by painters in coffin decoration. Furthermore, this gleaming coating stabilized the pigments,

allowing the depiction of minute details which would simply fade away without this protection.

This coating material was thus used as a substitute for black pitch as it could also be added during the rituals themselves. In the 'yellow' corpus the evidence of the selective use of varnish abounds, especially in inner objects such as the inner walls of the boxes or the mummy-boards, where often only the inscriptions and the deities are coated.[92] We certainly could not witness the outstanding development in the pictorial work of the coffins from the Ramesside period onwards without this technical innovation.

To put it simply, the coffins from Group B reveal a masterful use of varnish combined with skilful pictorial work, which is telling of the technical resources of these craftsmen. The use of these technical innovations betrays the deep engagement of coffin decorators in techniques associated with painting materials, which was only possible in a community of highly skilled artisans living next to each other. Moreover, they were able to put forward innovations created by themselves and for their own use.

Coffins from Group B thus provide a very interesting case regarding the impact of innovations introduced *from below*, i.e., from the artisans themselves and for their own use. This is the beginning of a new trend, which did not cease to grow during the 20th Dynasty and remained active throughout the 21st Dynasty, in which workshops seem to be increasingly autonomous and free to implement innovations and make conscious decisions on the layout of coffins.

The coffins from Group C seem to be contemporary with those from Group B. The workshops that produced these objects are deeply rooted in the Theban tradition of the black coffins and seem to be their natural followers. These workshops are more familiar with the use of precious materials than with varnish, and it is possible that they still may have used black pitch. Although paying attention to the innovations put forward by the artisans from Group B, namely by adopting the deceased in the iconographic programme of the open-work boards, the craftsmen in Group C produced less innovative objects. Moreover, the use of the deceased's images mostly in the open-work boards, thus in a hidden location, suggests a certain 'unease' in the use of this innovative repertoire.

Although objects from Groups B and C might have been produced separately, the subsequent use and reuse of these materials dictated some kind of osmosis between them. This is detectable in the coffin set of Weretwahset (Brooklyn Museum, 37.47E-a), where a coffin from the Group A was used together with a mask and open-work board that would be otherwise typical from a set of Group C. The differences in style and craftsmanship speak for themselves and clearly show that this set results from an opportunistic assemblage of objects with different provenances, which is consistent with the evidence of the reuse of the object (re-inscribed for Bensuipet).

In other situations, we may witness a certain 'contamination': features of one group may eventually influence the production of another one. In Group B, which excels in innovation, the coffin set of Khonsu, a son of Sennedjem, is the only one of this group to use a nested assemblage of two coffins: instead of a full-length board showing the deceased as living, the set uses an inner coffin. This solution seems clearly to have been borrowed from Group C and adapted to the specific pictorial setting of this workshop.

This 'contamination' eventually dictated the fusion of both traditions. The objects from Group D, which are the first true yellow coffins, reflect this new reality in the Theban workshops. First, they show the unification of the main trends previously in use in the Theban necropolis. The mummy-board, a defining object of the yellow type, was introduced in the archaeological record by combining the layout of the mummy-boards from Groups B and C: over the stylized depiction of the deceased in festive garments, the features of the funerary mask and the open-work board used in Group C were imprinted, creating a new arrangement. The layouts of the lids of these coffins were consequently dictated by this new design reached on the mummy-board.

The increasing coherence and consistency detected in the scheme of decoration of this emerging trend suggest that Theban workshops became unified or centralized in some way. This implies that the workshops from the late Ramesside period gathered the royal craftsmen from Deir el-Medina and the artisans who previously worked for the Theban high elite. In this process, it is clear that the inputs from the latter workshops played an important role: the pattern of using double sets of coffins was adopted in the yellow coffins, as well as the prevalent use of yellow to paint the skin of the deceased and the depiction of the crossed forearms. And more than anything else, the layout of the lid/mummy-board followed the combined layout of the mask and the open-work board.

These elements show that the traditions from Group C were fully acknowledged in this integration. However, the role that innovation plays in the yellow type betrays the prevalence of the royal artisans of Deir e-Medina in these workshops. This is particularly clear in the arrangement of the decoration in autonomous sections, both in the lid and the box. Each of these sections is treated as a composition of its own, revealing a remarkable degree of autonomy and a consistent set of rules, key features and principles of composition. This codification is one of the most distinctive features of the yellow type and one that shows the prevalent role performed by painters in this emerging type of coffins.[93] Moreover, the input from tomb decoration was transferred from the lid to the box, and from then onwards the design of the box leaves the scheme typically used in the black type, embracing the limitless visual repertoire of tomb decoration and funerary papyri.

Given the extension of the iconographic repertoire used in yellow coffins, it is clear that these workshops were managed by an educated elite, one that was familiar with royal compositions. In our view, these craftsmen could not be other than the artisans of the pharaoh from Deir el-Medina.

Once established, the layout of the yellow type was the most complex ever seen in Egyptian coffin decoration. Unlike previous models of coffins, the yellow type does not have a static model. With the layout of the objects carefully arranged in autonomous sections, innovative inputs were continuously added to the composition, either by joining new key features or by changing the layout of the scenes. The seriation of these compositions clearly reveals that innovations were not introduced randomly and that new arrangements were always built upon the former developments.[94] So much so that each single 'yellow' coffin presents a distinctive layout. The evolving nature of the yellow type thus played a crucial role in its craftsmanship.

Due to this *modus operandi*, the scheme of decoration of the yellow type continued to be continuously expanded during the 21st Dynasty, reaching levels of extreme complexity. The craftsmanship of these objects truly became a cutting-edge industry, presenting an entirely different nature from the phenomenon previously observed in Theban coffin decoration.

In the first place, the tremendous growth of complexity required a totally different organization of labour. The number of key features ruling each sector of a coffin was already so high that a careful plan of the coffin as a whole was required. All these factors combined would risk turning coffin decoration into a chaotic enterprise. However, such risk was mitigated by establishing very clear principles ruling the composition of each section and by implementing methods for introducing innovations. This allowed both to avoid entropy and to make progress in reaching increasingly higher levels of complexity.

As suggested elsewhere, these developments would certainly require a separation of the workshops of the painters from those of the carpenters.[95] On one hand, the workshops of the painters grouped the privileged circle of master artisans, who were deeply knowledgeable in the iconographic and textual repertoire of tomb decoration, funerary papyri and temple decoration that was formerly used during the Ramesside period. Moreover, the miniaturization implied in the pictorial work of coffins required outstanding technical skills, which was further enhanced by the introduction of the use of *pastiglia*. In contrast to this level of expertise, carpenters perform a totally secondary role, so much so that the carpentry techniques involved in the manufacture of the coffins became highly standardized and unspecific.

As ever, coffins still play a strong socio-political role in Thebes. However, this function is no longer dictated by the pharaoh, and rather reflects the direct association of the individual with the sacred dimension. In other words, the emerging yellow coffins manifest the ideals of personal piety regarding the afterlife. In a way, they can be seen as a funerary development of this religious trend that shaped the cultural atmosphere of the Ramesside period.[96]

It is most interesting to find this phenomenon rooted in the reign of Tutankhamun. The royal artisans – the very same ones who worked in Amarna for Akhenaten[97] – created a synthesis in Saqqara between the black and the festive dress type and that would deeply shape the subsequent cultural evolution that took form during the Ramesside period under the skilful work of their descendants, who settled in Deir el-Medina during the reign of Seti I.[98] This learned synthesis allowed Ramesside craftsmen to achieve a new agency, becoming the leading protagonists in a process that would deeply renovate the Egyptian funerary material culture and prevent it from falling into an endless repetition of the old traditional schemes.

The body of light: on the meaning of black pitch, gold and varnish

All these features suggest that this highly skilled community of painters had successfully incorporated the know-how of the Ramesside tomb decorators into the manufacture of coffins. The very significance of the yellow background in these objects betrays the deep engagement of these artisans in tomb decoration. At Saqqara, the high elite necropolises dating from the late 18th Dynasty include superb examples of monochromatic decoration in the underground chambers,[99] showing the magnificent reliefs uniformly painted in yellow. These innovations will be further developed in Deir el-Medina, in the so-called monochrome tombs, all of them dating from the early 19th Dynasty.[100] In these tombs, the burial chambers are decorated with scenes outlined in black against a white background and summarily painted in yellow. This monochrome style is even detected in royal tombs, seemingly with the purpose of suggesting gilded decoration,[101] normally associated with shrines holding deities of the netherworld. Plate 16 shows a section of painted decoration from the tomb of Seti II (KV 15), where a full set of these shrines is presented. This set includes the jackal form of Anubis, a king navigating a barque with a harpoon, a royal statue carried by a panther, the avian forms of the god Sokar and even the god Ihy playing the sistrum. Shrines exactly like these were conspicuously found in the so-called 'Treasury' of the tomb of Tutankhamun (Fig. 5.15b). Thus, yellow decoration seen in tombs, both royal and private, from the reign of Tutankhamun onwards is deeply rooted in the divine imagery of the Amduat which, before the reign of Tutankhamun, was associated with the use of black pitch, particularly in the Valley of the Kings, where it was used to coat the images of the divine beings of the netherworld. The Amarnian reform suspended this practice and the evidence provided by the tomb of Tutankhamun suggests that a new pattern emerged, with these deities covered in gold foil instead of black pitch to enhance the solarization of the netherworld.

Despite this prevalence of gold, black pitch is to be seen on a number of highly significant objects. The famous 'guardian statues' of Tutankhamun head this group of objects (Fig. 5.15a). Found in the antechamber and flanking the entrance to the burial chamber, they show a masterful combination of black pitch and gold foil, with the former used to coat the skin of the king and the latter used in the garments, adornments and cosmetic lines. This resourceful combination of gold foil and black pitch certainly enhanced the magical agency of both materials to irradiate light. The result is an outstanding depiction of Tutankhamun as a mighty king, as he is shown in possession of royal symbols of power and dignity, such as the long staff and mace. Moreover, their position is highly meaningful as they stand next to the ritual couches that stage the different moments in the re-birth process,[102] thus alluding to the newly born king in his nightly manifestation. This characterization of the king complements his depiction as a solar winged deity in the nested assemblage of *rishi* coffins kept in the burial chamber. It is noteworthy that, also in this latter context, black pitch was abundantly used to coat these objects, particularly the innermost golden coffin, as we mentioned above (Fig. 2.19, Plate 10).

This group of objects also includes an outstanding figure of the god Ihy, entirely coated in black pitch (Fig. 5.16). This statue of the infant god Ihy is particularly interesting, showing what can be truly considered as a divine manifestation of the king as a newly born god rising from the netherworld in his active manifestation as player of the sistrum, i.e., as a creator of music and harmony.

Other objects show the use of black pitch mainly associated with figurations of animal deities, such as the panthers carrying the king on their back (Fig. 5.15b) on his way through the netherworld. Other animal forms, such as the goose (Fig. 5.15c), the jackal form of Anubis (Fig. 5.15d) and the bovine head of Hathor (Fig. 5.15e) clearly refer to the association of these deities to the netherworld. The goose alludes to the primeval manifestation of Amun and his creative powers, while the jackal and the bovine forms allude to liminal aspects of the Theban necropolis as contact points with the netherworld. In all these objects, the use of black pitch enhances the association of these entities with the primeval regenerative powers of the netherworld.

All these elements show that the significance conferred to the black pitch during the first half of the 18th Dynasty was by no means reduced in the tomb of Tutankhamun, but it was in some way 'transmuted' into the materiality of gold. In this way, the prevalence of gold detected in the funerary materials of Tutankhamun, particularly in the shrines nested around the sarcophagus and in all the ritual objects set up in the burial chamber (Fig. 4.9), may well have been

a

b

c

d

e

Fig. 5.15. Wooden statues partially coated with black pitch. (a) Statue of Tutankhamun, Carter no. 22; (b) Royal statues over panthers, Carter no. 289; (c) Goose, Carter no. 176; (d) Anubis, Carter no. 261; (e) Hathor, Carter no. 264. Photos: © Griffith Institute, University of Oxford.

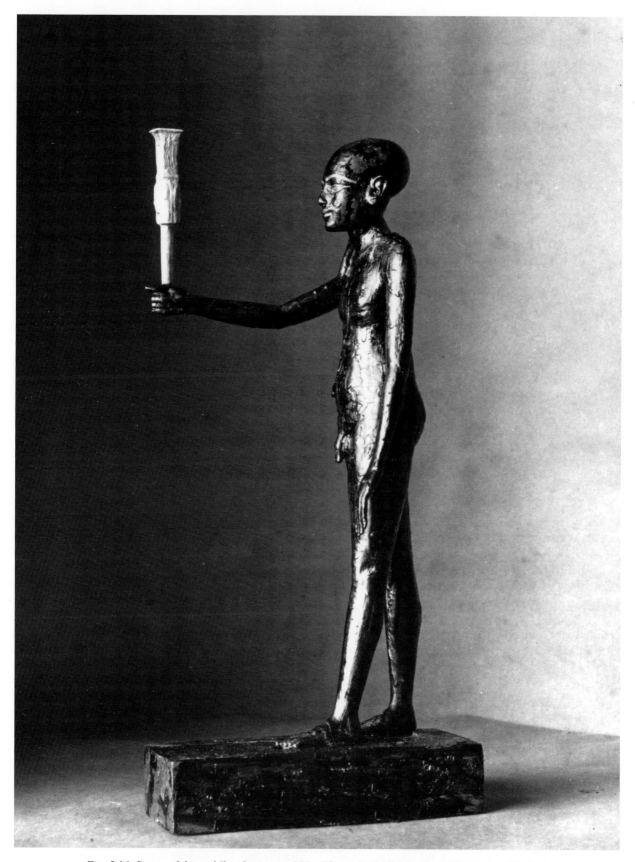

Fig. 5.16. Statue of the god Ihy, Carter no. 275a. Photo: © Griffith Institute, University of Oxford.

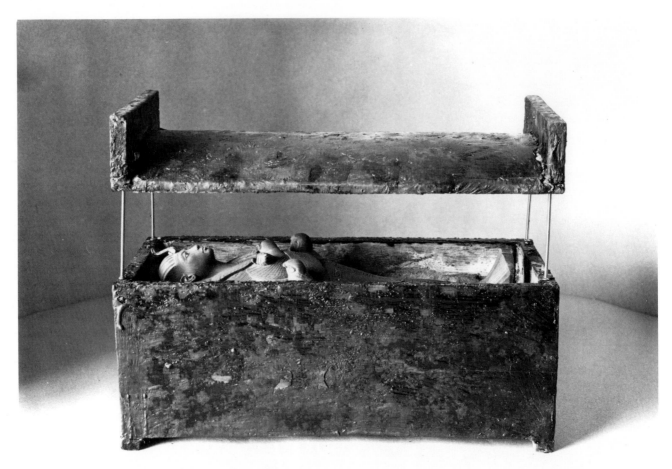

Fig. 5.17. Shabti figurine and model coffin, Carter no. 331a. Photo: © Griffith Institute, University of Oxford.

unprecedented.¹⁰³ Thus, previous royal burials probably may have used black pitch in much greater quantity than gold. The prevalent use of yellow paint both in tomb decoration and in coffins detected henceforth is obviously rooted in this same trend which aimed at expressing the solarization of the hereafter.

Black pitch, gold and varnish were thus used in association with light. All of these substances conferred a solar godlike radiance to the deceased, showing him/her as a deity irradiating sunlight. Interestingly enough, the treatment with varnish was not restricted to the coffin and was extended to the mummy itself, as Aidan Dodson pointed out of the materials from TT 1.¹⁰⁴ In fact, lavish use of resin in mummification is common in the New Kingdom, being applied both over the skin and inside the body cavities, such as the cranium. In the case of Tutankhamun, the consecration unguents poured over the mummy of Tutankhamun were in such quantity that it was firmly glued to the innermost coffin (Plates 9–10).¹⁰⁵ When unwrapped, the mummy of Tutankhamun revealed the same overabundance of black resin applied over the skin, giving it a very dark coloration and glow (Fig. 5.18). In this respect, the amount of resin

found in the royal mummy seems to have been unparalleled, even if we compare it with other royal burials. Moreover, this black resin also filled the space between the two coffins (Fig. 2.19). In a very literal way, resins seem to have been used in the burial of Tutankhamun to establish a magical link between the mummy and the coffin, as if the latter had become a radiant extension of the former.¹⁰⁶

The massive use of black pitch seems to be related to the funerary rites performed during the royal burial itself, perhaps in association with the Opening of the Mouth Ritual, as other ritual items surrounding the royal burial were found with the same treatment.¹⁰⁷ In short, black pitch (and later on varnish) seems to have been used as a magical substance to transform the body (and the items associated with it) into a radiant form, i.e., a body of light.

Contemporary faience shabtis, mummiform¹⁰⁸ or carved after the festive dress type,¹⁰⁹ show further evidence that might be helpful in understanding this trend, as they often bear the inscription *sḥḏ Osiris N.* ('To make shine the Osiris N.'), sometimes using the sun disk as determinative (N 8 in Gardiner's list) pointing out the solarization of the Osirian afterlife and depicting the deceased as a solarized god. The

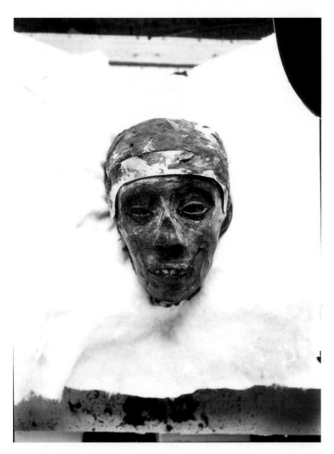

Fig. 5.18. The mummy of Tutankhamun (head). Photo: © Griffith Institute, University of Oxford.

use of faience in these objects is fully justified by its gleaming properties and even when terracotta is used varnish is sometimes added to assure a similar result.[110] Either through faience,[111] gold foil or black pitch, illumination and radiance were thus sought as the ultimate expression of a glorious afterlife and the gleaming coating provided to the funerary equipment expressed this pursuit of light, as expression of deification.

A similar idea is also expressed in Ramesside funerary figures by showing the deceased clad in festive garments,[112] at times embracing his own *ba*-bird, who nests himself over his chest (Fig. 5.5c).[113] At times these figurines seem designed as statues of the *ka* of the deceased (Fig. 5.5b),[114] but they actually may also be seen as shabtis as they can be depicted with hoes.[115] This ambiguity may well be the result of the original reading of these objects, which may have been designed by Akhenaten as substitutes for the traditional shabtis. Unlike the latter, these figurines would not serve the deceased in the Osirian Fields of *Iaru*, but they were probably crafted to replace him in the tasks involved in the sacred festivals of Akhetaten. The shabti of Hatsherit, dating from the reign of Akhenaten (Fig. 5.5a),[116] is a good

example of such an object. Figurines like these thus could have been seen as shabtis, although with a slightly different purpose: instead of working in the mythical fields of the netherworld, they were supposed to perform ritual tasks in the festivals of the Aten. This probably explains why this type of object was eventually integrated in the regular production of shabtis through the model of the overseer who, unlike the regular shabtis, is dressed in festive garments and it is not supposed to 'work'.

The shabtis depicting the deceased in festive garments thus seem to have been used to convey his solarized form, one under which he would go forth by day and through which he could engage himself in the temple activities.

Thus, the rise of yellow coffins should not be seen as an isolated phenomenon, but rather as the natural outcome of a broader trend, where the afterlife is designed as a realm of light. Under this inspiration, the depiction of the deceased in priestly garments was integrated in coffin decoration to highlight his/her agency in contact with the deities of the netherworld. Henceforth, the decorative scheme of anthropoid coffins became open to a dynamic, ever-changing process, where the deceased plays an active role before the gods and becomes himself/herself a divine being associated both with Osiris and the reborn sun. In short, yellow coffins feature the deceased as someone who not only goes forth to the light in his form of Ba, but as a truly illuminated being, who shines in the netherworld.

This same idea is consistent with the pictorial depiction of Ramesside coffins. As we noticed above, unlike black coffins, which are often depicted in tomb decoration in a very realistic way showing black background and many of their usual iconographic details, Ramesside murals show the mummy, rather than the container itself, as if the coffin had become invisible. This 'invisibility' of the coffin superbly reflects its association with light, as if the heavy pictorial compositions depicted in its walls formed nothing but a gleaming wrapping of light around the mummy itself, a phenomenon which Éva Liptay beautifully described as the 'transparency effect'.[117]

The yellow type of coffins revolves around the solarization of the netherworld, implying both the illumination of the body and the visibility of the Duat, and these aspects seem to result from the integration of solar beliefs in the Osirian framework. From the reign of Tutankhamun onwards, the royal tombs themselves showcased this transformation superbly, with the unseen dominance of polychrome decoration painted over yellow background.[118]

The scope of this transformation reveals how important the reign of Tutankhamun was to create a balanced and creative integration of originally antithetic visions, but also to firmly ground a new way to see the Duat as a realm of light. Despite his young age, the king himself must have been actively involved in this speculative trend, or at least very supportive of it, as his tomb is the first in the Valley of the Kings to showcase this new vision of the hereafter, not only in the mural decoration,[119] but also in its burial equipment. However, the most conspicuous piece of evidence of the personal involvement of the king in this process is found in the king's mummy itself, which stands out as a unique and extreme example of a black pitched body.[120] This 'gleaming body' truly became the core from which the enlightened form of the king would eventually rise to shine through the Duat, exactly as he is depicted in the so-called 'guardian' statues (Frontispiece).

In a way, the king's mummy figures as the most accomplished result of a religious transformation embraced by Tutankhamun himself, one that would entirely reshape the funerary material culture in Egypt until the beginning of the 22nd Dynasty. This silent legacy is perhaps the most accomplished endeavour of his reign.

Documental corpus

Black coffins

Anonymous coffin of a prince (From Deir El-Medina, JE 49549)

- Unpublished.

Anonymous coffin of a prince (Royal Cache, CG 61007)

- Daressy 1909, pl. X.

Coffin of Henutwedjbu (University Gallery of Art, Washington, inv. no. 2292)

- Kozloff, Bryan, Berman, and Delange 1993, 270–275.

Coffin sets of Kha and Merit (Museo Egizio, Turin, inv. no. S.8210/S.8516/S.8517/S.8429/ S.8470)

- Ferraris 2018, 56–65.
- Sousa 2019, 76–81.

Coffin sets of Yuya and Thuya. From KV 46 (Egyptian Museum, Cairo, inv. no. CG 51003-51006).

- Reeves, Wilkinson 1996, 177.
- Jouguet 1930, pls II–X.

Inner coffin of Maherpra (Egyptian Museum, Cairo, inv. no. CG 4219)

- Ikram and Dodson 1998, 211.

Sarcophagus of an unknown man reused for Psusennes I, from Tanis NRT III (Egyptian Museum, Cairo, inv. no. JE 85911)

- Ikram and Dodson 1998, 226.
- Montet 1951, pls XCIV–XCVII.

Coffin of Teti (Brooklyn Museum, inv. no. 37.14E)

- Bleiberg 2008, figs 34, 114.
- Dodson 2000.

Sarcophagi of Merymes (British Museum, London, inv. no. EA 1001)

- Kozloff, Bryan, Berman, and Delange 1993, 276–280.

Coffin of Kent (Museo Egizio in Florence, inv. no. 6526)

- Guidotti 2001, no. 1-A.
- Guidotti 2015, no. 66.

Coffin of Nebtaui (Museo Egizio in Florence, inv. no. 6525)

Coffin of Tentamentet (British Museum, EA 54521)

Fragment of coffin (Eton College Museum, Windsor, inv. no. 1876)

- Spurr, Reeves and Quirke 1999, 24.

Festive dress coffins

Coffin of Amenemhat (Metropolitan Museum of Art, New York, inv. no. 19.3.207a, b)

- https://www.metmuseum.org/art/collection/search/545660.

Coffin of Tairsekheru (Royal Museum of Scotland, Edinburg, inv. no. 1887.597)

- Taylor 1989, 37.
- Manley and Dodson 2010, 30–31.

Festive dress lids from Saqqara

Lid of anonymous man. Probably from Saqqara (Brooklyn Museum of Art, inv. no. 37.1520 E)

- Cooney 2007, figs 198–201.

Lid of anonymous man. Probably from Saqqara (Nationalmuseet, Copenhagen, inv. no. Aaa 67)

- Cooney 2007, fig. 205.

Lid of anonymous woman. Probably from Saqqara (Michael Carlos Museum, Atlanta, inv. no. L2003.14.38)

- Cooney 2007, fig. 206.

Anonymous male mask (Musées royaux d'Art et d'Histoire, Brussels, inv. no. E.6884)

- Cooney 2007, fig. 202.

Mask reused by Kanefernefer (Art Museum, St Louis, inv. no. 19:1998)

- Cooney 2007, fig. 287.

Proto-yellow coffins

Group A – Festive dress lid and black type box

Coffin of Isis. From TT 1 (National Museum of Egyptian Civilization, Cairo, inv. no. JE 27309)

- Malek, *Egypt*, 241.
- Saleh and Sourouzian 1987, fig. 218.

Coffin of Weretwahset *re-inscribed for Bensuipet* (Brooklyn Museum of Art, inv. no. 37.47E-a)

- Cooney 2007, figs 65–70.

Coffin of Henutwati. (Louvre Museum, Paris, inv. no. E 18848)

- Cooney 2007, figs 125–128.

Group B – coffin set with a festive dress full-length board

Coffin set of Sennedjem. TT 1 (National Museum of Egyptian Civilization, Cairo, inv. no. JE 27308)

- Cooney 2007, figs 96–105.

Coffin set of Iyneferty. From TT 1 (Metropolitan Museum of Art, New York, inv. no. 86.1.5)

- Cooney 2007, figs 54–62.

Coffin set of Tamakhet. From TT 1 (Ägyptisches Museum und Papyrus Sammlung, Berlin, inv. no. 10832)

- Cooney 2007, figs 54–62.

Coffin of Khonsu. From TT 1 (Metropolitan Museum of Art, New York, inv. no. 86.1.1 a–b)

- Cooney 2007, figs 130–138.

Coffin of Paherpet. From the Royal Cache (Egyptian Museum, Cairo, inv. no. JE 26223/CG 61022)

- Cooney 2007, figs 78–86.

Mummy-board of Khay (Musées Royaux d´Art et d´Histoire, Brussels, inv. no. E.6878)

- Taylor 1989, 71–74.

Mummy-board of Piay (Egyptian Museum, Cairo, inv. no. JE 2156)

- Cooney 2007, figs 75–76.

Anonymous male mummy-board. Auguste Rodin Museum, Paris (unknown number).

Group C – Coffin set with an open-work board

Coffin set of Tamutneferet (Musée du Louvre, Paris, inv. nos. N 2631, N2571, N 2623, N 2620)

- Cooney 2007, figs 38–53.

Coffin set of Henutmehyt (British Museum, London, inv. no. EA 48001)

- Cooney 2007, figs 1–20.
- Taylor 1999.

Coffin set of Takayt (Städtische Galerie Liebighaus, Frankfurt am Main, inv. no. 1651 a–f)

- Cooney 2007, figs 25–37.

Mask and board of Ram (Hermitage, St. Petersburg, inv. no. 787)

- Cooney 2007, fig. 124.

Yellow coffins

Group D – Coffin set with a mummy-board

Mummy-board of Hory (August Kestner Museum, Hanover, inv. no. 1977.1)

- Sousa and Loeben forthcoming.

Coffin of a child. From Bab el-Gasus (A.79). (Egyptian Museum, Cairo, inv. no. CG 6019/6020)

- Niwiński 1995, pl. 1.

Mummy-board of Khaemipet. Private collection of B.P. Harris

- Cooney 2007, fig. 213.

Coffin of Sitkames. From the Royal Cache (Egyptian Museum, Cairo, inv. no. JE 26220/CG 61011)

- Cooney 2007, figs 175–179.
- Daressy 1909, pl. XII.

Ramesside coffin from an intrusive deposit in TT 97. Present location unknown

Ikram and Dodson 1998, 228.

Coffin of Nesyamun (Leeds Museum, inv. no. D. 426–426a.1960)

- Niwiński 1988, 14.
- Cooney 2007, figs 187–191.

Coofin set of Panebmontu (Louvre Museum, Paris, inv. no. E 13029, 13046)

- Seipel 1989, nos. 472–473.

Coffin set of Tabasety (Museum of Ancient Art and Archaeology, Aarhus, inv. no. O 303)

- Sousa and Nørskov 2018.

Notes

1. I would like to acknowledge the precious contribution of Aidan Dodson for the careful review of this text. I also would like to thank to Maissara Hussein and Wolfram Grajetsky for the interesting discussions revolving around the materials from the tomb of Sennedjem.
2. Sousa 2020b, 1.
3. Coffin sets of Kha and Merit (Museo Egizio, Turin, S.8516/ S.8429/S.8470).
4. Mummy-board of Tjuiu, from KV 46 (Egyptian Museum, Cairo, no. CG 51011).
5. Mask of Merit (Museo Egizio, Turin, S. 8473).
6. Occasionally, the lid receives further decoration, such as the figure of Anubis in jackal form, the *wedjat*-eye or the mourning goddesses. See anonymous black coffin today in the British Museum, London, in Robins 1997, 147.
7. Taylor 2016, 52.
8. Taylor 2016, 53.
9. Taylor 1989, 34.
10. Coffin of Henutwedjbu (Washington University Gallery of Art, 2292); Coffin set of Kha (Egyptian Museum, Turin, S.8429, 8316/1).
11. Van Walsem 2014, 16. See burial assemblages of Yuya and Thuya (Egyptian Museum, Cairo, CG 51003–51006).
12. Fragment from the coffin of Amenhotep (Eton College Museum, Windsor, 1876), gilded inner coffin of Maherpra (Egyptian Museum Cairo, no. CG 24003-4). In anthropoid sarcophagi, this attribute is more often found: outer and inner sarcophagi of Merymes (British Museum, London, no. EA 1001), reused anthropoid sarcophagi of Psusennes I (Egyptian Museum, Cairo, no. JE 85911).
13. Van Walsem 1997, 29.
14. Sarcophagi of Merymes (British Museum, London, EA 1001).
15. Coffin of Merit (Museo Egizio, Turin, S.8470)
16. Coffin of Teti (Brooklyn Museum of Art, 37.14E).
17. Coffins of Kent and Nebtaui (Museo Egizio in Florence); Coffin of Tentamentet (British Museum, EA 54521).
18. Taylor 2010, 200–201.
19. Reeves and Wilkinson 1996, 98.
20. Ikram and Dodson 1998, 211.
21. Tomb of Pairi (TT 130); Tomb of Nebamun and Ipuki (TT 181).
22. Assmann 2003, 219–222.
23. Davies 1905.
24. Stevens 2018, 155. Anna Stevens also points out that in the same necropolis fragments with traditional deities had been bound. The fact that coffins were a rare commodity in Amarna may explain the persistence of the old schemes.
25. Martin 1989.
26. Sousa 2018, 33–37; 2019, 114–115; 2020a; Grajetzky and Sousa forthcoming.
27. Sarcophagus of Djehutymes (Kaiser Wilhelms-Universität, Strasbourg, no. 1393, Museo Camposanto, Pisa, 2) in Grajetsky and Sousa forthcoming.
28. Gender differentiation is episodically detected in Middle Kingdom funerary masks, but this seems to be the result of local innovations and did not seem to have played any role in the mainstream of coffin production: cartonnage masks of

a woman and a man from Asyut, 11th Dynasty (Pelizaeus Museum, Hildsheim, no. 6227/6226) in Eggebrecht 1996, 44–45. Gender differentiation of coffins is detected in the *rishi* corpus, particularly in the royal context: coffin of Queen Ah-hotep (Egyptian Museum, Cairo, no. CG 28501) in Hornung, Bryan 2002, 108–109. Again, this remained an exceptional feature.

29. Manley and Dodson 2010, 30–31.
30. Sousa 2018.
31. Saleh and Sourouzian 1987, fig. 171.
32. Coffin of Tentamentet (British Museum, London, EA 54521).
33. Shabti and model coffin of Amenhotep called Huy (Egyptian Museum, Cairo, JE 88902) in Saleh, Sourouzian 1987, fig. 151.
34. Unpublished (from Deir el-Medina, JE 49549). See also a child coffin from the Royal Cache (Daressy 1909, pl. X).
35. Stevens et al. 2019.
36. British Museum, EA 8644.
37. Note, in particular, the famous scene on the back of the throne of Tutankhamun where the queen's exposed skin is red, exactly as that of the king (Manniche 2016).
38. Sousa 2014.
39. A set of miniature coffins contained a lock of hair of Queen Tiye; see Reeves 1990, 168.
40. Sousa and Loeben forthcoming.
41. Reeves 1990, 72.
42. Sousa 2020b, 5–7; Grajetzki and Sousa forthcoming.
43. Taylor 1989, 39.
44. Brooklyn Museum of Art (37.1520 E), Nationalmuseet, Copenhagen (Aaa 67), Michael Carlos Museum, Atlanta (L2003.14.38).
45. The disappearance of the boxes may be due to the use of ordinary sycamore wood for these objects, which did not resist the poor conditions of preservation of these tombs. The resilience of the lids supposes a better quality of the wood used in their craftsmanship. The lid at the Michael Carlos Museum (inv. no. I.2003.14.38) is made of tamarisk (face) and yew (lower body) (Cooney 2017, 284).
46. It is likely that most of the undecorated objects have been cleaned by modern antiquities dealers aiming to highlight the high quality of the wood. See lid of anonymous woman (Michael Carlos Museum, Atlanta, I.2003.14.18).
47. See anonymous male lid (Brooklyn Museum of Art, 37.1520E), anonymous male lid (Nationalmuseet, Copenhagen, AA67) and coffin set of Ninetjer in Cooney 2017, 285.
48. Anonymous male lid (Museo Egizio, Turin, 5424), anonymous male lid (Christies 5488), fragment of male lid (Sale 2232, Lot 13) in Cooney 2017, 284.
49. Cooney 2017, 282.
50. Although used in royal context, thus integrated in a rishi coffin set, Tutankhamun's funerary mask is a good example of this new layout.
51. Sarcophagus of Khay (National Museum of Egyptian Civilization, Cairo, JE 36454 [lid]; 36525 [box]) in Grajetzky and Sousa forthcoming.
52. Sarcophagus of Senqed (Egyptian Museum, Cairo, unknown number) in Grajetzky and Sousa forthcoming.
53. Sarcophagus of Ramessu (Egyptian Museum, Cairo, JE 72203) in Saleh and Sourouzian 1987, fig. 200.

54 Niwiński 1988, 12–13.
55 Coffin of Teti (Brooklyn Museum of Art, 37.14E). See Dodson 2000.
56 Sousa 2018, 37–42; 2020b, 5–7.
57 Coffin of Isis (National Museum of Egyptian Civilization, Cairo, JE 27309).
58 See coffin set of Isis (National Museum of Egyptian Civilization, Cairo, JE 27309). The coffin of Weretwahset (Brooklyn Museum, 37.47E-a) is associated with a mummy adorned with a mask and an open-work funerary board showing patterns of craftsmanship which are otherwise consistent with Group B. As we will see below, this most likely is an association that resulted from a later reuse of objects with different provenance.
59 Daressy 1909, pl. XXIV; Cooney 2007, fig. 81.
60 Coffin set of Sennedjem (National Museum of Egyptian Civilization, Cairo, JE 27308).
61 Coffin and shabti inscribed for Amenmes. Friedman, Borromeo and Leveque 1998, 152.
62 Sousa 2018, 40.
63 Coffin set of Iyneferty. From TT 1 (Metropolitan Museum of Art, New York, inv. no. 86.1.5).
64 Taylor 2016, 57.
65 Incense's designation in Egyptian is *sntr*, 'that which makes divine'; in Taylor 2016, 57.
66 Valbelle 1985, 294–298.
67 Van Walsem 1997, 361.
68 Liptay 2017, 261.
69 Sousa 2019, 124.
70 Aidan Dodson relates the development of polychrome decoration in coffins with the development of this same trend in royal tombs, a phenomenon particularly clear during the reign of Seti I (Dodson 2000, 99–100).
71 Open-work funerary board of Tjuiu (Egyptian Museum, Cairo, no. CG 51011).
72 Funerary board of Henutmehyt (British Museum, London, EA 48001).
73 Mask of Henutmehyt (British Museum, London, EA 48001).
74 The mask and mummy-board of Ram figures as an exception to this rule (Hermitage, St Petersburg, no. 787).
75 Unpublished mask and open-work board found in October 2023 at Al-Gharifa, Tuna el-Gebel. This find suggests that the objects from Group C were taken as a model for other necropolises.
76 Sarcophagi carved after this layout are sometimes difficult to distinguish from a black-type sarcophagus. See sarcophagus of Bakenkhonsu in Liverpool Museum (M13864; Schmidt 1919, 122).
77 Occasionally, some lids show this layout. Coffin of a child (A.79: Egyptian Museum, Cairo, CG 6019/6020).
78 Mummy-board of Hory (August Kestner Museum, Hanover, inv. no. 1977.1).
79 Mummy-board from TT 97 in Ikram and Dodson 1998, 228.
80 Mummy-board of Khaemipet. Private collection of B.P. Harris. Mummy-board of Nesyamun (Leeds City Museum, D. 426–426a.1960) and mummy-board of Panebmontu (Louvre Museum, E 13029, 13046).
81 Mummy-board of Hory (August Kestner Museum, Hanover, inv. no. 1977.1).
82 Schreiber 2018, 199. However, he wrongly interpreted this design as deriving from the mummiform shape.
83 Coffin of Sitkames (Egyptian Museum, Cairo, no. CG 61011). Ramesside coffin from an intrusive deposit in TT 97 in Ikram and Dodson 1998, 228.
84 Mummy-board of Nesyamun (Leeds City Museum, D. 426–426a.1960) and mummy-board of Panebmontu (Louvre Museum, E 13029, 13046).
85 The depiction of the goddess of the West is first attested in the interior of the royal sarcophagi from the New Kingdom. See anthropoid alabaster sarcophagus of Seti I (Taylor 2017, 73–75).
86 Sousa 2011.
87 Bryan 2002; Hornung 2002.
88 Although some coffins have been uncovered recently in the South Tombs Cemetery, these cannot be representative of the burial customs of the highest elite from Amarna.
89 Van Dijk 2009.
90 Cooney 2017.
91 Taylor 2016, 57.
92 Mummy-cover of Tabasety (Museum of Ancient Art and Archaeology, Aarhus, no. inv. O 303).
93 Sousa and Hansen 2022, 4–5.
94 Sousa 2018. For a typology of these compositions, see Sousa 2020c, 2022.
95 Sousa 2023.
96 Assman 1997.
97 Löhr 1974, 186.
98 Hornung and Bryan 2002, 144.
99 Tomb of Maya in Saqqara. Martin 1991, 177–188.
100 Tombs of Khabekhnet (TT 2), Penbuy (TT 10), Khawy (TT 214), Paneb (TT 211), Neferabu (TT 5), Nebenmaat (TT 219) and Nakhtamun (TT 335); in Vandier 1935; Maystre 1936; Bruyère 1952.
101 Tomb of Seti II (KV 15); see enshrined images of the king in Reeves and Wilkinson 1996, 152.
102 See Schutz's chapter above in this book in her discussion on the ritual couches of Tutankhamun (Figs 3.9–11).
103 In the tomb of Seti II the same figures that in the tomb of Tutankhamun are coated in black pitch (note the god Ihy and the panthers (Figs 5.15b–5.16) appear painted in yellow, as if they were gilded (Plate). This suggests the intermutability of roles between gold and black pitch.
104 Dodson 2000, 99.
105 See Chapter 2; see also Ikram and Dodson 1998, 118.
106 The exceptional character of Tutankhamun's mummification can be detected in the very significance of the so-called 'embalming caches' associated with this king (KV 54 and KV 63). For the latter, see Sousa 2014.
107 See Chapter 2, the reference to the ritual Kiosks and *peseshkef* found in the Burial Chamber (Fig. 2.18).
108 Shabti of Khabekhnet, from TT 1; see Hornung and Bryan 2002, 143.
109 Shabti of Sunur; see Taylor, 2001, 123.
110 Shabtis of Padiamun, Khonsuemheb and Khonsumes from the Bab el-Gasus; in Sousa 2022, 432.
111 Some of the earliest attestations of faience shabtis are found in the tomb of Thutmose IV, together with the objects coated in black pitch; see Reeves and Wilkinson 1996, 107.

112 Sennedjem funerary figure (National Museum of Egyptian Civilization, Cairo, JE 27221/CG 4744); in Hornung and Bryan 2002, 144.

113 Shabti of Wepwautmes (National Museum of Antiquities, Leiden, AH 117). See also Shabti of Iuredef in Martin 1991, 137.

114 This is clearly the case of the figure crafted for Sennedjem. The statuette shows the deceased in festive garment, with his arms along the body in the *dw3* gesture also adopted in his mummy-board. An inscription reads: 'Everything which goes forth upon the offering table of Amun in *Ipt-Swt*, for the ka of Sennedjem, justified, happy in peace'; in Hornung and Bryan 2002, 144.

115 Shabti of Iuredef in Martin 1991, 137. The use of the Spell 6 of the Book of the Dead has not been attested by this author on these objects, but this use seems rather incompatible with the overall shape of the garments.

116 British Museum, London, EA 8644.

117 Liptay 2017, 269.

118 Dodson 2000, 100.

119 The tomb of Ay (WV 23) often said to be originally prepared for Tutankhamun, presents a similar layout although on a larger scale.

120 No other royal mummy has revealed such an amount of unguent coating as Tutankhamun's. In this respect it is interesting to note that the use of black coating in royal mummies during the 18th Dynasty is consistent with the rise of the black type of coffins, reaching its apex in Tutankhamun's burial. This use tends to decrease in Ramesside times.

Bibliography

Assmann, Jan. 1997. 'Gottesbeherzigung. Persönliche frömmigkeit als religiöse strömung der ramessidenzfjt'. In *L'Impero Ramesside. Convegni Internazionale in Onore di Sergio Donadoni*, 17–44. Vicino Oriente. Roma: Università degli Studi *di* Roma La Sapienza.

Assmann, Jan. 2003. *The Mind of Egypt: History and Meaning in the Time of the Pharaohs*. Cambridge and London: Harvard University Press.

Bierbrier, Morris. 1982. *The Tomb-builders of the Pharaoh*. London: British Museum Publications.

Bleiberg, Edward. 2008. *To Live Forever: Egyptian Treasures from the Brooklyn Museum*. Brooklyn and London: Brooklyn Museum, Giles Ltd.

Brunner-Traut, Emma, Hellmut Brunner and Johanna Zick-Nissen. 1984. *Osiris Kreuz und Halbmond: Die drei Religionen Ägyptens*. Mainz am Rhein: Verlag Philipp von Zabern.

Bruyère, Bernard. 1952. *Tombes Thébaines de Deir el Médineh à Décoration Monochrome*. Cairo: Institut Français d'Archéologie Orientale.

Bruyère, Bernand, and Charles Kuentz. 1926. *Tombes Thébaines. La nécropole de Deir-el-Medineh. La Tombe de Nakht-Min et la Tombe de d'Ari-Nefer*. MIFAO 54. Cairo: Institut Français d'Archéologie Oriental.

Bryan, Betsy. 2002. 'Art for the Afterlife'. In *The Quest for Immortality: Treasures of Ancient Egypt*, edited by Erik Hornung and Betsy Bryan, 52–73. Washington: National Gallery of Art.

Cooney, Kathlyn. 2007. *The Cost of Death: The Social and Economic Value of Ancient Egyptian Funerary Art in the Ramesside Period*. Egyptologische Uitgaven 22. Leiden: Nederlands Instituut voor het Nabije Oosten.

Cooney, Kathlyn. 2017. 'Ramesside Body Containers of Wood and Cartonnage from Memphite Necropolises'. In *Imaging and Imagining the Memphite Necropolis: Liber Amicorum René van Walsem*, edited by Vincent Verschoor, Arnold Jan Stuart and Cocky Demarée, 279–292. Leiden and Leuven: Nederlands Instituut voor het Nabije Oosten – Peeters Publishers.

Daressy, Georges 1909. *Catalogue Général des Antiquités Égyptiennes du Musée du Caire: Cercueils des Cachettes Royales (Nos 61001–61044)*. Cairo: Institut Français d'Archéologie Orientale.

Davies, Norman de G. 1905 (Reprinted 2004). *The Rock Tombs of El-Amarna*. London: The Egypt Exploration Society.

Delvaux, Luc, and Isabelle Therasse (eds). 2016. *Sarcophages. Sous les Étoiles de Nout*. Bruxelles: Musées royaux d'Art et d'Histoire.

Dodson, Aidan. 2000. 'The Late Eighteenth Dynasty Necropolis at Deir el-Medina and the Earliest Yellow Coffin of the New Kingdom'. In *Deir el-Medina in the Third Millenium AD: A Tribute to Jac. J. Janssen*, edited by Robert Demarée and Arno Egberts, 89–100. Egyptologische Uitgaven 14. Leiden: Nederlands Instituut Boor Het Nabije Oosten.

Eggebrecht, Arne (ed.). 1996. *Pelizaeus Museum Hildesheim: The Egyptian Collection*. Mainz: Verlag Philipp von Zabern.

Farid, Hany, and Samir Farid. 2001. 'Unfolding Sennedjem's Tomb'. In *KMT: A Modern Journal of Ancient Egypt*, 1–8.

Ferraris, Enrico. 2018. *La Tomba di Kha e Merit*. Turin: Museo Egizio.

Friedman, Florence, Georgina Borromeo and Mimi Leveque (eds). 1998. *Gifts of the Nile: Ancient Egyptian Faience*. New York: Thames and Hudson and RISD Museum.

Grajetsky, Wolfram, and Rogério Sousa. Forthcoming. 'Contextualizing the Sarcophagus of Khay (JdE 36454)'. In *From Objects to Histories: Studies in Honour of John Taylor*, edited by Nigel Strudwick and David Aston, 173–190. Wallasey: Abercromby Press.

Guidotti, Maria Cristina. 2001. *Le mummie del Museo Egizio di Firenze*. Firenze: Ministerio per i Beni e le Attivita Culturalli.

Guidotti, Maria Cristina. 2015. *Egyptian Museum of Florence: Masterpieces and More*. Livorno: Sillabe.

Hornung, Erik. 2002. 'Exploring the Beyond'. In *The Quest for Immortality: Treasures of Ancient Egypt*, edited by Erik Hornung and Betsy Bryan, 24–51. Washington: National Gallery of Art.

Hornung, Erik, and Betsy Bryan (eds). 2002. *The Quest for Immortality: Treasures of Ancient Egypt*. Washington: National Gallery of Art.

Ikram, Salima, and Aidan Dodson. 1998. *The Mummy in Ancient Egypt: Equipping the Dead for Eternity*. Cairo: The American University in Cairo Press.

Jouguet, Pierre. 1930. *Catalogue Général des Antiquités Égyptiennes du Musée du Caire (Nos 51001–51191): Tomb of Yuaa and Thuiu*. Cairo: Institut Français d'Archéologie Orientale.

Kozloff, Arielle, Betsy Bryan, Lawrence Berman and Elisabeth Delange (eds). 1993. *Amenophis III, le Pharaon-Soleil*. Paris: Réunion des Musées Nationaux.

Liptay, Éva. 2017. 'The Ancient Egyptian Coffin as Sacred Space: Changes of the Sacred Space during the Third Intermediate Period'. In *Proceedings of the First Vatican Coffin Conference, 19–22 June 2013*, Vol. 1, edited by Alessia Amenta and Hélène Guichard, 259–270. Vatican: Edizioni Musei Vaticani.

Löhr, Beatrix. 1974. 'Aḫanjāti in Memphis'. *Studien zur Altägyptischen Kultur* 2: 139–187.

Manniche, Lise. 2016. 'Body Colour in Amarna Art'. In *Artists and Colour in Ancient Egypt: Proceedings of the Colloquium Held in Montepulciano, August 22nd–24th, 2008*, edited by Valérie Angenot and Francesco Tiradritti, 60–71. Studi Poliziani di Egittologia 1. Montepulciano: Missione Archeologica Italiana a Luxor.

Martin, Geoffrey. 1989. *The Royal Tomb at El-'Amarna, Vol.* II. *The Reliefs, Inscriptions, and Architecture*. London: Egypt Exploration Society.

Martin, Geoffrey. 1991. *The Hidden Tombs of Memphis: New Discoveries from the Time of Tutankhamun and Ramesses the Great*. London: Thames and Hudson.

Maystre, Charles. 1936. *La Tombe de Nebenmât (No. 219)*. Cairo: Institut Français d'Archéologie Orientale.

Montet, Pierre (avec un chapitre et des notes d'Alexandre Lézine, Pierre Amiet, Édouard Dhorme). 1951. *Les Constructions et le Tombeau de Psousennès à Tanis*. Paris.

Niwiński, Andrzej. 1988. *21st Dynasty Coffins from Thebes: Chronological and Typological Studies*. Mainz am Rhein: Verlag Philipp von Zabern.

Niwiński, Andrzej. 1995. *Catalogue Général des Antiquités Égyptiennes du Musée du Caire: La Seconde Trouvaille de Deir el-Bahari (Sarcophages)*. Cairo: Conseil Suprême des Antiquités de l'Égypte.

Quibell, James Edward. 1908. *Tomb of Yuaa and Thuiu: Catalogue Général des Antiquitiés Égyptiennes du Musée du Caire, nos. 51001–51191*. Cairo: Imprimerie de l'Institut Français d'Archéologie Orientale.

Reeves, Nicholas. 1990. *The Complete Tutankhamun: The King, the Tomb, the Royal Treasure*. London: Thames & Hudson.

Reeves, Nicholas, and Richard Wilkinson. 1996. *The Complete Valley of the Kings: Tombs and Treasures of Egypt's Greatest Pharaohs*. London: Thames & Hudson Ltd.

Robins, Gay. 1997. *The Art of Ancient Egypt*. Cambridge: Harvard University Press.

Saleh, Mohamed, and Hourig Sourouzian. 1987. *The Cairo Egyptian Museum: Official Catalogue*. Mainz: Verlag Philipp von Zabern.

Schreiber, Gábor. 2018. 'Mummy-boards from a Theban Group Burial Dating to Dynasty 20'. In *Ancient Egyptian Coffins: Craft, Traditions and Functionality*, edited by John Taylor and Marie Vandenbeush, 186–200. Leuven, Paris and Bristol: Peeters Publishers.

Schmidt, Valdemar. 1919. *Sarkofager, Mumiekister og Mumiehylstre I det Gamle Aegypten*. København: J. Frimodt.

Schmidt, Valdemar. 2022. *Sarcophagi, Mummy Coffins, and Mummy Cases in Ancient Egypt: Typological Atlas*. Translated by Ziff Jonker. Albany: The Ancient Egyptian Heritage and Archaeology Fund.

Sousa, Rogério. 2011. *The Heart of Wisdom: Studies on the Heart Amulet in Ancient Egypt* (IS 2211). Oxford: British Archaeological Reports.

Sousa, Rogério. 2014. 'Coffins Without Mummies: The Tomb KV 63 in the Valley of the Kings'. In *Body, Cosmos & Eternity: New Research Trends in the Symbolism of Coffins in Ancient Egypt*, edited by Rogério Sousa, 197–203. Oxford: Archaeopress.

Sousa, Rogério. 2018. *Gleaming Coffins: Iconography and symbolism in Theban Coffin Decoration (21st Dynasty)*. Coimbra: Coimbra University Press.

Sousa, Rogério. 2019. *Gilded Flesh: Coffins and Afterlife in Ancient Egypt*. Oxford and Philadelphia: Oxbow Books.

Sousa, Rogério (ed.). 2020a. *Yellow Coffins from Thebes: Recording and Decoding Complexity in Egyptian Funerary Arts (21st–22nd Dynasties)*. Oxford: BAR Publishing.

Sousa, Rogério. 2020b. 'Anthropoid Coffins before the Yellow Type'. In *Yellow Coffins from Thebes: Recording and Decoding Complexity in Egyptian Funerary Arts (21st–22nd Dynasties)*, edited by Rogério Sousa, 1–10. Oxford: BAR Publishing.

Sousa, Rogério. 2020c. 'Yellow Coffins: Definition and Typology'. In *Yellow Coffins from Thebes: Recording and Decoding Complexity in Egyptian Funerary Arts (21st–22nd Dynasties)*, edited by Rogério Sousa, 11–26. Oxford: BAR Publishing.

Sousa, Rogério. 2022. 'The Lot XVI: An Overview'. In *The Tomb of the Priests of Amun: Burial Assemblages in the National Museum in Copenhagen*, edited by Rogério Sousa and Anne Haslund Hansen, 431–473. Gate of the Priests Series 2. Leiden and Boston: Brill Publishers.

Sousa, Rogério. 2023. 'Os ataúdes amarelos: as novas práticas oficinais tebanas da XXI dinastia'. In *Revista del Instituto de Historia Antigua Oriental* 24: 242–260.

Sousa, Rogério, and Anne Haslund Hansen (eds). 2022. *The Tomb of the Priests of Amun: Burial Assemblages in the National Museum in Copenhagen*. Gate of the Priests Series 2. Leiden and Boston: Brill Publishers.

Sousa, Rogério, and Vinnie Nørskov. 2018. 'Tabasety, the Temple Singer in Aarhus'. *Trabajos de Egiptologia: Papers on Ancient Egypt* 9, 207–224.

Sousa, Rogério, and Christian Loeben. Forthcoming. *The Egyptian Mummy Board of Hori at the Museum August Kestner in Hannover*. Hanover.

Spurr, Stephen, Nicholas Reeves and Stephen Quirke. 1999. *Egyptian Art at Eton College: Selections from the Myers Museum*. New York: The Metropolitan Museum of Art.

Stevens, Anna. 2018. 'Beyond Iconography: The Amarna Coffins in Social Context'. In *Ancient Egyptian Coffins: Craft, Traditions and Functionality*, edited by John Taylor and Marie Vandenbeush, 139–160. Leuven, Paris and Bristol: Peeters Publishers.

Stevens, Anna, Corina E. Rogge, Jolanda E.M.F. Bos and Gretchen R. Dabbs. 2019. 'From Representation to Reality: Ancient Egyptian Wax Head Cones from Amarna'. *Antiquity* 93: 1515–1533.

Taylor, John. 1989. *Egyptian Coffins*. Aylesbury: Shire Egyptology Series.

Taylor, John. 1999. 'Burial Assemblage of Henutmehyt: Inventory, Date and Provenance'. In *Studies in Egyptian Antiquities: A Tribute to T.G.H. James*, edited by William Davies, 59–72. Occasional Papers 123. London: British Museum.

Taylor, John. 2001. *Death and Afterlife in Ancient Egypt*. London: British Museum Press.

Taylor, John (ed.). 2010. *Death and the Afterlife in Ancient Egypt*. Chicago: University of Chicago Press.

Taylor, John. 2016. 'Coffins from the Middle Kingdom to the Roman Period'. In *Death on the Nile: Uncovering the Afterlife of Ancient Egypt*, edited by Helen Strudwick and Julie Dawson, 49–74. Cambridge and London: The Fitzwilliam Museum, D. Giles Ltd.

Taylor, John. 2017. *Sir John Soane's Greatest Treasure: The Sarcophagus of Seti I*. London: Pimpernel Press Ltd.

Valbelle, Dominique. 1985. *Les Ouvriers de la Tombe: Deir el-Médineh à l'Époque Ramesside*. Cairo: Institut Français d'Archéologie Orientale du Caire.

Van Dijk, Jacobus. 2009. 'The Death of Meketaten'. In *Causing His Name to Live: Studies in Egyptian Epigraphy and History in Memory of William J. Murnane*, edited by Peter Brand and Louise Cooper, 83–88. Leiden and Boston: Brill Publishers.

Van Walsem, René. 1997. *The Coffin of Djedmonthuiufankh in the National Museum of Antiquities at Leiden: Technical and Iconographic/Iconological Aspects*, Vol. I. Egyptologische Uitgaven 10. Leiden: Nederlands Instituut Boor Het Nabije Oosten.

Van Walsem, René. 2014. 'From Skin Wrappings to Architecture: The Evolution of Prehistoric, Anthropoid Wrappings to Historic Architectonic Coffins/Sarcophagi; Separate Contrasts Optimally Fused in Single Theban Stola Coffins (c. 975–920 BC)'. In *Body, Cosmos & Eternity: New Research Trends in the Symbolism of Coffins in Ancient Egypt*, edited by Rogério Sousa, 1–28. Egyptology Series 3. Oxford: Archaeopress.

Vandier, Jacques. 1935. *La Tombe de Nefer-Abou*. Cairo: Impremerie de l'Institut Français d'Archéologie Orientale.

6

'Absolutely new in type': the anthropomorphized signs on the monuments of King Tutankhamun

Ghada Mohamed

Abstract

Despite their prominence in different aspects of ancient Egyptian life, little attention has been paid to anthropomorphized forms of hieroglyphic signs. This distinctive form is a fundamental component in the ancient Egyptian writing system, and plays a key role, both iconographically and textually, in both ancient and modern cultures. Through anthropomorphism, inanimate signs acquire not only human limbs/characteristics, life and vital power, but also the ability to move, perform various tasks independently and consciously and replace/represent different persons. The aim of this paper is to discuss the objects and depictions that employ anthropomorphized signs, in both material from the tomb of Tutankhamun, and on other monuments dated to his reign, particularly at Karnak and Luxor. These include scenes of the anthropomorphized ankh, djed *and* was-*signs as bearers of fans, standards and sacred staves of the gods 'pꜣ mdw špsy', behind and/or before the king, or the pedestals of the sacred barques of the Theban triad in the reliefs of the Opet Festival. Furthermore, the single* ankh *holding a fan behind the king is found on the golden fan of Tutankhamun as well as on one of the embossed gold applications from his tomb. Additionally, the* ankh-*sign in this form was selected to replace one of the figures of an Amarna ruler, probably Tutankhamun, by a later king on the Third Pylon in Karnak. Interestingly, four unique anthropomorphized* ankh-*signs made of bronze, described by Carter as 'absolutely new in type', were found in the king's tomb and used as torch-holders to light the underworld for the king. Moreover, an* ankh *holding two* was-*sceptres is also a component in one of the king's magnificent alabaster vases.*

Examination of the significance, symbolism and function of these anthropomorphized signs on the monuments of Tutankhamun contributes to the study of traditional and innovative usages of this form of sign following the Amarna period.

Keywords: Tutankhamun, anthropomorphized signs, torch-holders, *ankh*, *djed*, *was*-signs

Introduction

Anthropomorphism, i.e., granting human attributes and characteristics, both in form and behaviour[1] to a non-human entity, is one of the means used by humans to reflect or imitate their own thoughts and actions on such elements (e.g., animals, plants and inanimate objects). It allows them to be integrated into similar (inter)active contexts to facilitate making use of them in their own environment or using them to achieve a specific purpose. A wide range of ancient and modern cultures have employed anthropomorphism in both textual and iconographic contexts. Despite ancient Egyptian hieroglyphs' widespread use, comparatively little attention has been paid to the symbolism and significance of their anthropomorphized form.[2] From Egypt's Pre- and Early Dynastic periods onward, anthropomorphized signs have played a prominent role, both iconographically and textually,

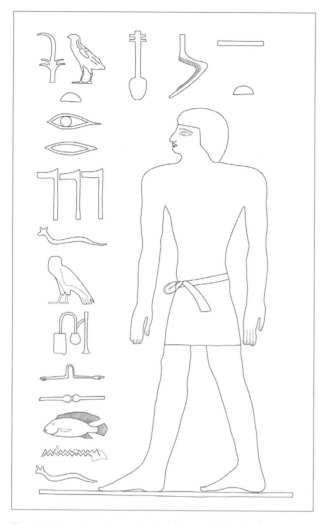

Fig. 6.1. Scene from the Tomb of Nefermaat (Mastaba 16, Meidum). Drawing: Ghada Mohamed.

often serving several purposes simultaneously. Once anthropomorphized, inanimate signs acquire human limbs, life and vitality,[3] as well as the capability to perform multiple tasks and replace/represent different entities in a broader context, especially in the religious and ritual spheres.[4] The main focus of this paper is to study the anthropomorphized signs found on Tutankhamun's monuments in order to elucidate the traditions and innovations concerning this kind of sign after the Amarna period.

Brief overview over the anthropomorphism of the ancient Egyptian hieroglyphic signs

According to ancient Egyptian perception, the hieroglyphic signs (or *mdw-nṯr*: Gottesworte,[5] divine words) were attributed to a divine source. Moreover, hieroglyphs were more than a mere communication system: they were also regarded to be living beings with divine powers of their own. The text

accompanying a unique scene from the tomb of Nefermaat and his wife Itet at Meidum[6] emphasizes this specific nature of signs (Fig. 6.1):[7] '[h]e (Nefermaat) is the one who made his gods (i.e., hieroglyphs) in a script which cannot be erased'. Another reference to 'living signs' and their ability to interact with their creator is mentioned in the later Book of Thoth (Pap. Berlin P 15531): '[t]he signs revealed their forms. He called to them, and they answered to him'.[8]

This textual evidence distinctly describes the signs as gods endowed with power, as well as newborn living characters that possess their own images and phonetic values. Obviously, they also have the ability to communicate by being able to hear, understand and respond. Furthermore, many hieroglyphs were provided with explicitly human attributes and behaviour so that they could be capable of (inter)acting autonomously, as illustrated in many scenes. Thus, the sign turns from an inactive static element into an active dynamic object and interacts effectively in a wider context wordlessly, directly and clearly. This concept includes the possession of certain abilities, such as physical movement or vital powers.[9] It is logical to assume that this form was applied and shaped from a human perspective. On the other hand, animalization, i.e., representing humans with animal characteristics and attributes, is likewise considered to be a highly significant manifestation in support of the right of legitimate rulers, when kings are provided with animal qualities and compared visually and textually with powerful animals, such as bulls and lions.

The present evidence of the humanized signs demonstrates that they were not merely space-filling components, but rather effective elements in scenes/contexts as they perform specific, not only practical but also symbolic, tasks. They combine concepts, texts and images together in order to achieve a certain content and effect. The anthropomorphized signs may be divided into the following three categories:

A. Anthropomorphized signs with phonetic value: this category contains signs that have a phonetic value and are mainly used as phonetic characters in textual evidence.

B. Living hybrid creatures: this category includes the anthropomorphized signs that represent non-human living beings with human limbs, characteristics and behaviour (e.g., *bꜣ-* and the *rḫyt*-bird as well as snakes with arms and legs in the Books of the Underworld).

C. Inanimate characters: inanimate objects which are anthropomorphized by granting life and human attributes and by adding human limbs to the sign fall under this category.

The signs in the last two categories appear as visual components in iconographical representations as well as in three-dimensional works of art. They stand independently or as a group of two or more signs, take various forms and perform various functions.[10]

The anthropomorphized signs on the monuments of King Tutankhamun

Despite their limited number, Tutankhamun's instances of anthropomorphized signs display great variety in form and function. Most of them were found in his well-known tomb (KV 62) in 1922, presenting some completely new and unparalleled cases of humanized signs so far.

The gilded wooden Ostrich-Hunt Fan

The first study case is taken from on the well-known gilded wooden ceremonial fan (Cairo JE 62001) (Fig. 6.2).[11] It was found between the third and fourth shrines within the burial chamber of the king, together with remains of white and brown ostrich feathers which have been evidently fitted alternately to the 30 holes pierced into the semi-circular palm of the fan.[12] Both sides of the fan are decorated with ostrich-hunt scenes, which according to the text, are taking place near Heliopolis. These show the king riding his chariot and shooting arrows at the frightened ostriches on one side, and the return of the king with his prey carried on the shoulders of his followers on the other side.[13] Behind Tutankhamun while hunting on the first side is a humanized sign of life which is strongly reminiscent of those that are to be found on the chariot of Thutmose IV.[14] The *ankh* is fully visible, provided with both arms and running legs, and imitates human behaviour.[15] The hands hold a fan realistically and the wrists are adorned with bracelets. With the heel of the back foot raised slightly upwards, the sense of running has been enhanced, giving an effective visual impression of movement, and emphasizing the idea that the *ankh* is following the king. This detail is not to be seen in earlier examples, since the two feet of the sign holding the fan normally rest steady and horizontally on the standing line.

There is also a kind of visual duplication on this fan, as a fan and its bearer are depicted on the king's actual ceremonial fan (Fig. 6.3). Despite the fact that the fans and divine standards had already appeared in the times of kings Scorpion and Narmer, they were still carried by human bearers.[16] However, the earliest evidence of the humanized *ankh* and *was* as fan- and standard-bearers dates to the reign of Djoser and is found on his six limestone panels that were installed under both the Step Pyramid and the South Tomb of the king, which depict Djoser performing *Heb-Sed* rituals.[17]

From this point of time onwards, such anthropomorphized signs became a royal tradition, a privilege that was maintained until the Greco-Roman period. They were used in various contexts, not only at festivals, ceremonies and religious rituals, but also in battle and hunting scenes.

Among all signs, the *ankh* dominates over the other bearer-signs. In ancient Egypt, fans are essentially associated with royalty and high prestige, larger examples acting as sunshades.[18] In addition, fans are closely related to the images of the deities in their various cult forms.[19]

They were used to cool the king while performing his duties and provide him with fresh air and shade.[20] Even though it is invisible, air is regarded as a significant component of creation in ancient Egypt, since without the air ('Breath of life': *ṯȝw n ʿnḫ/ṯʿw nḏm n ʿnḫ*)[21] no living creature can exist. Thus, fans and their fronds are clearly related to the concept of giving life, because they grant air, shade and new life.[22] Shadow also possesses an enlivening effect, an association that is easy to understand in the heat of Egypt. Various deities occasionally granted this shadow, such as Behedet or Nekhbet and Wadjet, who very often hover above the ruler with spread wings and various symbols held in the claws, like *ankh*, *was*, *shen*-ring, *heb*-sign, etc. As the shadow of the gods falls on and resides in the person of the ruler, fans were interpreted by some scholars as a manifestation of the divine presence of the deity.[23] Therefore, the fronds in the hands of the humanized *ankh* and *was* may well be compared to the effect (power and life) of the shadow of a deity.[24] This symbolism clarifies the close association of the *ankh*-sign holding the fan behind Tutankhamun, and the accompanying text emphasizes this concept as it states: '(May) all the protection and life be behind/around him' (*sȝ ʿnḫ nb ḥȝ .f*).

The king's gold-sheet appliqué

Another similar anthropomorphized *ankh*-sign holding the fan behind Tutankhamun is found on one of the king's surviving gold-sheet appliqués from his tomb (Cairo TR 30.3.34.52; Carter 122x), showing, however, a few differences (Plate 7).[25] The context, in this instance, is the well-known smiting of the enemy, in which the king decapitates an Asian foe with the *khepesh*-sword. Moreover, the large *ankh*-sign here is merely provided with two relatively long human arms,[26] while legs are absent. In addition, the accompanying text emphasizes once again the concept of granting life eternally, but with a different formula: *di ʿnḫ mi Rʿ*, 'given life like Re'. Interestingly, the earliest evidence of the *ankh*-sign holding a fan behind the king in this context dates to the time of Amenemhat III and appears on a pectoral found in Princess Mereret's burial at Dahshur.[27] The pectoral takes the form of the temple facade and depicts a traditional scene of smiting of the enemies. Under the outstretched wings of the vulture goddess is a vertical column with hieroglyphs in the middle, recording the royal titulary of Amenemhet III,[28] dividing the representations on the pectoral into two almost symmetrical scenes. Each half represents the fighting king, holding the hair of a kneeling, bearded foe and smiting him with a mace.[29] Behind Amenemhat III, and on its own base-line, is an *ankh*-sign with

Fig. 6.2. The anthropomorphized ankh-*sign on the gilded wooden Ostrich-Hunt Fan. Photo: © Griffith Institute, University of Oxford.*

Fig. 6.3. The running ankh-*sign behind Tutankhamun on his golden fan. Drawing: Ghada Mohamed.*

two arms, carrying a fan raised as if it is wafting air towards the king or, perhaps more likely, providing him with shade. Depictions of the anthropomorphized *ankh* holding fans behind the king, while he is fighting or hunting, developed then into a very popular tradition in the New Kingdom onwards and this subject was occasionally represented in more complex forms.[30]

The four bronze torch-holders

Among the lamps and torches found in Tutankhamun's tomb, the most unprecedented objects so far discovered are four bronze torch-holders (JE 62356, Carter no. 41) (Fig. 6.4).[31] Carter found these unique items on the ritual lion-headed bed in the tomb's antechamber and described them as 'absolutely new in type'[32] (Fig. 6.3b). However,

Carter believed that they were originally stored in a plain wooden box discovered in the north-east corner of the Treasury (JE 61474, Carter no. 361),[33] together with other metal implements. They had then been relocated by the tomb robbers in the antechamber, who took only the components they found valuable. Carter also assumed that, in the dim light, the robbers had erroneously thought they were made of gold, but they realized the mistake before leaving the tomb, and so left the pieces in the antechamber.[34] Carter supports his hypothesis by emphasizing that the dimensions of the four torch-holders and the space they occupy correspond well with the capacity of the box. In addition, the pieces are incomplete, some parts are missing and also there are traces of black resinous material on the bottom of the box, similar to the material covering the wooden bases of the torch-holders.[35]

Each of the four pieces is approximately 23 cm tall[36] and consists of a bronze *ankh*-sign with two human arms, set on a rectangular, wooden base. The arms grow out, as usual, from the intersection point between the loop and the vertical lower part, and in this case on each of the four torch-holders the traces of metal welding of the arms at the crossing point are visible from behind, giving an indication of the technique used to produce the objects. The arms were designed separately and then attached at the crossing point on either side of the body of the sign.[37] According to their arm positions, the four torch-holders can be divided into two groups:

Group A (torch-holders with cup torches)

This group includes two pieces with arms aligned, wide open and almost at the same level (Fig. 6.5).[38] Both arms bend slightly at the elbow inward to support the torch cup, while the two hands surround it.[39] The lost cups between the hands were probably made of gold and filled with grease or oil, in which the wicks were floated, but they were apparently stolen by tomb robbers in ancient times.[40] A small, modern ceramic cup has been made and placed in front of one of the two torch-holders to demonstrate their original appearance.[41]

Group B (torch-holders with conical torches)

In this group, the arms of the two life-signs are located at different levels to fit a tubular torch (Fig. 6.5, Plate 8).[42] One of them is intact and still has the original torch, which consists of twisted conical linen, bound spirally by a strip of linen and inserted into a holder made of gilded bronze. Traces of a yellow, oily liquid with acidic properties required for the burning process were found in the linen wick and its metal holder. However, according to Carter, its amount was too small to be identified (Fig. 6.6).[43] From the second torch, only the gilded container survives, while the twisted linen wick has been lost (Plate 8).

Fig. 6.4. The four torch-holders under the ritual lion-headed bed in Tutankhamun's antechamber. Photo: © Griffith Institute, University of Oxford.

Fig. 6.5. The four torch-holders of King Tutankhamun. Photo: © Griffith Institute, University of Oxford.

As in Group A, both arms bend at the elbow inward to hold the torch, but on two levels. The left arm is produced in the higher position in both pieces, causing the acute angle of the left elbow, in contrast to the right arm, which bends to a lesser degree. Furthermore, the open fists and the fingers bend flexibly around the wick holders. In fact, this arm and hand position is not entirely new, since it is already documented in the representations of the anthropomorphized signs bearing fans, standards and sacred staffs (*mdw špsy*). However, here the implementation of this form is produced in two unique, three-dimensional pieces. Despite their small size and, above all, the small dimensions of the arms and hands, no detail escaped the artist's attention. This includes the fine fingers, which are superbly executed in the four objects.

It is not entirely certain whether or not there were similar torch-holders before the reign of Tutankhamun, as none have been found so far. They seem to the writer to be a direct result of the strong solar character of the Amarna reform, which still continued to have a powerful impact after Akhenaten's death, when the young king was raised and was surely influenced by it.

There is no doubt that there is a profound bond in ancient Egyptian beliefs between light and granting life, as the light was strongly associated with activity, movement and vitality, while darkness was related to death, silence, stillness and dangerous creatures. The repeated representation of the Aten during the Amarna period as a sun-disc holding many signs of life in his delicate hands emphasizes this concept visually, and confirms the relevance of the sun, or rather the light, to the *ankh*-sign. By providing light, these torches assist dispelling darkness in the tomb or rather in the underworld, ensuring the resurrection and eternal life of the deceased king. The continuity of this perception in the Egyptian consciousness after the end of the Amarna period was, in my opinion, the essential motivation to produce this unusual form of torch-holders.

On the other hand, these unique torch-holders may be associated as well with Chapter 137 of the Book of the Dead, which deals with provision of light to the deceased by torches and their ritual extinguishing.[44] Two versions are attested from different sources, namely Chapter 137A (the long version) entitled: 'You shall make four basins of clay beaten up with incense and filled with milk of a white cow; the torches are to be quenched in them', and Chapter 137B (the short version) entitled: 'Spell to light the torch for Osiris NN'.[45] The purpose of the chapter is to bring the torches – occasionally, the text explicitly mentions four torches – and the Eyes of Horus, which shine like Re on the horizon, to the Ka and the Ba of the deceased and subsequently to guarantee protection against enemies.[46] Moreover, appeals are made to the four sons of Horus to protect their father Osiris- Khentiamentiu/Osiris NN Horus 'so that he

Fig. 6.6. The torch-holder with conical torch as twisted linen. Photo: © Griffith Institute, University of Oxford.

may live with the gods'. The chapter also mentions that the four torches are made of red linen and soaked in the finest Libyan oil. They were also carried in the hands of four men identified with the four Sons of Horus and lit at sunset: as a consequence, the deceased will not perish, and his Ba will live forever.[47]

In view of the above-mentioned considerations, it may be assumed that the unusual torch-holders of Tutankhamun share the same long-lasting concept of light as a key element of life and resurrection. Furthermore, they could represent a continuity in content and form of the anthropomorphized sun, the Aten, and the many *ankh*-signs in his hands, and could also be related to Chapter 137 of the Book of the Dead. Humanizing the life-signs corresponds to this concept and allows them to both offer the torch themselves as a bearer of life, as well as to contribute their own symbolic significance for the benefit of the deceased. Moreover, the four torches are associated with the protective four Sons of Horus and with the four cardinal points, and thus surround Osiris/the deceased king and provide him with light from all cardinal directions. This carries with it the concept of protection by encircling and embracing the deceased as well. Since the four Sons of Horus relate to the four protective goddesses, Isis, Nephthys, Neith and Selket, the purpose of the king's torch-holders in this particular, unique form primarily aims to protect him and guarantee his resurrection by annihilating both darkness and enemies of the deceased, both practically and symbolically.

The alabaster vase

One of the most common variants of the anthropomorphized life-sign is the *ankh*-sign on the central vertical axis, with human arms on either side and two objects held in its fists. This composition can be found in various sources in the New Kingdom and is occasionally depicted on a *neb*-sign. The items held by the sign's hands vary between *was*- and *sekhem*-sceptres, *maat*-feathers, palm fronds and bowls.

The next case study of anthropomorphized signs from Tutankhamun's tomb is represented on one of the alabaster vases (JE 62118), which were placed between two of the ritual beds in the antechamber (Fig. 6.7).[48] The piece consists of two unevenly joined alabaster parts; the vase and the stand. In the middle of the top part is a long-necked jar covered with floral motifs, the pectoral of goddess Hathor and the royal titulary of King Tutankhamun. This centrepiece is flanked symmetrically by the lily (symbol of Upper Egypt) and papyrus (symbol of Lower Egypt) knotted firmly at the neck of the vase, evoking the unification of the Two Lands, *smꜣ-tꜣwy* (Fig. 6.8). On the far sides there are two palm fronds (*rnpt* = years), which rest on the signs of the Tadpole (*ḥfn* = 100,000) and the *shen*-ring (= eternity and infinity), symbolizing eternal years of ruling the united Egypt.[49] The lower part representing the base is characterized by a central support in the middle and on either side one *ankh*-sign provided with human arms and holding *was*-sceptres.[50] Unusually, the horizontal bar between the loop and the vertical part in both signs is entirely missing. Moreover, the arms were not carved separately, as common in such pieces, but as one piece with the sign body. The remarkable fine details of the hands and fingers wrapped around the sceptres have been carefully executed. This composition, which occasionally rests on the *neb*-sign, is frequently represented in various ancient Egyptian sources.[51] It can be read from the middle to either right or left as *ꜥnḥ wꜣs nb*, meaning 'all life, dominion/welfare'. The group of signs thus plays both an ornamental and a meaningful role in terms of content. It can be concluded that thereby all life and well-being should be donated to the owner of the objects, in this case the king, or to the depicted individuals in the scene.

The Third Pylon at Karnak

One of the most impressive depictions of the *ankh*-sign as a fan-bearer is found on the east face of the north tower of the Third Pylon at Karnak, which was built by Amenhotep III and decorated in the last years of his reign.[52] The scene illustrates a river procession of sacred barks during the annual Opet-Festival, in which the king himself participates. On the main bark of Amun-Re, Userhat, there is a shrine of the divine statue flanked by two large figures of Amenhotep III, with his heads are now missing. Two smaller figures follow the king, however, both deliberately erased in antiquity and replaced by other motifs. The outlines reveal royal figures wearing the blue crown.[53] On the left side, a huge offering table, and on the right side, a relatively large, anthropomorphized *ankh*-sign holding a long semi-circular fan have replaced the deleted persons (Fig. 6.9). It has been variously argued that these depict Amenhotep III himself,[54] Amenhotep IV (Akhenaten),[55] Semenkhkare, Tutankhamun[56] and Ay, and were erased and replaced by Horemheb after the Amarna period.[57]

Analysis of the remaining traces of the royal cartouches and the reliefs suggests that they most likely belong to King Tutankhamun, who tried repeatedly to associate himself with Amenhotep III after the end of the Amarna period and the return to Thebes. This tendency can also be observed in Tutankhamun's scenes of the Opet-Festival on the walls of the Great Colonnade in Luxor-Temple, where the image of Amenhotep III is frequently depicted on the bark of Amun-Re. It would therefore appear that Tutankhamun inserted his figures behind those of his grandfather to link himself to the last orthodox ruler before Amarna. Horemheb subsequently removed his images later and replaced them with an offering table and an anthropomorphized *ankh* holding a large, semi-circular fan.[58] This was clearly seen as an optimal alternative to the omitted royal figure, since this form of the life-sign with two human arms holding the fan behind the ruler was, as previously mentioned, a concept going back to the Old Kingdom. The life-sign is proportionately larger than in analogous instances to correspond with the erased human figure that it replaces. Furthermore, attention should be drawn to the fact that the group of anthropomorphized *ankh*, *djed* and *was* is once again represented in royal and private sources after a long interruption during Akhenaten's reign.

The Colonnade Hall of the Luxor Temple

The Great Colonnade in Luxor-Temple was first constructed under Amenhotep III and finished and inscribed by Tutankhamun, Horemheb and then Sethy I with episodes of the well-known Opet festival. However, the reliefs of Tutankhamun and Ay were widely and systematically usurped by Horemheb at the end of the 18th Dynasty, who replaced their cartouches with his own.[59] Some of these scenes present a further function for the anthropomorphized signs from the reign of Tutankhamun. The reliefs on the walls of both short ends of the Colonnade Hall depict the king leaving the royal palace, and being

Fig. 6.7. The alabaster vases in the king's antechamber. Photo: © Griffith Institute, University of Oxford.

Fig. 6.8. One of the alabaster vases of the king with the base formed as anthropomorphized ankh-*signs holding* was. *Photo: © Griffith Institute, University of Oxford.*

Fig. 6.9. The anthropomorphized ankh-*sign behind the king on the Third Pylon of Karnak. Photo: Ghada Mohamed.*

greeted by Amun-Re and Mut (Figs 6.10–6.11).[60] The king is preceded by three divine standards of Wepwawet, the so-called Khonsu-Emblem,[61] and a Behdeti-falcon, which are held by the anthropomorphized *ankh*, *was* and *ankh* respectively. Analysis of anthropomorphized signs down to the end of the Late Period indicates a likely connection between specific divine standards and certain anthropomorphized signs that frequently carry them. This connection most probably emerged through the repeated arrangement of both standards and anthropomorphized signs as bearers. Therefore, the sign of life, which usually leads the sign-group, frequently holds the standard of Wepwawet, which often stands as foremost of the standards. The *was*-sceptre usually bears the standard of Khonsu, which generally comes second, etc. This order

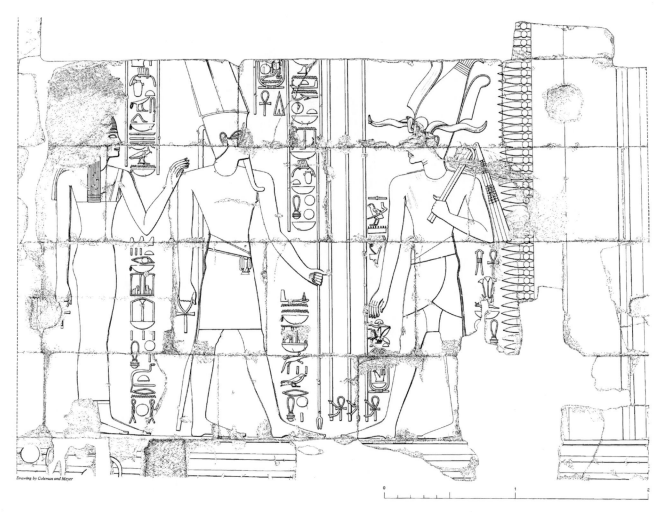

Fig. 6.10. The humanized ankh- *and* was-*signs holding divine standards before the king in the great Colonnade Hall of Luxor Temple. Drawing: Epigraphic Survey 1994, pl. 3.*

is attested as far back as the earliest attested appearance of the humanized hieroglyphs as standard-bearers under Djoser.[62] However, in some cases the arrangement was reversed, and the standard of Khonsu is unusually placed in front of that of Wepwawet, the *was*-sceptre being thus now at the front of the bearer-group.[63] As a result, some scholars have proposed that the standard of Khonsu and the anthropomorphized *was* were closely related.[64] Despite the possibility of such a link, the study demonstrated that it could not be confirmed definitively, as there exist scenes in which the jackal standard comes first and is followed by that of Khons, but the *was*-sceptre precedes the sign of life and holds the Wepwawet standard,[65] and vice versa.[66]

Finally, the reliefs of the barks of the Theban triad on the east wall of the colonnade depicting the ceremonial procession returning from Luxor temple to Karnak show the anthropomorphized *ankh* and *was* performing a further

task. This is that of bearing the sacred staffs *mdw-špsy* alternately behind the base on which the bark of Amun-Re rests (Fig. 6.12).[67] The earliest evidence for this function dates to the reign of Hatshepsut and Thutmose III. Furthermore, it is noteworthy that the sacred staffs *mdw-špsy* carried by the anthropomorphized signs are attested frequently with the main bark of Amun-Re and, albeit quite rarely, with the barks of Mut and Khonsu. They can be essentially observed behind,[68] or both behind and before the pedestal of the sacred bark. Starting from the reign of Hatshepsut and Thutmose III, the humanized *djed*-pillar joined the *ankh* and *was* as a bearer of the divine standards and the sacred staves *mdw-špsy*. The *djed* is usually flanked by the *ankh*- and *was*-signs and therefore, it occasionally carries the standard of Khonsu.[69] The Egyptians realized the frequent sequence of the signs represented in this group of bearers, i.e., *ankh*, *djed* and *was* respectively, as it became a long-term tradition. This concept is emphasized

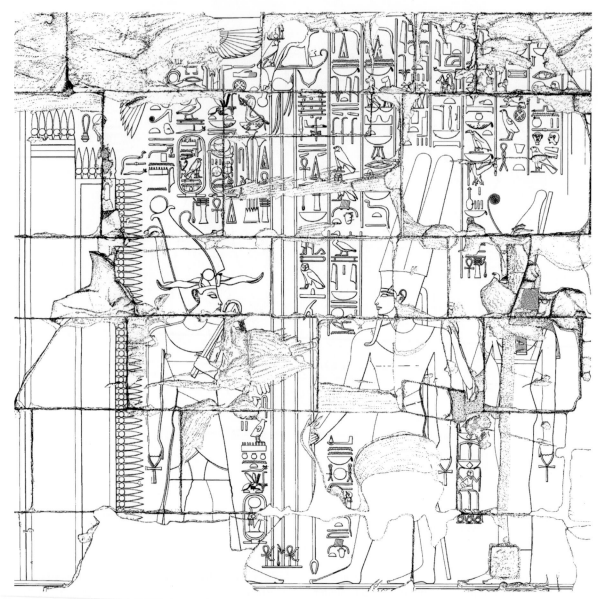

Fig. 6.11. The humanized ankh- *and* was-*signs holding divine standards before the king in the great Colonnade Hall of Luxor Temple. Drawing: Epigraphic Survey 1994, pl. 119.*

by the red marks of the later, Ramesside restorers in the temple of Hatshepsut at Deir el-Bahari on the partly damaged signs bearing divine standards to serve as a guideline during work (Fig. 6.13).[70]

Conclusion

Taking everything into account, ancient Egyptians considered the hieroglyphic signs to be living beings possessing divine and magical powers of their own. Visually and textually, many signs have been anthropomorphized and provided with human characteristics in terms of form and behaviour to become capable of (inter)acting independently

and to replace deities, kings and private individuals. It should be emphasized that anthropomorphism is applied and formed in the first place from a purely human perspective. The anthropomorphized *ankh* and *was* became a royal privilege during the Old Kingdom and continued until the Greco-Roman period: even kings of foreign origin adopted this long-enduring royal custom in their reliefs. However, this tradition was abandoned during the Amarna period, when only ordinary individuals are portrayed accompanying the king as fan- and standard-bearers. Then, the young Tutankhamun revived the concept after Akhenaten's death and after restoring the old beliefs. In addition, the findings of the latter's tomb representing the anthropomorphized

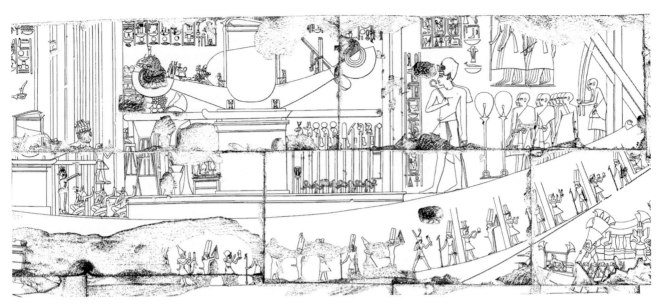

Fig. 6.12. The humanized ankh- *and* was-*signs holding the sacred staves behind the pedestal of the sacred bark of Amun-Re, Colonnade Hall of Luxor Temple. Drawing: Epigraphic Survey 1994, pl. 78.*

Fig. 6.13. Scene from the Temple of Hatshepsut at Deir el-Bahari. Photo: Ghada Mohamed.

signs reveal not only a very interesting diversity but also demonstrate tradition and innovation in function and form. Many instances follow earlier traditions, such as bearing fans and standards, while others represent an entirely new shape and function, such as the four torch-holders from Tutankhamun's tomb. The latter unique pieces are highly significant, as they represent one of the very few models of anthropomorphized signs in three-dimensional works, and may also reflect a direct, continuous influence from Atenism on light as life donor and on the images of the sun-disc with the life-signs in its hands. A particularly noteworthy aspect of King Tutankhamun's monuments is the prominence of the anthropomorphized *ankh* over the other signs. However, it is essentially associated with the task which was performed in order to give life to the dead king. In conclusion, Tutankhamun's case studies provide a valuable link for understanding the development and use of the anthropomorphized signs during the New Kingdom in general, and after the controversial Amarna period in particular.

Notes

1 'Anthropomorphis', Merriam-Webster, https://www.merriam-webster.com/dictionary/anthropomorphism; 'Anthropomorphic', Merriam-Webster, https://www.merriam-webster.com/dictionary/anthropomorphic (last accessed 1 June 2022); Peters 2004, 418.

2 In my doctoral dissertation, recently defended at the University of Bonn in Germany, the anthropomorphized form of Egyptian hieroglyphs until the end of the Late Period is examined in detail. Eleven selected case studies of anthropomorphized inanimate signs are intensively investigated in various sources until the Late Period. Among these case studies are *ankh, djed, was, tit, 'Imnt.t, iȝbt.t,* the sun-disc, the *wadjet*-eye, the name rings of foreign lands, the royal serekh/cartouche and divine standards (Mohamed 2020).

3 Otto 1975, 311; Te Velde 1986, 66.

4 Pries 2016, 449–450.

5 Wb II, 180 (13)-181 (6); Faulkner 1991, 122; Hannig 2015, 401.

6 Tomb No. 16; see PM IV, 92–94; Petrie 1892; Harpur 2001, 21–47, 55–94.

7 Petrie 1892, 24, pl. XXIV; Spiegelberg 1930, 119; Te Velde 1986, 63; Urk. I, 7; Harpur 2001, 83–4, figs 84, 169, 177, pl. 27; Pries 2016, 452; Ritner 2018, 88.

8 Pries 2016, 457. See also Quack 2007, 276.

9 Otto 1975, 311; Te Velde 1986, 66.

10 For an intensive study of the significance and categories of the anthropomorphized hieroglyphs in ancient Egypt, see Mohamed forthcoming.

11 An inscription on the fan's mast states that it is made of ostrich feathers obtained from hunting in the desert of Heliopolis. Edwards 1974, No. 23; Reed and Osborn 1978, 274, fig. 1; Decker and Herb 1994, vol. 1: Text, 346–347; vol. 2, pl. CLXXVIII.

12 http://www.griffith.ox.ac.uk/gri/carter/242-c242-1.html (accessed 1 May 2023); Carter 2014b, 32–33, pls LXI–LXII.

13 Edwards 1974, No. 23; Houlihan 1986, 1–2, fig. 1; Sabbahy 2012, 192; http://www.griffith.ox.ac.uk/perl/gi-ca-qmak-edeta.pl?sid=212.201.79.61-1497719765&qno=1&df-nam=242-c242-1 (accessed 20 December 2018); Reed and Osborn believe that the hunted birds on this fan are not ostriches but bustards. They give the following reasons for this interpretation: 'The birds do not look like ostriches; they have three toes on each foot instead of the two normal to an ostrich, the tail and wings carry stiff feathers instead of plumes, and the necks are feathered rather than nearly naked. Also, these birds are small for ostriches, and the necks and legs lack the length typical of an ostrich. The birds look like bustards'; Reed and Osborn 1978, 275–276.

14 Cf. Carter and Newberry 1904, pls X–XI.

15 Edwards 1974, No. 23; Houlihan 1986, 1.

16 On king Scorpion's well-known mace-head, the king is preceded by two standard-bearers and followed by two fan-bearers. Two fan-bearers on the Narmer mace-head stand next to the high podium, while four standard-bearers walk in the opposite direction towards the king. See Hendrickx 2012, 1072.

17 Friedman 1995, 1–42.

18 Kees 1912, 126–128; Fischer 1977, 81.

19 Bell 1985, 31–33. Kees, followed by Bell, mentions that the fans are rarely depicted behind the deities in their human form. However, investigating the anthropomorphized signs as fan bearers in my study demonstrates that Egyptian gods and goddesses in anthropomorphic form were frequently accompanied by diverse kinds of fans, mainly ⸗ and ⸗, which were occasionally carried by anthropomorphized *Ankh* and *Was*. Instances include Reshep, Anukis, Hathor, Osiris, Amun-Re and the deified Amenhotep I. Cf. Kees 1912, 127; Bell 1985, 33; Mohamed 2020, 209–212, 251–252.

20 Kees 1912, 126; Friedman 1995, 20–21. The shadow was represented in ancient Egypt as a black human form or fan ⸗, and was believed to be a component of man. Likewise, shadow was regarded as coolness, air, protection from heat and as an essential element for life. See George 1970, 4, 6–11, 15–17, 116; about the sexual aspect of the shadow, George 1970, 112–117; Schenkel 1984, 535–536.

21 Wb V, 350–352; e.g., 'Der Wind…, dessen Stimme man hört, ohne dass man ihn sehen kann'; see Westendorf 1980, 1098.

22 Feucht 1981, 110. This paper mentions that the fronds/fans have replaced the king himself in rare depictions. This can be observed in the temple of Deir el-Bahari where the frond is depicted on Hatshepsut's throne; see Naville 1901, pls LXXXVIII, LXXXIX, XCI.

23 Kees 1912, 127; Bonnet 1952, 178, 675; Bell 1985, 33; Hartwig 2004, 66; 2023, No. 24.

24 Feucht 1981, 111; Bell 1985, 33.

25 https://phys.org/news/2017-11-treasures-tutankhamun-tomb.html (accessed 1 May 2023); Carter No. 122x, http://www.griffith.ox.ac.uk/gri/carter/122x.html (accessed 1 May 2023). Carter found this piece among other similar gold sheets in Tutankhamun's tomb, but they have not yet been conclusively examined or processed. The aim of a joint project (funded by the DFG) of the Egyptian Museum in Cairo, the Institut für die Kulturen des Alten Orients (IANES) at the University of Tübingen, the German Archaeological Institute in Cairo (DAI) and the Römisch-Germanischen Zentralmuseum (RGZM) in Mainz are the restoration and analysis of these decorated gold sheets. For more information about this project, see https://uni-tuebingen.de/fakultaeten/philosophische-fakultaet/fachbereiche/altertums-und-kunstwissenschaften/ianes/forschung/vorderasiatische-archaeologie/projekte/die-goldbleche-aus-dem-grab-des-tutanchamun-untersuchungen-zur-kulturellen-kommunikation-zwischen-aegypten-und-vorderasien-dfg/ (accessed 1 May 2023); https://publications.dainst.org/journals/efb/1951/6092 (accessed 1 May 2023); https://phys.org/news/2017-11-treasures-tutankhamun-tomb.html (accessed 1 May 2023); https://blog.selket.de/aus-den-museen/goldbleche-aus-tutanchamuns-grabschatz-erstmals-ausgestellt (accessed 1 May 2023). I would like to express my gratitude to Dr Christian Eckmann from the Römisch-Germanisches Zentralmuseum in Mainz, Germany, for providing me with a recent colour photography of the Gold-Sheet Appliqué in question.

26 Carter No. 122x, http://www.griffith.ox.ac.uk/gri/carter/122x-c122vgg.html (accessed 1 May 2023).

27 De Morgan 1895, 63–64; Kees 1912, 233 (85); Bell 1985, 47 (74).

28 De Morgan 1895, 64, pls XX–XXI.

29 De Morgan 1895, 64; Schulz and Seidel, 2004, 116. The hieroglyphs describe the action of the king, while the vulture goddess supports the king and grants him life and stability to his arm to win his battle.

30 E.g., Naville 1908, pl. CLX; The Epigraphic Survey 1986, pl. 3, 28–29, 31, 82; Calvert 2013, 64, fig. 17.

31 http://www.griffith.ox.ac.uk/gri/carter/, No. 41 a–d; http://www.griffith.ox.ac.uk/gri/carter/041a-p0022.html (accessed 1 May 2023).

32 Reeves 1990, 196; Carter 2014a, 104, 241, pl. LXXV.

33 http://www.griffith.ox.ac.uk/gri/carter/316.html (accessed 1 May 2023).

34 Reeves 1990, 196; Carter 2014c, 65. Several indications suggest that the box in question was robbed, the lid being partly open and moved to the side. Moreover, the rope tied around the box had already been cut and the seal on it had been broken. Furthermore, some metal implements were found on the floor in front of the box or inside with their handles apart. See Carter 2014c, 65; http://www.griffith.ox.ac.uk/gri/carter/316-c316-1.html (accessed 4 January 2024).

35 Carter 2014c, 65; http://www.griffith.ox.ac.uk/gri/carter/316-c316-1.html (accessed 1 May 2023).

36 Reeves 1990, 196; http://www.globalegyptianmuseum.org/record.aspx?id=15035 (accessed 1 May 2023).

37 http://www.griffith.ox.ac.uk/gri/carter/041a-p0454.html (accessed 1 May 2023).

38   http://www.griffith.ox.ac.uk/gri/carter/041a-p0453a.html (accessed 1 May 2023).
39   http://www.griffith.ox.ac.uk/gri/carter/041a-c041a-2.html (accessed 1 May 2023).
40   Carter 2014a, 241.
41   Carter 2014a, 104, 241.
42   http://www.griffith.ox.ac.uk/gri/carter/041a-p0453a.html (accessed 1 May 2023).
43   Carter 2014b, 125; http://www.griffith.ox.ac.uk/gri/carter/041a-c041a-2.html; http://www.globalegyptianmuseum.org/record.aspx?id=15035 (accessed 1 May 2023).
44   Saleh 1984, 75; Hornung 1990, 271; von Dassow 1994, 119.
45   Faulkner 1985, 127; Hornung 1990, 266–271. See also Naville 1886: Einleitung, 196. Luft distinguishes a third version of the chapter, which occurred from the 26th Dynasty to the Ptolemaic period, and calls it 'Tb 137 spät'. This category contains a combination of the texts of the two early versions and has the same content, but 'in neuem strukturellen Gewand'. Therefore, it does not receive a new, independent chapter number, see Luft 2009, 10, 29–30, 71–72, 115–119, 146–155, 158, 221–230, 315–341.
46   Hornung 1990, 266–267; von Dassow 1994, 119.
47   Hornung 1990, 267; von Dassow 1994, 119.
48   Edwards 1974, No. 3; Carter 2014a, pl. XXII; Manniche 2019, 20–21, pls XX, XXII; http://www.globalegyptianmuseum.org/record.aspx?id=15137 (accessed 1 May 2023).
49   Edwards points out that the royal name on the body of the vase is partially misspelled. See Edwards 1974, No. 3.
50   Edwards 1974, No. 3.
51   E.g., Petrie 1914, pl. III (No. 30a–f); Breasted 1940, pl. 246–II; The Epigraphic Survey 1957, pl. 255. In rare instances the anthropomorphized djed-pillar replaces the life-sign and holds two was-sceptres on either side, and rests on the neb-sign. This composition is depicted alternately with the usual group with the ankh-sign or with tit-knot; see Davies 1933, pl. XXX; Vandier 1935, pl. XXI.
52   Murnane 1979, 11; PM II, 59; https://www.memphis.edu/hypostyle/tour_hall/third_pylon.php (accessed 1 May 2023).
53   Murnane 1979, 11–12.
54   Murnane 1979, 12.
55   Barguet suggests that the fan in this scene belonged to the erased figure and thus this character may refer to the Fan-bearer on the Right Side of the King. Murnane disagrees with this suggestion and claims that the fan is obviously cut later over this human figure. Cf. Barguet, 1962, 82 (3); Murnane 1979, 12. In addition, this scene was interpreted by some scholars as a representation of Amenhotep IV and thus a reference to a co-regency between him and his father, Amenhotep III. See Saad 1970, 191; Aldred 1973, 18–19; Murnane 1977, 162–169; PM II, 61 (183).
56   Murnane 1977, 167–168; 1979, 15.
57   Murnane 1979, 15.
58   Murnane 1977, 167–168; 1979, 16–18. See also Johnson 1994, 133–144.
59   Johnson 2009, 126.
60   The Epigraphic Survey 1994, 1, 42, pl. 3, 119. For the scenes of departing from the palace, see Barguet 1986, 51–54.
61   On the meaning and interpretation of the standard, see Seligmann and Murray 1911, 168–171; Blackman 1916, 235–249;

Munro 1961, 62–63; Posener 1965, 198–200; Lurker 1974, 183; Brunner 1975, 960; Morenz 2002, 277–283.
62   Cf. Murnane and Nelson 1981, pl. 37, 50–51; Friedman 1995, 1–42; Burgos and Larché 2006, 78, 103; LD III, 36-a.
63   E.g., Gabolde 1998, pl. XXVII; Burgos and Larché 2006, 239.
64   Seligmann and Murray 1911, 167.
65   Larché 2019, pl. 58-a.
66   Gardiner 1958, pl. 15, 21, 24.
67   The Epigraphic Survey 1994, pls 68, 76–80; Johnson 1994, 138, fig. 9.1.
68   Sethos II, Tf. 5 (oben); Murnane and Nelson 1981, pls 76, 178; Pawlicki 1999, 129.
69   Gardiner 1935, pl. 5 (above), 36; Breasted 1940, pl. 228; Murnane and Nelson 1981, pl. 76, 151; Burgos and Larché 2006, 61; Masquelier-Loorius 2017, 397, fig. 6.
70   Cwiek and Sankiewicz 2008, figs 1, 3.

Bibliography

Aldred, Cyril. 1973. *Akhenaten and Nefertiti*. New York: Brooklyn Museum.

Barguet, Paul. 1962. *Le Temple d'Amon-Rê à Karnak: Essai d'Exégèse*. RAPH 21. Le Caire: Institut Français d'Archéologie Orientale.

Barguet, Paul. 1986. 'Note sur la sortie du roi hors du palais'. In *Hommages à François Daumas*, vol. I, edited by Antoine Guillaumont, 51–54. Orientalia Monspeliensia 3. Montpellier: Université Paul Valéry.

Bell, Lanny. 1985. 'Aspects of the Cult of the Deified Tutankhamun'. In *Mélanges Gamal ed-Din Mokhtar*, vol. 1, edited by Paule Posener-Kriéger, 31–59. Bibliothèque d'Étude 97. Cairo: Institut Français d'Archéologie Oriental.

Blackman, Aylward M. 1916. 'The Pharaoh's Placenta and the Moon-God Khons'. *Journal of Egyptian Archaeology* 3: 235–249.

Bonnet, Hans. 1952. *Reallexikon der Ägyptischen Religionsgeschichte*. Berlin: de Gruyter.

Breasted, James H. (ed.). 1940. *The Epigraphic Survey, Medinet Habu IV: Festival scenes of Ramses III*. OIP 51. Chicago: Oriental Institute of the University of Chicago.

Brunner, Hans. 1975. 'Chons'. In *Lexikon der Ägyptologie I*, edited by Wolfgang Helck and Wolfhart Westendorf, 960–963. Wiesbaden: Harrassowitz.

Burgos, Franck, and François Larché. 2006. *La Chapelle Rouge: Le Sanctuaire de Barque d'Hatshepsout: Facsimilés et photographies des scènes*, Vol. I. Paris: Recherche sur les civilisation.

Calvert, Amy M. 2013. 'Vehicle of the Sun: The Royal Chariot in the New Kingdom'. In *Chasing Chariots. Proceedings of the First International Chariot Conference (Cairo 2012)*, edited by André J. Veldmeijer and Salima Ikram, 45–71. Leiden: Sidestone Press.

Carter, Howard. 2014a. *The Tomb of Tutankhamun: Search, Discovery and the Clearness of the Antechamber*, Vol. I. London: Bloomsbury Academic.

Carter, Howard. 2014b. *The Tomb of Tutankhamun: The Burial Chamber*, Vol. II. London: Bloomsbury Academic.

Carter, Howard. 2014c. *The Tomb of Tutankhamun: The Annexe and Treasury*, Vol. III. London: Bloomsbury Academic.

Carter, Howard, and Percy Edward Newberry. 1904. *Catalogue Général des Antiquités Égyptiennes du Musée du Caire (Nr. 46001/46529): The Tomb of Thoutmôsis IV*. Westminster: Archibald Constable and Co.

Ćwiek, Andrzej, and Sankiewicz, Marta. 2008. 'The Scene of "Going Round the Wall" on the North Wall of the Portico of the Birth'. *Polish Archaeology in the Mediterranean* 18: 290–294.

Davies, Norman de Garis. 1933. *The Tomb of Nefer-hotep at Thebes*, Vol. I. New York: The Metropolitan Museum of Art.

Decker, Wolfgang, and Michael Herb. 1994. *Bildatlas zum Sport im alten Ägypten: Corpus der bildlichen Quellen zu Leibesübungen, Spiel, Jagd, Tanz und verwandten Themen, Teil 1: Text und Teil 2: Abbildungen*. Leiden: E.J. Brill.

Edwards, Iorwerth Eiddon Stephen. 1974. *The Treasures of Tutankhamun*. London: Joseph.

The Epigraphic Survey. 1957. *Medinet Habu V. The Temple Proper, Part I: The Portico, the Treasury, and Chapels Adjoining the First Hypostyle Hall with Marginal Material from the Forecourts*. OIP 83. Chicago: Oriental Institute of the University of Chicago.

The Epigraphic Survey 1986. *Reliefs and Inscriptions at Karnak IV: The Battle Reliefs of King Sety I*. OIP 107. Chicago: Oriental Institute of the University of Chicago.

The Epigraphic Survey 1994. *Reliefs and Inscriptions at Luxor Temple 1: The Festival Procession of Opet in the Colonnade Hall, with Translations of Texts, Commentary, and Glossary*. OIP 112. Chicago: Oriental Institute of the University of Chicago.

Faulkner, Raymond O. 1985. *The Ancient Egyptian Book of the Dead*. London: British Museum Publications.

Faulkner, Raymond O. 1991. *A Concise Dictionary of Middle Egyptian*. Oxford: Griffith Institute/Ashmolean Museum.

Feucht, Erika. 1981. 'Relief Scheschonqs I. beim Erschlagen der Feinde'. *Studien zur Altägyptischen Kultur* 9: 105–117.

Fischer, Henry George. 1977. 'Fächer und Wedel'. In *Lexikon der Ägyptologie*, Vol. II, edited by Wolfgang Helck and Wolfhart Westendorf, 81–85. Wiesbaden: Harrassowitz.

Friedman, Florence Dunn. 1995. 'The Underground Relief Panels of King Djoser at the Step Pyramid Complex'. *Journal of the American Research Center in Egypt* 32: 1–42.

Gabolde, Luc. 1998. 'Le «Grand Château d'Amon» de Sésostris Ier à Karnak. La Décoration du Temple d'Amon-Rê au Moyen Empire'. *Mémoires de l'Académie des Inscriptions et Belle-Lettres* 17: 143–158.

Gardiner, Alan H. (ed.). 1935. *The Temple of King Sethos I at Abydos: The Chapels of Amen-Re, Re-Harakhti, Ptah, and King Sethos*, Vol. II. Chicago: The Oriental Institute of the University of Chicago.

Gardiner, Alan H. (ed.). 1958. *The Temple of King Sethos I at Abydos: The Second Hypostyle Hall*, Vol. IV. Chicago: The Oriental Institute of the University of Chicago.

George, B. 1970. *Zu den altägyptischen Vorstellungen vom Schatten als Seele*. Bonn: Habelt.

Hannig, Rainer. 2015. *Die Sprache der Pharaonen. Großes Handwörterbuch Ägyptisch–Deutsch (2800 bis 950 v. Chr.)*, Marburger edition. Hannig Lexica 1, Kulturgeschichte der Antiken Welt 64. Mainz: Philip von Zabern.

Harpur, Yvonne. 2001. *The Tombs of Nefermaat and Rahotep at Maidum: Discovery, Destruction and Reconstruction*. Prestbury: Oxford Expedition to Egypt.

Hartwig, Melinda K. 2004. *Tomb Painting and Identity in Ancient Thebes, 1419–1372. BCE*. Monumenta Aegyptiaca 10. Turnhout: Brepols.

Hartwig, Melinda K. (ed.). 2023. *Life and the Afterlife Ancient Egyptian Art from the Senusret Collection*. Atlanta: Michael C. Carlos Museum.

Hendrickx, Stan et al. 2012. 'The Earliest Representations of Royal Power in Egypt: The Rock Drawings of Nag el-Hamdulab (Aswan)'. *Antiquity* 86: 1068–1083.

Hornung, Erik. 1990. *Das Totenbuch der Ägypter*. Zürich: Artemis.

Houlihan, Patrick F. 1986. *The Birds of Ancient Egypt*. Warminster: Aris & Phillips.

Johnson, W.R. 1994. 'Honorific Figures of Amenhotep III in the Luxor Temple Colonnade Hall'. In *For His Ka: Essays in Memory of Klaus Baer*, edited by D.P. Silverman, 133–144. SAOC 55. Chicago: Oriental Institute of the University of Chicago.

Johnson, W.R. 2009. 'A Sandstone Relief of Tutankhamun in the Liverpool Museum from the Luxor Temple Colonnade Hall'. In *Causing his Name to Live Culture and History of the Ancient Near East. Essays in Memory of William J. Murnane*, edited by Peter Brand and Louise Cooper, 125–128. Leiden and Boston: Brill.

Kees, Hermann. 1912. *Der Opfertanz des ägyptischen Königs*. Leipzig: J.C. Hinrichs'sche Buchhandlung.

Larché, François. 2019. *L'anastylose des Blocs d'Amenhotep Ier à Karnak*. Études d'Égyptologie 18, 4 vols. Paris: Soleb.

Lepsius, Karl Richard Lepsius. 1849–1859. *Denkmäler aus Ägypten und Äthiopien*, 6 Bd. Berlin: Nicolaische Buchhandlung.

Luft, Daniela C. 2009. *Das Anzünden der Fackel. Untersuchungen zu Spruch 137 des Totenbuches*. Studien zum Altägyptischen Totenbuch 15. Wiesbaden: Harrassowitz.

Lurker, Manfred. 1974. *Götter und Symbole der Alten Ägypter*. Bern: Barth.

Masquelier-Loorius, Julie. 2017. 'The Akh-menu of Thutmosis III at Karnak. The Sokarian Rooms'. In *Proceedings of the XI International Congress of Egyptologists Florence Egyptian Museum: Florence, 23–30 August 2015*, edited by M. Cristina Guidotti and Gloria Rosati, 394–398. Oxford: Archaeopress.

Mohamed, Ghada. 2020. 'Menschenhafte Zeichen: Die Anthropomorphisierten Sakralzeichen im Pharaonischen Ägypten'. Unpublished dissertation, Bonn.

Mohamed, Ghada. Forthcoming. '*The Signs Revealed their Forms. He called to Them and They Answered to Him*: The Anthropomorphized Hieroglyphs as (Inter)active Image-text Compositions in Ancient Egypt'. In *Proceedings of Rethinking the Visual Aesthetics of Ancient Egyptian Writing Conference* (18–20 November 2021).

Morenz, Ludwig D. 2002. 'Die Standarten des Königsgeleits Repräsentanten von Abydos und Hierakonpolis als Denbeiden Herrscherlichen Residenzen?'. *Studien zur altägyptischen Kultur* 30: 277–283.

Morgan, Jacques de. 1895. *Fouilles à Dahchour. Mars–Juin 1894*. Vienne: Holzhausen.

Munro, Peter. 1961. 'Bemerkungen zu einem Sedfest-Relief in der Stadtmauer von Kairo'. *Zeitschrift für ägyptische Sprache und Altertumskunde* 86: 61–74.

Murnane, William J. 1977. *Ancient Egyptian Coregencies*. SAOC 40. Chicago: The Oriental Institute of the University of Chicago.

Murnane, William J. 1979. 'The Bark of Amun on the Third Pylon at Karnak'. *Journal of the American Research Center in Egypt* 16: 11–27.

Murnane, William J., and Harold Hayden Nelson (eds). 1981. *The Epigraphic Survey: The Great Hypostyle Hall at Karnak: The Wall Reliefs*, Vol. I, Part 1. Oriental Institute Publications 106. Chicago: Oriental Institute of the University of Chicago.

Naville, Édouard. 1886. *Das Altägyptische Totenbuch der XVIII. bis XX. Dynastie: Aus Verschiedenen Urkunden Zusammengestellt. Text und Vignetten*, Vol. I; *Einleitung*, Vol. II. Berlin: Asher.

Naville, Édouard. 1901. *The Temple of Deir el-Bahari: The Shrine of Hathor and the Southern Hall of Offerings*, Vol. IV. London: Egypt Exploration Fund.

Naville, Édouard. 1908. *The Temple of Deir el-Bahari: The Lower Terrace, Additions and Plans*, Vol. VI. London: Egypt Exploration Fund.

Otto, E. 1975. 'Anthropomorphismus'. In *Lexikon der Ägyptologie*, Vol. I, edited by Wolfgang Helck and Wolfhart Westendorf, 311–318. Wiesbaden: Harrassowitz.

Pawlicki, Franciszek. 1999. 'Deir el-Bahari: The Temple of Queen Hatshepsut 1997/1998'. *Polish Archaeology in the Mediterranean* 10: 119–130.

Pawlicki, Franciszek. 2000. *The Temple of Queen Hatshepsut at Deir el-Bahari*. Cairo: Supreme Council of Antiquities.

Peters, Pam. 2004. The *Cambridge Guide to English Usage*. Cambridge: Cambridge University Press.

Petrie, W.M. Flinders. 1892. *Medum*. London: Nutt.

Petrie, W.M. Flinders. 1914. *Amulets: Illustrated by the Egyptian Collection in University College*. London: Constable & Company Ltd.

Posener, Georges. 1965. 'Le Nom de l'Enseigne Appelée "Khons"'. *Revue d'Égyptologie* 17: 198–200.

Pries, Andreas. H. 2016. 'ἔμψυχα ἱερογλυφικά I. Eine Annäherung an Wesen und Wirkmacht Ägyptischer Hieroglyphen nach dem Indigenen Zeugnis'. In *Sapientia Felicitas. Festschrift für Günter Vittmann zum 29. Februar 2016*, edited by Sandra L. Lippert, Maren Schentuleit and Martin A. Stadler. *Les Cahiers Égypte Nilotique et Meditérranéenne* 14: 449–488.

Quack, Joachim Friedrich. 2007. 'Ein Ägyptischer Dialog über die Schreibkunst und das Arkane Wissen'. *Archiv für Religionsgeschichte* 9: 259–294.

Reed, Charles A., and Dale J. Osborn. 1978. 'Taxonomic Transgressions in Tutankhamun's Treasures'. *American Journal of Archaeology* 82: 273–283.

Reeves, Nicholas. 1990. *The Complete Tutankhamun: The King, the Tomb, the Royal Treasure*. London: Thames and Hudson.

Ritner, Robert Kriech. 2018. 'Relief of Nefermaat and Itet'. In *Highlights of the Collections of the Oriental Institute Museum*, edited by Jean M. Evans, Jack Green and Emily Teeter, 88. Chicago: The Oriental Institute of the University of Chicago.

Saad, R. 1970. 'Les Travaux d'Aménophis IV au IIIe Pylône du Temple d'Amon Rê à Karnak'. *Kêmi. Revue de Philologie et d'Archéologie Égytiennes et Coptes* 20: 187–193.

Sabbahy, Lisa. 2013. 'Depictional Study of the Chariot Use in the New Kingdom'. In *Chasing Chariots. Proceedings of the First International Chariot Conference (Cairo 2012)*, edited by André J. Veldmeijer and Salima Ikram, 191–202. Leiden: Sidestone Press.

Saleh, Mohamed. 1984. *Das Totenbuch in den Thebanischen Beamtengribern des Neuen Reiches: Texte und Vignetten*. Archäologische Veröffentlichungen 46. Mainz am Rhein: Philip von Zabern.

Schenkel, W. 1984. 'Schatten'. In *Lexikon der Ägyptologie* V, edited by Wolfgang Helck and Wolfhart Westendorf, 535–536. Wiesbaden: Harrassowitz.

Schulz, Regine and Matthias Seidel. 1997. *Ägypten. Die Welt der Pharaonen*. Köln: Könemann.

Seligmann, C.G., and M. A. Murray 1911. 'Note Upon an Early Egyptian Standard'. *Man* 11: 168–171.

Spiegelberg, Wilhelm. 1930. '*nṯr.w* "Götter" = "Bilder"'. *Zeitschrift für ägyptische Sprache und Altertumskunde* 65: 119–121.

Te Velde, Herman. 1986. 'Egyptian Hieroglyphs as Signs, Symbols and Gods'. *Visible Religion* 4–5: 63–72.

Vandier, Jacques. 1935. *Tombes de Deir el-Médineh: La Tombe de Nefer-Abou*. Mémoires de l'Institut Français d'Archéologie Orientale 69. Le Caire: Institut Francais d'Archéologie Orientale.

von Dassow, Eva (ed.). 1994. *The Egyptian Book of the Dead: The Book of Going Forth by Day*. San Francisco: Chronicle Books.

Westendorf, Wolfhart. 1980. 'Luft'. In *Lexikon der Ägyptologie*, Vol. III, edited by Wolfgang Helck and Wolfhart Westendorf, 1098–1102. Wiesbaden: Harrassowitz.

Abbreviations

PM

Porter, Bertha, and Rosalind L.B. Moss. 1927–1951. *Topographical Bibliography of Ancient Egyptian Hieroglyphic Texts, Reliefs and Paintings*, Vols I–VII. Oxford: The Griffith Institute.

Wb

Erman, Adolf, and Hermann Grapow. 1926–1931. *Wörterbuch der Ägyptische Sprache*, Vols I–V. Berlin: Akademie-Verlag.

'Tut-mania' through the iconography of Egyptomaniac ex libris[1]

Valentin Boyer

Abstract

The production of ex libris featuring motifs relating to ancient Egypt, and more specifically linked to Tutankhamun, may be seen as a manifestation of Tut-mania. However, it is important to distinguish between ex libris that are more related to Egyptophilia (and therefore Tut-philia) and those that are more related to Egyptomania (and therefore Tut-mania). When there is re-creation, re-appropriation and re-adaptation of motifs from the Tutankhamun treasure, it may be considered to be Tut-mania.[2] This profusion of examples representing real archaeological objects, sometimes integrated into totally fanciful compositions, was the starting point for this study. It focuses on bookplates deriving their motifs from Tutankhamun, a tiny subset of the several hundreds of thousands of bookplates that must exist. The search for archaeological sources improves our understanding of the diffusion of certain motifs, which enhances our understanding of the reception of Tut-mania.

Keywords: bookplates, ex libris, Egyptomania, Egyptian Revival, bibliophilia, history of Egyptology, Tut-mania, engraving

Introduction

There are hundreds of ex libris with Egyptian patterns, some exhibiting considerable originality, whereas others consist simply of a few patterns evoking ancient Egypt, together with more widespread clichés. The reception and representation of Tutankhamun through bookplates, an artistic medium generally reserved for the sphere of bibliophiles, provide an interesting insight into the mechanisms of the development and the perception of the iconography of Tut-mania. Since the discovery of Tutankhamun's tomb by Howard Carter on 4 November 1922, the king, and particularly his funerary mask and other treasures of his virtually intact tomb, has been a widespread source of fascination. Tutankhamun has also evoked the 'mysterious East', and been a portal to a distant past, revealed by a tomb that had been concealed for centuries. The mask of Tutankhamun has become a cultural referent that evokes ancient Egypt at first sight.

Ex libris are, in general, gummed printed paper name-plates fixed inside the covers of books to indicate to whom they belong. Book lovers have used them for centuries, not just to specify ownership, but to enhance the beauty of their book collection. 'Ex libris', from the Latin, translates simply as 'from the library of'. With 'ex bibliotheca', the formula 'ex libris' is the most used in Latin languages, but there are also many other formulations, e.g., 'this book belongs to' (English), 'boek van' (Dutch), 'z knih' (Czech), 'из книг' (Russian), 'denna bok tillhör' (Swedish), 'könyve' (Hungarian), 'dos livros de' (Portuguese), etc. Tut-mania has not escaped the world of bibliophiles and the ex libris has become an interesting medium for revisiting this fascinating pharaoh, not only through representations of his mask, but also of a number of finds from his tomb. Bookplate artists may demonstrate a certain originality by revisiting and reinventing the patterns thanks to their subjective sensibility.

Between Tut-philia and Tut-mania

The treasures in Tutankhamun's tomb created a widespread craze for both Tutankhamun and ancient Egypt, fed by the overflowing imaginations of people obsessed with these sparkling wonders. Combining the fulfilment of every archaeologist's dream, analogy with Ali Baba's cave, the mystery of a virtually intact tomb and a new window on the Pharaonic past, a myth was created.

The production of ex libris featuring motifs relating to ancient Egypt, and more specifically linked to Tutankhamun, are a manifestation of this Tut-mania. However, it is important to distinguish between ex libris that are more akin to Egyptophilia (and therefore Tut-philia) and those that are more related to Egyptomania (and therefore Tut-mania). When there is re-creation, re-appropriation and re-adaptation of motifs from the Tutankhamen treasure, it may be considered to fall under the heading of Tut-mania.[3]

The time of discovery, creation of 'modern triads'

Tut-mania is also characterized by the creation of 'modern triads'. That most closely related to the discovery of the tomb brings together Tutankhamun, Howard Carter and Lord Carnarvon, while the next associated almost inevitably ancient figures of Tutankhamun, Akhenaten and Nefertiti.

Tutankhamun, Carter and Carnarvon

The discovery of the tomb of Pharaoh Tutankhamun by the British archaeologist Howard Carter (1874–1939) and his patron and compatriot, the 5th Earl of Carnarvon (1866–1923) is the most famous and mythic find in the history of archaeology. The ex libris of Wolfgang Pungs (Fig. 7.1), made in 1996 by the Belgian artist Pauwels Hedwig, illustrates the three figures of this discovery. The funerary mask of Tutankhamun is easily recognizable. The portrait of Howard Carter in the upper right-hand corner of the ex libris is a detail from a painting, oil on canvas,[4] with gilded wood frame, belonging to the Griffith Institute at Oxford University.[5] It was painted by his older brother William Carter (1863–1939), who was a professional portrait artist. Signed and dated by William, the painting was probably commissioned shortly after the discovery of the tomb of Tutankhamun and completed in 1924. Carter's British home was in London and this painting was displayed there. This painting was donated to the Griffith Institute by Carter's favourite niece and heir, Phyllis Walker, in 1959 and is displayed in the Archive of the Griffith Institute in Oxford. The portrait of Lord Carnarvon, reading on the veranda of Carter's house at Elwat el-Dibbân on the Theban west bank, is a detail of a photograph in the Griffith Institute,[6] probably made by Harry Burton (1879–1940), the British archaeological photographer, best known for his photographs of the excavations in the Valley of the Kings.

Tutankhamun, Akhenaten and Nefertiti

Three ancient figures are regularly associated: Tutankhamun, Akhenaten and Nefertiti. This association is not insignificant. In the ex libris of Iain Boyd (Fig. 7.2), made by Czech artist Pavel Hlavaty (b. 1943), it is an assumed genealogy with a representation of a colossal sandstone statue of Akhenaten (when still Amenhotep IV) from Karnak, now in the Egyptian Museum, Cairo.[7] This colossus of is one of a number discovered by Maurice Pillet in 1925 to the east of the temple enclosure. This colossal statue bears the *khat* adorned with a uraeus and surmounted by the double-crown. Part of his left arm and his legs from the knees down are missing. It is here associated in this ex libris with the famous bust of Queen Nefertiti in the Ägyptisches Museum in Berlin.[8] These modern triads pay homage to an event or family group, and should be seen as manifestations of Egyptophilia.

Creation of a modern icon: the mask of Tutankhamun

Is the mask of Tutankhamun truly an iconic image? The gold mask of Tutankhamun might not be the first object that comes to mind when one thinks of the wonders of Egypt, but it is arguably one of the most famous ones. The receptivity of this world-famous image is indisputable. This powerful image has been widely taken up, adapted and re-appropriated to such an extent that it has almost been stripped of its original nature. Ever since its discovery, the funerary mask of Tutankhamun has become a universal symbol that evokes an ostensible understanding, a feeling of familiarity, of a known reference. A truly universal cultural referent, it has become part of international visual culture, permeating every social class, every culture and every artistic medium. In ex libris, when the figure of Tutankhamun is chosen, the mask generally becomes the main and central motif of the vignette, apart from a few exceptions where it is relegated to the background, or even simply suggested by its silhouette.

By its silence and unfathomable expression, this mask fascinates and impresses. The technical finesse of its creation, the preciousness of its materials and the strange sense of eternity that emerges from this artefact hypnotize the viewer. A symbol of aesthetics, craftsmanship, preciousness, balance and composition, this object of fascination captivates the attention and feeds the imagination, maintained from the discovery of the tomb by a disproportionate media promotion which one can qualify as over-mediatization. A little-known king who reigned for a very short time, Tutankhamun alone embodies the Pharaonic civilization. This mask, the most emblematic object in the entire funerary treasure, helped grip the world with an Egyptian fever.

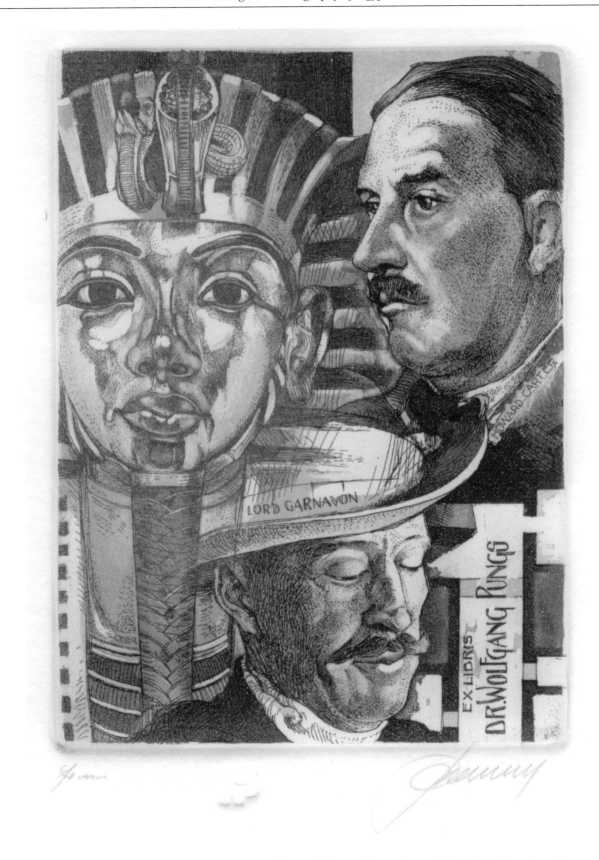

Fig. 7.1. Ex libris of Wolfgang Pungs made by Pauwels Hedwig, 1996, aqua fortis and aquatint (C3+C5), Sammlung Museum Schloß Burgk, No. XXVI-53169. © Museum Schloß Burgk.

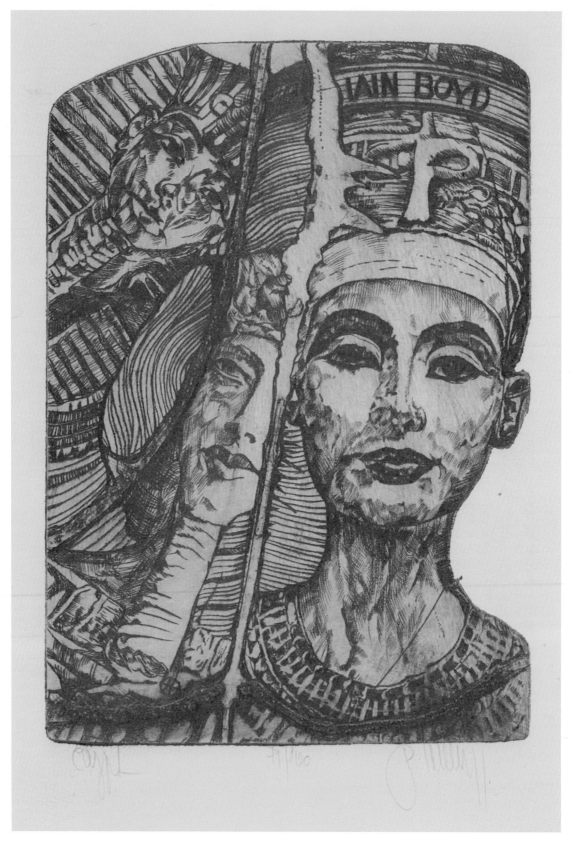

Fig. 7.2. Ex libris of Iain Boyd made by Pavel Hlavaty, 1987, aqua fortis (C3), H. 129 mm, W. 89 mm. Frederikshavn Kunstmuseum & Exlibrissamling, Collection Klaus Rödel (cassette: 32 No. 17). © Frederikshavn Kunstmuseum & Exlibrissamling.

Fig. 7.3. Ex libris of Riet de Haas made by Harry Jürgens (1949–), 1996, aqua fortis (C3), H. 210 mm, W. 150 mm. Print 96/100, Private collection, No. 2021_242. © Photo Valentin Boyer.

Fig. 7.4. Ex libris of Valerie made by Gulicska Lőrinc, 1972, linocut (X3), H. 155 mm, W. 104 mm. Private collection, No. 2021_175. © Photo Valentin Boyer.

The ex libris of Riet de Hass (Fig. 7.3), made by Estonian artist Harry Jürgens (b. 1949), depicts a sequence from the second act of the opera *Aida*, by Giuseppe Verdi (1813–1901). Packed with detail, the scene is that of the triumph of Radames. The long, upright trumpets open this triumphal entry, providing a heroic thrill, while echoing the long spears pointing skywards. The tumult of the scene gradually reveals the dancers, musicians and spoils of war in the procession. In this scene of jubilation and festivities, three deities stand out in the foreground: Horus, Sekhmet and Seth. The protagonists, Aida and Radames, dominate the scene on either side of King Tutankhamun's mask, a timeless evocation of the figure of the pharaoh.

Thus, this 'Tut-mania' does not escape the world of bibliophiles, and ex libris becomes a privileged artistic medium for revisiting this icon. Despite its re-appropriation and re-adaptation in different styles and on different media, the image of Tutankhamun's funerary mask is immediately understood here, which is characteristic of iconicity, the relationship between the form of a sign, such as a word or symbol, and its meaning. The shape, dimensions and, in other cases, the colours used, the materials and the regalia of the pharaoh are all analogical characteristics allowing an immediate identification of this mask. On the ex libris of

Valerie (Fig. 7.4), made by the Hungarian artist Gulicska Lőrinc, the famous mask of King Tutankhamun[9] is immediately recognizable, although the false beard here is much shorter than on the original mask.

On the ex libris example for Gernot Blum (Fig. 7.5), made by the Czech artist Vladimír Pechar (b. 1931), the ex libris honours Tutankhamun with a representation in profile of the second coffin with sceptres.[10] The background is covered with hieratic text. Although not an exact duplicate, it could be an extract from vignette 1 of the Hunefer Papyrus (New Kingdom, 19th Dynasty) in the British Museum,[11] comprising Spell 15 of the Book of the Dead, relating to the Adoration of Amun-Ra.

The icon, with a high degree of iconicity, is purely referential. It is a universally and easily recognizable sign. As a paradigm of Egyptian royalty, Egyptian technical know-how and Pharaonic civilization, the mask has been elevated to the rank of universal icon, and thus, arbitrarily and unconsciously, to that of visual symbol, stereotype and allegory – albeit a restrictive one – of ancient Egypt.

Fig. 7.6. Ex libris of Klaus Hermanns made by Ukrainian artist Gennady Pugachevsky, 1996, plastic engravings with pressings / relief-printed engraving of other materials, for example synthetic ones (X6/8), Opus 72, H. 88 mm, W. 86 mm. Private collection, No. 2022_008. © Photo Valentin Boyer.

A patchwork of patterns

One may wonder why Tutankhamun is so often used on ex libris, and in particular his mask, which becomes an almost immutable representation. Over the course of the 20th century, Tutankhamun acquired an enviable position as a universal icon which concentrates, through the sole representation of his mask, not only his own identity but also, and above all, an evocation of the whole of ancient Egypt.

'Egyptomania' means first of all a reuse of decorative elements borrowed from ancient Egypt by our contemporary societies without necessarily caring about the original context. This corresponds to a cultural re-appropriation through the re-creation of objects that sometimes have nothing to do with the pharaonic civilization. It is not enough for the Egyptian forms to be copied. They need to be re-created with the sensitivity of the artists who thus reflects a history of aesthetic taste specific to their time. As can be seen on the ex libris of Jan Karásek (Fig. 7.7), made by Czech artist Bohuslav Knobloch (1924–1998), the mask and the pyramid evoke ancient Egypt at first glance alongside other works, the Taj Mahal and a statue of a dancer, perhaps from Karnataka, and a representation of a Bavarian-looking hunter, perhaps more Czech if we consider the origin of the ex libris holder.

In the ex libris of Z. Benýšek (Fig. 7.8), made by Czech artist Renata Kaiserová (b. 1962), the mask of Tutankhamun

Fig. 7.5. Ex libris of Mario de Filippis made by Vladimír Pechar (1931–), 1987, offset (P7), Opus 741, H. 108 mm, W. 82 mm. Private collection, No. 2021_219. © Photo Valentin Boyer.

The mask of Tutankhamun has quite naturally taken its place as a symbol of Egypt in the collective imagination, becoming a cultural referent, making it possible to evoke ancient Egypt at first sight. As can be seen here, many ex libris depict Tutankhamun's funerary mask, the most famous object in his treasure. These works are truly 'Egyptomania', as they involve a reinvention of the mask, a re-appropriation, a re-adaptation of the motif in very different styles (Fig. 7.6).

Whatever the degree of stylization, simplification and abstraction of the representation of Tutankhamun's funerary mask, its resemblance to the original artefact remains unmistakable. It is easily recognizable and understandable by the similarities it maintains with its referent, the original artefact. This almost immediate identification reveals a high degree of iconicity. This true 'Tut-mania' is equivalent to the fascination with the bust of Nefertiti and its impact on Egyptophile bibliophiles. Now tutelary and iconic images of ancient Egypt, there is a shift in their perception. From purely Egyptological figures, they become 'Egyptianized' by the collective imagination which appropriates and universalizes them.[12]

Fig. 7.8. Ex libris of Z. Benýšek made by Renata Kaiserová (1962–), 2005, aquafortis + drypoint + mezzotint (C3 + C4 + C7), Opus 153, EditioiusiI./ X., H. 230 mm, W. 165 mm. Private collection, No. 2021_012. © Photo Valentin Boyer.

The same pectoral is used as pattern in the ex libris of J. Rünstuk (Fig. 7.9), made by Bohuslav Knobloch, but associated with a depiction of the goddess Isis, a scene inspired by the north-east corridor of the vestibule of Nefertari's tomb (QV 66). Dressed in a sheath dress, wearing an *wesekh*-collar, a *menat*-necklace and holding an *was*-sceptre, the goddess Isis is wearing a tripartite wig topped with two cows' horns enclosing a solar disk coiled with an *uraeus*. On the right, the column of hieroglyphs *ḥmt-nsw wrt [nb]t tȝwy* (Great Royal Wife, Lady of the Two Lands). Within the cartouche, Nefertari's name is replaced by the word 'Exlibris', followed by the hieroglyphs *mȝꜥ-ḥrw* (true of voice).

Tutankhamun's treasure, a treasure trove of patterns

But Tut-mania is not just Tututankhamun's legendary funerary mask. More subtlety in the representation in the ex libris of Arno Kupka (Fig. 7.10), made by Ukrainian artist Gennady Pugachevsky in 1998. In this case it is not the funerary mask but the upper part of Tutankhamun's

Fig. 7.7. Ex libris of Jan Karásek made by Bohuslav Knobloch, date unknown, aquatint (C5), H. 182 mm, W. 63 mm. Private collection, No. 2021_092. © Photo Valentin Boyer.

is associated with a composite *wadjet*-eye pectoral in Cairo[13] which served as the inspiration. In this pectoral, the eye is flanked by the cobra-goddess, Wadjet, wearing the crown of Lower Egypt, and the vulture of Nekhbet with the *atef*-crown, as the representative goddess of Upper Egypt. The whole ensemble is made of gold and inlaid for the most part with polychrome glass interspersed with some carnelian and lapis lazuli.

Fig. 7.9. Ex libris of J. Rünštuk made by Bohuslav Knobloch (1924–1998), c. 1970–1989, lithography (L/4), H. 227 mm, W. 107 mm. Private collection, No. 2021_146. © Photo Valentin Boyer.

Fig. 7.10. Ex libris of Arno Kupka made by Gennady Pugachevsky, 1998, plastic engravings with pressings / Relief-printed engraving of other materials, for example synthetic ones (X6/9), H. 101 mm, W. 69 mm. Opus 97, Private collection. © All rights reserved.

innermost anthropoid coffin,[14] recognizable by its all-gold *khat* and blue glass-framed eyes.

The study of the phenomenon of Tut-mania in the bibliophilic medium of ex libris is particularly interesting through references to Tutankhamun other than by representations of his funerary mask. It seems that true Egyptophilia (or Tut-philia) involves the creation of

works paying homage to artefacts from Tutankhamun's tomb that are perhaps less well known to the neophyte public. Although the funerary mask has been revived in all its forms throughout the twentieth and twenty-first centuries, there are ex libris honouring other objects from the Tutankhamun treasure that one should highlight. An example is the ex libris of Helmer Fogedgaard, made by German artist Jürgens Dost[15] and printed on Ingres paper.[16] The vignette depicts two figures: Tutankhamun holding a pear-shaped mace in one hand, and the god Osiris clad in a shroud, arms crossed over his chest, holding two sceptres and wearing the *atef*-crown. Tutankhamun can be identified by the cartouche of his prenomen, *Nb-ḫprw-Rˁ*. Another cartouche is not legible but would probably correspond to his nomen. This scene is a detail from a mural representation on the north wall of the burial chamber of the tomb in the Valley of the Kings. But are there other things to see other than the funerary mask or the tomb? 'Yes, wonderful things!' Boxes, chests, pectorals, fans, jewellery and many other objects that give an account of the diversity of representations borrowed from the Tutankhamun treasure

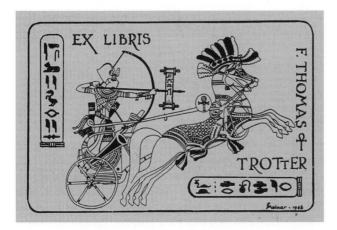

Fig. 7.11. Ex libris of F. Thomas Trotter made by Istvan Molnar (1974–), 1968, linear zincotyping (P1), H. 37 mm, W. 56 mm. Frederikshavn Kunstmuseum & Exlibrissamling, Collection Jensen Tusch (cassette 385, No. 88). © Frederikshavn Kunstmuseum & Exlibrissamling.

in order to understand the impact of this discovery on bibliophile Egyptophiles.

Various objects: chests

In the ex libris of Gernot Blum, made by Dutch artist Ludovicus Arnoldus (Lou) Strik (1921–2001),[17] could be the representation of Ankhesenamun borrowed from the lid of the ivory-inlaid chest from the tomb.[18] This elaborate chest was found by Carter in the Annexe. Made of a red wood, almost every part of the outer surface is either inlaid, gilded, covered or veneered. Ebony, ivory, faience, calcite and gilt are the materials that richly decorate the surface and adhere to it by means of glue and, in a few cases, copper nails. In the centre, surrounded by borders of stained ivory, is a scene depicting the king and queen in the marshes. She is here dressed in a white tunic, over which she wears a pleated dress-coat, tightened by a pleated belt with long floating sides. A large *wesekh*-collar hugs the top of her bust. She wears a short wig, to which is added a sidelock of youth falling on the side. She holds out with both hands a bouquet of papyrus and lotus.

A very rare representation in the production of ex libris with an iconography related to ancient Egypt is the representation of Tutankhamun in his chariot massacring enemies. The ex libris of F. Thomas Trotter (Fig. 7.11), made by Hungarian artist Istvan Molnar (b. 1947), is inspired by a wooden chest. It is one of the most intricately decorated objects in the tomb which was found in the Antechamber and illustrates the innovation of the frenzied battle. A fierce confrontation takes place on both sides of the box. The king shoots his arrows into the fray. This is the only known representation of Tutankhamun in a chariot in an ex libris, the others representing exclusively Rameses II at the battle of Qadesh.

Fig. 7.12. Ex libris of L.K.S. made by Jan Otava, date unknown, H. 140 mm, W. 105 mm. Private collection. © All rights reserved.

Various objects: pectorals

Many of the ex libris depict scarabs, almost exclusively scarabs from the jewels from Tutankhamun's tomb. On the ex libris of L.K.S. (Fig. 7.12), made by Czech artist Jan Otava (b. 1950), an Egyptian scarab holding the moon is inspired from a pectoral decorated in a complex way.[19] The central part of the pectoral, which represents the pre-nomen of the king, is placed in the middle of a large lapis lazuli scarab. Below it is a hieroglyphic *nb*-sign, inlaid with blue glass. Above is the lunar disk made of electrum. On another ex libris, of Gernot Blum (Fig. 7.13), made by Vladimír Pechar in 1985, inspired by another pectoral,[20] lunar disc and crescent replace the conventional sun-disc. Because of its solar nature, the scarab (often winged) surmounted by the sun played a key role in Tutankhamun's funerary furniture, and this iconography used on these two ex libris is particularly interesting. The funerary treasure contains scarabs surmounted by the moon (represented by the crescent and the full moon). This symbol represented regeneration. The identification of the king with the moon is obvious, revealing that Tutankhamun was revered as a lunar god. Words and images thus demonstrate that the king possesses both the divine character of the sun and that of

Fig. 7.13. Ex libris of Gernot Blum made by Vladimír Pechar, 1985, rotogravure (P4), H. 100 mm, W. 125 mm. Frederikshavn Kunstmuseum & Exlibrissamling, collection Jensen Tusch (cassette 321, No. 64). © Frederikshavn Kunstmuseum & Exlibrissamling.

the moon; in this way, his daily and monthly regeneration is guaranteed in the afterlife.[21]

The fan of Tutankhamun

The ex libris of Willem Karel de Bruijn (Fig. 7.14), made by Spanish artist Elfi Osiander de Lewin-Richter (1912–1999) in 1983, represents a hunting scene. The king is shown riding a light chariot pulled by a team of horses. The reins are wrapped around his hips to leave his hands free to draw his bow. Behind the chariot runs a sign of life, with human legs and arms, carrying in his hands a long-handled fan whose shape[22] corresponds to the one shown here, a detail also transcribed on the ex libris. He draws his bow to shoot yet another arrow in order to hit a gazelle, already overtaken by a hunting dog. This scene is faithfully inspired by the iconography of King Tutankhamun's fan,[23] except for the hunted prey, which is a gazelle on the ex libris, whereas it is ostriches on the original fan. The long-handled fan features a semi-circular or semi-elliptical plate on which the feathers were arranged in an arc. This fan with a representation of

Fig. 7.14. Ex libris of Willem Karel r. a de Bruijn made by Elfi Osiander de Lewin-Richter (1912–1999), 1983, aqua fortis (C3), H. 125 mm, W. 174 mm. Private collection, No. 2021_038. © Photo Valentin Boyer.

Fig. 7.16. Ex libris of Antoniego Brosza made by Jan Hasso Agopsowicz (1915–1982), 2003, mixed technique (Tm4), H. 138 mm, W. 120 mm. Zamość, Muzeum Zamojskie, No. EX-2153. © Muzeum Zamojskie.

Fig. 7.15. Ex libris of Klaus Hermanns made by Elly de Koster (1948–), 1989, aqua fortis and aquatint (C3+C5), Opus 206, 26/100, H. 119 mm, W. 110 mm. Private collection, No. 2021_205. © Photo Valentin Boyer.

an ostrich hunt was found in the burial chamber of Tutankhamun's tomb on the floor between the third and fourth chapels. On a gilded wooden bow case[24] there is a hunting scene with caprids but the position of these does not correspond to that represented on de Bruijn's ex libris, which is perhaps due to the artist's creativity. The original fan was found in the Burial Chamber, between the two innermost shrines; from the remains of its feathers, it was clear that it had been fitted with 30 ostrich feathers, white and brown, alternately set.

A wooden shabti reflecting the state of conservation

The ex libris of Klaus Hermanns (Fig. 7.15), made by the Dutch artist Elly de Koster (b. 1948), represents one of the shabtis of Tutankhamun,[25] recognizable with wings spread over his chest. The wooden statuette represents the deceased as Osiris, wrapped in a shroud, wearing the *nemes* and holding just the flail-sceptre. The artist has transcribed the grain of the wood on the face and the cracks in the wood on the *nemes*.

Since the original excavation records show both crook- and flail-sceptres in place, the absence of the crook-sceptre is particularly intriguing and suggests that the shabti was used as a model, while the sceptre had been mislaid. A crook-sceptre is currently seen in place on the shabti as exhibited in the Egyptian Museum in Cairo. A crook-sceptre,

albeit longer and thinner than the current one, was in place during the early 1970s, as attested by the publication of a photograph of the shabti in the catalogue *Treasures of Tutankhamun* published in 1972.[26] On the other hand, the sceptre is missing in the exhibition catalogue *Götter und Pharaonen*, published in 1978–1979,[27] and described as 'lost'.[28] Given that the ex libris was made in 1989, this indicates that it was based on the state of conservation of the shabti between the late 1970s and early 1980s.[29] It could thus probably be that the model was the photograph published in the 1978–1979 catalogue.

The seat of power: Tutankhamun's thrones

On one example, the scene on the ex libris of Antoniego Brosza (Fig. 7.16), made by Polish Armenian artist Jan Hasso Agopsowicz (1915–1982), is inspired by a wooden chair with finely carved back.[30] The back consists of a scene representing Heh, the personification of a million years and eternity. Heh is always represented in a crouching position, raising his hands to the sky. The chair is decorated at the top with the winged solar disk, which is not represented on the ex libris. However, there are several modifications, such as a re-creation of the original pattern. The scene is re-adapted for the function of the ex libris. Indeed, the inscriptions have been omitted to allow the artist Jan Hasso Agopsowicz to have a little more space to enlarge the two cartouches of Tutankhamun. On the other hand, some other inscriptions have simply been replaced by the name of the ex libris holder (Antoniego Brosza) and the essential words: 'ex' and 'libris'.

The ex libris of Auguste and Madeleine Pickar,[31] made by Belgian artist Marie-Louise Albessart (1907–1999) in 1984,[32] and of Axel Leier,[33] made by Hungarian artist Ladislav Vincze in 1989, show the same clearly recognizable scene from the back of Tutankhamun's famous throne[34] but without the representation of Ankhesenamun.

A contemporary Portuguese ex libris of Ana Cristina Nunes Martins[35] (Plate 22), made by Portuguese artist David Fernandes da Silva, was displayed in the exhibition 'Tutankhamon em Portugal. Relatos na Imprensa Portuguesa (1922–1939)' at the National Library of Portugal (Academia Portuguesa de Ex-Libris) in Lisbon. This exhibition was the direct result of a research project of the Egyptologists Susanna Mota and José Sales, within the context of the reception of ancient Egypt, entitled 'Tutankhamen in Portugal'.[36] A special table with ex libris was displayed in this exhibition, as a demonstration of Egyptomania and Egyptophilia in Portugal. The various examples of ex libris were often depicted with the Great Sphinx and the pyramids of Giza, but this one is about or connected with Tutankhamun. This ex libris of Ana Cristina Nunes Martins is a partial representation of the panel on the throne of Tutankhamun (Egyptian Museum in Cairo), with his name on two cartouches.

Conclusion

Carter's discovery sparked a wave of 'Tut-mania' across the world and this Tut-mania has not escaped the world of bibliophiles; the ex libris has become a privileged medium for revisiting this fascinating pharaoh, not only through representations of his mask but also several specific archaeological artefacts from his tomb. Although the artefacts of Tutankhamun's treasure are well known and have been published many times, in all countries of the world, the representations of objects other than the funerary mask are difficult to identify for the neophyte. The choice of these objects is part of a certain Egyptophilia among holders, owners and artists of ex libris, because these are not intended to be shown but to remain stuck in books and discovered by chance by other people if the book is lent or given. An ex libris is confidential. In the 21 ex libris discussed in this article, three of them were made in the 21st century and the others were made in the 20th century. One was designed in 2022, after the 2019 exhibition in Paris and probably commemorating the bicentenary of the discovery of the tomb. Most of the others were therefore made from the 1970s to the 1990s. With a larger corpus, their relationships to the various exhibitions (Paris 1967; USA 1976–1979; Canada 1979–1980; Germany 1980–1981 [Berlin, Cologne, Munich, Hanover and Hamburg]) can be studied. The reception of this Tut-mania is also international and is reflected in the production of ex libris for which the holders, owners and artists come from a wide variety of countries. In the 21 ex libris presented in this article, the owners and artists come from Belgium, Czech Republic, Denmark, Estonia,

Germany, Hungary, Netherlands, Poland, Portugal, Spain and Ukraine.

The profusion of examples representing real archaeological objects, sometimes integrated into totally fanciful compositions, was the starting point for this study, focused exclusively on bookplates taking their motifs from Tutankhamun, a highly specific theme when compared to the production of bookplates in general, which must amount to several hundreds of thousands of examples. The search for archaeological sources improves our understanding of the diffusion of certain motifs more than others, and the study of these motifs is a study of the reception of Tut-mania.

Notes

1   Tribute to Jean-François Chassaing, Honorary President of AFCEL (Association Française pour la Connaissance de l'Ex-Libris), who passed away on 22 June 2023.
2   Boyer 2023.
3   Boyer 2023.
4   William Carter, *Portrait of Howard Carter*, oil on canvas, 139 × 111 cm, Oxford, Griffith Institute Archive.
5   Carter MSS viii.2.
6   Burton photo: pkv93.
7   JE49529.
8   ÄM 21300.
9   Cairo JE 60672.
10 Czosnyka 1992, 7, No 76.
11 British Museum EA 9901.
12 Humbert 2022, 49–66.
13 Cairo JE 61901.
14 Cairo JE 60671.
15 Ex libris of Helmer Fogedgaard made by Jürgen Dost (b. 1939), longitudinal woodcut or linocut (X1 or X3), H. 131 mm, W. 107 mm, Private collection, No. 2021_065. © Photo Valentin Boyer.
16 Type of drawing paper. It is a laid finish paper of light to medium weight.
17 Ex libris of Gernot Blum made by Ludovicus Arnoldus (Lou) Strik (1921–2001), copper engraving or aqua fortis and aquatint (C2 or C3 + C5), 1982, H. 149 mm, W. 112 mm, Private collection, No. 2021_019. © Photo Valentin Boyer.
18 Cairo JE 61477.
19 Cairo JE 61890.
20 Cairo JE 61887.
21 Hornung and Staehelin 2004, 81–82. Many thanks to Florence Doyen for providing me with this bibliographical reference.
22 Hornung and Staehelin 2004, 318–320.
23 Cairo JE 62001.
24 Cairo JE 61502.
25 Cairo JE 60828, Carter No. 330j.
26 *Treasures of Tutankhamun*, London, British Museum, 1972, No. 11.
27 Roemer-Pelizaeus-Museum 1979, No. 41.
28 '[…] der Krummstab, einst von der linken Faust gehalten, ist verloren', Roemer-Pelizaeus-Museum 1979, No. 41.
29 Many thanks to Christian Loeben for bringing this valuable information to my attention.

30 Cairo JE 62029.
31 Ex libris of Auguste and Madeleine Pickar made by Marie-Louise Albessart, 1984, linear zincotyping (P1), Sammlung Museum Schloß Burgk, No. XVIII–23936.
32 Ex libris displayed in 2022 in the exhibition 'Égypte et ex-libris' at the Maison de l'Imprimerie in Thuin (Belgium) in collaboration with the Musée royal de Mariemont (curators: Valentin Boyer and Arnaud Quertinmont).
33 Ex libris of Axel Leier made by Ladislav Vincze, 1989, linocut (X3), Sammlung Museum Schloß Burgk, No. XXVII-42098.
34 Tutankhamen's Throne, New Kingdom, 18th Dynasty, Reign of Tutankhamun, Cairo, Grand Egyptian Museum, No. JE 62028.
35 Chair of the *Academia Portuguesa de Ex-Libris*, a non-profit association based in Lisbon, which is dedicated to the promotion, study and dissemination of ex libris.
36 Many thanks to Susanna Mota and José Salas for bringing this Portuguese ex libris to my attention and for sending me a photograph of it.

Bibliography

Blum, Gernot. 1992. *Antike im Exlibris: Aegypten im Exlibris*, Teil 1. Exlibrispublikation 276. Frederikshavn: Exlibristen.

Boyer, Valentin. 2023 (in print). 'Reflet de 200 ans d'Égyptologie: L'Archéologisation de l'Imaginaire dans les Ex-libris Égyptisants'. *Annales du Service des Antiquités de l'Égypte* 89: 18 pages.

Boyer, Valentin. 2023. 'Ancient Egypt in Exlibris. Objects and Images: Egyptological and Archaeological Sources'. In *Current Research in Egyptology 2022: Proceedings of the 22nd Annual Symposium, Université Paul-Valéry Montpellier 3, 26–30 September 2022*, edited by Amel Bouhafs, Linda Chapon, Marion Claude, et al., 46–60. Oxford and Montpellier: Archaeopress and CENiM 36.

Boyer, Valentin, and Arnaud Quertinmont (eds). 2022. *Égypte et Ex-libris: Entre Fantasme, Archéologie et Imaginaire*. Témoins d'Histoire 9. Brussels: Éditions Safran.

Capart, Jean. 1935. 'Les Ex-libris d'Aménophis III'. *Chronique d'Égypte* 10, Fasc. 19: 23–25.

Czosnyka, Józef Tadeusz. 1992. *Antyczny Egipt w ekslibrisach Vladimira Pechara*. Biblioteka Ekslibrisu XX Wieku, 3. Kraków: Dzielnicowy Ośrodek Kultury Kraków Podgórze.

Hornung, Erik, and Elisabeth Staehelin. 2004. 'La Vallée des Rois à la XVIIIe dynastie'. In *Toutankhamon, l'Or de l'Au-delà. Trésors Funéraires de la Vallée des Rois*, edited by André Wiese and Andreas Brodbeck, 57–82. Paris: Cybèle.

Humbert, Jean-Marcel. 2022. 'Néfertiti et Toutânkhamon. Deux Icônes du XXe siècle'. In *Égypte et Ex-libris: Entre Fantasme, Archéologie et Imaginaire*, edited by Valentin Boyer and Arnaud Quertinmont, 49–66. Coll. Témoins d'Histoire 9. Brussels: Éditions Safran.

Konrad, Kirsten. 2015. *Exlibris der Ägyptenrezeption und Ägyptomanie. Zur Sammlung des Gutenberg-Museum in Mainz*. Philippika 90. Wiesbaden: Harrassowitz.

Konrad, Kirsten, and Peter Pamminger. 2014. *Exlibris von Ägyptologen*. Göttinger Miszellen Beihefte 7. Göttingen: Alfa Druck & Vermittlung.

Laboury, Dimitri. 2022. 'Toutankhamon, Icône Moderne de l'Ancienne Égypte'. In *Égypte, Éternelle Passion. Exhibition Catalogue. Musée royal de Mariemont, Morlanwelz, September 2022*, edited by Arnaud Quertinmont, 160–166. Morlanwelz: Musée royal de Mariemont.

Neureiter, Manfred (ed.) 2009. *Lexikon der Exlibriskünstler*. Berlin: Pro BUSINESS.

Parkinson, Richard. 1999. 'Two or Three Literary Artefacts: British Museum EA 41650/47896, and 22878–9'. In *Studies in Egyptian Antiquities. A Tribute to T.G.H. James*, edited by W.V. Davies, 51–53. British Museum Occasional Paper 123. London: British Museum Press.

Roemer- und Pelizaeus-Museum. 1979, *Götter und Pharaonen*. Exhibition catalogue, 29 May–16 September 1979. Hildesheim: Roemer- und Pelizaeus-Museum.

Van Laethem, Marie-Paule, and Tony Oost 2013. *Goden, Graven en Farao's: Het Oude Egypte in het Exlibris*. Sint-Niklaas: Stedelijke Musea.

Hearts of glass: the styles and sources of the Neiger Brothers' Egyptian Revival jewellery and the identification of two Neiger Tutankhamun pendants

Jasmine Day

Abstract

Max and Norbert Neiger produced some of the finest examples of Bohemian glass jewellery in Gablonz (Jablonec nad Nisou) in the early 20th century. Their repertoire included stunning Egyptian Revival beads and cabochons. The advent of eBay and other online marketplaces has popularized Neiger jewellery among collectors worldwide, yet records of its production have been lost and little is known about the range, dates and sources of its Egyptianizing motifs. Even distinguishing Neiger pieces from works by other Gablonz manufacturers is speculative. Through stylistic analysis of my comparative collection of Egyptian Revival jewellery amassed over 20 years, I will tentatively identify key Neiger pieces, suggest their Egyptological sources and attempt to reconstruct their production sequence. The influence of the discovery of Tutankhamun's tomb upon the designs – even the careers – of the Neiger brothers will be demonstrated.

Keywords: jewellery, Neiger, Tutankhamun

Introduction

For centuries, a vibrant glass jewellery industry thrived around the town of Gablonz (Jablonec nad Nisou) in northern Bohemia. It originated when local landlords invited German craftsmen and merchants to settle in the area and revitalize its industries in the wake of the destruction wrought by the Husite Wars (1419–1436).[1] Glassworking and costume jewellery making (known as *bijouterie*) survived subsequent conflicts in the region, and by the late 19th century Gablonz had grown into a large, affluent town in a region that was now a cornerstone of the economy of the Habsburg empire.[2] It was famed worldwide for its beautiful glass beads and cabochons (flat-backed imitation gemstones for attachment to metal jewellery elements). Bohemian glassmakers neither cut nor cast their beads and cabochons as earlier European makers had done; instead, they heated and press-moulded glass canes. Craftsmen refined the work by cutting and polishing it, sometimes applying a gilded or enamelled finish.[3] Gablonz *bijouterie* and loose beads and cabochons were exported worldwide, the latter often incorporated into jewellery by designers including Coro, Miriam Haskell and Trifari,[4] yet since most Bohemian glass was unsigned, its makers' names are unknown.[5]

Of the makers whose names do survive, nowadays the best known are the Neiger Brothers, Norbert and Max Moritz Neiger, whose work has lately become fashionable among collectors and antique dealers and now fetches high sums on eBay and RubyLane. The Neigers founded their company around 1900 in the basement of their family home. Nineteen-year-old Norbert, a recent graduate of the Gablonz Technical School's *bijouterie* course, produced popular designs and moved his workshop into town. There he was joined by his younger brother Max.[6] One of the Neigers' first designs was a long Egyptian-themed necklace featuring mummy-shaped beads and strung on knotted silk cord. Such pieces, although expensive, sold well[7] and resembled contemporary necklaces by French designers such as Lalique. After the First World War, the Neiger company produced designs conceived predominantly by Max.[8] Exotic designs from Asia and Egypt were popular in the 1920s and Max's Egyptian Revival and *chinoiserie* pieces set a trend,[9] although Max was careful to design within the limits of current fashions, dictated by American clients who visited Gablonz after Paris and requested that he imitate Parisian styles.[10] British and American demand for Neiger products prompted further expansion of the company, which now employed over two dozen people in addition to cottage workers.[11] The Neigers presented their jewellery to clients with remarkable flair in annual presentations of *Linie*, collections of pieces with a common design element. The 1935 collection was hidden beneath a sheet, which was whisked away to reveal 150 pieces of jewellery.[12]

After the late 19th century, rising European nationalisms that culminated in the First World War split Gablonzers into those with German sympathies and those who identified as Czech.[13] After the war, Gablonz was absorbed into the new Czechoslovakian Republic.[14] During the Great Depression, Adolf Hitler exploited the despair of unemployment that many Gablonzers experienced, but instead of bestowing upon them the self-determination they longed for, he annexed the Sudetengerman region of Czechoslovakia in 1938. Persecution of Jewish Gablonzers followed; some escaped abroad, while those who stayed lost their international markets as American and Jewish buyers boycotted Germany.[15] The Nazis belittled Bohemian jewellery as tawdry trinkets unfit to be worn by German women,[16] eventually converting many *bijouterie* factories into munitions works.[17] By 1946 three million Sudetengermans had left the region; it was the end of an era for the Bohemian jewellery industry.[18]

For all their success, the Neigers could not evade the political morass of Gablonz. When the Nazis seized the Sudetenland, the Jewish brothers fled with a handful of employees to the Czech region of Bohemia and continued a small-scale jewellery operation. They were arrested in 1941 in Prague. In 1942 the brothers and their family members were transported to Poland and murdered.[19] The Neiger Brothers have no grave, but their jewellery is their memorial. It is scattered in private collections around the world, some pieces broken to fragments through constant wear, some lovingly restored by enthusiasts, some crudely restrung to save them; others unworn and forgotten, then rediscovered in near-pristine condition. Neiger adorns the internet, acclaimed by collectors after recovery from basements and bottom drawers.[20] Neiger jewellery is popular once more, but since little has been published on the subject – especially in English – few collectors and dealers know much about it beyond the facts researched by the Bohemian jewellery historian Sibylle Jargstorf, which I have recounted previously. The Neiger information circulating online, most of which cites no sources, can be traced back to a two-page account

in Jargstorf's 1993 book *Baubles, Buttons and Beads: The Heritage of Bohemia*, which is based upon Rudolf Zitte's discussion of the Neigers in his 1958 book *Geschichte der Gablonzer Schmuckindustrie (History of the Jewellery Industry in Gablonz)*.[21] Some sellers on eBay and online antique vendors such as RubyLane advertise jewellery pieces incorrectly as Neiger, and many incomplete, repaired or modified Neiger pieces as original. Despite the surge in academic studies of Egyptomania, research into Egyptian Revival jewellery is limited, probably because the expense and rarity of the subject matter makes it difficult to acquire large comparative collections.[22] With the exception of the Muzeum Skla a Bižuterie (Museum of Glass and Jewellery) in Jablonec nad Nisou,[23] museums have shown little interest in collecting more than the occasional, upmarket piece of Egyptian Revival jewellery, even though works by designers such as Neiger were far more common than bespoke works by Cartier or Lalique. Although the international retailers who purchased costume jewellery from Gablonz often sold it at a high price, the *bijouterie* industry manufactured pieces to suit every budget, including a small percentage of its output reserved for the local market.[24]

Here, then, is our first opportunity to compare many Bohemian Egyptianizing glass jewellery pieces and draw some tentative conclusions about their makers, relationships, production sequences and design sources. An overview of trends in Egyptian Revival design in Victorian and Edwardian jewellery will demonstrate some ways in which Neiger designs were inspired by, but also varied from, their predecessors. Then, by combining the limited surviving information about the Neiger Brothers' production with the relatively better documentation of some major archaeological discoveries, it will be possible to date some Neiger pieces precisely and reveal the extent of the influence that Egyptology – especially the discovery of Tutankhamun's tomb – had upon Max and Norbert Neiger.

Precedents

The advent of European tourism in Egypt in the 19th century gave rise to amateur antiquarianism. In an age prior to the effective implementation of laws prohibiting the illicit excavation and export of antiquities, untold numbers of portable artefacts were removed from Egypt as curiosities bound for mantlepieces and writing desks. While the legal and illegal export of larger items such as mummies has been studied, many of the small souvenirs acquired by travellers in the late 19th to mid-20th century await systematic research. Most of them have found their way not into museums but into attics, basements, estate sales and, ultimately, online auctions and antique shops.

Notable among these old souvenirs are artefacts mounted into Victorian, Edwardian and Art Deco jewellery, most commonly amulets and scarabs. Scarabs were common talismans of spiritual resurrection after death in ancient Egypt, worn by both the living and the dead. Carved from plain or semi-precious stones or moulded in faience, scarabs were often pierced along the length of their bodies to be worn as beads. Ancient scarabs were exported from Egypt to Europe for the jewellery trade; some Egyptian antiquities dealers owned shops overseas or travelled to Europe or the United States.[25] The Cairo Museum's 'rejects' were sold in its shop, as were small antiquities in shops in Cairo and Luxor licensed by the Cairo Museum.[26] Some of the latter items were mounted into jewellery.[27] The Italian craftsman Giuseppe Parvis, whose Cairo workshops produced Arabesque furniture beloved by European buyers, also manufactured Egyptianizing jewellery set with ancient scarabs.[28] Parvis's displays of Arabesque and Egyptianizing furnishings at various international expositions included stalls at the 1867 Paris International Exposition and 1876 Universal Exhibition of Philadelphia,[29] which may have heightened the long-term demand for Egyptian Revival jewellery among the Neigers' American clients who visited Gablonz via Paris.[30]

A prominent example of Egyptianizing antiquarian jewellery that set the scene for the rise of the Neiger style was a necklace manufactured in London by Hancocks, commissioned in about 1870 by Edward, Prince of Wales (later Edward VII) for his mistress, the actress Lillie Langtry. Resembling a museum assemblage more than an authentic Egyptian necklace, the giant festoon featured hanging strings of faience scarabs, coral amulets and ancient beads. It was worn by Langtry in her debut as *Cleopatra* in 1890; thereafter, she wore a replica onstage. The piece was reacquired by Hancocks at auction in 2003 for US $43,750.[31] The antiquarian trend of Victorian and Edwardian jewellery continued into the era of Art Deco, notably in the work of the British jewellers Cartier. Their 1920s bespoke pieces for wealthy clients such as Linda Lee Porter (wife of composer Cole Porter) combined scarabs and faience amulets with gold, diamonds, rubies and sapphires.[32] Many of the Egyptian artefacts incorporated into these pieces were broken, but Cartier's brilliant designs disguised this damage, elevating second-rate artefacts into miniature works of art that continue to fetch astounding prices at auction.

Innovation

With antiquarian jewellery a well-established tradition popular in Europe, Britain and the United States throughout the late 19th and early 20th centuries, it seems probable that the Neigers' Egyptianizing beads were not merely meant to look Egyptian, but specifically to look old – to imitate with modern mass-production the ancient artefacts mounted in more costly bespoke jewellery. The most common types of Neiger Egyptian beads were scarabs,[33] which were also the most frequent inclusions in antiquarian jewellery. Further evidence for intentional imitation of artefacts was the use of

an enamel wash. Neiger enamelling was not always painted directly onto the jewellery but sometimes wiped off while wet to leave a residue in the designs' recesses.[34] In the case of Egyptianizing beads and cabochons, this technique filled the recesses with a replica patina. Although natural patina tones such as brown were used, other brighter wash colours were employed to contrast with the beads' colours and harmonize with the colours of spacer beads and silk cords. The Neigers did not limit their designs to authentic Egyptian tones but produced a variety of bright colours. Uranium, which had been used to colour glass from the late 18th century,[35] is found in some Neiger Egyptian designs; their white beads fluoresce in ultraviolet light. By the 1920s, gemstone colours and patterns reproduced in glass became popular, including imitation malachite, lapis lazuli, carnelian and coral;[36] these soon appeared in Neiger's Egyptianizing pins.

Bohemian jewellers worked in close cooperation with the region's metalsmiths, who produced *Gürtler* work.[37] Intricate filigree *Gürtler* products had been introduced to Bohemia in the second half of the 19th century[38] and the Neigers ensured that the reverse sides of their jewellery pieces were as attractive as the fronts.[39] Neiger *Gürtler* designs were European, not Egyptian, the latter being only one of various ethnic themes that could be signified by attaching an appropriate combination of cabochons and pressed metal elements to the front of a pin, pendant or bracelet. Like the Langtry necklace, they were more museum like than authentically Egyptian, striving not for pedantic authenticity but to conjure an idea of Egypt by selecting elements from its visual repertoire such as sphinxes, pyramids, obelisks and pharaohs' faces for insertion into European decorative schemes.[40] As a museum case displays artefacts, so a piece of jewellery frames and presents Egyptian motifs to their best advantage, even if this means taking them out of their original contexts and depriving them of their original meanings.

Some of the Egyptianizing Neiger *Gürtler* pins were based upon scenes of musicians in private tombs, likely copied from unidentified Egyptology books; I suggest that the musician pins, if not also the other jade cabochon pins, were part of a single *Linie* collection. A sphinx, with a lion's mane instead of the usual *nemes* headcloth, appeared on a pendant I consider to be Neiger,[41] which was clearly modelled after several distinctive sphinxes of Amenemhat III in the Cairo Museum. By contrast, many of the pharaohs, queens, gods and goddesses depicted in Bohemian glass by a variety of manufacturers had generic faces and torsos disembodied in the fashion of European portraiture but framed and made distinctively Egyptian by iconic wigs and headdresses. Geometrically shaped pendants probably made by Neiger catered to European tastes but were Egyptianized with the addition of a 'stone block' background. However, the ultimate stone block design had already been invented. The heavy stone architecture and

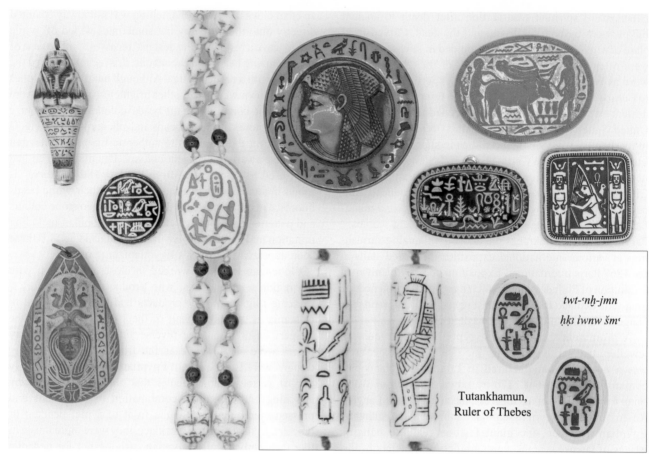

Fig. 8.1. A selection of cabochons, pendants and beads by Neiger and other manufacturers featuring mockhieroglyphic inscriptions. Inset: Beads and cabochons bearing the name of Tutankhamun. The lower line of text on the left bead also bears the pharaoh's epithet ḥḳꜣ iwnw šmꜥ, 'ruler of Thebes'. Author's collection. Photos: S. Kirkham.

sculpture of Egypt was miniaturized in glass, its grandeur contained and rendered delicate in a tiny, seated colossus, the little pharaoh's three dimensions foreshortened into a necklace pendant.[42]

Art Deco Egyptian Revival jewellery designs spoke to an audience familiar with and attracted to images from ancient Egypt, albeit often with limited understanding of their meaning. Some of the most prestigious jewellery artists attempted to incorporate or respond to the original meanings of the motifs referenced in their work, such as Cartier's clever conversion of a detached shabti figurine's head into the visage of the god Nefertem by mounting it within a bejewelled lotus flower.[43] By contrast, most Bohemian artists appear to have simply chosen and combined motifs according to aesthetics as, for instance, Hancocks had done before. Jewellers' engagement with ancient Egypt was primarily aesthetic, any meanings attached to its motifs being derived more often from modern European ideas about Egypt than from the ideas of the ancient Egyptians.

A case in point is the use of hieroglyphic inscriptions on Bohemian beads and cabochons. The majority are composed partly or entirely of pseudo-hieroglyphic squiggles or badly rendered hieroglyphs. Others are 'alphabet soup', a random combination of glyphs to fill a space. It took the intense publicity surrounding the Tutankhamun discovery to familiarize glassmakers with the correct spelling of one pharaoh's name (Fig. 8.1). Just as the prospect of wearing the name of this now famous king might have been a selling point, so the mystery of not knowing (or caring) what other inscriptions said might previously have added to the mystique and allure of Egyptianizing jewellery. Long after the decipherment of the ancient Egyptian script, European popular lore clung to the idea of hieroglyphs as an impenetrable code, and Egypt as beckoning but unknowable, an exotic and mysterious land forever.

Evolution

It can be difficult positively to identify Neiger Egyptianizing jewellery, given the loss of the Neiger's manufacturing archives and the imitation of its most successful designs by other companies.[44] Since Neiger utilized the *Gürtler* work of estamperies such as Scheibler, other *bijouterie* makers could use the same estamperies' metalwork to produce faux-Neiger

TUTANKHAMEN ON HIS THRONE: A WALL-PAINTING FROM THE TOMB OF HUY, HIS GOVERNOR OF ETHIOPIA, FOUND IN A HILL NEAR THEBES.

Fig. 8.2. A scene from the tomb of Amenhotep called Huy, sourced from Lepsius's Denkmäler *and reproduced in a newspaper article about Tutankhamun by Percy Newberry.* The Illustrated London News, *30 December 1922. Griffith Institute. Photo: J. Day.*

jewellery.[45] Yet this imitation had its limits; the Neigers successfully shut down the *Gürtler* factory of one of their former employees who made copies of their designs.[46] Thus it would appear that the Neiger Brothers forbade others to use their bead and cabochon designs. The jade cabochon pins are the only Egyptianizing pieces identified as Neiger by Jargstorf aside from mummy bead necklaces.[47] She also depicts a type of flat double-sided scarab bead[48] commonly attributed to Neiger by online dealers and collectors but does not make any specific attribution of manufacture – even though these scarabs appear on the mummy necklaces. Jargstorf remarks that Neiger works were of superior quality[49] and mentions that the company's 1935 collection featured geometrically shaped pieces with octagonal, oval and circular bases, gilding and the use of different shades of enamel.[50] Taking these few points into account and comparing various Bohemian Egyptian Revival cabochons, beads and necklaces, it is possible to speculate about the designs, sources and sequences of some key pieces.

One early Neiger design, a long Egyptian-themed necklace, featured mummy-shaped beads and was strung on knotted silk cord.[51] Necklaces with these beads also feature

the flat scarab beads and some include a seated pharaoh droplet-shaped pendant; therefore, these must also be Neiger (Plate 17).[52] The quality of their production and their characteristic colour wash support this attribution. The seated pharaoh droplet pendant is remarkably detailed, suggesting that it has been faithfully copied from some specific source. At the Griffith Institute in Oxford in 2018, while searching through original copies of 1922–1923 press articles about the discovery of Tutankhamun's tomb, I found an image of the pharaoh in the *Illustrated London News* (30 December 1922)[53] that matched the one on the Neiger pendant exactly (Fig. 8.2). An article about objects likely to be found in the newly discovered tomb, written by Percy Newberry, the botanist in Howard Carter's excavation team, included a slide of an illustration in Karl Richard Lepsius's 1849–1859 *Denkmäler aus Ägypten und Äthiopien*[54] of one of the three scenes of Tutankhamun[55] from the Tomb of Amenhotep called Huy, Viceroy of Kush to Tutankhamun (TT40 at Qurnet Murai, Luxor, New Kingdom, 18th Dynasty, ca. 1330 BCE) (Plate 18). The positions of the implements in the king's hands, the details of his costume and the number of vertical bands on the mat under the base of the throne on

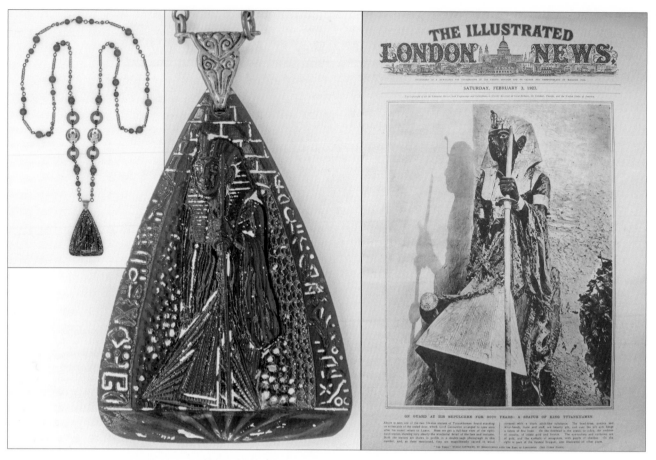

Fig. 8.3. Neiger Gürtler *necklace depicting one of the guardian statues in Tutankhamun's tomb. Author's collection. Photos: S. Kirkham. / Harry Burton's photograph of a guardian statue* in situ *introduced the public to Tutankhamun's treasures.* The Illustrated London News, *30 January 1923. Griffith Institute. Photo: J. Day.*

both the newspaper image and the pendant were identical. While scenes of enthroned pharaohs under canopies were generic, each one varied in its details, so the Neiger pendant had clearly been based upon the specific scene reproduced in the newspaper. The convex sides of the pendant reflect and extend the curving trajectory of the upper edge of Amenhotep Huy's raised feather staff as he bows toward his king, as if this graceful arc in the ancient composition suggested the pendant's shape to its designer.

Elizabeth Fleming identified the tomb that was the source of the image in Newberry's slide; given that it was not fully published until 1926[56] and Lepsius's mid-19th century illustration captured the complete painting before it was extensively damaged,[57] I think it probable that the Neigers copied Newberry's Lepsius slide, whether from the *Illustrated London News* or another newspaper that circulated the image.[58] Published on 30 December 1922, soon after Carter's 4 November 1922 discovery but before the release of Harry Burton's photographs of artefacts from the tomb depicting Tutankhamun on and after 30 January 1923, Newberry's Lepsius slide would have been one of the first images of the pharaoh circulated in the press.

The attractiveness, delicacy and archaeologically accurate detail of pieces such as the seated Tutankhamun pendant suggest that one person – in my view Max Neiger – designed them. What are we, then, to make of the aforementioned cruder, but prolific, series of geometrically shaped Egyptianizing beads and pendants? They share a stone block background and may thus be the work of a single company. The Max pieces and the stone block pieces would appear to have been designed by two different companies, were it not for one rare, translucent burgundy pendant on an intricate *Gürtler* chain. Unlike other stone block pendants and beads, this one features not two-dimensional wall carvings (possibly copied from books with line illustrations of Egyptian art) but a three-quarter profile view of one of the guardian statues in Tutankhamun's tomb, specifically the figure wearing a *nemes* headdress.[59] Its pendant image was copied directly from Harry Burton's photograph of the Tutankhamun guardian statue,[60] which had featured in *The Times*'s 30 January 1923[61] issue in which the public first glimpsed the king's treasures through Burton's photographs. Other newspapers also carried the guardian image on their covers that day (Fig. 8.3). A ragged ancient cloth still hanging over the statue's arm that appears in Burton's photograph is reproduced precisely upon the arm of the figure on the pendant. The cloth was later removed by Carter's team. This suggests that the *Gürtler* necklace, based upon one of the first published photographs of the tomb taken soon after its discovery, was rushed into production in or shortly after February 1923 to capitalize upon the new 'Tut' fad. The seated Tutankhamun necklace, by comparison, could have gone into production as early as January 1923 after Newberry's publication of Lepsius's drawings at the end of the previous year.

Several of the Tutankhamun-inspired Art Deco jewellery pieces loaned by various collectors to the *Discovering Tutankhamun* exhibition featured either the *nemes* guardian statue or scenes from the sides of a painted box depicting the young pharaoh hunting and in battle. His incarnation on the ends of the box as an androsphinx trampling Egypt's enemies attracted as many imitations as the main sides did (Fig. 8.4). Both the guardian and the box were found in the tomb's antechamber, the box *in situ* near the feet of the *nemes* guardian so that they appeared together in some photographs. These two objects became popular inspirations for artists and jewellers – the first 'hero' images from the tomb – prior to the revelation of even more spectacular treasures in Tutankhamun's burial chamber.[62]

If we accept that the beautifully crafted Tutankhamun pendant *Gürtler* necklace and the painstakingly accurate enthroned Tutankhamun pendant can only have been the work of Max Neiger, this could mean:

1. That the stone block series and Max series were both the work of the Neiger company.
2. That the cruder style of the stone block series had a different designer to the Max series, very likely Norbert Neiger.
3. That the stone block series largely or completely pre-dated the Max series, which appeared when Max took over from Norbert as principal designer.
4. That the Tutankhamun *Gürtler* necklace was a crossover piece either co-designed by the brothers or designed by Max to match the existing stone block series.
5. That the Tutankhamun discovery, along with associated images in the press such as Lepsius's artwork and Harry Burton's photographs that inspired designers worldwide, was the impetus for the transition from Norbert to Max as principal designer for the Neiger company.
6. That this transition occurred in or soon after January 1923, such that Neiger's most refined Egyptianizing designs may be dated to the early to mid-1920s.

Conclusion

Although my conclusions are speculative, it is probable that the Tutankhamun *Gürtler* necklace and the enthroned Tutankhamun pendant date to 1923 and, if they are Neiger pieces, they are among the first Neiger jewellery that can

Fig. 8.4. Above: Tutankhamun's double incarnation as an androsphinx tramples the enemies of Egypt on the ends of the painted box from the pharaoh's tomb. The New York Times, 10 March 1923b. Griffith Institute. Photo: J. Day. Below: Large cabochon duplicating the androsphinx scene from the painted box, manufacturer unknown. Author's collection. Photo: S. Kirkham.

be securely dated. This means that we might not only be able to reconstruct part of the Neiger production sequence but also show that the Tutankhamun discovery played a significant role in the evolution and success of the Neiger company. Further investigation of the Egyptological sources of Neiger and other companies' Egyptian Revival jewellery may reveal more information about the history of Bohemian glass jewellery production. Histories of Egyptology are integral to many other kinds of history, so many of which await excavation.

Notes

1   Jargstorf 1993, 5.
2   Jargstorf 1993, 7–8.
3   Jargstorf 1993, 17.
4   Jargstorf 1993, 4.

5   Jargstorf 1993, 8.
6   Jargstorf 1993, 89.
7   Jargstorf 1993, 89 after Zitte 1958, 148.
8   Jargstorf 1993, 89.
9   Jargstorf 1993, 93.
10 Jargstorf 1993, 90.
11 Jargstorf 1993, 89.
12 Jargstorf 1993, 88.
13 Jargstorf 1993, 10.
14 Jargstorf 1993, 13.
15 Jargstorf 1993, 14.
16 Jargstorf 1993, 14–15.
17 Jargstorf 1993, 14.
18 Jargstorf 1993, 14.
19 Jargstorf 1993, 90 states that the Neiger brothers were murdered at Auschwitz while Zitte 1958, 150 names only Norbert and his wife as Auschwitz victims. However, the Institut Terezínské Iniciativy (Terezín Initiative Institute) 2016 notes that Max was killed at Łódź on 17 July 1942, his mother Temerle at Terezín on 6 October 1942 and his daughter Zuzana, wife Anna and brother Norbert on unknown dates at unknown locations. Sheil 2016 adds that Norbert's wife Margareta and Anna's mother Emilie Bachnerova were taken to the Łódź Ghetto in Poland, but their dates and locations of death are also unknown.
20 One of my first Neiger purchases was a lilac-toned scarab necklace recovered by a dealer from a greasy garage floor somewhere in Europe.
21 Zitte 1958, 148–150; Jargstorf 1993, 89–90.
22 I began collecting Neiger and other Bohemian glass Egyptian Revival jewellery in the 1990s on eBay. At that time, lower prices and fewer bidders made it easy to acquire large numbers of items. The advent of eBay must have coincided with a wave of sales of 1920s estates, as Art Deco Egyptian Revival jewellery was plentiful. It is now harder to find, often of lesser quality and up to three or four times the 1990s price.
23 Muzeum Skla a Bižuterie 2023.
24 Jargstorf 1993, 20.
25 Hagen and Ryholt 2016, 39.
26 Hagen and Ryholt 2016.
27 In 2020, using Hagen and Ryholt 2016, 41, 68, 69 fig. 45, 118–119, 234–235, 284, I identified the retailer of a scarab mounted in a silver pin purchased in Cairo in 1942. Jeff Hemsley, the nephew of the purchaser, retained the pin's certificate of authenticity, which named Maguid Sameda of the Buddha Store, antiquities dealer license #108 issued by the Cairo Museum. This is a later example of the longstanding former practice of mounting antiquities in touristic jewellery. An earlier example is a faience lotus tile from Tell elAmarna mounted in a silver pendant with customcut pieces of polychrome glass from 'Behnessah' (elBahnasa, Roman period Oxyrhynchus), accompanied by a letter of authenticity from the Nassar Brothers, 'Curators of Artistic Jewellery' and 'Antiquity Dealers' of Khan elKhalili Bazaar, Cairo, dated 21 April 1914 (author's collection).
28 For example, a gold flying scarab pin inlaid with an ancient scarab in its original display box labelled 'Parvis' (Steven Sher collection).
29 Grillot 2014.
30 Jargstorf 1993, 90.
31 Christie's 2023; Gere and Rudoe 2010, 386.
32 *The Illustrated London News* 1924, reproduced by Collins and McNamara 2014, 75; Ruiz 2015.
33 Some Neiger necklaces consist entirely of flat scarabs produced in a variety of glass and enamel wash colours.
34 Jargstorf 1993, 91.
35 Jargstorf 1993, 26.
36 Jargstorf 1993, 24.
37 Jargstorf 1993, 17, 20.
38 Jargstorf 1993, 25.
39 Jargstorf 1993, 91.
40 Jargstorf 1993, 93 illustrates this style, identifying it as Neiger, and I have many other examples of this style in my collection.
41 This Amenemhat III sphinx pendant appears on the same sample card as several other Egyptianizing pendants I regard as Neiger, including the seated pharaoh type and a block background type, both of which are discussed later in this paper. The sample card, in the collection of the Muzeum Skla a Bižuterie (Museum of Glass and Jewellery) in Jablonec nad Nisou and illustrated by 'floorkasp' on the Bead Collector Network website, appears to represent a selection of (mostly Egyptianizing) pendants produced by Neiger, although their varied styles may not correspond to a single *linie*.
42 My collection includes the portrait cabochons, stone block beads and miniature (likely Neiger) colossus pendant necklace described here. More portrait cabochons are illustrated by Jargstorf 1993, 165.
43 Ziegler 1994, 537.
44 Jargstorf 1993, 91.
45 Jargstorf 1993, 90.
46 Jargstorf 1993, 90.
47 Jargstorf 1993, 93.
48 Jargstorf 1993, 164.
49 Jargstorf 1993, 91.
50 Jargstorf 1993, 89.
51 Jargstorf 1993, 89 after Zitte 1958, 148. It is unclear whether Zitte and Jargstorf refer to mummy-shaped bead necklaces with giant scarab pendants, with seated pharaoh pendants or both (see Fig. 8.2). Zitte claims that the mummy-shaped beads were used as pendants, but this is likely an error, as I have only seen these strung on the sides of necklaces. This omission makes it unclear in what sequence the variant designs were produced, or whether they were issued simultaneously. Given my argument in this paper that earlier Neiger Egyptianizing designs were less refined than later ones, I suggest that the giant scarab pendant variant was released first, with the seated pharaoh variant merely a substitution of a new pendant into the ongoing production of a standardized necklace design.
52 These pieces are sometimes strung in slightly different arrangements according, perhaps, to the supply of beads or whim of the person stringing the beads. They include generic spacer beads that in turn link other necklaces with the same spacers to Neiger. The other necklaces feature further, spectacular Egyptianizing pendant designs that can thence be attributed to Neiger, along with additional types of spacers that link to yet more pendants, and so forth. An example of the use of recurring bead types to identify Neiger necklaces is that the flat scarab beads found in many of them occasionally accompany fat scarabs with scalloped rims, so that necklaces

with fat scarabs alone are identifiable as Neiger. It follows that other types of pendants and beads strung alongside flat or fat scarabs are Neiger.

53   Newberry 1922.

54   Lepsius 1849–1859a, Abtheilung III, Band VI, Blatt 115 (Book 3, Section 6, pl. 115).

55   Specifically, the Asian tribute scene on the west wall, north side of the transverse hall, Benderitter 2023, 3. On entering the tomb, the remains of this now badly damaged scene are located opposite the front door on the right side of the entrance to the passage to the columned hall.

56   Davies and Gardiner 1926.

57   Damage to the tomb during the modern era resulted from its use as a stable by the villagers living in houses above and, after the 1960s, from attempts to steal sections of paintings from the walls; Benderitter 2023, 1.

58   After Newberry's publication of the three Amenhotep Huy images of Tutankhamun, they reappeared in complete or cropped form in other newspapers, such as *The New York Times* 1923a, 1–2 and *The New York Times Book Review and Magazine*, de Kay 1923, 11. They were also reprinted in books written by noted Egyptologists for the popular market including Budge 1923, pl. 1 and Elliot Smith 1923, 40 fig. 4. It is therefore unsurprising that the Neigers – and likely other jewellers and artists – used TT 40 as a source.

59   The *nemes*, an iconic headdress synonymous with the pharaohs, is a striped cloth that falls in two frontal lappets. The other statue in this pair wears a bobbed *khat* headdress, which appealed less to modern designers.

60   Liam McNamara, pers. comm.

61   *The Times* 1923, cover. This truncates the statue's kilt, which is included on the Neiger *Gürtler* necklace pendant, but some other newspapers published Burton's photograph at full-length on the same day as *The Times*, which held exclusive reportage rights to the excavation and syndicated Burton's photographs to other newspapers; see for instance *Daily News* (London) 1923, 1. Presumably, the Neiger Brothers accessed images of Tutankhamun via their ubiquitous reproduction in newspapers, whether from British sources or syndicated articles in European newspapers.

62   Collins and McNamara 2014, 76; McNamara, pers. comm. Another motif from Tutankhamun's antechamber, a scene carved on the back of the pharaoh's throne depicting the god Heh kneeling atop the hieroglyph for gold (*nub*), appears on a square two-hole bead strung with an assortment of other fancy beads in the Albert Sachse collection in the Muzeum Skla a Bižuterie (Museum of Glass and Jewellery) in Jablonec nad Nisou, illustrated by 'floorkasp' on the Bead Collector Network website. The manufacturer of this bead is unknown, but a tiny cabochon of similar size, colour and style in my collection that bears the seated Tutankhamun motif might indicate that both pieces were made by Neiger.

Bibliography

Benderitter, Thierry. 2023. 'TT40, the Tomb of Amenhotep, Surnamed Huy'. *Osirisnet: Tombs of Ancient Egypt.* https://osirisnet.net/tombes/nobles/houy40/e_houy40_03.htm (last accessed 1 August 2023).

Budge, Ernest. 1923. *Tutānkhåmen: Amenism, Atenism and Egyptian Monotheism.* London: Martin Hopkinson & Co. Ltd.

Christie's. 2023. 'An Egyptian Revival Coral, Multi-gem and Gold Necklace'. *Live Auction 2390 – Rare Jewels and Objets d'Art: A Superb Collection.* 21 October 2009. https://www.christies.com/lot/lot-5250240?ldp_breadcrumb=back&intobjectid=5250240&from=salessummary&lid=1 (last accessed 1 August 2023).

Collins, Paul, and Liam McNamara. 2014. *Discovering Tutankhamun.* Oxford: Ashmolean Museum.

Daily News (London). 1923. 'New Revelation'. 30 January, 1.

Davies, Nina M. de Garis, and Alan H. Gardiner. 1926. *The Tomb of Huy, Viceroy of Nubia in the Reign of Tutankhamun (No 40).* The Theban Tombs Series 4. London: Egypt Exploration Society.

de Kay, Charles. 1923. 'Most Famous of Pharaohs'. *The New York Times Book Review and Magazine*, 2 September, 11.

Elliot Smith, Grafton. 1923. *Tutankhamen and His Tomb.* London and New York: George Routledge & Sons, Ltd and E.P. Dutton & Co.

'Floorkasp'. 2012. 'Open Forum – Jablonec 2012: Trip Report'. *Bead Collector Network.* http://beadcollector.net/cgi-bin/anyboard.cgi?fvp=%2Fopenforum%2F&cmd=iYz&aK=87581&iZz=87581&gV=0&kQz&aO=1&iWz=0#87581 (last accessed 1 August 2023).

Gere, Charlotte, and Judy Rudoe. 2010. *Jewellery in the Age of Queen Victoria.* London: The British Museum Press.

Grillot, Marie. 2014. 'Giuseppe Parvis: Le "Designer" Italien du Khédive'. *Égyptophile*, 29 December. http://egyptophile.blogspot.com.au/2014/12/giuseppe-parvis-le-designer-italien-du.html (last accessed 1 August 2023).

Hagen, Fredrik, and Kim Ryholt. 2016. *The Antiquities Trade in Egypt 1880–1930: The H. O. Lange Papers.* Scientia Danica, Series H, Humanica 4, Vol. 8. Copenhagen: Det Kongelige Danske Videnskabernes Selskab.

The Illustrated London News. 1923. 'On Guard at his Sepulchre for 3000 Years: A Statue of King Tutankhamen'. 30 January, cover.

The Illustrated London News. 1924. 'The "Tutankhamen" Influence in Modern Jewellery'. 26 January, 143.

Institut Terezínské Iniciativy. 2016. 'Moritz Neiger'. *Holocaust. cz.* https://www.holocaust.cz/en/database-of-victims/victim/143690-moritz-neiger/ (last accessed 1 August 2023).

Jargstorf, Sibylle. 1993. *Baubles, Buttons and Beads: The Heritage of Bohemia.* Atglen, PA: Schiffer.

Lepsius, Karl. 1849–1859. *Denkmäler aus Ägypten und Äthiopien, Abtheilung III: Neues Reich*, Band VI. Berlin: Nicolaische Buchhandlung.

Muzeum Skla a Bižuterie. 2023. *Muzeum Skla a Bižuterie v Jablonci nad Nisou.* https://www.msb-jablonec.cz (last accessed 1 August 2023).

The New York Times. 1923a. 'Tutankhamen's Inner Tomb is Opened, Revealing Undreamed of Splendors, Still Untouched after 2,400 Years'. 17 February, 1–2.

The New York Times. 1923b. 'Tut-Ankh-Amen Tramples upon his African Enemies'. 10 March, Fotogravure Picture Section.

Newberry, Percy. 1922. 'Tutankhamen in Art – and Objects that May Be Found'. *Illustrated London News*, 1056, 30 December.

Ruiz, Michelle. 2015. 'The King Tut-inspired Gemstones Even Museums Can't Afford'. *Vanity Fair*, 15 June. http://www.vanityfair.com/style/2015/06/king-tut-inspired-gems-art-deco-egyptian-revival (last accessed 1 August 2023).

Sheil, Inger. 2016. 'The Neiger Brothers: Enduring Beauty'. *The Nouveau Flapper*, 11 February. https://sydneyflapper.word-press.com/2016/02/11/the-neiger-brothers-enduring-beauty/ (last accessed 1 August 2023).

The Times. 1923. 'In Pharaoh's Tomb: First Pictures'. 30 January, cover.

Ziegler, Christiane. 1994. '"God on a Lotus Flower" Brooch'. In *Egyptomania: Egypt in Western Art 1730–1930*, English edition, edited by Jean-Marcel Humbert, Michael Pantazzi and Christiane Ziegler, 536–537. Ottawa: National Gallery of Canada.

Zitte, Rudolf. 1958. *Geschichte der Gablonzer Schmuckindustrie.* Kaufbeuren-Neugablonz: Verlag.

Tutankhamun the pop idol: the Tut-mania phenomenon and its influence on the wider public

Valentina Santini

Abstract

From a general and popular standpoint, Tutankhamun is undoubtedly the most famous pharaoh of all. Since the 1920s, he has become a star, a legend, a proper VIP, and everyone – even just by hearsay – knows his name. Now – 100 years since the discovery of his tomb, the so-called 'boy pharaoh' has become almost a mythical being. Novels, comics, movies and even furniture have been influenced by the king, the tomb and its contents. How and why has this archaeological find determined such a massive image return? How is it that this unimaginable success continues after 100 years? This paper aims to answer these and other queries, by reviewing the most significant cases of the Tut-mania, and discusses Tutankhamun and his fame, in the light of his constant and continuous influence on the general audience.[1]

Keywords: Tutankhamun, Tut-mania, general public

Introduction

The discovery of the famous 'first steps' on 4 November 1922 was just the beginning: when KV 62 was brought to light, the marvellous objects found within the burial place and – even more – the owner of the tomb became an overnight sensation. People wanted to learn more about Tutankhamun, his life and his magnificent funerary equipment. They skulked in the proximity of KV 62, hoping to see some of those beautiful items being carried out from the tomb, or recognize the man in charge of such delicate work – Howard Carter.[2] Fundamentally, they wanted to bear witness to one of the biggest discoveries in the history of Egyptology, and somehow take part in it. This archaeological finding triggered a mania for ancient Egypt, a deep enthusiasm for the pharaonic civilization that has influenced various aspects of our contemporary culture – some of whose most iconic expressions will be described in detail in this paper.

The discovery of the tomb of Tutankhamun, however, was not the first to produce a profound love for ancient Egyptian culture, especially in the so-called 'Western world'. Even decades before the discovery of the tomb of the young pharaoh, Egyptomania had affected many different arts (fashion, architecture, literature, etc.), especially after the publication of Vivant Denon's *Voyage dans la basse et la haute Égypte* in 1802, and then the *Description de l'Égypte* during 1809–1829, containing the results of the scientific side of Napoleon Bonaparte's military campaign to Egypt during 1798–1799.[3]

The main difference between the Egyptomania that exploded during the 19th century and the one that arose after the discovery of KV 62 concerns the *target* of the fascination: while the strong interest for ancient Egypt due to Denon and the *Description de l'Égypte* was toward the entire civilization on the Nile, the focus after 1922 was notably on a specific character – Tutankhamun – and his funerary equipment.

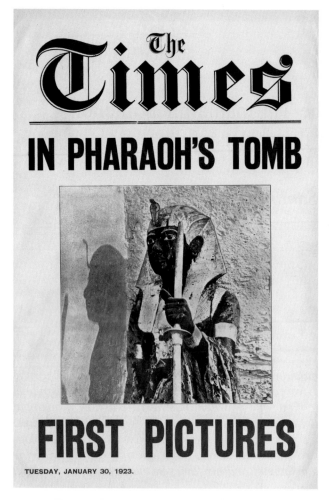

Fig. 9.1. Cover of The Times, *30 January 1923.*

As stated by *The New York Times* in 1923: 'There is only one topic of conversation […] One cannot escape the name of Tut-Ankh-Amen anywhere. It is shouted in the streets, whispered in the hotels, while the local shops advertise Tut-Ankh-Amen art, Tut-Ankh-Amen hats, Tut-Ankh-Amen curios, Tut-Ankh-Amen photographs'.[4] A few months after the discovery of the first steps leading to the main entrance of KV 62, a new version of Egyptomania was born, which, even after 100 years, is still more alive than ever.

Since the identification of his tomb, Tutankhamun has become a truly mythic being. Among the general public, Tutankhamun is today probably the most popular pharaoh of all. Even more: his character and some of the objects found among his funerary equipment (such as the golden mask discovered covering his face) have become *de facto* symbols of the entire ancient Egyptian culture.

If, before the identification of KV 62, the name of Tutankhamun was basically known only among scholars, after the discovery of the tomb, he started being a legend, a celebrity, a true pop idol. As previously stated, this paper aims to analyse the importance acquired by Tutankhamun

for the general public and examine the most significant examples of the so-called Tut-mania, which has assumed many different forms during the course of the years.

The influence of Tut-mania on the wider public

This subject is usually barely addressed by scholarly publications. Tutankhamun, his history, his tomb and his funerary equipment have been intensely investigated in the past century, but what is still little examined from a scientific point of view is the impact that the discovery of the burial place of the young pharaoh has had on the wider public. It is possible that this topic is considered (or *was* considered, especially in the past) somehow 'detached' from the academic purpose of learning more about the 'real' Tutankhamun. Research and projects strictly dedicated to this subject are accordingly scarce and usually little discussed. As noted by Abraham I. Fernández Pichel (Centro de História da Universidade de Lisboa) during the presentation of the *Egypopcult* project, 'Ich mache mir die [ägyptische] Welt wie sie mir gefällt' ('I'm making the [Egyptian] World as I like it').[5] This was during the International Colloquium 'Tutankhamun and Carter: Assessing the Impact of a Major Archaeological Find', held in Lisbon from 15 to 16 February 2023,[6] and implied that the main sources for Tut-mania and the influence of the young pharaoh on the general public do not belong to scientific publications, but – most of the time – to popular magazines or websites. For the writing of this very paper, online forums, encyclopaedic works compiled by TV or comics fandoms, and fashion periodicals have proved crucial. Luckily, scholars have recently started to consider the production of so-called 'pop culture' as an important aspect for analysis and examination in light of a new multi- and interdisciplinary approach to the study of Egyptology.[7] Therefore, this growing interest in the influence of ancient Egypt (or Tut-mania, in this particular case) on the general audience may provide a new critical approach in the Egyptological field.

In wake of this renewed interest on the interconnection between Egyptology and the reception of ancient Egypt by the wider public, the topic of the influence of Tutankhamun on the general audience will be addressed starting from the basis of Tut-mania: why did this young pharaoh gain so much importance during the 1920s and why is he still celebrated as an idol?

Undoubtedly, the event that generated Tut-mania was the rediscovery of the pharaoh Tutankhamun and, in particular, of his extremely rich funerary equipment (Fig. 9.1). Howard Carter, by finding KV 62, had unconsciously created a celebrity or – even better – two celebrities, because both the young pharaoh and also Carter himself were overwhelmed by fame (Fig. 9.2).

This whole curiosity, however, was natural: an extraordinary tomb belonging to a pharaoh had just been discovered,

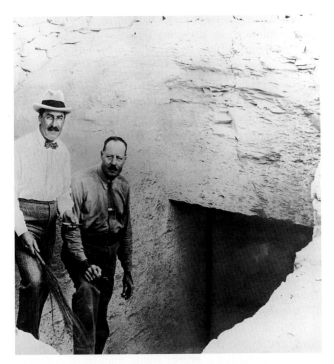

Fig. 9.2. Howard Carter and his assistant Arthur Callender on the steps leading to the Tomb of Tutankhamun (1922). © Griffith Institute, University of Oxford.

and people's fantasies had inevitably been unleashed. Many childhood dreams concern wonderful adventures to search for a 'pirate's treasure'. Carter was seen as the adventurer who actually made it: he was the great hero of the 'interior child' of many, the one who was able to correctly read the map left by the pirates and dig in the right spot, under the giant 'X'. He had found the greatest and richest treasure, and, for this reason, people celebrated him as a champion. The importance acquired by this discovery is still perceived nowadays, not only among scholars, but also by the general audience – people who have never studied archaeology or Egyptology, and also those who are not even interested in ancient Egypt; they all know the figure of Tutankhamun and at least some of the objects belonging to his funerary goods. Why, after 100 years, are the wider public still talking – a lot! – about Tutankhamun? The tomb of the young sovereign mesmerized not only contemporary people's fantasy, but also that of following generations: the richness of the equipment, the adventurous discovery of the burial place and the (allegedly) 'mysterious' life of the young pharaoh are just a few of the many elements that are still fascinating and intriguing not only for scholars, but also for common people.

Music

The first examples of Tut-mania come from the musical sphere. In the 1920s, directly after the KV 62 discovery, some delightful songs were created. Of course, many of

those mention Tutankhamun without actually knowing anything about this young pharaoh (whose age was not known until his mummy was autopsied), also because many of the studies dedicated to this figure had not been conducted at this time, a few months after the discovery.

From *King Tut Blues* (by Eddie Green)[8] to *Three Thousand Years Ago* (by Jack Egan and Alex Gerber),[9] passing through *Tut-Ankh-Amen* (by Carlo and Sanders),[10] the young pharaoh became one of the preferred subjects of music composers. Among the various songs released in 1923, *Old King Tut Was a Wise Old Nut* (by Lucien Denni and Roger Lewis) was probably one of the most successful (Plate 19). This song, an irreverent and ironic *vaudeville*, clearly represents the effect that the discovery of the tomb of Tutankhamun had on the general public:

Along the valley of the Nile, tonight a torch is flamin'
Because two excavators found the tomb of Tut Ankh Hamen.
They searched and searched for years and years at last they found the king
And while they Jesse Jamesed his tomb, these royal ghouls would sing.

Old King Tut was a wise old nut to sleep three thousand years,
He never gave a checkroom Jane six bits to check a two-bit cane,
Within a room they called a tomb he went away to sleep
He took along a wealth of jewels, Egyptian cows and sheep.
Old King Tut was a wise old nut to snore away in peace
No landlord ever chased him there, he had a good long lease.
They stored his tomb with beef and wine to help his journey on,
Today we find the beef is there but all the wine is gone.
Old King Tut was a wise old nut, so let the King sleep on.

Old King Tut was a wise old nut to sleep three thousand years,
He never had to pawn his throne to buy a meal for some Salome,
Within a room next to his tomb he gamboled for a lark,
Invited all the ladies there because the tomb was dark.
Old King Tut was a wise old nut, there's not the slightest doubt
The tomb was not to keep him in but keep the pikers out.
They buried him and all the men were jealous of the King,
They left him twenty dancing girls and they had ev'rything,
Old King Tut was a wise old nut, O death where is thy sting?

Old King Tut was a wise old nut to sleep three thousand years,
He never had an ache or pain or had to ride an Erie train,
He drank some old Egyptian wine, it was his private brew,
It had some kick and only now the King is coming to.
Old King Tut was a wise old nut, He had a great old time
Three thousand years upon the Nile, And never spent a dime.
He got into his royal bed three thousand years, B.C.
And left a call for three o'clock in nineteen twenty three,
Old King Tut was a wise old nut, Oh, wouldst the King were me!

Old King Tut was a wise old nut to sleep three thousand years,
He never had the chills or croup or gargle Kosher noodle soup,
Within a room next to his tomb one night he gave a ball
The Pharaohs all played Faro but it wasn't fair at all.

Old King Tut was a wise old nut, with the pyramids on top
He had a show there ev'ry night no Ku Klux Klan could stop
The day he died they stored a thousand jugs of wine away.
With moonshine twenty bucks a quart what's his stuff
worth today?
Old King Tut was a wise old nut, Come where the Yits
Yoks play.[11]

Those lyrics distinctly exemplify the wider public's stand-point on this gigantic event: Tutankhamun and his tomb were seen as a sort of 'gold mine', and those who were responsible for the discovery were considered similar to 'relic hunters' ('[…] while they Jesse Jamesed his tomb […]').

This same impression can be perceived by another song, in the same style of the latter: *Old King Tut: In Old King Tutenkhamen's Day* (Plate 19). Written by William Jerome and set to music by Harry Von Tilzer, it was first published in 1923,[12] but had many rearrangements over the years. In fact, this quite successful melody was even played in an episode of the award-winning *Boardwalk Empire*. This TV series, starring Steve Buscemi as Enoch Malachi 'Nucky' Thompson – a politician, but also a criminal boss of Atlantic City – is set during America's prohibition era, and the first episode of the third season (2012) celebrates Tut-mania with this version of the song, sung by Stephen DeRosa and Meg Steedle.[13] The lyrics run as follows:

Three thousand years ago, In history we know,
King Tutenkhamen ruled a mighty land;
He ruled for many years, 'Mid laughter, song and tears,
He made a record that will always stand;
They opened up his tomb the other day and jumped with glee,
They learned a lot of ancient history.

In old King Tut-Tut-Tut-enkhamen's day,
Beneath the tropic skies King Tut-Tut-Tut was very wise,
Now old King Tut-Tut-Tut was always gay,
Cleopatra she sat upon his knee, Pat! That's where she sat.
Now old King Tut was just a nut as you can see,
Still proud was Tut about his Beechnut ancestry.
A thousand girls would dance each day,
With lots of hip-hip-hip-hooray,
In old King Tut-Tut-Tut-Tut-Tut-Tut, King Tutty's Day.

His tomb instead of tears, Was full of Souveniers,
He must have travelled greatly in his time;
The gold and silver ware, That they found hidden there,
Was from hotels of ev'ry land and clime.
While going thru' his royal robes they found up in his sleeve,
The first love letter Adam wrote to Eve.

In old King Tut-Tut-Tut-enkhamen's day,
The dancers then in style
Would even make the old Sphinx smile,
In old King Tut-Tut-Tutenkhamen's day,
On the desert sand old King Tutty's band
Played while maidens swayed.
They'd dance for old King Tut 'neath moonlit skies so warm,
They wore such happy smiles and were in perfect form.

They'd dance for him both fat and thin,
He didn't care what shape they're in,
In old King Tut-Tut-Tut-Tut-Tut-Tut, King Tutty's Day.[14]

As with the previous one, this song presents a series of evident inaccuracies (for instance, the co-existence of Tut-ankhamun and Cleopatra!), partially because of the irony of the song itself, partially because of the little information about Tutankhamun available to the general audience. As already noted, these songs usually had little to do with the 'real' Tutankhamun (starting from the title, where the young pharaoh is called *old* – even if this term could also refer to Tutankhamun being from ancient Egypt), but nonetheless they acquired a certain success and melodies dedicated to Tutankhamun continued to be produced even in the following years.

Indeed, moving forward in time, some songs dedicated to Tutankhamun were published during the 1970s as well. The most famous one – titled *King Tut* – was released in 1978 by Steve Martin. The acclaimed actor – who starred in *The Father of the Bride*, *The Pink Panther*, among other films, and in the very recent series *Only Murders in the Building* – realized a proper ironic mini-show dedicated to the young pharaoh, on the occasion of the most famous exhibition *Treasures of Tutankhamun* in the USA.[15] The song *King Tut* was part of the sketch – it was presented for the very first time on 22 April 1978 on *Saturday Night Live* – but quite soon it became a hit single and ended up in the Top 20 chart, selling over a million copies.[16]

One of the most recent songs inspired by Tutankhamun dates to 2015. It is quite different from the various melodies dedicated to the young sovereign over the years, since it is a children's song, presented at the Italian Zecchino d'Oro festival. It is one of the most important Italian song contests reserved to young singers (3 to 10 years old), and, in its 58th edition, a composition entitled *Tutanc'mon* was presented.[17] The title is a sort of *crasis* between the name of the young pharaoh and the English expression *c'mon*, and the song – sung by Giuditta Meawad – is bilingual, since its lyrics are partly in Arabic and partly in Italian. Tutankhamun is depicted as a sleepy child, who must be encouraged to wake up, in order to see the vastness of curiosities that are in the world.[18]

Literature and comics

However, music is just one of the many arts where the figure of Tutankhamun became a pivotal source of inspiration. Another example is literature, with books, novels and even comics clearly influenced by the young pharaoh. Since 1922, and even more since 1923, when the Tut-mania had already exploded everywhere, especially in the West, Tut-ankhamun turned into the main character of many volumes belonging to various genres. Those genres also included romances, and the young sovereign became the protagonist of books such as *The Kiss of Pharaoh: The Love Story of Tutankhamen*, written by Richard Goyne and published in 1923 (Plate 20), and *King Tutankhamen: His Romantic History*, written by Archie Bell and published in the same year.[19] These books, obviously pure fiction, mark once more the importance acquired by Tutankhamun for the general public from the very beginning of his emergence into the general consciousness.

Tutankhamun was chosen as the main character of mystery books as well, especially because of the 'enigmatic atmosphere' that arose around the figure of the young pharaoh. One of the very first examples of Tut-mania in this genre dates back to 1924 and comes from Portugal: *A Profecia ou O Mistério da Morte de Tut-Ank-Amon*, written by Fernando Val do Rio de Carvalho Henriques and focused on Tutankhamun and his supposedly obscure death (Fig. 9.3).[20]

However, probably the most peculiar literary production, written right after the discovery of the tomb of Tutankhamun, was the tale *Imprisoned with the Pharaohs*, by Howard Phillips Lovecraft in collaboration with the illusionist Harry Houdini. The story is not actually strictly related to Tutankhamun, but the tale was created *because* of the publicity surrounding Tutankhamun and his tomb, and Houdini – who wanted to ride the wave of success of the discovery of KV 62 – also arranged an escapology trick (one of his classical 'Buried Alive' ones) to be in some way set in ancient Egypt.[21]

Houdini's name is also linked to Tutankhamun because of a series of statements he made after the death of Lord Carnarvon, in 1923. In particular, the magician stood against the spiritistic theories sustained by Sir Arthur Conan Doyle, an illustrious writer, but also a profound supporter of spiritualism. According to the latter, Carnarvon died because of a curse imposed to him by a spirit placed in the tomb by ancient Egyptians to protect the young pharaoh,[22] whereas Houdini was strongly opposed to this view. As the escapologist declared to the *Los Angeles Examiner*:[23] 'If, as Sir Arthur says, an avenging spirit, placed at the tomb to prevent its disturbance, probably was the cause of the explorer's death, why is it that other Egyptologists never likewise have been slain? Hundreds of these ancient tombs have been opened; but, so far as I know, no one concerned in the opening afterward was the victim of such supernatural watchmen' (Fig. 9.4).

Apart from tales and novels, Tutankhamun also became an important source of inspiration for comics. Even though the young pharaoh was featured in a plethora of comics (*Kid Eternity: Terror from the Tomb*, 1946 [Fig. 9.5];[24] *Zio Paperone e il tesoro di Tutank-Paperon*, 1979;[25] *Papyrus: Toutânkhamon, le Pharaon assassiné*, 1994,[26] to name a few), perhaps the most remarkable example comes from the DC Universe.[27] Even if far less famous than the Joker,

Fig. 9.3. A Profecia ou O Mistério da Morte de Tut-Ank-Amon, *by Fernando Val do Rio de Carvalho Henriques, 1924.*

Penguin or Poison Ivy, 'King Tut' appears as one of the antagonists of Batman. Before becoming a character of Batman comics, however, King Tut made his first appearance in the TV series dedicated to the same hero. In the series, King Tut is the evil *alter ego* of an illustrious professor of Egyptology at Yale University (named William Omaha McElroy and played by Victor Buono), who – when he is hit on his head – forgets his real identity, believes he is Tutankhamun's reincarnation and wants to make Gotham worship him as a pharaoh. This villain appears in many episodes released between 1966 and 1968, as well as in two animated movies based on the 1960s series[28] (*Batman: The Return of the Caped Crusaders*, 2016,[29] and *Batman v/s Two-Faces*, 2017[30]). However, in comics, 'King Tut' is the *alter ego* of an Egyptologist and criminal, who leaves riddles – similar to that of the Sphinx – at the scenes of his crimes. The convict behind this villain is named Victor Goodman, in honour of the actor who played King Tut in the TV series, 'Goodman' being the English literal translation of the artist's surname, Buono.[31] The character of King Tut is still extant, a Funko POP figure was produced of him, as was one in Lego.[32]

HOUDINI SCOFFS AT TUT GHOST

Famous Magician Takes Issue With Conan Doyle on Carnarvon Death; Irvine Gets Message

Houdini vs. Conan Doyle.

Did a poisonous insect or an avenging spirit cause the death of Lord Carnarvon?

The Cairo cable telling of the death of the explorer of the tomb of Pharoah Tut-Ankh-Amen states "death was due to blood poisoning through the bite of an insect."

Sir Arthur Conan Doyle, famous English novelist and noted student of spiritualism, says he is strongly inclined to believe that the titled archaeologist died under a curse imposed upon him by an "elemental" or guardian spirit placed at the pharoah's tomb by ancient Egyptian priests.

Harry Houdini, world-famous magician, says Sir Arthur, in his estimation, is the victim of a sincere but senseless delusion, if he thinks Carnarvon was thus a victim.

TELLS OF SPIRIT MESSAGE

Clark Irvine, student of psychic phenomena, announced last night that news of Carnarvon's death was conveyed to him here through psychic channels Wednesday evening, or several hours before the information was received by Los Angeles newspapers.

Houdini, in his dressing room at the Orpheum yesterday, dismissed the controversy with the assertion that his lordship's death, like many others, should be attributed to the insect in question.

"This insect," he said, "is very poisonous, due to ages-old unsanitary conditions generally where it is found in Egypt.

"A friend of mine also was a victim of this insect while touring Egypt. He survived, but has never recovered from the sting, his neck and shoulders still being much swollen.

WHY NOT OTHER VICTIMS?

"If, as Sir Arthur says, an avenging spirit, placed at the tomb to prevent its disturbance, probably was the cause of the explorer's death, why is it that other Egyptologists never likewise have been slain?

"Hundreds of these ancient tombs have been opened; but, so far as I know, no one concerned in the opening afterward was the victim of such supernatural watchmen."

Now listen to Irvine:

"Wednesday evening a group of five students of psychic manifestation were at my house, 7017 Watseka street, Culver City," he said.

"We were holding a meeting—a little group sincerely seeking the truth.

"In the midst of the meeting my grandfather's spirit came to us and told us that Lord Carnarvon had just died, and that his death was due to the agency of spirits placed at his tomb to prevent its desecration."

Fig. 9.4. Interview given by Houdini, Los Angeles Examiner, 7 April 1923.

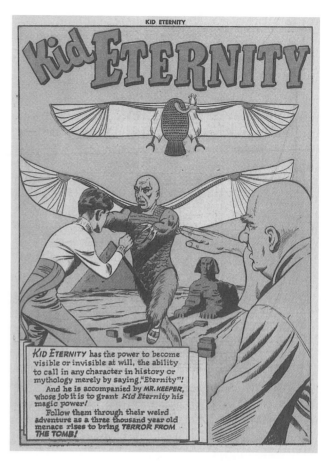

Fig. 9.5. Kid Eternity: Terror from the Tomb, *1946.*

Toys and games

Having raised the matter of the Funko POP and Lego figures, a few words are necessary on other toys and collectable items. Tut-mania is solidly manifested in this popular sector as well, with teddy bears, board games, action figures and a range of other items all linked with Tutankhamun.[33] Among the toys that achieved the greatest success, a key example is the so-called King Tut (Plate 21), produced by Franco American Novelty during the 1940s. Franco was a pioneering company in terms of illusionism, and created a little mummiform Tutankhamun – made of plastic – to be inserted in his coffin. The item was thought of as a sort of magic trick: thanks to a series of magnets, the figure could stay inside the coffin or 'come alive' and 'jump out' of it. Franco sold over 10 million examples of King Tut, modernizing and upgrading the packaging for a number of decades, at least until the 1960s.[34]

Two decades from the first production of this object, another important item related to Tut-mania was realized: the King Tut pinball machine, distributed by Bally Manufacturing during the 1960s. Bally, one of the most famous companies producing electronic coin-operated games, released between 1968 and 1969 a pinball entirely inspired by the figure of Tutankhamun. With the score displayed within the bodies of four canopic jars and a close-up on the golden mask, 1,000 machines were produced, and is today in high demand among collectors worldwide.[35] King Tut was but one of many arcade items born because of Tut-mania and the influence of the young pharaoh on a broad audience.

Moving forward in time, in 1982 another quite important coin-operated game became available, in which an explorer raids Tutankhamun's tomb. It is titled Tutankham and produced by the Konami Corporation (Fig. 9.6).[36] The video game was originally to be called Tutankhamun, but due to a rearrangement of the game's physical layout, which reduced the of space available in the cabinet header, the title had to be shortened by two letters.[37] The game was a major success and, in fact, was an inspiration for follow-on video games, such as Time Bandit in 1983.[38]

It would be impossible to mention all the other video games related to Tutankhamun produced over the years. The presumed 'mystery' around his figure, the 'golden treasure' found in his tomb and, even more, the myth of the curse that is conventionally attributed to his mummy are perfect ingredients at the heart of many different adventure games, which are still being produced. One of the most recent creations dates to 2020 and is titled Emily Archer and the Curse of Tutankhamun.[39] Developed by HH Game, it is set in Egypt during the 1920s and revolves around the enigmatic death of Lord Carnarvon and the stealing of the funerary mask of Tutankhamun. Lady Archer, a friend of the deceased Lord Carnarvon, has to find the culprit and recover the golden mask before it is too late. As the title suggests, the game is partially based on the alleged curse of the pharaoh and makes this rumour the pivot around which the whole investigative story twists.

As mentioned above, however, Tutankhamun was (and still is!) an inspiration not only for video games, but also for other kinds of entertainment, which have distinctive 'Tutankhamun versions'. This includes some iconic toys, such as Trolls. These plastic dolls with their peculiar colourful hair, created by Thomas Dam and produced by Russ Berrie and Co., became particularly well known between the 1960s and the 1990s. There were all kinds, including the magician, the gladiator, the pirate and – of course – the Egyptian one. The Troll inspired by Tutankhamun was ideally paired with the one inspired by Queen Nefertiti. Both Troll-Tutankhamun and Troll-Nefertiti are characterized by shiny and sparkling golden clothing elements, recalling the richness of the burial equipment of the young pharaoh.[40]

Fashion

As *The New York Times* wrote, '[we had a] complete change in furniture, decorations, jewellery and women's dress [...] as a result of the discoveries in the tomb of Tutankhamun'.[41] Indeed, since the 1920s, Tut-mania has embraced fashion.

Fig. 9.6. Tutankham, by Konami Corporation, 1982.

Fashion is probably one of the arts where Tut-mania gave its best, because, from the very moment of the discovery of KV 62 – and its funerary goods – clothes and accessories inspired by ancient Egypt and the young pharaoh were produced and sold in large quantities. Even Margot Asquith, wife of the former British Premier, Herbert Henry Asquith, yielded to this trend, and on 10 March 1923 the *Literary Digest* remarked that 'Mrs. Asquith [...] appeared in London recently wearing this gown draped in the manner popular when King Tut ruled'.[42]

The fame of Tutankhamun forced stores to include decorations inspired by ancient Egyptian style in their collections, since the young pharaoh was the trend of the moment, and people wanted to be dressed according to 'Tut-fashion'. The firm Lefkowitz & Pitofsky (a shop at 500 Seventh Avenue, in Manhattan) sent a telegram to Lord Carnarvon to seek his permission to buy the rights to the garments included the funerary equipment of Tutankhamun:

> For exclusive style rights of garments, embroideries, and colorings on all apparel found in the tomb of TutankhAmen will make a most generous offer. Will deposit $100,000 with American representative to bind offer. Member of firm leave immediately to close on receipt of your cable. Divide equally all profits derived from transaction with a museum you name. Believe your discovery will revolutionize style world. We are considered among leading creators and would like to sponsor newest sensation.[43]

Another marvellous example of the influence of the young pharaoh on dresses and ornaments is the pocket watch Tutankhamun, produced around 1925 by Cartier. The item was on display in 2017 at the Cooper Hewitt, Smithsonian Design Museum, during the temporary exhibition *Jeweled Splendors of the Art Deco Era: The Prince and Princess Sadruddin Aga Khan Collection*.[44] Viewing just the dial, the reason for the Tutankhamun name seems obscure, but turning it over, the reason behind the choice of this name becomes evident. Here, an image of the young pharaoh's golden mask completely covers the rear part of this extremely precious watch.[45] During the 1920s, the public was profoundly fascinated by the fact that such ancient designs and decors seemed extraordinarily modern. This sense of wonder on one hand caused the wider audience to be affected by Tut-mania but, on the other hand, it probably also helped people feel a sense of closeness to that young pharaoh who had lived over 3,000 years before but who was seemingly not so different from them.[46]

The great success of the Tut-style, however, is not confined to the past since, even today, Tutankhamun is still considered a source of inspiration for designers and fashion houses, such as Chanel (2018)[47] and Dior – just to mention two of the most recent examples. The latter, in 2004, organized a fashion show in Paris entirely dedicated to ancient Egypt.[48] Shiny dresses, covered in gold; blue and yellow cloths (to recall the Nile and the desert of Egypt); bandages used to wrap the models as mummies: all the elements clearly recalled ancient Egyptian culture. However, the most exemplary reference to Tutankhamun was, of course, the golden mask, replicated in detail and placed on the face of one of the models.[49]

Movies, cartoons and TV series

Another art where the Tut-mania has raged – and is still raging – is, obviously, cinema. Plenty of movies, TV series and cartoons have been created around Tutankhamun and his myth. It would be impossible to comprehensively cover the titles inspired by the young pharaoh here; we will therefore just mention some of the most iconic movies and series linked to Tut-mania.

The first major example of Tut-mania in movies dates to 1932: *The Mummy*, with Boris Karloff, with plenty of references to Tutankhamun (such as the name of the woman Imhotep is in love with, Ankhesenamun, named after the Great Royal Wife of Tutankhamun).[50] The 1932 movie started the long series of films with the similar titles and dedicated to the 'curse of the mummy'. However, Tutankhamun not only *inspired* movies: sometimes he also became the main character of them, one example being in *The Curse of King Tut's Tomb*. In this movie, a combination of horror, fantasy and adventure released in 2006, Tutankhamun is even summoned to fight against Seth and free humankind.[51] The title of the movie recalls an older film (released in 1980) where, however, the curse of the mummy is considered responsible for some suspicious deaths, but Tutankhamun himself is not a character.[52]

Tutankhamun also stars in animated movies, where – however – he is usually perceived not only as a pharaoh who rules Egypt, but also as a spoiled child. An example is given by *Mr Peabody & Sherman*, produced by DreamWorks

Animation and released by 20th Century Fox in 2014.[53] Here, the young pharaoh is one of the antagonists of the heroes (Sherman and the brilliant dog, Mr Peabody, who travel together through time and space)[54] and is depicted as a pampered sovereign, who presumes to have a right to everything he desires.[55] A very similar perspective on the character (who, however, unlike the above-mentioned movie, in this case is a positive figure) is discernible in *Tutenstein*, the animated series streamed for the very first time in 2003, on Discovery Kids in the USA. *Tutenstein* is none other than the pharaoh 'Tut-ankh-en-set-amun' who came back to life and now lives through hundreds of adventures together with his friend, Cleo Carter (whose surname is a clear reference to Howard Carter himself).[56]

Tut-mania embraces TV shows and series more widely as well. For instance, the 2015 mini-series *Tut* is set during the reign of Tutankhamun and stars the Oscar winner Ben Kingsley (who plays Ay, Tutankhamun's successor). The plot is not wholly based on historical facts, and is significantly fictionalized and novelized. Tutankhamun is depicted as a weak sovereign, inadequate to properly rule the 'great Egyptian empire' but, throughout fights and alliances, the young pharaoh acquires charisma and ability, even if his tragic end is just around the corner.[57] Although still fictionalized, a plot more closely aligned to historical facts around Tutankhamun is found in another TV series, released in 2016 and entitled *Tutankhamun* (starring Max Irons and Sam Neill). Despite the title, the episodes are focused on Howard Carter and the discovery of the tomb of the young pharaoh, not on Tutankhamun himself. However, as well as *Tut*, this series proves that the myth of Tutankhamun is more alive than ever, and Tut-mania – even after 100 years – is still all around us.

Conclusions

So, why has Tutankhamun become a pop idol? How is it that his fame is still celebrated all over the world, so much that even toys and games have been created to recall the young pharaoh?

The list of case-studies could be much longer, but this paper has deliberately focused on some specific examples which can reveal clues behind the reason why Tutankhamun has become a proper myth.

The 'adventurous' and sudden (at least, for the wider public) discovery of his tomb was a fundamental piece in the puzzle of the Tut-mania as the various songs produced during the 1920s clearly exemplify, but this is not the only element to consider. The richness of the funerary equipment is another fundamental aspect to take into account – Cartier and Dior creations are perfect examples of this – as well as the fact that Tutankhamun was very young when he ascended the throne. Moreover, his youth was used in literature and cinema as a sort of 'justification' for this character's childish behaviour. However, the most emblematic factor that transformed Tutankhamun into a proper myth for the general public is the infamous legend of the curse, a lead player in novels, movies, comics and games.

Nonetheless, behind the multifaceted figure of Tutankhamun there are many other possible reasons why the young pharaoh became a superstar: his life and the many unsolved questions issues regarding it; the fact that he ascended the throne during the controversial Amarna period; the mediatic echo of the discovery of his tomb … Therefore, perhaps, there is not one single answer to the question 'Why is Tutankhamun a celebrity?'; perhaps the uniqueness of this young pharaoh is given by the sum of all these elements; or, perhaps, everyone has their personal reason to celebrate Tutankhamun. Whichever the explanation is, Tutankhamun was and still is a pop idol, and Tut-mania has been – for 100 years, whether we want it or not – all around us.

Notes

1   I am extremely grateful to the editors of this volume and the anonymous reviewers for their valuable comments and suggestions, which have helped improve the quality of this paper.
2   Reeves and Taylor 1992, 155.
3   Thiry 1973; Laurens 1997; Day 2005, 296.
4   *The New York Times*, 18 February 1923.
5   To learn more about the project, see http://www.centrodehistoria-flul.com/abertura/projecto-egypopcult-i-mache-mir-die-agyptische-world-as-i-like-it-comeca-as-suas-atividades.
6   Pichel 2023.
7   See, for instance, Fryxell 2017.
8   Arab Kitsch, 'King Tut Blues' (https://arabkitsch.com/business-directory/581/king-tut-blues/ [last accessed 4 May 2023]).
9   Digital Commons at the University of Maine, USA (UMaine), 'Three Thousand Years Ago' (https://digitalcommons.library.umaine.edu/mmb-vp/5275/ [last accessed 15 April 2023]).
10 Stanford Libraries, 'Tut-Ankh-Amen' (https://searchworks.stanford.edu/view/13570651 [last accessed 24 April 2023]).
11 Arab Kitsch, 'Old King Tut Was a Wise Old Nut' (https://arabkitsch.com/business-directory/735/old-king-tut-was-a-wise-old-nut/ [last accessed 30 March 2023]); Brier 2015, 171–172.
12 Digital Commons at UMaine, 'Old King Tut. In Old King Tutenkhamen's Day' (https://digitalcommons.library.umaine.edu/mmb-vp/1304/ [last accessed 3 May 2023]).
13 Boardwalk Empire Wiki, 'Tutankhamun' (https://boardwalkempire.fandom.com/wiki/Tutankhamun [last accessed 24 April 2023]).
14 Arab Kitsch, 'Old King Tut. In Old King Tutenkhamen's Day' (https://arabkitsch.com/business-directory/733/old-king-tut/ [last accessed 30 March 2023]).
15 To learn more about the exhibition, https://libmma.org/digital_files/archives/MacManus_Tutankhamun_records_b18131165.pdf (last accessed 9 May 2023]).
16 Perkins 2023.
17 Zecchino d'Oro, 'Tutanc'mon' (https://zecchinodoro.org/canzone/tutancmon [last accessed 4 May 2023]).
18 Santini 2022, 251.
19 Sales and Mota 2020b, 608 n. 97.
20 Sales and Mota 2020a, 407–408.
21 Mancini 2019.
22 Reeves 1990, 62–63; Luckhurst 2012, 3–24.
23 *Los Angeles Examiner*, 7 April 1923.
24 DC Database, 'Kid Eternity Vol. 11' (https://dc.fandom.com/wiki/Kid_Eternity_Vol_1_1 [last accessed 23 April 2023]).
25 Comic Vine, 'Topolino #1256' (https://comicvine.gamespot.com/topolino-1256-zio-paperone-e-il-tesoro-di-tutank-p/4000-166737 [last accessed 03 March 2023]).
26 Comic Vine, 'Papyrus #17' (https://comicvine.gamespot.com/papyrus-17-toutankhamon-le-pharaon-assassine/4000-734799/ [last accessed 01 March 2023]).
27 The DC Universe (also known as DCU) is the shared universe where most stories published by DC Comics are set.
28 Batman Fandom, 'King Tut' (https://batman.fandom.com/wiki/King_Tut [last accessed 1 May 2023]).
29 Batman Fandom, 'Return of the Caped Crusader' (https://batman.fandom.com/wiki/Batman:_Return_of_the_Caped_Crusaders [last accessed 17 April 2023]).
30 Batman Fandom, 'Batman vs. Two-Face' (https://batman.fandom.com/wiki/Batman_vs._Two-Face [last accessed 5 May 2023]).
31 Batman Fandom, 'King Tut' (https://batman.fandom.com/wiki/King_Tut [last accessed 1 May 2023]).
32 King Tut appears as a cameo also in *The Lego Batman Movie* (2017).
33 Just to mention one of the most recent, in 2021 Figma produced an action figure of the mummy of Tutankhamun wearing the famous golden mask (https://www.figma.jp/en/products/tag/figma/announced/2021 and https://www.goodsmile.info/en/product/11913/figma+Tutankhamun.html [last accessed 29 May 2023]).
34 Santini 2022, 275.
35 Internet Pinball Database, 'King Tut' (https://www.ipdb.org/machine.cgi?id=1378 [last accessed 25 March 2023]).
36 Lamera 1984, 52–54; and Atari Mania, 'Tutankham' (http://www.atarimania.com/game-atari-2600-vcs-tutankham_7534.html [last accessed 18 May 2023]).
37 Progetto E.M.M.A., 'Tutankham' (https://web.archive.org/web/20160808054723fw_/http://www.progettoemma.net/gioco.php?game=tutankhm [last accessed 8 November 2019, via Wayback Machine]).
38 DBG 2003.
39 Curtis 2021.
40 Santini 2022, 277–278.
41 Rekas 2000; 'The King in Fashion' 2022; *The New York Times*, 27 February 2023, 6.
42 Literary Digest, 9 March 1923; American Studies at the University of Virginia, 'Fashion Is King' (https://xroads.virginia.edu/~ug00/rekas/tut/king.htm [last accessed 5 May 2023]).
43 'Miscellany' 1923.
44 Aga Khan et al. 2017.
45 Cooper Hewitt Collection, 'Pocket Watch, Tutankhamun' (https://collection.cooperhewitt.org/objects/420577291/ [last accessed 12 April 2023]).
46 McAlister 1923, 167–169; Fryxell 2017, 525–529.
47 Cartner-Morley 2018.

48 John Galliano for Dior (Alexander 2004). Previously, Galliano designed another Egyptian-inspired collection (Borrelli-Persson 1997).

49 Mower 2004.

50 Vieira 2003, 55–58.

51 IMDb, 'The Curse of King Tut's Tomb' (https://www.imdb.com/title/tt0464799/ [last accessed 17 March 2023]).

52 IMDb, 'The Curse of King's Tut's Tomb' (https://www.imdb.com/title/tt0080582/ [last accessed 20 March 2023]).

53 IMDb, 'Mr. Peabody & Sherman' (https://www.imdb.com/title/tt0864835/ [last accessed 12 April 2023]).

54 Dreamworks, 'Mr. Peabody & Sherman' (https://www.dreamworks.com/movies/mr-peabody-and-sherman [last accessed 5 May 2023]).

55 Peabodyverse Encyclopedia, 'King Tut' (https://mr-peabody-sherman.fandom.com/wiki/King_Tut [last accessed 26 April 2023]).

56 Her name is possibly a reference to Cleopatra as well. IMDb, 'Tutenstein' (https://www.imdb.com/title/tt0386986/ [last accessed 7 April 2023]).

57 IMDb, 'Tut' (https://www.imdb.com/title/tt3214310/ [last accessed 12 March 2023]).

Bibliography

Aga Khan, Catherine, Pierre Rainero, Évelyne Possémé, Stephen Harrison, Sarah D. Coffin and Sarah Davis. 2017. *Jeweled Splendors of the Art Deco Era: The Prince and Princess Sadruddin Aga Khan Collection*. New York: Thames & Hudson.

Alexander, Hillary. 2004. 'Paris Haute Couture: Dior Reincarnates Queens of the Nile'. *The Telegraph*, 20 January 2004. http://fashion.telegraph.co.uk/news-features/TMG4795936/Paris-haute-couture-Dior-reincarnates-queens-of-the-Nile.html (last accessed 19 April 2023).

American Studies at the University of Virginia. https://xroads.virginia.edu/ (last accessed 5 May 2023).

Arab Kitsch. Exploring Middle Eastern Stereotypes is American Music. https://arabkitsch.com/ (last accessed 31 March 2023).

Atari Mania. http://www.atarimania.com/index.html (last accessed 18 April 2023).

Baber, Tessa T. 2016. 'Ancient Corpses as Curiosities: Mummymania in the Age of Early Travel'. *Journal of Ancient Egyptian Interconnections* 8: 60–93.

Batman Fandom. https://batman.fandom.com/wiki/Batman_Wiki (last accessed 5 May 2023).

Boardwalk Empire Wiki. https://boardwalkempire.fandom.com/wiki/Boardwalk_Empire_Wiki (last accessed 24 April 2023).

Borrelli-Persson, Laird. 1997. 'John Galliano: Fall 1997 Ready-to-Wear'. *Vogue*, 14 March 1997. https://www.vogue.com/fashion-shows/fall-1997-ready-to-wear/john-galliano (last accessed 30 April 2023).

Brier, Bob. 2013. *Egyptomania: Our Three Thousand Year Obsession with the Land of the Pharaohs*. New York: St Martin's Press.

Cartner-Morley, Jess. 2018. '"Only Karl Can Do This": Lagerfeld Blends Egypt and Manhattan for Chanel'. *The Guardian*, 5 December 2018. https://www.theguardian.com/fashion/2018/dec/05/only-karl-can-do-this-lagerfeld-blends-egypt-and-manhattan-for-chanel (last accessed 5 May 2023)/

Cep, Casey. 2022. 'Why King Tut Is Still Fascinating'. *The New Yorker*, 7 February 2022. https://www.newyorker.com/magazine/2022/02/14/why-king-tut-is-still-fascinating (last accessed 31 March 2023).

Comic Vine. https://comicvine.gamespot.com/ (last accessed 3 March 2023).

Cooper Hewitt, Smithsonian Design Museum, Collection. https://collection.cooperhewitt.org/ (last accessed 12 April 2023).

Curtis, Mel. 2021. 'Emily Archer and the Curse of Tutankhamun'. *BDG – Big Daddy Gaming*, 11 May 2021. https://bigdaddygaming.co.uk/emily-archer-and-the-curse-of-tutankhamun-review-nintendo-switch/ (last accessed 3 May 2023).

Day, Jasmine. 2005. 'Mummymania: Mummies, Museums and Popular Culture'. *Journal of Biological Research* 80 (1): 296–300.

DBG. 2003. 'Interview with Harry Lafnear'. *Atari Legends: Legends Never Die*, 5 September 2023. https://www.atarilegend.com/interviews/4 (last accessed 29 May 2023).

DC Database. https://dc.fandom.com/wiki/DC_Comics_Database (last accessed 2 May 2023).

Digital Commons at UMaine, University of Maine. https://digitalcommons.library.umaine.edu/ (last accessed 4 May 2023).

DreamWorks. https://www.dreamworks.com/ (last accessed 5 May 2023).

Figma. https://www.figma.jp/ja/figma (last accessed 29 May 2023).

Fryxell, Allegra. 2017. 'Tutankhamen, Egyptomania, and Temporal Enchantment in Interwar Britain'. *Twentieth Century British History* 28 (4): 516–542.

Good Smile Company. https://www.goodsmile.info/en/ (last accessed 29 May 2023).

IMDb – Internet Movie Database. https://www.imdb.com/?ref_=nv_home (last accessed 15 April 2023).

Internet Pinball Database. https://www.ipdb.org/sear.pl (last accessed 25 March 2023).

'The King in Fashion'. 2022. *Pashion. The Modern Arab Woman's Fashion Source*, 12 November 2022. https://pashionmagazine.com/the-king-in-fashion/ (last accessed 5 May 2023).

Lamera, Danilo. 1984. 'Tutankham'. *Videogiochi* 17: 52–55.

Laurens, Henry. 1997. *L'expédition d'Égypte (1798–1801)*. Paris: Seuil.

Luckhurst, Roger. 2012. *The Mummy's Curse: The True History of a Dark Fantasy*. Oxford: Oxford University Press.

Mancini, Mattia. 2019. 'Houdini e l'antico Egitto'. *Djed Medu: Blog di Egittologia*, 30 January 2019. https://djedmedu.wordpress.com/2019/01/30/houdini-e-lantico-egitto/ (last accessed 31 March 2023).

McAlister, Mary. 1923. 'Ancient Costume and Modern Fashion'. *Art and Archaeology* 15: 167–175.

Metropolitan Museum of Arts Archives, 'Irvine MacManus Records Related to "Treasures of Tutankhamun" Exhibition, 1975–1979'. https://libmma.org/digital_files/archives/MacManus_Tutankhamun_records_b18131165.pdf (last accessed 29 May 2023).

'Miscellany'. 1923. *Time*, 9 March 1923. https://content.time.com/time/subscriber/article/0,33009,846468,00.html (last accessed 9 April 2023).

Mower, Sarah. 2004. 'Christian Dior Spring 2004 Couture'. *Vogue*, 19 January 2004. https://www.vogue.com/fashion-shows/

spring-2004-couture/christian-dior (last accessed 31 March 2023).

Peabodyverse Encyclopedia, https://mr-peabody-sherman.fandom. com/wiki/Peabodyverse_Encyclopedia (last accessed 26 April 2023).

Perkins, Dennis. 2023. '45 Years Ago: Steve Martin's "King Tut" Becomes a Super Hit'. *UCR Classic Rock & Culture*, 22 April 2023. https://ultimateclassicrock.com/steve-martin-king-tut/ (last accessed 24 April 2023).

Progetto E.M.M.A. – Emulatore Multiplo Macchine Arcade. https://web.archive.org/web/20191113205846fw_/http://www. progettoemma.net/titolo.php# (last accessed 8 November 2019).

Projecto Egypopcult. 'Ich mache mir die (ägyptische) Welt wie sie mir gefällt' começa as suas atividades'. 2023. http:// www.centrodehistoria-flul.com/abertura/projecto-egypopcult-i-mache-mir-die-agyptische-world-as-i-like-it-comeca-as-suas-atividades (last accessed 11 April 2023).

Reeves, Nicholas. 1990. *The Complete Tutankhamun. The King; the Tomb; the Royal Treasure*. London: Thames & Hudson.

Reeves, Nicholas, and John Taylor. 1992. *Howard Carter before Tutankhamun*. London: The Trustees of the British Museum.

Rekas, Mary. 2000. 'Old World, New World: America Meets Tutankhamen'. https://xroads.virginia.edu/~ug00/rekas/tut/ paper/tutpaper.htm#N_68 (last accessed 20 April 2023).

Riggs, Christina. 2022. *Treasured: How Tutankhamun Shaped a Century*. London: Atlantic Books.

Sales, José das Candeias, and Susana Mota. 2020a. 'Fernando Val do Rio de Carvalho Henriques (1897–1962): o primeiro romancista-egiptólogo português'. In *El Próximo Oriente antíguo y el Egipto faraónico en España y Portugal: viajeros, pioneros, coleccionistas, instituciones y recepción*, edited by Lucía Brage Martínez and Juan-Luis Montero Fenollós, 407–420. Barcelona: Publicacions i Edicions de la Universitat de Barcelona.

Sales, José das Candeias, and Susana Mota. 2020b. 'Tutankhamun in Portugal. Reports in the Portuguese Press (1922–1939)'. *Aegyptiaca: Journal of the History of Reception of Ancient Egypt* 5: 565–609.

Santini, Valentina. 2022. *I segreti di Tutankhamon: Storia di un Faraone tra Mito e Realtà*. Milano: Longanesi Editore.

Stanford Libraries, Stanford University. https://library.stanford. edu/ (last accessed 24 April 2023).

Thiry, Jean. 1973. *Bonaparte en Égypte*. Paris: Berger-Levrault.

Vieira, Mark A. 2003. *Hollywood Horror: From Gothic to Cosmic*. New York: Harry N. Abrams.

Williams, Ann R. 2022. 'How Tutankhamun Conquered Pop Culture'. *National Geographic*, 2 November 2022. https://www. nationalgeographic.co.uk/history-and-civilisation/2022/11/ how-tutankhamun-conquered-pop-culture (last accessed 31 March 2023).

Wireless to *The New York Times*. 1923. 'Tomb Treasures of Tut-Ankh-Amen Beyond Reckoning'. *The New York Times*, 18 February 1923, 1.

Zaki, Asaad A. 2017. 'Tutankhamun Exhibition at the British Museum in 1972: A Historical Perspective'. *Journal of Tourism Theory and Research* 3 (2): 79–88.

Zecchino d'Oro. https://zecchinodoro.org/ (last accessed 4 May 2023).

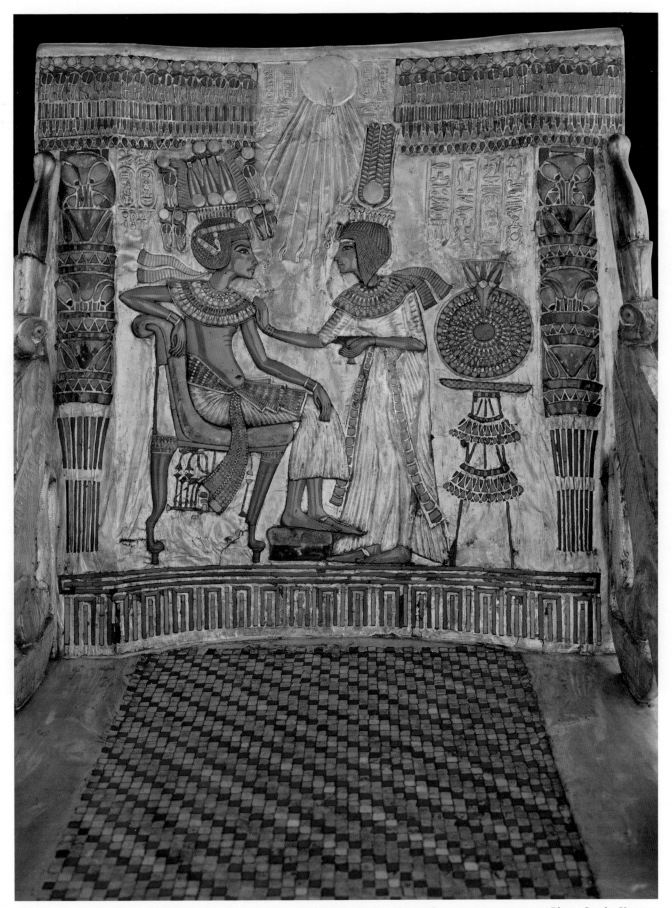

Plate 1. The Golden Throne of Tutankhamun: a depiction on the backrest displays the royal pair in an intimate pose. Photo: Sandro Vannini.

Plate 2. The pectoral of Nut showing the goddess in the centre spreading her wings over the inscription, Photo: Christian Eckmann, Leibniz-Zentrum für Archäologie. Courtesy of the Egyptian Museum Cairo.

Plate 3. Pectoral depicting the goddess Nut as a vulture. Photo: Christian Eckmann, Leibniz-Zentrum für Archäologie. Courtesy of the Egyptian Museum Cairo.

Plate 4. The mummy bands with one of the two necklaces that used to be fixed to the gold mask of the king, the Ba-*bird amulet, and the gold hands holding a crook and flail. Photo: Sandro Vannini. Courtesy of the Egyptian Museum Cairo.*

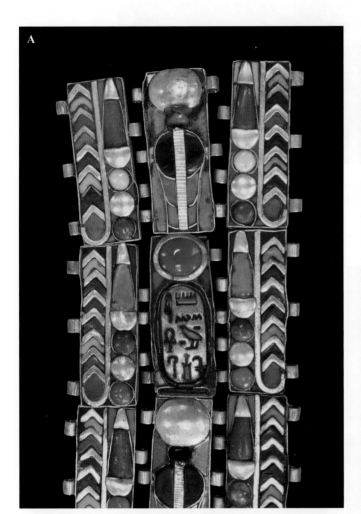 

Plate 5. Segments of the side straps, front view (a), back view (b). The gold sheets that camouflage the newly inserted cartouches were not inscribed to replace the now missing text. Photo: Eid Mertah, Egyptian Museum Cairo. Courtesy of the Egyptian Museum Cairo.

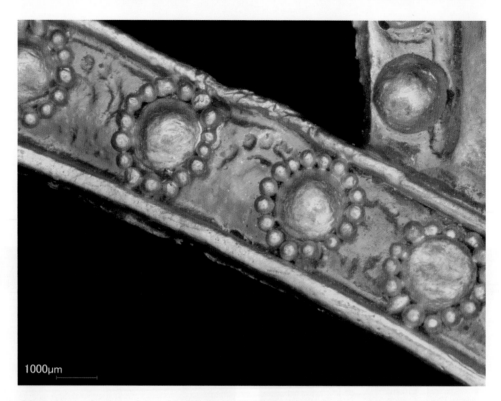

Plate 6. *One out of four pieces of openwork in gold with details highlighted by granules and small gold details (Carter 44a). The base sheet shows the vibrant, glossy pink red layer. The thicker it is, the more it turns from pink to a deep cherry red. Of course, this colouring is a decorative technique and not an accidental phenomenon. Photo: Christian Eckmann, Leibniz-Zentrum für Archäologie. Courtesy of the Egyptian Museum Cairo.*

Plate 7. *The anthropomorphized* Ankh *on one of Tutankhamun's gold-sheet appliqués. Photo: © Christian Eckmann, Römisch-Germanisches Zentralmuseum Mainz/Germany.*

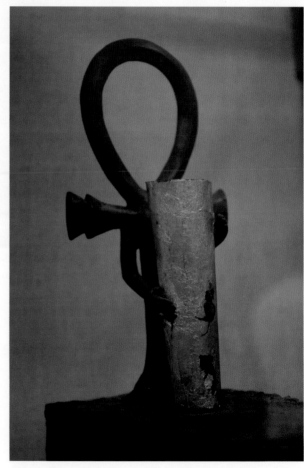

Plate 8. *The torch-holder with lost conical torch. Photo: Ghada Mohamed.*

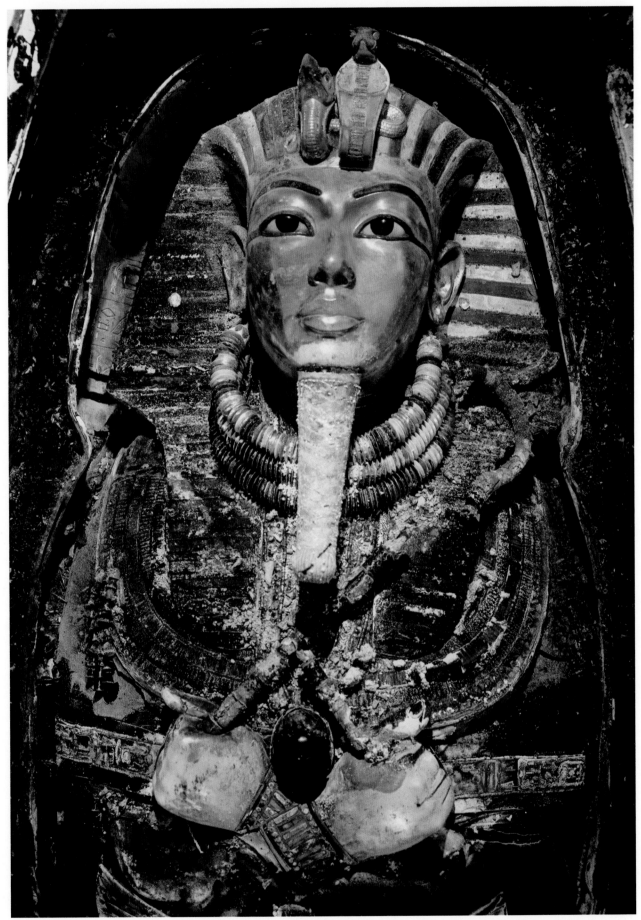

Plate 9. The funerary mask of Tutankhamun in situ *(colourised digitally). Photo: © Griffith Institute, University of Oxford.*

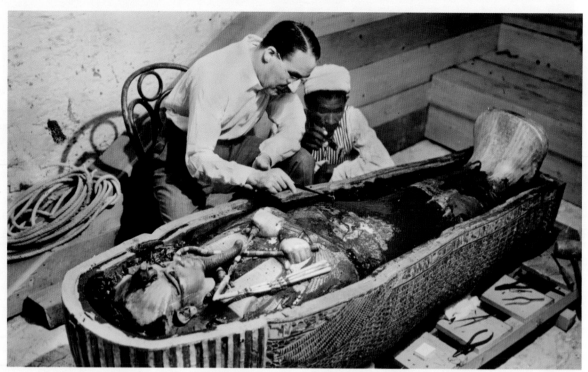

Plate 10. Howard Carter cleaning the third coffin of Tutankhamun (colourised digitally). Photo: © Griffith Institute, University of Oxford.

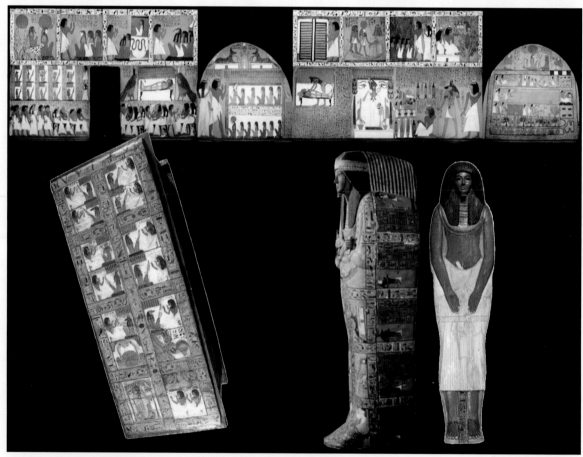

Plate 11. Nested burial assemblage of Sennedjem and the pictorial decoration of his tomb (TT 1). Composition by Rogério Sousa. Diagram of Sennedjem's Tomb courtesy of Hany Farid.

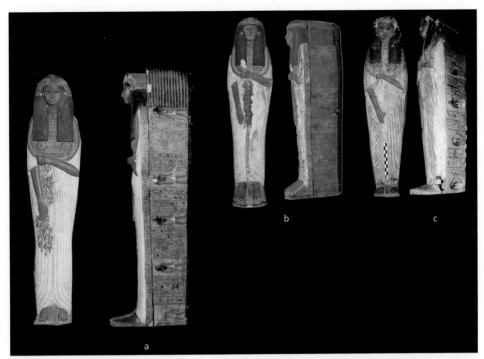

Plate 12. Coffins from Group A. Composition by the author. (a) Coffin of Isis, from TT 1 (National Museum of Egyptian Civilization, Cairo, JE 27309); (b) Coffin of Weretwahset (Brooklyn Museum of Art, inv. no. 37.47E-a); (c) Coffin of Henutwati (Louvre Museum, Paris, inv. no. E 18848).

Plate 13. Coffins from Group B. Composition by the author. (a) Coffin set of Sennedjem (National Museum of Egyptian Civilization, Cairo, JE 27308); (b) Coffin set of Iyneferti (Metropolitan Museum of Art, New York, inv. no. 86.1.5); (c) Coffin set of Tamakhet. from TT 1 (Ägyptisches Museum und Papyrus Sammlung, Berlin, inv. no. 10832); (d) Coffin of Khonsu, from TT 1 (Metropolitan Museum of Art, New York, inv. no. 86.1.1 a-b); (e) Coffin of Paherpet, from the Royal Cache (Egyptian Museum, Cairo, CG 61022); (f) Mummy-board of Khay (Musées royaux d'Art et d'Histoire, Brussels, inv. no. E.6878); (g) Mummy-board of Piay (Egyptian Museum, Cairo, inv. no. JE 2156); (h) Anonymous male mummy-board (Auguste Rodin Museum, Paris).

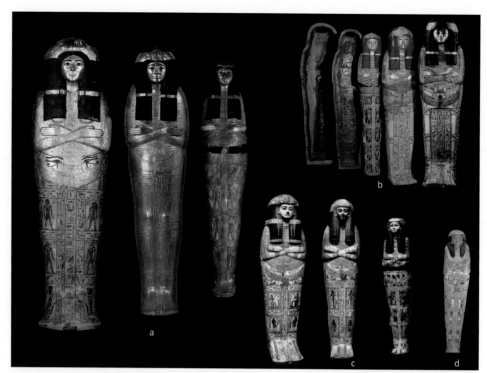

Plate 14. Coffins from Group C. Composition by the author. (a) Coffin set of Henutmehyt (British Museum, London, inv. no. EA 48001); (b) Coffin set of Tamutneferet (Musée du Louvre, Paris, inv. nos. N 2631, N2571, N 2623, N 2620); (c) Coffin set of Takayt (Städtische Galerie Liebieghaus, Frankfurt am Main, inv. no. 1651 a–f); (d) Mask and board of Ram (Hermitage, St Petersburg, inv. no. 787).

Plate 15. Coffins from Group D. Composition by the author. (a) Ramesside board from an intrusive deposit in TT 97. Present location unknown; (b) Coffin of a child,. from Bab el-Gasus (A.79) (Egyptian Museum, Cairo, inv. no. CG 6019/6020); (c) Mummy board of Hory (August Kestner Museum, Hanover, inv. no. 1977.1); (d) Coffin of Nesyamun (Leeds Museum, inv. no. D. 426-426a.1960); (e) Coffin of Sitkames. From the Royal Cache (Egyptian Museum, Cairo, inv. no. JE 26220/CG 61011); (f) Coffin set of Panebmontu (Louvre Museum, Paris, inv. nos. E 13029, 13046); (g) Mummy-board of Khaemipet. Private collection of B.P. Harris.

Plate 16. Above: Yellow decoration in the tomb of Seti II (KV 15). Below: Corresponding objects from the tomb of Tutankhamun. Photos: © Griffith Institute, University of Oxford.

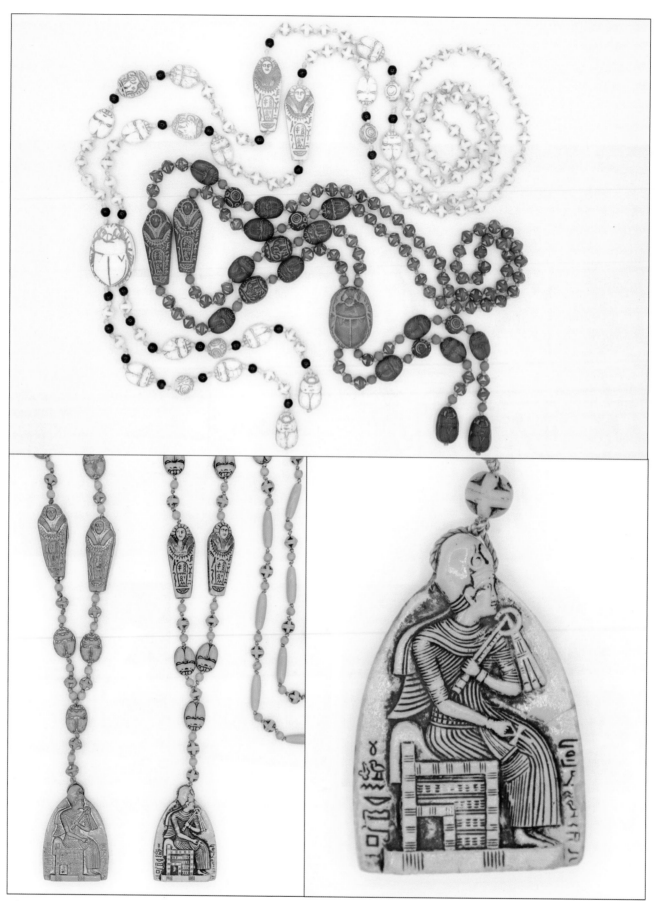

Plate 17. Above: An early Egyptianizing Neiger necklace featuring mummy shaped beads, flat scarab beads and a large double hole scarab pendant suspending twin tails terminating in long scarabs. Below: An Egyptianizing Neiger necklace design featuring mummy shaped beads, flat scarab beads and a seated pharaoh pendant. Author's collection. Photos: S. Kirkham.

Plate 18. Left: The original, now badly damaged scene of Amenhotep Huy bowing before Tutankhamun in TT40. Photo: J. Day. Right: The same scene recorded by Lepsius 1849–1859. Karl Richard Lepsius 1849–1859.

Plate 19. Old King Tut Was a Wise Old Nut, *by Lucien Denni & Roger Lewis and* Old King Tut: In Old King Tutenkhamen's Day, *by William Jerome, 1923.*

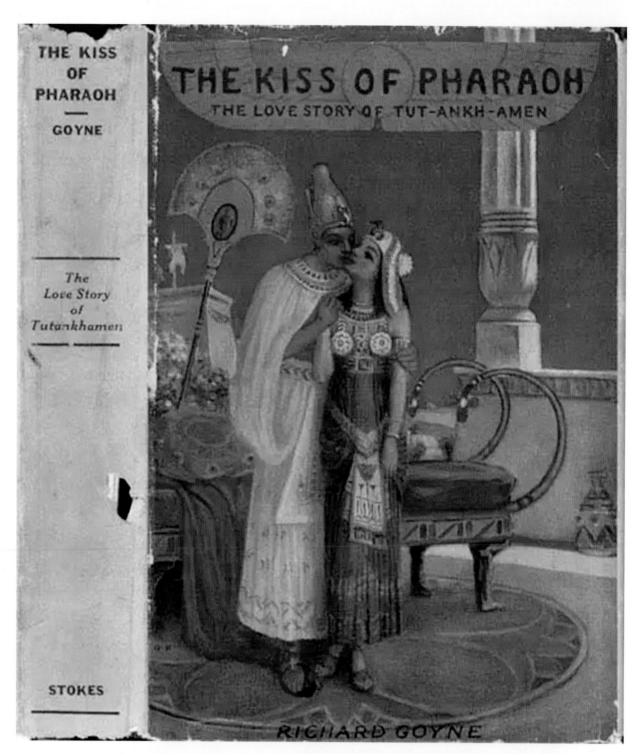

Plate 20. The Kiss of Pharaoh: The Love Story of Tutankhamen *by Richard Goyne, 1923.*

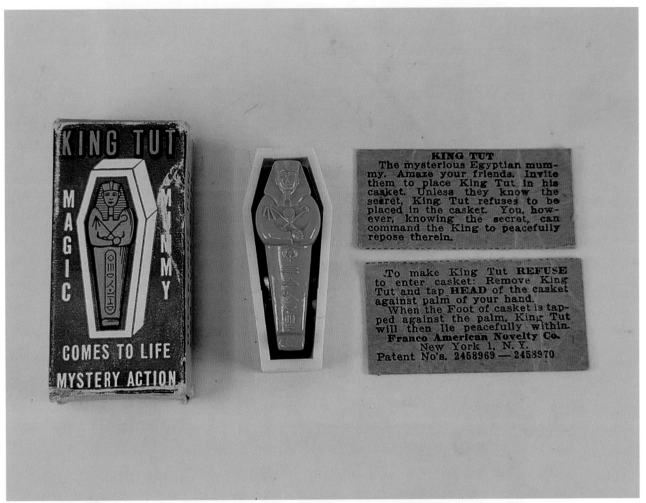

Plate 21. The King Tut magic trick produced by Franco American Novelties starting from the 1940s. Courtesy of Kimberly K Auction, LLC of Boyertown, Pennsylvania.

Plate 22. Ex libris of Ana Cristina Nunes Martins made by David Fernandes da Silva, 2022, zincography (L3). © Ana Cristina Nunes Martins.